Ireland Since 1939

Henry Patterson was born in Coleraine, County Londonderry, in 1947. He was educated at Queen's University, Belfast, and Nuffield College, Oxford. He is the author and co-author of ten books on modern Irish history, including *Class Conflict and Sectarianism* (1980), *Seán Lemass and the Making of Modern Ireland* (1982), *The Politics of Illusion: Republicanism and Socialism in Modern Ireland* (1989) and *Modern Ireland 1921–2001: Political Forces and Social Classes* (2001). He is Professor of Politics at the University of Ulster at Jordanstown.

Ireland Since 1939

The Persistence of Conflict

HENRY PATTERSON

PENGUIN
IRELAND

0674406

PENGUIN IRELAND

Published by the Penguin Group
Penguin Ireland, 25 St Stephen's Green, Dublin 2, Ireland
(a division of Penguin Books Ltd)
Penguin Books Ltd, 80 Strand, London WC2R ORL, England
Penguin Group (USA) Inc., 375 Hudson Street, New York, New York 10014, USA
Penguin Group (Australia), 250 Camberwell Road,
Camberwell, Victoria 3124, Australia (a division of Pearson Australia Group Pty Ltd)
Penguin Group (Canada), 90 Eglinton Avenue East, Suite 700, Toronto, Ontario, Canada M4P 2Y3
(a division of Pearson Penguin Canada Inc.)
Penguin Books India Pvt Ltd, 11 Community Centre,
Panchsheel Park, New Delhi – 110 017, India
Penguin Group (NZ), cnr Airborne and Rosedale Roads, Albany,
Auckland 1310, New Zealand (a division of Pearson New Zealand Ltd)
Penguin Books (South Africa) (Pty) Ltd, 24 Sturdee Avenue,
Rosebank, Johannesburg 2196, South Africa

Penguin Books Ltd, Registered Offices: 80 Strand, London WC2R ORL, England

www.penguin.com

First published 2006
1

Copyright © Henry Patterson, 2006

Set in 11.25/14pt Monotype Bembo
Typeset by Palimpsest Book Production Limited, Polmont, Stirlingshire
Printed in Great Britain by Clays Ltd, St Ives plc

A CIP catalogue record for this book is available from the British Library

ISBN-13: 978–1–844–88103–1
ISBN-10: 1–844–88076–1

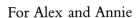

For Alex and Annie

Contents

Acknowledgements

This book could not have been written without the support, intellectual and otherwise, provided by fellow researchers, colleagues and friends. The project itself was suggested by my friend Paul Bew, who has continued to be a major source of ideas and stimulation, as has my colleague Arthur Aughey. Particular parts of the text have benefited from the work and helpful suggestions of Rogelio Alonso, George Boyce, Paul Dixon, David Fitzpatrick, Tom Garvin, Paddy Gillan, Gordon Gillespie, Arthur Green, Graham Gudgin, Ellen Hazelkorn, Greta Jones, Dennis Kennedy, Steven King, Martin Knox, Anthony McIntyre, Deirdre McMahon, Peter Mair, Patrick Maume, Paul Teague and Graham Walker. C.D.C. Armstrong provided research assistance and information based on his own independent scholarship. Professor Máiréad Nic Craith, Director of the Academy for Irish Cultural Heritages at the University of Ulster, provided generous support for visits to archives and teaching relief. I am grateful for the assistance of the staff in the Public Record Office of Northern Ireland, the Public Record Office at Kew, the National Archives, Dublin, the Library at the University of Ulster, Jordanstown, the Linenhall Library, Belfast, the National Library of Ireland and the Grand Orange Lodge of Ireland, Schomberg House, Belfast, and to the Party Officers of the Ulster Unionist Council for granting me access to the UUC papers in the PRONI. Eoghan Harris gave encouragement during a difficult period, and Brendan Barrington was an exemplary editor at Penguin Ireland who combined enthusiasm for the book with detailed and productive criticism. Linda Moore was a major source of support throughout.

Introduction

Eric Hobsbawm observed that 'Nobody can write a history of the twentieth century like that of any other era, if only because nobody can write about his or her lifetime as one can (and must) write about a period known only from the outside.'[1] My own lifetime has coincided with most of the period covered in this book, and I can date my own first awareness of Irish public affairs to a summer day in 1958. My father had parked our car off the main road from Newry to Dundalk, just south of the border. As my mother got out the flask and sandwiches, she wondered aloud about whether we should have stopped so near the border in the middle of an ongoing IRA campaign. We were on our way to the annual conference of the Irish Congress of Trade Unions in Killarney, where the family would combine our summer holiday with my father's attendance as a delegate. We lived in the largely Protestant town of Bangor in north Down, which was, like much of Northern Ireland, largely unaffected by the IRA campaign. This was a period when the dominant community in Northern Ireland was at least as likely to be exercised by class issues of unemployment, redundancies and rent rises as by the threat from the Republic or the Catholic Church. I now know that intra-Protestant divisions were much more liable to show themselves at times when Protestant–Catholic relations were more relaxed, and there was no strong perceived threat to the 'Constitution'.

Those of us who came of age before 1968 have the inestimable advantage of knowing that pre-'Troubles' Ireland was another country, with sensibilities and projects that now appear strange and quixotic. Unionist attitudes to the Republic had a complexity that events after 1968 would brutally simplify. Of course many accepted the Stormont regime's focus on official anti-partitionism and confessionalism when they looked across the border. Others, including my father's elder brother, an Orangeman and bin-lorry driver, were only too happy to set off to tour the lakes of Killarney or the Ring of Kerry during the annual fortnight's holiday for the 12th of July. While my uncle's image of the Republic may have been over-determined by the propaganda of the Irish tourist board, my father's took account of more material realities.

The Irish trade union movement was a thirty-two-county one that included many delegates from British-based unions in Northern Ireland. Some of them would have been, like my father, supporters of the Northern Ireland Labour Party, which looked to the arrival of a Labour government in London to shake up the Stormont regime. They were low-key unionists with a simple 'live and let live' attitude to community relations. They were better placed than many northern Protestants to appreciate the epochal economic changes that were being introduced in the Republic at the end of the 1950s. As an official in the hosiery workers' union, my father was well aware that the factories established by US and British firms in the late forties and early 1950s had come to Northern Ireland, in part at least, because of the restrictions on foreign investment that were in place in the Republic. From the early 1960s this northern advantage was removed. Decades of partition and official propaganda that dwelt on the 'inward-looking' and backward South meant that the revolutionary implications of Seán Lemass's dismantling of the protectionist regime he had done so much to create in the 1930s were invisible to many in Northern Ireland.

This included many Catholics. As an undergraduate at Queen's University in the year of the fiftieth anniversary of the Easter Rising, I found that a number of my Catholic peers who took an interest in politics saw the republican movement as a collection of old men in a time-warp and mainstream nationalists as ineffectual 'Green Tories'. Anti-partitionism was very definitely as passé as the music of Irish showbands. The Irish Republic, traditionally disparaged by unionists, was also now viewed with contempt by many younger, educated northern Catholics for its political class's kowtowing to the Catholic Church and its inferior social services. Lemass was more likely to be seen as a superannuated survivor of the 1916 Rising than as the pragmatic and modernizing twenty-six-county nationalist that he most emphatically was. The dominant imaginings of what the future held were of political realignments and a shift to the left. It is all too easy to dismiss these perspectives as a local version of the frothy excesses of 1968 student radicalism. Naive in the extreme they very soon turned out to be; yet at their core was the recognition that the prosecution of conflicting nationalist agendas was a sure recipe for regression. This was implicit in the political projects of the two modernizing premiers of the period, Terence O'Neill and Lemass, who we were all too ready to dismiss at the time. While O'Neill's project failed, Lemass's succeeded, with profound long-term implications for both Irish states.

The story of Lemass and the Republic's dominant party, Fianna Fáil, is central to this study; the book returns to, while developing and amending, the analysis that Paul Bew and I put forward over two decades ago in *Seán Lemass and the Making of Modern Ireland*. We wrote with access to government archives available only up to the late 1940s; here I have been able to refer to the archives up to and beyond Lemass's retirement. I have also benefited from the major work that has since been done on Lemass and his party by other scholars, particularly Joe Lee, Brian Girvin, Richard Dunphy and John Horgan. The book starts with the high point of de Valera's Ireland: the demonstration of Irish sovereignty through the neutrality policy during the Second World War. By deepening the North–South divide and isolating the Free State from the international post-war economic expansion, neutrality created formidable institutional and ideological obstacles to change. However, a profound economic and demographic crisis in the mid fifties propelled the modernizers into the driving seat. That the Irish state had experienced and resolved its crisis at least a decade before the outbreak of the 'Troubles' was a fact of profound significance for the subsequent history of the island. For it meant that, although as late as the early seventies the British Ambassador to the Republic could refer to the 'Isle of Wight syndrome'[2] – the tendency of the British political class to forget that the Republic was an independent state – the Republic's post-1959 economic transformation and its associated membership of the EEC made it increasingly attractive as a partner, junior or otherwise, in Britain's search for a solution in Northern Ireland.

Much of what has been termed 'revisionism' in the writing of Irish history has consisted of an attempt to purge it of political partisanship in the service of a nationalist or unionist project. Anyone who has lived on the island and who attempts to write a history of Ireland for all or part of the past century faces a related problem: that their direct experience of public and private life will have been predominantly a southern or northern one, with the attendant dangers of mental partitionism. Of course there is a degree of scholarly interchange and dialogue, but it is still true that historians of twentieth-century Ireland, or at least those based on the island, have tended to focus on their 'own' state. I have noticed that my students in Belfast, whether republican, nationalist, unionist or loyalist, are generally united in relative intellectual indifference to what goes on in the Republic. Northern tunnel vision was matched for decades by a view from the Republic of Northern Ireland as a place sunk in repetitive and destructive passions. But, just as it is impossible to comprehend the self-confidence of the Ulster Unionist ruling elite in the 1950s without reference to the economic crisis of the Republic, so it is impossible to comprehend the end of the 'Troubles' without a grasp of the Republic's shift from a thirty-two-county anti-partitionist nationalism to a twenty-six-county state patriotism.

This book was written and then revised over a period that coincided with the signing and enactment of the Belfast Agreement, which seemed to herald an historic political accommodation between unionism and nationalism and between Northern Ireland and the Republic. Eight years after the Agreement, with the dominant political parties in Northern Ireland led by the Reverend Ian Paisley and Gerry Adams, and much evidence of an increasingly segregated society, it is clear that a great deal of the immediate post-Agreement optimism was a product of wishful thinking. The Agreement did see some remarkable developments, particularly the republican movement's endorsement, however hedged around by ambiguity, of what their fundamentalist critics denounced as a 'partitionist settlement'. This followed the IRA's ceasefire declarations of 1994 and 1997, which have ensured that dozens of people are alive today who would not have been if the 'armed struggle' had continued. Deaths are still meted out by paramilitary groups, including the IRA, but they have been mercifully few, and, as a former adviser to successive Fianna Fáil leaders on Northern Ireland has put it, 'For the first time since 1922, Irish democracy is no longer seriously challenged by any armed group.'[3]

The government of the Irish Republic, whose right to be involved in the affairs of Northern Ireland had been officially rejected by successive British governments up to the 1980s, has since the Anglo-Irish Agreement of 1985 been accorded an institutionalized role in the governance of the province. It played a central role in the 1990s in the development of the peace process and in the negotiations that led to the Belfast Agreement. These developments occurred at a time when the growth rates in the economy of the Irish Republic have destroyed for ever the perception of it as a poor nation on the fringe of Europe. In 1997 real per capita GDP was 3.6 times what it had been in 1960,[4] and much of this was down to the spectacular growth rates of the 1990s. There was much talk of a new self-confident and more pluralist and inclusive Irish identity. Decades of membership of the European Union reduced the economic dependence on the UK and provided a broader framework in which to renegotiate both Anglo-Irish and North–South relations.

As early as 1995 Bertie Ahern, the new leader of Fianna Fáil, declared that 'Irish nationalism has changed. Irredentism is dead. I know of no one who believes it is feasible or desirable to attempt to incorporate Northern Ireland into the Republic against the will of a majority there, either by force or coercion.'[5] Such sentiments reflected one of the major processes that has occurred since the 1960s: the deepening of the perception in the Republic of the North as a place apart, one riven by primordial sectarian animosities and with an economy sustained only by a massive subvention from the British Exchequer. If the Republic had once been too poor to afford unity, now the prospect of unity with Northern Ireland could be seen as a sort of Banquo's ghost threatening to disrupt the consumerist celebration of the 'Celtic Tiger'. This is one reason why there is a much larger degree of realism in the official discourse of the Republic about the limits of what is possible in Northern Ireland and in North–South relations.

An element of unionist hostility to post-ceasefire republicanism lay in the feeling that the republican movement had been successful in propagating an image of pre-'Troubles' Northern Ireland as an 'apartheid state'. This book, based in part on the archives of the state itself and also on those of its ruling party, depicts a regime that, contrary to some unionist apologetics, did practise discrimination. The extent and the intensity of that discrimination, and the degree of inequality for which the state at both local and central level was responsible, have sometimes been exaggerated. However, what cannot be denied was the incapacity of the Stormont regime to provide an opportunity for Catholics to feel themselves as a respected and valued part of the community. Too many unionists, even of the liberal variety, tended to dwell on the undoubted material advantages of being part of the UK, as if these in themselves excused a state that remained encrusted with ethnic particularism. Yet neither the inequalities nor the discrimination that existed in Northern Ireland provided any justification for the IRA's disastrous and futile resort to the 'armed struggle'.

Out of the crisis provoked by the attempt to reform Northern Ireland in the 1960s came the quarter century of what is euphemistically termed the 'Troubles'. But, as two political scientists have pointed out,[6] given the number of casualties compared to Northern Ireland's population, a true linguistic rendering of that horrendous experience would be to term it a war. A comprehensive accounting of that period is only beginning to be written. But already a self-serving 'conflict-resolution' paradigm has been imposed on Northern Ireland's recent history. From this perspective the violence flowed ineluctably from the structural inequalities, discrimination and oppression of the Northern Ireland state in its heyday.

This provides a convenient denial of any significant responsibility on the part of the paramilitary organizations that practised violence. It also has the distorting effect of treating the history of Ireland, North and South, before 1969 as little more than an antechamber to the 'Troubles'. This book tries to view the earlier decades in their own terms. The Republic in the 1960s under Seán Lemass and Northern Ireland with Terence O'Neill as Prime Minister bore a closer resemblance to the Free State under William Cosgrave and the North of Sir James Craig than they do to Ireland, North and South, in the early years of the new millennium.

Since the 1970s the economy of Northern Ireland has become heavily dependent on the public sector. In the 1960s the North had a thriving manufacturing sector, employing over 30 per cent of the workforce and returning the highest rates of productivity growth amongst the UK regions. Since then deindustrialization has devastated the manufacturing sector, while the onset of the 'Troubles' insured that the British state adopted more interventionist policies to prevent massively high levels of unemployment with their potential to exacerbate levels of violence. The British Treasury's subvention to Northern Ireland, which was tiny in the 1970s, had become huge by the 1990s, standing at about £3.7 billion.[7] The result was what the Secretary of State for Northern Ireland, Peter Hain, described in 2005 as an economy that 'was not sustainable in the long term'.[8] Referring to the fast rates of growth in the Republic, Hain added that 'in future decades it is going to be increasingly difficult to look at the economy of north and south except as a sort of island of Ireland economy.'

While such sentiments might be music to the ears of Irish republicans, one of the lessons of the period covered in this book is that just as there is no violent way to Irish unity, neither is there an economically determinist one. For all the growing maturity of political debate on Northern Ireland in the Republic, there remains the danger that its economic success story will be used to reinvigorate a traditionalist nationalist narrative. This holds great dangers, as it has been all too easy to represent the history of Northern Ireland since the 1960s as one of Protestant loss. The arch-exponent of this narrative of decline and betrayal has been Ian Paisley. There is much in what follows about the various attempts to modernize both states, but, whereas 'modernization' is often associated with the growth of liberalism and the decline of religious sectarianism, the Irish experience, particularly that north of the border, has been more complex and bleaker than this term would suggest.

1. The Legacy of Partition

The Dynamics of Unionist Rule

On the eve of the Second World War, the two states that had emerged out of the conflicts between Irish nationalism and the British state and between nationalism and Ulster Unionism appeared even more deeply antagonistic to each other than they had at the time of their formation. The Ulster Unionist Party had come quickly to embrace the devolved institutions of government created by the Government of Ireland Act (1920). These institutions had been established not in response to a movement for self-government in the north of Ireland but rather as a part of the British government's attempt at a general settlement of the Irish question. The provisions in the Act for a separate parliament and administration in Northern Ireland had been accepted reluctantly by unionists, whose struggle against Irish nationalism was motivated by a desire to maintain the status quo of British governance from Westminster, not by any positive vision of regional self-government. However, even before the Northern Ireland parliament had shifted from its temporary accommodation in a Presbyterian theological college to the overblown grandeur of a new building with a classical façade in the Stormont estate in East Belfast in 1932,[1] the attractions of devolution for the Unionist Party had become compelling.

In part, the change in attitude was a product of their experience during the negotiation of the Anglo-Irish Treaty (1921). The Treaty, which provided for a twenty-six-county state with the status of a dominion within the British Empire, split Sinn Féin, the revolutionary nationalist movement that had led the political and military campaign against British rule in the War of Independence (1919–21). Lloyd George had for a time attempted to persuade the unionists to accept Irish unity in order to ensure that what was perceived to be the less anglophobic section of Sinn Féin would triumph over the more militant section of the nationalist movement.[2] Fears of 'betrayal' by British politicians increased the attractiveness of an institutional buffer between Belfast and London. A related but distinct concern was to be as untrammelled as possible in dealing with what was perceived to be a hostile Catholic minority.

Although the Government of Ireland Act asserted, in Section 75, the ultimate sovereignty of the Westminster parliament, which also retained all the crucial fiscal powers, it extended to the devolved parliament 'power to make laws for the peace, order and good government'. Law and order issues were at the centre of the Northern Ireland government's concerns from the inception of the state, for reasons that stemmed from the nature of unionism as an organized movement and also from the specific conditions in which the new state was created.

From the emergence of the Home Rule threat in the 1880s Ulster Unionists had reserved the right to resist rule from Dublin, seen as both economically and socially regressive and hostile to their Protestant and British identities, by force if necessary. The formation of the Ulster Volunteer Force (UVF) in 1913 as part of the Ulster Unionist Council's strategy of opposition to the Liberal government's Home Rule Bill was the most substantial manifestation of unionism's conviction that proposals that would alter radically their citizenship of the United Kingdom dissolved normal conditions of loyalty to the constitution.[3] The UVF's drilling and subsequent importation of arms had the unintended consequence of assisting radical nationalists in their challenge to the still-dominant constitutionalist tradition of John Redmond and the Irish Parliamentary Party. Although Redmond had maintained control of the paramilitary Irish Volunteers, which had been formed in response to the creation of the UVF, his support for the British war effort led to a radical nationalist scission that was to provide the nucleus for the armed insurrection in Dublin at Easter 1916. The insurrection and the subsequent execution of its leaders did much to strengthen the forces making for the militarization of Irish politics, which, by the time the Government of Ireland Act was passed, had produced in Sinn Féin and the IRA much more implacable opponents for unionists.

The post-Rising upsurge of revolutionary nationalism had powerful reverberations for the Catholic and nationalist minority in the new state in the North. They had opposed partition not only because it would put them under a Protestant regime but also because of its violation of the unity of the 'historic Irish nation'. Catholics comprised a third of the population of the new state, although they were a majority in two of the six counties – Tyrone and Fermanagh – and in the second city, Derry. Their political affiliations were divided between the Nationalist Party led by Joe Devlin, a Belfast politician who had been one of Redmond's chief lieutenants before 1914, and Sinn Féin, the party that had displaced it in the rest of Ireland in the 1918 Westminster election.

The survival of Redmondism in Northern Ireland reflected the distinctive history of the region's Catholics, which has been well described by Enda Staunton: 'The hemmed-in situation of northern Catholics, the weakness of their middle class and the consequently disproportionate clerical influence left them strongly insulated from trends in the rest of Ireland.'[4] From the inception of the state an important basis for the strength of constitutional nationalism lay in the fear amongst a sizeable sector of Catholics that Sinn Féin's political militancy and the IRA's activities would contribute to sectarian violence from which the Catholic community, particularly in Belfast, would be the main losers.

In 1918 Sinn Féin had not asked for a mandate for the use of force against British rule, but its identification with the 1916 insurrection allowed its military wing, the IRA, to initiate its armed struggle in 1919 with a substantial degree of popular acquiescence, if not active support. But in Ulster the IRA's armed campaign, based on the simplistic assumption that the only substantial obstacle to Irish self-determination was British rule, ignited a sectarian conflagration, which, beginning with the mass expulsion of Catholics from the shipyards and engineering plants in Belfast in July 1920, would over the next two years result in 453 deaths, 7,500 expulsions from workplaces and 5,000 evictions from homes.[5] The majority of victims were Catholics.

The shipyard expulsions and much of the subsequent Protestant violence were the work of unofficial 'vigilance' groups and armed gangs. However, the decision of the fledgling government to control and discipline Protestant reaction to the IRA through the integration of such groups and the recently reconstituted UVF into a Special Constabulary would colour Catholic attitudes to the security apparatus of the state for decades to come. Although unionist leaders would at times accept that there was no necessary connection between being a Catholic and being 'disloyal', the three-tier Special Constabulary was from formation to dissolution an almost totally Protestant force. At its high point of mobilization against the IRA in 1922–3, its three sections had a total of 14,200 Specials mobilized, while the RUC was only 1,200 strong.[6] Even when any substantial IRA threat had disappeared in the later 1920s, the part-time 'B Specials' had a membership of 12,000. This dwarfed the RUC, which, when it reached its full complement, had 3,000 members.[7]

A departmental committee established by the Minister of Home Affairs had recommended that the full complement for the RUC should be 3,000 and that one third of the force should be Catholic. This led to almost a third of the force's NCO/junior-officer level being Catholic.

Catholic representation at rank-and-file level was considerably less at 13.7 per cent. Overall, the Catholic share of the police would stagnate in the inter-war period and begin to decline from the 1950s when the RIC generation began to retire.[8] This, in part, reflected the partisan flavour given to the state's security apparatus by the Specials and the sanctioning by the government of a request by some members of the RUC to be allowed to form an Orange lodge.

The populist and sectarian dimensions of the new regime must be related to the violent and threatening conditions of its early years. A British government official sent to Belfast in 1922 described the dominant unionist mentality: 'The Protestant community of the North feels that it is an outpost of civilisation set precariously on the frontiers of Bolshevism. It believes that the British government has betrayed it and at best that its cause is misunderstood in England.'[9]

Sir James Craig, the Ulster Unionist Prime Minister, had met Michael Collins, the IRA leader and head of the new provisional government in Dublin, in January 1922, in an attempt to establish a *modus vivendi* between the two states. The first Craig–Collins pact exchanged Collins's calling off of a southern economic boycott of Belfast for Craig's commitment to have expelled Catholic workers reinstated in the shipyards. However, Collins continued to support Catholic schoolteachers and nationalist-controlled local authorities who refused to recognize the new Northern Irish state. He also secretly approved a series of IRA raids across the border into Fermanagh and Tyrone, which led to the kidnapping of forty-two prominent loyalists who were to be used as bargaining counters to secure the release of IRA prisoners. IRA killings of B Specials and violent loyalist reprisals in Belfast, including a bomb attack that killed six children, were part of a deteriorating situation in the North, which in March claimed the lives of thirty-five Catholics and eighteen Protestants.[10]

In a desperate effort to halt the escalation of violence, the two leaders met at the end of March and agreed a second and more far-reaching pact. At its core was a proposal that police patrols in religiously mixed areas of Belfast would be composed of equal numbers of Protestants and Catholics and that all Specials not needed for this force should be stood down. There was also provision for an Advisory Committee of Catholics to assist in the recruitment of their co-religionists for the Specials. The British government was to provide £500,000 for relief works to employ expelled workers. Here there was the outline of a non-sectarian Northern Ireland as far as security and employment policy was concerned. It was in line with a declaration by Craig in February 1921 that 'The rights of the minority must be sacred to the majority . . . it will only be by broad views, tolerant ideas and real desire for liberty of conscience that we here can make an ideal of the parliament and executive.'[11] As J. J. Lee has pointed out, Craig 'could at times show physical and even moral courage well above the ordinary'.[12] He had chosen a liberal unionist, Lord Londonderry, as his first Minister of Education, and the Londonderry Education Act of 1923 had attempted to provide for a secular, integrated system of primary education. Although it failed, largely because of the united and bitter opposition of Catholic and Protestant Churches, it had reflected a genuine desire on the Prime Minister's part for reconciliation of the two religious traditions.

The non-fulfilment of both Craig–Collins pacts and Craig's failure to deliver on his early non-sectarian rhetoric were largely a product of two factors. One was the regime's fear of divisions in the Protestant community and a resultant propensity to indulge grass-roots loyalism. As the British official sent to investigate nationalist allegations of police involvement in murderous reprisals for IRA attacks noted, 'Ministers are too close to their community and cannot treat their ministries as from a distance.' The other factor was reflected in his conclusion that the basic reason for the collapse of the second pact was the failure of the IRA to abide by Clause 6 of the Craig–Collins pact, which provided for a cessation of armed activity in the North.[13] Instead the IRA had killed one Unionist MP and burnt the houses of others, and the Irish Army had added its contribution by an 'invasion' of Fermanagh in May 1922.

The period of state formation established a negative and long-lasting dialectic between the sectarian and populist aspects of the northern regime and an aggressive and threatening approach from Dublin, both of which undermined conciliatory tendencies within northern nationalism. Key Ulster Catholic leaders, particularly in Belfast, had initially favoured some form of recognition of Craig's regime, but support for such a strategy was weakened by IRA attacks and unofficial Protestant reprisals. The tone of nationalist politics was increasingly set by the more militant and rejectionist voices from the border areas where Catholics were in a majority. The result was disastrous for the Catholic community. They did not contest the gerrymandering of the local government election boundaries by the electoral commission set up in 1922 under the control of the Minister of Home Affairs' nominee, Sir John Leech. The 1924 election revealed the vital importance of the commission's work. As Michael Farrell notes, 'Some of the results were bizarre. In the Omagh Rural Council area with a 61.5 per cent Catholic majority, the

nationalists had won the council in 1920 with twenty-six seats to thirteen. After Leech's endeavours the Unionists held it with twenty-one
seats to eighteen.'[14] The nationalist boycott of the Leech commission
gave the Unionists a ready-made excuse. Thus when the British Council
of Jews asked the British Home Secretary how it was that 59,000
Protestants in Tyrone elected sixteen representatives to the county council,
while 74,000 Catholics elected only eleven, a senior official in the Ministry
of Home Affairs explained: 'When electoral areas were being fixed the
Nationalists absolutely refused to take any part in the inquiries or to
come and state their case and it was completely impossible for the persons
who were holding the inquiry to look after their interests in these areas.'[15]
The gerrymandering naturally increased opportunities for discrimination
in local government employment. As one official admitted, 'There can
be little doubt that in those areas where there was a Protestant majority
in the councils, in practice posts do not often go to Catholics.'[16] The
unionist leadership was not totally united on this issue. The head of the
Northern Ireland Civil Service (NICS), Sir Wilfrid Spender, hoped that
it would be possible to induce some of the councils to use their powers
of co-option to secure a better representation of minorities (and claimed
that Craig did too). He also opposed discrimination against Catholics by
local government agencies.[17] Such doubts and reservations within the
unionist leadership were to prove of little significance in the absence of
Catholic attempts to exploit them.

　　While discriminatory practices were most developed in unionist-
controlled local authorities in the west of the province, central government
was also affected. Although a number of Catholics were appointed to
senior posts in the NICS, there were instances of discrimination from the
beginning, and over sixty appointments were made without normal selection procedures being observed at all. At the Ministry of Home Affairs,
the Minister, Robert Dawson Bates, refused to allow Catholic appointments. In 1926 the Minister of Labour and future Prime Minister, John
Andrews, found two 'Free Staters' in his ministry when he returned from
holiday and immediately initiated a tightening of regulations to disqualify
such candidates. In 1927 the Minister of Agriculture boasted that there
were only four Catholics in his ministry.[18] Spender and successive Ministers
of Finance, perhaps because of their annual negotiations with the Treasury,
were concerned that such ostentatious sectarianism could produce a destabilizing intervention from London. They were also strongly pre-Keynesian
and critical of the regime's propensity to make 'extravagant' public expenditure commitments to solidify communal solidarity.

But Craig's populist policy of 'distributing bones' to Ulster Unionism's supporters, while it was the despair of the officials at the Ministry of Finance,[19] reflected the fact that his political life, particularly in his later and least impressive years, had been dominated by the fear of Protestant schism. From its inception his government was attacked for not being sufficiently 'Protestant' and for its failure to shield its working-class supporters from the depressed economic conditions of the inter-war years. Divisions along class and intra-sectarian fissures were most threatening in the heartlands of proletarian unionism in Belfast.

The city, with a population of 437,000 in 1937[20] – nearly one third of the total for the province – had from the beginning of the previous century suffered periodic outbursts of sectarian violence. While these were often sparked by political developments in the broader conflict between unionism and Irish nationalism, they also reflected competition over employment and housing amongst Protestant and Catholic workers. The development from the mid nineteenth century of shipbuilding and engineering industries with a workforce dominated by skilled Protestant artisans contributed strongly to a less open labour market than in the older linen industry where Catholics had been represented more equally. Together with the city's increasingly unenviable record for sectarian violence, which acted as a deterrent for Catholic migrants from the Ulster countryside, Belfast's emergence as a major centre of heavy industry helped to explain the decline of the Catholic proportion of Belfast's population from 34 per cent in 1861 to 23 per cent in 1911.

The history of the shipyards showed much evidence of a strong class consciousness manifest in industrial militancy, but also of the most brutal sectarianism. In 1919 shipyard and engineering workers had brought the city's economic activity to a halt by a general strike for shorter hours. But the Unionist Party leadership, aghast at the possibilities of a divided Protestant community, was soon able to use the intensifying IRA campaign as an object lesson in the need for communal solidarity. More extreme loyalist voices alleged that the shipyards and engineering plants had suffered a process of 'peaceful penetration' by Sinn Féiners and extreme socialists when 'loyal' workers had been serving king and country.

The Unionist Party's linkage with the Orange Order provided it with ready access to the fears and grievances of working-class Protestants. The Order had been founded in 1795 in County Armagh as a sort of primitive trade union of Protestant weavers concerned to exclude Catholic competitors from the developing linen industry. Organized in county and district lodges, it had won the patronage of the landlord class, who saw it as a major resource against a feared Catholic *jacquerie*. Its annual parades on 12 July to commemorate the victory of William of Orange at the Battle of the Boyne (1690) were seen by its critics as a prime cause of sectarian conflict. Down to the 1880s it had been based on an alliance between the landlords and clergy of the established Church of Ireland and farmers, labourers and weavers: an institution within which lower-class Protestants could mix with their 'betters' in the defence of the Protestant interest in Ireland and ultimately of the Union itself. Politically it acted as an electoral machine for the Conservatives. The province's Presbyterian, Liberal tradition, strongly represented amongst the bourgeoisie of Belfast and the tenant farmer class, had been cool or hostile to the Order because of its links with the Tories and the Church of Ireland. However, the common threat of Home Rule had led to the fusion of Tories and Liberals, and to a Presbyterian influx to the Order, which came to be seen as the best grass-roots defender of the constitutional status quo. When the directing body of Unionism, the Ulster Unionist Council, was set up in 1905, the Orange Order was provided with a substantial representation, and its membership expanded rapidly during the mobilization against Home Rule. Its political importance resided not simply in that it had representation as of right in the party at all levels, or that the overwhelming bulk of Unionist MPs and cabinet members were members, but also in its ability to criticize the party and the government if they were seen to deviate from the defence of Protestant interests.

During the mobilizations against Home Rule, liberal unionists had been careful to emphasize that the unionist case should be put in secular terms, fearing that too much emphasis on Orange and Protestant themes would undermine support in the rest of the United Kingdom.[21] At the core of the secular unionist argument had been the economic success of the north-east of Ireland under the Union, symbolized above all by the shipyards, engineering factories and linen mills of Belfast. After 1921 secular unionism went into recession as depressed economic conditions challenged the Unionist Party's ability to contain the force of plebeian Protestant discontent within its ranks, and this was a major factor in encouraging the stridently anti-Catholic rhetoric that disfigured the speeches of leading unionist politicians in the 1930s.

The industries that had been at the core of Ulster Unionists' self-confidence before 1914 were to experience major problems in the inter-war period. Although the shipyards had performed creditably in the 1920s given a situation of worldwide overcapacity, the slump in world trade after 1929 hit the two firms hard, with employment in the winter of 1932–3 at only a tenth of its 1929–30 level and an unemployment rate of over 80 per cent. The smaller of the two yards, Workman Clark, closed down in 1935, and, although the Harland and Wolff enterprise absorbed some of its plant and labour force and made serious efforts to diversify production, shipbuilding employment at the outbreak of war was still only 10,000 – an improvement on the mere 2,000 at the depth of the depression but just half of the figure for 1929.[22] The engineering sector was given an injection of energy with the establishment of the Short and Harland aircraft factory in 1937, an enterprise that employed over 6,000 by May 1939. Shipbuilding and engineering had begun to pull out of recession by 1939, but the region's largest employer of manufacturing labour, the linen industry, faced the bleaker prospect of changes in fashion and lifestyle that consigned linen to the status of a luxury product. There was a contraction in employment in the industry from 75,000 in 1924 to 57,000 in 1939, and by the latter date 20 per cent of its workers were unemployed.

Agriculture, which in 1926 employed a third of the male and a quarter of the total labour force, suffered like shipbuilding and linen production from adverse international trends: overcapacity and a sluggish growth in demand. The industry was dominated by small farms (70 per cent were under 30 acres and 86 per cent under 50), and its concentration on dairying and livestock, where prices declined less than cereals, was the main reason for a slight improvement in its position in the inter-war period relative to the industry in the rest of the UK. Per capita output, which was 46 per cent of the British level in 1924–5, had reached 53 per cent by 1939. Nevertheless, rural Ulster remained miserably poor. In 1930 Keynes had described the living standards of the region's small farmers as 'almost unbelievable', and the wages of farm labourers in the 1930s were less than the unemployment benefit paid to an unemployed married man.[23] Despite migration to the towns, the level of unemployment in agriculture was over 20 per cent in 1939. The economy as a whole experienced persistently high unemployment rates, with on average 19 per cent of the insured labour force unemployed between 1923 and 1930 and 27 per cent between 1931 and 1939. In 1939 the figure was 23 per cent, compared with 10 per cent in Britain.[24]

The increasingly sectarian tone of the northern state in the 1930s reflected the internal tensions that unemployment and poverty created for a governing party that was committed to the notion of 'parity' in a range of social services with the rest of the UK. As unemployed Protestant and Catholic workers rioted together against Belfast's niggardly system of outdoor relief in 1932, the unionist elite worried that the capacity of the Orange Order to bind together the classes in the Protestant community was weakening. The Order found its membership in decline as the new state firmly established itself and unemployment sapped the commitment of its working-class members.[25] This thinning of the ranks in the heartland of working-class loyalism was a major concern to the unionist leadership, although they still looked to the Ulster Unionist Labour Association, created in 1918 to counter socialistic influence on the Protestant working class, to win over the 'cream' of the working class.[26]

The gravity of the economic situation meant that the appeasement of sectarianism was not sufficient to deal with the threat of working-class disaffection. The 'anti-populists' such as Spender and Hugh Pollock, the Minister of Finance, had used the Loans Guarantee Act, by which the government guaranteed loans made to business concerns, as a means of preserving employment in the shipyards. The government also continued to fund public works as a method of relieving unemployment after the Treasury had ceased to do so in the rest of the UK.[27] But, despite these economic responses, there was no escaping the sour sectarian edge of unionist politics in the 1930s.

A weakening of Orange influence was accompanied by the development of the more rabid, and less controllable, form of sectarian demands associated with the Ulster Protestant League (UPL), founded in 1931 to 'keep Ulster Protestant' by ensuring that Protestant employers took on only 'loyalists'. A loose alliance of lower-middle-class evangelicals and the poorest sections of the Protestant working class, it was allowed the use of the Unionist Party headquarters to hold its meetings and was patronized by leading members, most notably the Minister of Agriculture and future Prime Minister, Basil Brooke.[28] The UPL had thrived in the more febrile environment created by the victory of Eamon de Valera and Fianna Fáil in the 1932 elections in the South. De Valera's indulgence in the political theatre of intervention in the Stormont elections in 1933, when he was returned on an abstentionist ticket for South Down (another Fianna Fáiler won West Tyrone), contributed to a unionist obsession with the supposed threat of a large-scale inflow of 'disloyalists' across the border.

Basil Brooke, in the 1930s the only rising star in the unionist firmament, identified himself intimately with these concerns. Educated at Winchester and Sandhurst, he was a scion of the 'fighting Brookes', a County Fermanagh landowning family with a record of military service and, since the 1880s, of providing militant leadership against the advances of nationalism. Although his own service in India and the Boer War had confirmed his imperialism, action during the First World War had led him to consider the possibility of Irish unity as the price for whole-hearted Irish support against Germany; but his return to the role of local landlord and to the unionist and Orange leadership in Fermanagh found him adopting an increasingly parochial and sectarian tone in his politics. The organizational and leadership capacity that he had displayed in the establishment of the Special Constabulary in his area had brought him to Craig's attention and, combined with his relative youth, personal charm and strong family connections with the English military and landed elite, marked him out in a party whose leadership was ageing and suffering from a severe lack of ability. Entering parliament in 1929, he became Minister of Agriculture in 1933, providing the government with one of its few examples of policy activism and earning the reluctant admiration of Spender as one of the two competent members of the cabinet.

However, Brooke did not allow the regular visits to the cabinet room at Stormont to dilute his public commitment to the more fevered expressions of unionism in Fermanagh. The county was typical of those parts of Northern Ireland where Protestants were in a minority but still dominated local government through the creative drawing of constituency boundaries. In Fermanagh 25,000 unionists had seventeen seats on the county council, while 35,000 nationalists had only seven. Like other leading figures in border-county unionism, Brooke was fixated on the twin threats of 'infiltration' from the South and any potential weakening of Protestant unity by those who put economic grievances before communal solidarity. These included Protestant farmers encouraged by speculation that de Valera's government would abolish land annuity payments to demand that Stormont do likewise. Fear of possible independent farmers' candidates splitting the unionist vote led Brooke to denounce 'semi-Protestants and semi-loyalists'.[29] His subsequent political career would be dogged by the reputation for pugnacious sectarianism that he had acquired in the 1930s. Speaking to Fermanagh Orangemen in 1933, he urged Protestant employers to employ 'Protestant lads and lassies' and boasted of his own Catholic-free estate. He gave dire warnings of a plot to overturn the unionist majority in the North through 'infiltration' and 'peaceful penetration' from the South and of Catholics 'getting in everywhere' because of laxity and complacency amongst Protestant employers.[30]

This exclusivist tone was reflected at the centre of provincial government where Sir James Craig declared in a parliamentary debate in 1934 that Northern Ireland was a 'Protestant Parliament and a Protestant State'. The declaration was part of a response to a Nationalist MP who had raised the issue of discrimination against Catholics in state employment. Craig asked him to 'remember that in the South they boasted of a Catholic State. All I boast of is that we are a Protestant Parliament and a Protestant State.'[31] Perhaps conscious of giving a potent propaganda weapon to critics of his government, he claimed that he was not opposed to the employment of Catholics as long as they were loyal to the state. But the distinction between Catholic and 'disloyalist' was subverted by his own communal definition of the state and by the public pronouncements of senior ministers like J. M. Andrews, Minister of Labour, who assured ultra-Protestants, kept awake at night by the allegation that twenty-eight of the thirty-one porters at Stormont were Catholics, that he had investigated and found there to be only one Catholic, there on a temporary basis.[32]

The increasingly Catholic and nationalist tone of the Free State intensified sectarian animosities in the North. Events like the state-sponsored celebration of the centenary of Catholic Emancipation in 1929, the appointment of a minister at the Vatican in the same year and the holding of the international Eucharistic Congress in 1932 in Dublin were given heavy coverage in unionist newspapers and Orange platforms, as was the declaration by the Bishop of Down and Connor, Joseph MacRory, in December 1931 that it was doubtful if the Protestant Churches were part of the Church of Christ.[33] There was no shortage of Protestant clerics to respond in kind, and 1931 had already seen anti-Catholic riots in Portadown, Armagh and Lisburn.[34]

The intensifying sectarian tone was accompanied by concern at de Valera's continuing links with those who still insisted they had the right to wage war against the northern state. The IRA's support for Fianna Fáil during the 1932 election, the mass release of IRA prisoners as soon as de Valera took power, the organization's open drilling and recruiting, and the expression of violently anti-partitionist sentiments by some of de Valera's senior colleagues[35] all contributed to the perception of the South as having entered into a new and aggressive posture.

But while these factors may help explain the responsiveness of Craig's government to ultra-pressures throughout the 1930s, they do little to excuse it. After attacks on pilgrims travelling from Northern Ireland to the Eucharistic Congress, Dawson Bates arranged with the Attorney-General that the Protestant offenders should be treated leniently.[36] In Belfast, where discontent on issues of unemployment and housing could be exploited by both loyalist and labour critics, the attractions of assuaging such discontent through the patronage of ethnic militancy were obvious, but so were the dangers. The first sectarian killing of a Catholic since the 1920–22 period occurred in Belfast in 1933, and there was sectarian rioting in 1934 and during the celebrations of George V's Silver Jubilee in the spring of 1935. The febrile atmosphere had produced an unprecedented decision by Dawson Bates to ban all processions in the city, but, after the threat of open defiance from the Orange Order and the intervention of the Prime Minister, the ban was rescinded in time for the July processions. The parades sparked off the only prolonged and serious outbreak of violence in the city between 1922 and 1969: ten days of riots in which seven Protestants and three Catholics were killed. Apart from the deaths, the Catholic community bore the brunt of the violence, with 430 Catholic families being evicted compared to sixty-four Protestant families.[37] The result was the sort of press coverage in the Free State and the UK that the few critics of Craig's populism within the regime feared would spur Westminster to investigate the way devolved power was being exercised. When it did produce precisely this result, defenders of the government would turn the focus of discussion southward, attempting to explain away the blemishes of unionist rule through a lurid depiction of developments in the other Irish state.

Conservatism in Power: The Irish Free State 1922–1932

The 'Irish Revolution', as a number of scholars have pointed out, was a solely political one. Ireland's chance of a social revolution had been undermined by the land reforms sponsored by the British state, which created an increasingly conservative peasant proprietorship in the four decades before independence. An estimated two thirds to three quarters of Irish farmers had become owners of their land by the outbreak of the First World War. A leading member of the pro-Treaty section of Sinn Féin described the dynamics of this conservative revolution: 'Getting rid of foreign control rather than vast social and economic changes was our aim.'[38] The result is summed up by John M. Regan:

'The revolutionary and civil wars were fought over constitutional forms and symbols, fundamentally the republic versus the Crown, and ultimately on the source of sovereignty. Though there was undoubtedly a class component to both conflicts it did not come to dominate the issue of national sovereignty.'[39]

The fundamental priority that Sinn Féin attached to social consensus, with its conservative implications, goes far towards explaining the speed with which a stable society, complete with the structures of a democratic political system, was achieved after a decade of insurrection and civil war. The Irish Free State was governed, like its northern counterpart, by a bicameral parliament whose procedures were loosely modelled on those of Westminster. Its Constitution, negotiated with Britain after the Treaty in 1922, had created a form of parliamentary democracy. The lower house, named Dáil Éireann in order to maintain continuity with the revolutionary first Dáil composed of the Sinn Féiners victorious in the 1918 general election, was elected by proportional representation. The Constitution provided for a system of cabinet government: an Executive Council bound by collective responsibility and headed by a President.

The Constitution was able to come into effect only after the Civil War (1922–3), in which there were between 4,000 and 5,000 deaths (compared with 1,200 in the War of Independence).[40] The pro-Treaty victors had to create a new party from the top down using elements of existing political and politico-military organizations. From its inception Cumann na nGaedheal (from 1933 Fine Gael) defined itself as the party of the Treaty, law and order, and Commonwealth status. Its focus on the defence and consolidation of the state was understandable: the prosecution of the war had cost the state £17 million, and material destruction was estimated at about £30 million. Demilitarization was essential both to consolidate the fledgling democracy and to cut the large defence budget. A key decision had already been made during the Civil War: the new police force, the Garda Síochána, was to be unarmed. The decision to create a new army, breaking with ambiguities that had characterized civil–military relations between the Dáil and the IRA during the War of Independence, was a source of considerable resentment amongst sections of the pro-Treaty military, and the rapid demobilization and reduction in the army's size announced in 1923 produced a failed 'army mutiny' in 1924.

The government's economic and social philosophy was conservative, reflecting in large part the straitened circumstances of the early years of state building, but also its ties with the Catholic professional and business class and in the countryside with the larger farmers who had a strong vested interest in the maintenance of the existing relationship with the British market. Its dominant personality was not its leader, William T. Cosgrave, but Kevin O'Higgins, the Minister for Home Affairs.

O'Higgins was elitist, authoritarian, an enthusiast for the Commonwealth and an ardent believer in the moral virtues of balanced budgets; there was little surprise, therefore, when one of the early decisions of the government was to cut old-age pensions by a shilling a week. He was a strong supporter of the Department for Finance's imposition of best British Treasury practice. The government's hard-nosed image was encapsulated in the icy declaration by the Minister for Industry and Commerce, Patrick McGilligan, in 1924 that 'People may have to die in this country and die of starvation.'[41]

The Treatyites had been excoriated for their acceptance of British insistence that all members of the Dáil had to take an oath of allegiance to the British monarch, and the new government was condemned for other manifestations of its 'pro-imperialist' mentality. These included its use of the upper house, the Seanad, to make overtures to the Free State's rapidly dwindling Protestant population: Cosgrave had used his powers of nomination to the body to appoint sixteen former unionists. This, along with the existence of proportional representation, allowed the minority some voice in national politics but needs to be set against the radical shrinkage in the Protestant population, which occurred during the national revolution, and the increasingly Catholic ethos of public policy.

The census of 1926 showed that almost a third of Protestants in the twenty-six counties had gone since 1911. The Catholic population of the new state was 2,751,269, while there were just 220,723 non-Catholics.[42] Although the withdrawal of the British garrison after 1921 was in part responsible for the decline, the distinct sectarian edge of the national revolution was another. Thus in Cork, the most violent of all Irish counties during the War of Independence, Protestants made up 7 per cent of the population but 36 per cent of the 200 civilians shot by the IRA, and eighty-five of the 113 houses burnt belonged to Protestants. In just one night in April 1922 ten Cork Protestants were killed by the IRA allegedly as 'spies' or 'informers' but in reality as a sectarian reprisal for attacks on Catholics in Belfast. They included businessmen, farmers, a lawyer, a curate, a post-office clerk and a farm labourer. Hundreds of Protestants went into hiding or fled their homes, abandoning farms and shops. Many did not stop until they arrived in England or Belfast.[43]

Cosgrave's desire to reach out to the minority was commendable, but its positive effects were undermined by his and his colleagues' eagerness to reflect Catholic morality in legislation. In 1925 divorce was outlawed, leading W. B. Yeats to warn the government, 'You will create an impassable barrier between South and North.'[44] Protestants, North and South, subsequently saw the creation of the Censorship Board in 1930 as further evidence of the Catholicization of the public sphere in the Free State. This and the state's commitment to the creation of a 'Gaelic Civilization', through making the Irish language compulsory for the Intermediate and Leaving Certificate and for jobs in the civil service, would do little to help the realization of the first objective of its party programme: 'To secure the unity of Ireland and to unify the diverse elements of the Nation in a common bond of citizenship.'[45]

For all its contradictions, the desire of Cosgrave's government to work out a more harmonious relationship with the North was sincere. This was reflected in its acceptance of the demise of the Boundary Commission in 1925. Under Article 12 of the Treaty, the Commission had been given the task, if Northern Ireland exercised its right to secede from the Free State, of determining the boundaries between the two states as specified by the ambiguous formula 'in accordance with the wishes of the inhabitants, so far as it may be compatible with economic and geographic conditions'.[46] Held out by Lloyd George as a major tactical inducement to the Sinn Féin negotiators, it had encouraged them to hope for such substantial transfers of territory to the Free State that the North would be made unviable. However, when the Commission was eventually constituted in 1924, Lloyd George had departed the scene and Collins's death removed the Irish leader who would have been most able to press a tough position. With Craig firmly ensconced in power, refusing to nominate the North's representative but sure of the sympathy of the British government's substitute (the former editor of liberal unionist *Northern Whig*), the eventual report, which left the northern state virtually intact and even proposed some minor transfers from the Free State, was unsurprising, although still acutely embarrassing for Cosgrave.

Rather than implement the report, the three governments signed a tripartite boundary agreement on 3 December 1925. It confirmed the existing boundary and released the Free State from the financial liabilities it had incurred under the Treaty. Cosgrave's attempt to obtain concessions from Craig in the agreement on the treatment of Catholics in the North failed, although Craig did speak of a 'fair deal' for the minority.[47] The Council of Ireland, that provision for North–South co-operation under the Government of Ireland Act, had its powers transferred to the government of Northern Ireland, but the agreement provided for representatives of the two governments to meet to consider matters of mutual concern. The benign possibilities that might have flowed from

Dublin's recognition of the northern state were not to be realized. In part this reflected the northern regime's too-easy indulgence of sectarianism. South of the border it was a product of the growing political strength of those who had been defeated in the Civil War.

Fianna Fáil and the Republicanization of the South

There is no doubt that Fianna Fáil has been the dominant political force in modern Ireland. In the fifty-year period (1922–72) following the establishment of the Free State, the party held governmental office for no fewer than thirty-four years. For most of this period the party's success was intimately linked with its enigmatic and machiavellian leader, Eamon de Valera. Born in New York in 1882, de Valera had been sent back to Ireland at the age of two by his Irish mother when his Spanish father died. Brought up by relatives on a small farm in County Limerick, he was educated by the Christian Brothers and the Holy Ghost Fathers at Blackrock College, which produced many of the new state's religious and political elite. His early formation encouraged some of his key characteristics: industry, asceticism and self-discipline, accompanied by emotional distance and cold calculation. His rural petit bourgeois background, education and white-collar position made him typical of that generation of earnest young men and women whose nationalism had been deeply influenced by the movement to revive the Irish language. He joined the Gaelic League in 1908 and the Irish Volunteers in 1913. He was the oldest leader of the 1916 insurrection to survive, his death sentence being commuted because of his American birth.

After the Rising he became the President of the ascendant Sinn Féin Party and titular head of the Irish Volunteers, later the Irish Republican Army. He was the main political opponent of the Treaty and, after the Civil War, of the anti-Treatyite Sinn Féin, which in the first election to the Dáil after the conflict in 1923 won 27.4 per cent of the vote and forty-four seats to Cumann na nGaedheal's 39 per cent and sixty-three seats.[48] De Valera and his allies in the leadership of the anti-Treatyites were soon convinced that the new dispensation had enough popular legitimacy to make any attempt at its physical overthrow unthinkable, and this forced them into a parting of the ways with their more fundamentalist colleagues in Sinn Féin and the IRA, who wanted to maintain the twin policies of abstention from the Dáil and the underground preparation of the IRA for the overthrow of the states North and South.

The name Fianna Fáil – meaning 'Warriors of Destiny' – and its subtitle 'The Republican Party' demonstrated de Valera's determination to monopolize the legacy of 1916 and the national revolution. The first two aims set out in the party's constitution were the ending of partition and the restoration of the Irish language as the spoken language of the people.[49] The nationalist and Gaelic dimensions of the party's project were crucial in de Valera's determination to bring as many of the anti-Treatyites as possible with the new formation. Although the two aims might have appeared contradictory, given northern Protestants' generally disdainful attitude to the Irish language, they were essential in defining Fianna Fáil not just as a mere political party but rather, as de Valera portrayed it, as a movement for national redemption.

All this lofty nationalist idealism notwithstanding, the leaders of the new party demonstrated a ruthless pragmatism, a sure grasp of the material dimension of party appeal and a Leninist approach to organization and propaganda. The party was still committed not to take its seats in the Dáil until the oath of allegiance was removed. However, the assassination of Kevin O'Higgins, the government's strong man, by IRA dissidents in July 1927 forced de Valera's hand. Emergency legislation enforced the oath as a sine qua non of participation in constitutional politics and Fianna Fáil complied, telling their supporters that 'hardheaded common sense is not incompatible with true nationalist idealism.'[50]

Once it began to participate fully in constitutional politics, Fianna Fáil adopted a left-of-centre social and economic programme, opposing the government's conservatism and not simply its alleged pro-British orientation. In its first electoral contest in June 1927, Fianna Fáil had been attacked by the leader of the Labour Party for allegedly drawing twelve of its fifteen manifesto pledges from earlier Labour programmes.[51] Its electoral success was based on more than stealing Labour's clothes, for from its inception the party's leadership had poured all their energies into building a formidable political machine. At the core of the party-building process were the numerous old IRA companies that were transformed into local *cumainn* (branches). The famed discipline of the party, together with its lack of serious debate and the authoritarian tinge to its internal culture, derived from this militarist component in its formation. Founded in March 1926, the party had 460 *cumainn* by November, and by the summer of 1927 it had 1,000.[52] By contrast, Cumann na nGaedheal never grasped the possibilities inherent in mass organization, and many of its leaders maintained a patrician contempt for party branches, which were seen as a hindrance to the work of government. This elitist disdain for the demands of a competitive party system combined with the government's conservative economic and social policies to ease Fianna Fáil's road to power.

Although de Valera would periodically claim that he had been deeply influenced by the ideas of the socialist leader and 1916 martyr James Connolly and the party's progressive image, Fianna Fáil cultivated business support from its earliest days, promising a more radical regime of tariff protection and proclaiming its concern to govern in the national interest. It was with the support of those whom the party's national organizer referred to as its 200 or so 'wealthy friends',[53] together with their rich American friends, that the party was able to launch a daily paper, the *Irish Press*, in 1931.

Although Seán Lemass, architect of the party's electoral hegemony in urban areas, boasted of the 'slightly constitutional' nature of Fianna Fáil, de Valera demonstrated that there were strict limits to his willingness to accommodate those republicans who refused to accept the new constitutional order he set out to create when the party took office for the first time in 1932. Many members of the IRA had deserted the organization to join Fianna Fáil as it emerged as a radical nationalist challenger to what it depicted as the reactionary pro-British policies of Cumann na nGaedheal. The leadership of the IRA had instructed its members to work and vote for the party in the elections of 1932 and 1933, and the first two years of the new government saw an increase in IRA militancy and in the bitterness of political and ideological conflicts.

The new government was faced with an economy already suffering from the shock to the country's exports delivered by the Great Depression. The all-important cattle trade was experiencing major problems, and added to these economic concerns was a widespread fear of de Valera's 'communistic' agrarian policies amongst the larger farmers. It was from this class that most of the support for the short-lived Blueshirt movement derived: an unstable mixture of civil war animosities, fascist sympathies and economic self-interest.

Unionist newspapers would make much of the street clashes between Blueshirts and the IRA in the 1932–4 period, depicting the South as in a state of burgeoning chaos. In fact de Valera showed a willingness to use repressive measures in the form of military tribunals against what were depicted as opposing sets of extremists. After offering the IRA a number of carrots, from mass releases of prisoners in 1932 to employment in the state's security apparatus, and failing to extinguish its elitist vision of itself as the 'real' government of Ireland, he did not hesitate to outlaw the organization in 1936.

Like Craig, de Valera proved much more successful in marginalizing political challengers from the extremes than he did in delivering on the economic and social dimensions of his political project. As with his northern counterpart, constitutional questions would prove an important means of compensating for economic and social failures. He waged a relentless war of attrition against the vestiges of imperial subordination in the Treaty: the abolition of the oath of allegiance, the downgrading of the position of the Governor-General and the abolition of the right of appeal to the Judicial Committee of the Privy Council. The process culminated in the promulgation of a new Constitution, adopted by referendum on 1 July 1937. The Governor-General was replaced with an elected President, while the already abolished Free State Senate was replaced with a vocationally selected body with much reduced powers. The tonal shift was completed by renaming the Prime Minister, known as President of the Executive Council under the Free State Constitution, as the Taoiseach, meaning 'Chief' in Irish. However, much more significant were Articles 2 and 3, which laid territorial and jurisdictional claim to Northern Ireland. Together with the Constitution's indebtedness to Catholic social theory, a ban on divorce and, in Article 44, its recognition of the 'special position' of the Catholic Church, it deepened the North–South divide. Despite this, de Valera continued to pressurize the British government to reopen the partition issue and attempted to use the resolution of other unfinished business from the Treaty settlement to achieve this.

The refusal of de Valera in July 1932 to continue to transfer to the British Exchequer the annuity payments due from Irish farmers under the various British Land Acts provoked retaliatory British duties on Irish exports. The subsequent economic war, together with the already significant effects of the slump in international demand, saw the value of the most important single item in exports, live cattle, decline from £19.7 million in 1929 to £6.1 million in 1934.[54] The economic war and the adverse international conditions served to accelerate and at the same time to justify Fianna Fáil's own economic and social project, which it liked to portray, at least in the early 1930s, as broadly 'progressive'. In the countryside it stood for a generalized agrarian radicalism. In order to break Irish dependence on the British market, it was argued that tillage production should be favoured over a strong emphasis on livestock. Tillage was to be encouraged to meet domestic grain demand and help make the country self-sufficient in food. The party's rhetoric depicted the small farmer rather than the large rancher as the stable basis of the Irish nation. The Land Commission was to be used to redistribute land on a large scale to small farmers and landless men. As many families as possible were to be settled on the land. Radical agrarianism was complemented by a strong commitment to industrialize through the vigorous use of import tariffs and quotas. The protected home market was to be saved as much as possible for native capitalists by the Control of Manufactures legislation to limit the power of foreign businessmen. The programme was given a left-of-centre tone by a commitment to welfarist policies in areas including pensions, unemployment insurance and housing. De Valera, who was not averse to summoning up the ghost of James Connolly, the socialist martyr of the 1916 insurrection, had gone as far as declaring that his government's objective was to end the conditions that had forced hundreds of thousands of Irishmen to emigrate since the Great Famine of the 1840s.[55] By the end of the decade, if some of the undoubted achievements of the Fianna Fáil project were visible, so too were its limitations.

This was particularly clear in rural Ireland, where the government's agrarian radicalism sharply diminished as fear of a decline in living standards led to a growing emphasis on the need to trade with the nearest large market. In 1935 a Coal–Cattle pact was agreed with Britain, and from 1936 onwards there was a steady reintegration of Irish agriculture into the British market. The impact of Fianna Fáil efforts to alter radically Irish agriculture was slight. By 1939 the tillage acreage was a mere 2 per cent above its 1930 level, and cattle raising remained the dominant enterprise despite a severe price decline. The flight from the land continued, and the decline of the small farmer class was not arrested. The pace of land redistribution had slowed considerably by the late 1930s. Delegates to Fianna Fáil's annual conference in 1938 complained about the government's desertion of its small farmer constituency and a new political party, Clann na Talmhan ('Children of the Land'), was created that year as an expression of small-farmer discontent,[56] which was strong along the western seaboard and in the south-west, where there was a concentration of small farmers working poorer land in districts that were particularly hard hit by emigration.

By 1938 Fianna Fáil, which had come to power with a disproportionate reliance on the votes of small farmers and with a regional support base that was stronger in the west than in the centre and east of the state, had begun to acquire the status of a majority 'catch-all' party with an extremely wide and diverse electoral constituency. Its loss of some electoral support from disappointed farmers and landless men had been diminished by the 1933 Unemployment Assistance Act, which for the first time provided support to small farmers and farm labourers. These groups together with the urban working class were also beneficiaries of the most significant of the government's social improvements: a crash slum-clearance and house-building programme that led to the construction or renovation of 132,000 houses between 1932 and 1942. An average of 12,000 houses a year were built with state aid between those years, compared with fewer than 2,000 a year between 1923 and 1931. Housing was one area of social expenditure in which de Valera's government clearly outperformed Craigavon's.[57]

Central to Fianna Fáil's electoral success were those economic and welfare policies that allowed it to appeal to both the working class and an expanding manufacturing bourgeoisie. Although there is some dispute about whether official figures that show industrial employment rising from 162,000 in 1931 to 217,000 in 1938 may in part be a product of improved enumeration procedures,[58] even the sceptics agree that a substantial increase did occur.[59] This was complemented by the government's more frequent use of publicly owned corporations when private enterprise was unwilling or unable to develop national resources. These included an Irish Sugar Company, a Turf Development Board, an Industrial Credit Company, the Irish Tourist Board and a national airline, Aer Lingus. As more and more of the actual or aspirant manufacturing class shifted their political loyalties to a party once perceived as practically 'Bolshevist', the urban working class saw in the Fianna Fáil government a welcome break with the conservatism and pro-rural bias of its predecessor. Although some of the more radical impulses of Seán Lemass as Minister for Industry and Commerce were countered by the formidable conservatism of the officials in the Department of Finance, supported by the Minister Seán MacEntee, Lemass did much in the decade to establish his claim that the existence of Fianna Fáil made the Irish Labour Party unnecessary. Some of the leaders of the Irish trade union movement increasingly saw Fianna Fáil as an ally. As the membership of trade unions affiliated to the Irish Trade Union Congress grew from 95,000 in 1933 to 161,000 in 1938, this was unsurprising.[60] The pro-labour bias of the government was also perceived in measures designed to improve working conditions through the introduction of Joint Industrial Councils, Trade Boards and the Conditions of Employment Act (1936).

But the gains of this activism were almost exhausted by 1938. The limits of import-substitution industrialization on the basis of a small home market had been reached by the end of the 1930s. Consumers often paid for the undoubted employment gains with higher prices and inferior products. Small-scale and inefficient production meant much of the new industry would be incapable of selling abroad. What extra jobs were created were insufficient to absorb rural depopulation, and unemployment had reached 145,000 in January 1936.[61] The problem was in part a reflection of the fact that emigration, the traditional solution to the Irish economy's inability to employ its people, had been blocked by the Great Depression. Despite de Valera's claim in a speech to Irish emigrants in London in 1933 that 'We shall not rest until we have lifted the doom of exile which for so long has lain upon hundreds of thousands of Irishmen in every generation',[62] there was a major resumption of emigration to the United Kingdom from 1935 once that country's economy began to show signs of recovery.[63]

The Irish Labour Party hoped to benefit from the dissatisfaction of those who had looked to Fianna Fáil for a more radical set of policies on both the economy and the national question. Created in 1912 by the Irish trade unions, it had faced the daunting task of development in a political system where the predominant fault line in the 1920s and 1930s reflected a national and not a class issue. During the Civil War, Labour had deplored the excesses of both sides while trying to emphasize the primacy of socio-economic issues. In the 1920s the party continued to decry the concentration on constitutional issues left over from the Treaty and the Civil War. Before Fianna Fáil committed itself to constitutional politics and entered the Dáil, Labour was able to establish itself as a moderate, reformist alternative to Cumann na nGaedheal. In the election of 1923 it won 10.9 per cent of the vote and fourteen seats. In the next election, in June 1927, its support had risen to 12.6 per cent and twenty-two seats out of 153. However, once Fianna Fáil entered the Dáil the party was faced with an even more formidable competitor for the working-class vote. For, although the small size of the South's industrial working class (14.6 per cent of the workforce in 1936)[64] militated against the development of the party, it was also the case that even within this restricted constituency Labour was not the hegemonic force.

Most noticeable was its stark weakness in the two main urban centres, Cork and Dublin. From the 1920s until the 1960s, Labour's strongholds were in a number of largely agricultural counties in the east and southeast, where the state's agrarian proletariat was concentrated. Neglected by Fianna Fáil, whose agrarian policies were fixated on the needs of the small farmers, these labourers constituted a third of the agricultural workforce in twelve counties, and it was in these counties, including Wexford, Waterford and Tipperary, that Labour's most reliable support existed. Elsewhere the party's structure and plodding concentration on material issues narrowed its appeal.

Until 1930 it maintained its organic link with the trade union movement: of its forty-four candidates in the June 1927 election, twenty-seven were trade union officials. The trade union movement, which had expanded during the 1916–21 period, was badly hit by the depressed economic conditions of the 1920s, and its urban heartland in Dublin was seriously damaged by a bitter conflict within the country's largest union, the Irish Transport and General Workers' Union (ITGWU). At the heart of the dispute was the role of James Larkin, who had founded the union in 1908 and incarnated the spirit of intransigent revolutionary syndicalism that had manifested itself in his partnership with the Marxist founder of the Irish Labour Party, James Connolly, and in his charismatic leadership of the workers during the Dublin Lock-Out of 1913. Out of Ireland from 1914 to 1923, he returned to a radically different situation but showed no inclination to scale down what William O'Brien and the other moderate organization men who ran the ITGWU considered his unrealistically militant vision of trade union struggle. Bitter internal wranglings, a court case and finally Larkin's expulsion from the ITGWU in 1924 led to his formation of a rival union, the Workers' Union of Ireland.

Larkin's mythic status amongst the Dublin working class meant that the dispute had severe implications for Labour in the city. The ITGWU leadership's involvement in the party led to a bitter Larkinite assault on Labour's timidity and its moderation on constitutional issues. Larkin had been a strong opponent of the Treaty, and he echoed IRA taunts about the party's English leader, Thomas Johnson, being an imperialist who could not understand Irish nationalism.[65] Labour did move closer to Fianna Fáil from 1927 onwards, making it clear that it would be prepared to consider a coalition agreement with Fianna Fáil if that party entered the Dáil.[66] This strategy simply confused some of its supporters, while others who had been attracted by its pro-Treaty stance now deserted it. In the September 1927 election, the first after de Valera led his supporters into the Dáil, Labour's support dropped to 9 per cent and thirteen seats as the electorate polarized between the two major parties. It did particularly badly in Dublin, where a Larkinite assault resulted in Johnson losing his seat.

As long as Fianna Fáil's promises of a progressive, republican project were untested by office or, as in the early 1930s, in the first flush of realization, Labour faced a real danger of obliteration as a distinctive political force, as was evident in its electoral performance in 1932 when it won a mere 7.7 per cent.[67] Supporting de Valera's minority government in 1932 brought further decline as Fianna Fáil appealed for a secure majority with which to implement its programme, and in the snap 1933 election Fianna Fáil's support rose from 44.5 per cent to 49.7 per cent, while Labour was reduced to its worst-ever performance with a mere 5.5 per cent. Its new leader was a prominent trade unionist, William Norton, General Secretary of the Post Office Workers' Union. Norton's leadership was a sharp break with the past. He had played a central role in the severing of the link with the unions in 1930 to enable the party to appeal beyond such a sectional constituency. A convinced nationalist, he was friendly with de Valera and ditched Labour's neutrality on constitutional issues in favour of a straightforward acceptance of mainstream republicanism.[68] There were signs that as the limits of Fianna Fáil's social radicalism became clear, Norton's left-republicanism might bring gains. In the 1937 election Labour's support rose to 10.3 per cent and thirteen seats. Yet de Valera's capacity to exploit the unfinished business of Anglo-Irish relations to marginalize any Labour challenge was far from exhausted.

Here de Valera's triumph in the Anglo-Irish Agreement on 25 April 1938 was decisive. The British Prime Minister, Neville Chamberlain, was determined to do as much as possible, short of the coercion of the North, to put relations with de Valera on a new and amicable basis. In part this reflected a concern to end the bitterness of centuries, but he also saw success as a means of providing an example of appeasement in action.[69] The centrepiece of the Agreement was the return of those ports that Britain had retained control of under the Treaty: Cobh, Berehaven and Lough Swilly. Chamberlain's hope that de Valera might consider a defence treaty to allow Britain access to them in times of war proved illusory. The economic war was ended on terms extremely favourable to Ireland: the British agreed to drop their demand for a settlement of the financial dispute over the land annuities from £26 million to £10 million. Ireland was granted the same trade terms as other dominions, with the result that, while UK exports to Ireland were still subject to restrictions, Irish exports gained free entry to the British market.[70] British attempts to press Belfast's demand for lower duties on Ulster exports to the South were rebuffed with the claim that such a concession was impossible, given the oppression of Catholics in the North. For the first time since 1922, inquiries into the activities of the Stormont regime were carried out by the Home Office and the Dominions Office.[71]

Capitalizing on his triumph, de Valera called an election for June 1938 focusing on how the Agreement would make Irish neutrality possible in world conflict and claiming that he was much more optimistic about an end to partition than he had been in 1932.[72] The result was a major victory for Fianna Fáil, which won over 50 per cent of the vote, its share rising from 45.2 per cent to 51.9 per cent. As J. J. Lee has pointed out, de Valera was wise to seize the opportunity offered by the Agreement to snatch his election triumph. A deteriorating economic and financial situation was reflected in a harsh budget in May 1939.[73] The inquiries into the allegations of Stormont's ill-treatment of Catholics had produced a critical report by the Dominions Office: 'it is everywhere inimical to good and impartial administration where government and party are as closely united as in Northern Ireland.' However, the Home Office line of defence of the regime won out, in large part because Spender, as head of the Northern Ireland Civil Service, could point to increasing numbers of Catholic applications to the NICS.[74] Thus, despite the moribund nature of the northern government, it appeared that there was little chance of London destabilizing it, unless de Valera was prepared to barter the neutrality policy that was so popular in the South.

2. War and the Welfare State

Nationalists and the Second World War

The attitudes of northern nationalists to the war were heavily influenced by their fraught relation with the state. However, there were important differences of approach that reflected the longer-term division between the Nationalist Party and Sinn Féin. In the early years of the new regime nationalists in Belfast and the east of the province had been more inclined to support participation in parliament as a means of highlighting injustices and pressuring for redress, particularly in the area of education. Living in areas where Catholics were in a minority, and with the bitter experience of the inter-communal violence of the 1920–22 period, they were less likely to be supporters of republican militancy. The influence of Joe Devlin's constitutional and reformist populism had been decisive there. Support for abstentionism and Sinn Féin was much stronger in the west and south of Northern Ireland, where nearness to the border and the existence of local Catholic majorities had initially encouraged hopes of a strategy of exit from the state through repartition. Most northern republicans had been pro-Treaty and after the collapse of the Boundary Commission in 1925 had moved towards an uneasy coalition with the Devlinites and the Catholic Church to adopt a policy of qualified and fitful participation in the northern parliament. A new organization, the National League of the North, was set up in 1928 with Devlin as President and Cahir Healy, a Fermanagh insurance agent who had been a founding member of Sinn Féin, as Secretary.[1] Committed to the 'national reunification of Ireland', the new organization's initial tendency to support Devlin's policy of participation was from the start unpopular with a sizeable section of those from the pro-Treaty Sinn Féin tradition, and as the 1930s progressed the support for abstentionism grew.

Devlin's own participation in parliament had only ever been a partial and qualified one, the main purpose of which was to campaign for the defence of Catholic education in the North. On this question at least he had the support of the bitterly anti-unionist Archbishop of Armagh, Cardinal Joseph MacRory, and the other northern bishops. The universal concern of the Catholic Church that it control all aspects of the

education of Catholic children was in Northern Ireland complicated by
the distrust and antagonism felt by the hierarchy towards the new state.
The liberal Minister of Education, Lord Londonderry, had, in the
Education Act of 1923, tried to refashion the North's education system
along more integrated lines by excluding religious instruction while at
the same time creating three classes of elementary school, each enjoying
a different level of financial assistance. Only those that were fully
controlled by local authority education committees were fully funded
by the Ministry of Education for salaries, running costs and capital
expenditure. Those that accepted a management committee with four
members chosen by the school trustees and two representatives of the
education committee received all the cost of salaries, half the running
costs and a discretionary amount towards capital costs. The 'four and
two' committees were rejected as the thin end of the wedge of total
control by a Protestant state, and thus Catholic schools became part of
the 'voluntary' sector, where the Ministry paid the salaries but there was
no contribution to running and capital costs. Lord Londonderry's
genuine but abstract liberalism – he had naively considered the 'four
and two' committees as a compromise attractive to both the Protestant
and Catholic Churches – actually disadvantaged the Catholic Church,
which lost the grants it had received under the pre-partition provisions
amounting to two thirds of its building and equipment costs. Pressure
from the Protestant Churches and the Orange Order forced the government to modify the 1923 Act to ensure that schools controlled by the
local authorities were 'safe for Protestant children' by providing for representation of Protestant clergy on appointments committees and by
installing religious education. As compensation, the 1930 Education Act
provided Catholic schools with capital grants of 50 per cent.[2]

The 1930 Act had come as a result of a threat by the Catholic bishops
to take legal action against the 1923 Act, which they claimed violated
the provision of the Government of Ireland Act forbidding the endow-
ment of any Church. This victory, compared to the futile manoeuvrings
of Nationalist politicians, encouraged a process by which the Catholic
population of Northern Ireland increasingly focused its practical horizons on building a distinct civil society within a Protestant-dominated
state. The inter-war period had seen a proliferation of Catholic organizations: the Catholic Arts Guild, the Catholic Young Men's Society, the
Legion of Mary, the Catholic Boy Scouts and even a Catholic Billiards
League. At a time when the openly proclaimed policy of the government was that the state was a Protestant one, the seeming dead-end of

constitutional or semi-constitutional opposition, together with the flourishing Catholic 'state within a state', tended to increase the influence of abstentionist sentiment within nationalist politics.

The victory of Fianna Fáil in the 1932 election had strengthened republican optimism. IRA membership in the North rose dramatically while northern supporters of Fianna Fáil such as Eamon Donnelly, a former republican–abstentionist MP for Armagh, and pockets of 'anti-Treaty republicans' such as the National Defence Association in the Newry and south Armagh area, began to campaign vigorously against any recognition of the northern parliament. In the 1933 Stormont election the National League's candidate in south Armagh was defeated by a republican–abstentionist, and Eamon de Valera was nominated and returned unopposed by Nationalists in South Down.[3] Devlin himself saw his majority in Belfast Central cut into by a republican prisoner, and after his death in 1934 northern nationalism lacked any substantial figure who could have attempted to bring its fractious elements together.

The 1935 riots in Belfast inevitably strengthened northern Catholics' sense of themselves as a besieged minority within a hostile society and with a government that was, at best, indifferent to their fate.[4] Those such as Devlin's successor as MP for Belfast Central, the Catholic barrister T. J. Campbell, who continued to favour attendance at Stormont, were increasingly overshadowed by supporters of abstentionism either as a tactic or as a fundamental matter of principle. The government had responded to de Valera's success in the 1933 election by introducing legislation that required all candidates in Stormont elections to make a declaration that they would take their seat if elected. Republicans were still able to pressurize Healy and the other Nationalist MP for Fermanagh–Tyrone to step down in favour of abstentionist candidates in the 1935 Westminster election, but Healy was strongly opposed to any attempt to adopt a similar strategy for Stormont. However, northern sympathizers of Fianna Fáil led by Eamon Donnelly, now a Fianna Fáil TD, favoured a radical strategy of boycotting Stormont while allowing northern Nationalists to take seats in the Dáil. In the 1938 Stormont election the result of these divisions was that in three Nationalist constituencies the local organizations refused to nominate candidates, and the seats were lost, reducing Nationalist representation to eight MPs.

By the time of the 1938 Anglo-Irish negotiations, the dominant political tendency in northern nationalism was to look expectantly to de Valera to sort out partition as part of his negotiations with Chamberlain. Healy and other Nationalist MPs had travelled to London during the negotiations to meet de Valera and press him to ensure that partition was put at the centre of the negotiations. De Valera was told that it would be a betrayal if he settled the trade and defence disputes and ignored partition. But, as he had already demonstrated in his opposition to the proposal to allow northern MPs to sit in the Dáil, de Valera's primary concern was with the consolidation and defence of his twenty-six-county state, and he was not prepared to allow a settlement that so plainly favoured the Irish to be delayed or even prevented by pressure from the North.

Northern nationalist frustration and anger with the Fianna Fáil leader over the 1938 agreements with London were intense. Despite this, de Valera was able to get Healy to launch a series of anti-partition rallies in the autumn of 1938. He wanted to use these as part of his anti-partition campaign in Britain and the US,[5] but for de Valera the central purpose of the campaign was to establish internationally a clear sense of Irish grievance that would allow him to justify Irish neutrality in the coming conflict. Neutrality was the goal, not unity, and de Valera was hostile to any attempt, whether it came from Downing Street or nationalists in the six counties, to raise the unity issue.

Alienation from Fianna Fáil produced a fusion of its supporters in the North with the group of parliamentarians under the direction of Healy in a new organization, the Six Counties Men's Association. It was supported in the South by republican critics of de Valera, including the former chief of staff of the IRA, Seán MacBride, and the former Blueshirt leader and Nazi supporter, General Eoin O'Duffy. Three of its leading members in the North welcomed the possibility of a German victory, telling the German minister in Dublin that they were prepared to 'place the Catholic minority in the north under the protection of the Axis powers'.[6] Healy was interned in Brixton prison between July 1941 and September 1942 under an order signed by the Home Secretary, Herbert Morrison, because of suspicions of pro-German activities. Although Healy protested that he was neither anti-British nor pro-Nazi,[7] intercepted correspondence with a Fermanagh priest suggested a policy of collaboration in the event of a German invasion.[8]

Such pro-German sentiment was strongly developed in the ranks of the northern IRA. While support for the IRA dwindled in the South during the 1930s due to the attractive power of the initial period of Fianna Fáil radicalism, the organization grew in strength in Northern Ireland through a mixture of the misplaced hopes generated by de Valera's victory and the attendant intensification of sectarian passions in the North. Although most of the Belfast IRA was outside the city at a training camp in the South when the sectarian violence of 1935 began,[9] the organization's role as a communal defence force received a boost, much to the despair of some of the more left-wing republicans in the South who wanted the IRA to bridge the gap with the Protestant working class. The IRA's newspaper had complained that Belfast republicans were 'on the whole possessed of a bigotry that is dangerous to the cause they have at heart', and the left-republican Peadar O'Donnell bluntly proclaimed 'we haven't a battalion of IRA men in Belfast; we just have a battalion of armed Catholics.'[10] These rather pious criticisms simply missed the point that for many northern republicans the main enemy was not the abstractions of 'British rule' or 'imperialist domination' but the six-county Protestant state and what were seen as its repressive and discriminatory manifestations.

Northern republicanism was able to exploit the state's increasingly repressive response to republican marches and commemorations. Conflicts over the right to march had been a recurrent feature of the social and political history of the North for well over a century. Orangeism's determination to mark out as much as possible of northern territory as Protestant and unionist public space was periodically contested by both Catholic and nationalist organizations. The Ancient Order of Hibernians, which developed in the late nineteenth century as a defender of Catholic interests and a counter to Orangeism, had been closely linked to Devlin's party. Its acceptance of partition, coupled with the resurgence of republicanism after 1916, had seen it go into slow decline.[11] Its annual parades on St Patrick's Day and on the Feast of the Assumption in August were largely limited to predominantly Catholic villages and small towns. Although these parades could at times be the occasion of conflicts with local loyalists, they were generally not interfered with by the police. It was very different with public manifestations of republicanism, which were frequently prohibited under regulations of the Special Powers Act, even when they took place in areas like the Falls Road district of Belfast, which were predominantly nationalist.[12] Throughout the inter-war period, but particularly in the 1930s, the main manifestation of northern republicanism was the annual commemoration of the 1916 Easter insurrection. These parades, particularly the largest ones in Belfast and Derry, were regularly banned, and as a result the RUC found itself in conflict not simply with a few hundred republicans but with much larger numbers of Catholics who had gathered to watch the parades. In 1937 there were serious disturbances on the Falls Road when, in enforcing a ban, the RUC baton-charged the crowds of spectators.[13]

The rise in northern nationalist expectations during 1938, first during the Anglo-Irish negotiation and subsequently because of the de Valera-inspired anti-partition rallies in the autumn, produced a predictable increase in conflict with the state and sections of the unionist population. Grass-roots unionist annoyance at anti-partitionist demonstrations where the Irish national anthem, 'The Soldier's Song', was sung led to the government introducing a new regulation under the Special Powers Act banning it, despite the advice of the Inspector-General of the RUC that the enforcement of such a ban would exacerbate communal conflict and disorder.[14] As war approached, this pattern of nationalist and republican assertiveness, Protestant reaction and state repression established itself. The IRA's bombing campaign in England inevitably encouraged a unionist identification of nationalist politics as subversive. When the British government refused to extend conscription to the province in May 1939, Sir Basil Brooke blamed 'the minority in our midst . . . either afraid or too despicable to take a hand in the defence of the country . . . prepared to go to any lengths to prevent the loyal and brave men of this country from doing their duty'.[15] The IRA responded by a demonstration on the Falls Road, where there was a burning of thousands of recently distributed gas masks.[16] When war was declared, Catholic workers at Harland and Wolff were evicted by gangs of fellow employees and Catholic mill girls were forced to quit, while police escorts accompanied Protestant workers leaving Mackies Foundry on the Springfield Road in West Belfast.[17]

Anti-state sentiment was not simply a response to repression and discrimination. It was also an expression of an autonomous sense of Irish national identity produced through Church and school and reinforced in the institutions of Catholic civil society from newspapers to sporting and cultural organizations. At its core was a vision of Catholics, whatever their social class, as belonging to a victimized community. A report by the Irish National Council of the YMCA into the experience of young unemployed Catholics attending a work camp near Belfast in 1940 warned of the potentially explosive mixture of economic exclusion, anti-police sentiment and nationalism. The report claimed that 'quite good boys' who had been looking for jobs failed to get them in workplaces where the majority of workers were Protestant and where Protestant boys from the camp were being constantly taken on. Talking to the Catholic boys, they came across strong anti-RUC sentiment: 'To them the police were all prejudiced against the Catholic areas of the city, all laws were bad laws because they were English laws and every moral argument was propaganda.' One of the best boys in the camp, 'tidy, clean, above the average in intelligence, a good worker', was an ardent supporter of the IRA: 'he firmly believed that we would be better off under Nazi rule.'[18]

Cardinal MacRory might not have gone quite as far, although the Nazis believed that he was in favour of German action to end partition.[19] But he did nothing to encourage any softening of anti-state feeling, declaring that Catholics in Northern Ireland had neither freedom nor justice.[20] It is none the less important to register the complexity of Catholic attitudes. It was not true, as F. H. Boland of the Department of External Affairs claimed in April 1941, that 'the vast majority of Nationalists in the six-county area are absolutely pro-German on account of their unjustified treatment by the British government and its Belfast puppet.'[21] A delegation of northern nationalists who met de Valera in October 1940 provided him with a detailed analysis of three strands of opinion within the Catholic community: some supported the IRA, others wanted to assist the northern government in its defensive measures against a possible German invasion, and the third group was content to trust Fianna Fáil and support his policy by not cooperating with Stormont.[22]

Pro-Germanism tended to be secondary to anti-British and anti-Stormont feelings. The support for limited assistance to the government was strongest in Belfast, where the city's two Nationalist MPs were willing to sit on a defence committee created by Craigavon in the summer of 1940.[23] Although the Catholic community had been united in opposition to Craigavon's call for conscription, there is some evidence, particularly for Belfast, that a tradition of service in the British forces, a product more of economic necessity and the desire for action and adventure than of loyalty to the state, asserted itself during the war.[24] Northern Ireland's only Victoria Cross in the Second World War was won by a Catholic. The *Irish News*, Belfast's Catholic daily, maintained the Redmondite tradition and referred to IRA men who raided banks and post offices as 'bandits'.[25] Its coverage of the progress of the war was pro-Allied. Thus, although it was in Belfast that the IRA concentrated its efforts to disrupt the war effort and that it obtained its main martyr when Tom Williams was executed for the killing of a Catholic RUC man in West Belfast on Easter Sunday 1942, its Catholic community was not unified in hostility to the war effort.

The strong republican current that had been manifested in the early years of the war went into recession as the conflict progressed. This reflected the vigorous repression North and South and the disorientating effect of the 'Hayes Affair' in June 1941, when the Chief of Staff of the

IRA was arrested and interrogated by his own comrades, who believed he was a police informer.[26] The devastation of large parts of Belfast in four German air raids in April and May 1941 may have weakened the pro-German convictions of some northern Catholics. Brian Moore, whose novel *The Emperor of Ice Cream* portrays that grim and chaotic time in the city's history, has described how the Blitz destroyed his surgeon father's Axis sympathies: 'My father, who was pro-German, when he saw what the Germans were able to do, when he saw what modern warfare was really like, when they blow up your home, that was all, things were over.'[27] Cardinal MacRory, concerned that anti-British sentiment had been undermined by the Blitz, warned the German minister in Dublin that more attacks would stir up anti-German feeling.[28]

Although Craigavon's government had ensured that any possible Catholic participation in the Home Guard was minimized by basing it on the B Specials, there was some shared wartime experience when people took on civil defence activities and became air-raid wardens, fire-fighters and rescue workers.[29] The halting of Orange marches during the war – its critics claimed it was to avoid the embarrassment of the large numbers of loyalists of fighting age who had not joined up – substantially reduced possible occasions of sectarian conflict. The effective ending of unemployment by 1943, as a result of the massive expansion of the North's traditional industries brought about by wartime demand, softened the material edge of Catholic grievance. The Nationalist Party in Belfast had, since Devlin's death, become increasingly identified with the interests of the Catholic middle class of solicitors, teachers, doctors and publicans. Its conservatism at a time when even Northern Ireland was being affected by the UK-wide swing to the left lost it two of its councillors, who joined the Northern Ireland Labour Party in January 1942.[30] However, the interpenetration of class and sectarianism in the life of the city meant that the Nationalists' appeal to a predominantly working-class constituency could also be outflanked by more militant forms of anti-partitionism. When the sitting Nationalist MP for the Stormont constituency of Falls died in 1942, his proposed successor was defeated by Eamon Donnelly running on an abstentionist ticket. This reflected Catholic anger at the execution of Tom Williams, who was a native of the constituency. When a few months later the Catholics of West Belfast had a choice between an NILP candidate and an abstentionist for the Westminster constituency, they voted massively in favour of Jack Beattie of the NILP, who won the seat. Beattie was a strongly anti-partitionist socialist, and he was seen as the candidate most likely to defeat the

Unionist Party, which held the seat. Nevertheless, his victory indicated that the city's Catholic working class was inclined to express its nationalism in a pragmatic and left-of-centre way.

In Derry, despite the bitter Catholic resentment at the gerrymandered system of the city's government, the war years saw a lessening of local antagonisms. As in Belfast, this had a material basis in the unprecedented wartime prosperity of the local shirt-making and shipbuilding industries and the substantial amount of work associated with the creation of the US naval station, which became the Allies' most westerly base for repair and refuelling.[31] Local asperities were temporarily displaced with the influx of tens of thousands of American servicemen, whose superior resources and novelty value made them attractive to local women and earned them the resentment of Derry men irrespective of religious denomination. The city's Catholic bishop encouraged his flock to participate in the war effort by involving themselves in civil defence activities,[32] and, as in the Great War, Derry men of both traditions enlisted in the British forces.[33] Unlike Belfast, where the war years saw the emergence of a Labour and republican-Labour challenge to the Nationalist Party, which was maintained after 1945, in Derry traditional forms of nationalism went into temporary decline to be reinvigorated in the post-war period. The local injustice was such a glaring one that, although the worldwide cataclysm would temporarily diminish its significance, its continued existence ensured that by the end of the war Derry Nationalists would be in the forefront of attempts to relaunch a coherent northern Nationalist Party.

What little we know of nationalism outside Belfast and Derry in the war years seems to indicate a sense of disorientation and a lack of energy or direction. When the Nationalist MP for Mid Derry died in 1941, such was the apathy and enervation in party ranks that the writ for a by-election was not moved until 1945.[34] With only one Nationalist MP at Stormont for most of the war, it was unsurprising that Seán MacEntee, a prominent member of de Valera's government, could publicly criticize the Nationalist Party for condemning its supporters to 'political futility for 22 years'.[35]

Stormont and the Challenge of War

The lacklustre response of Craigavon's government to the outbreak of war confirmed the opinion of the head of the NICS, Sir Wilfrid Spender, that the devolved regime had become a threat to the cause of the Union.[36] Craigavon had been reduced by age (he was sixty-nine) and recurring illnesses to one hour of work a day, and his frequent long vacations outside the province did nothing to diminish his paternalist indulgence of the most sectarian and parochial strands of loyalist opinion. The increasingly rigid sectarian tone of unionism in the 1930s had reflected, the liberal Minister of Education, Lord Charlemont, believed, 'the gradual increase of pressure from independent organisations, leagues, Socialism; all the political expressions of Ulster individualism'.[37] When Craigavon called a general election in February 1938, ostensibly as a response to de Valera's raising of the partition issue in the Anglo-Irish negotiations, his main domestic concern was the challenge of a new Progressive Unionist organization. This had been founded in 1937 by a Westminster Unionist MP, W. J. Stewart, who had broken from the party to challenge the government's record on employment, housing conditions and agriculture. Not for the first or last time did southern irredentism powerfully contribute to the marginalization of challenges to Unionist Party hegemony. Support for the Unionist Party rose from 72,000 in the previous general election to 186,000, while the Progressive Unionists got 47,888 votes and won no seats.[38]

The despair of Spender at Craigavon's style of government could only have been deepened by the administration's inability to adjust to the demands of war. In part this reflected the deadening effects of two decades of unchallenged power. By the outbreak of war the average age of his cabinet was sixty-two and four of its seven members had been in government since 1921. John Andrews, Minister of Finance, was born in the same year as Craigavon and, despite signs of physical debility, was to be the Prime Minister's successor. From a family with major interests in flax spinning and railways, Andrews was President of the Ulster Unionist Labour Association and a strong supporter of running the state on communal lines. John Milne Barbour, whose undistinguished record as Minister of Commerce made him the butt of much Labour and Independent Unionist criticism, was seventy-one. Barbour, who had combined his Commerce position with that of Parliamentary Secretary to the Ministry of Finance, was amongst the few in the government (the Minister of Finance from 1921 to 1937, Hugh Pollock, was another) who had been unhappy with Craigavon's Protestant populism. Robert Dawson Bates, one of the younger members of the cabinet at sixty-two, was a rigid and strident proponent of the view that the state's first priority should be to guard against the internal and external nationalist threat.

Despite his exaggerated sense of the precarious position of his government, he persisted in living in the northern seaside town of Portrush,
seventy miles from his department. The result, as Spender bitterly noted,
was, despite fuel rationing, a yearly distance of over 30,000 miles for
his large official car and frequent and prolonged absences from his
department.[39]

Although persuaded by Chamberlain not to press the issue in the
broader interest of the war effort,[40] Craigavon and his ministers resented
the exclusion of Northern Ireland from conscription, particularly as they
saw in the decision an indication of British desire to conciliate de Valera
in the interests of possible Irish participation in the war. They were also
concerned that, without conscription, the unionist community's commitment to the war effort might be shown to be less than enthusiastic. In
the opening phase of the war recruits came forward at a rate of 2,500
per month, but this had fallen to fewer than 1,000 by the spring of 1940.
There was a brief upsurge in the aftermath of Dunkirk, but by December
1940 monthly recruitment levels had fallen to 600 and the long-term
trend was downward.[41]

Memories of the terrible losses of the Ulster Division at the Somme
in 1916 may have kept recruitment figures down. The local sectarian
dynamics of the northern state also played a part. Basil Brooke had
appealed early in the war for people to 'set aside the Orange and Green
dispute and co-operate fully with the government. If this war goes against
us the only flag that will fly over Belfast or Dublin will be the swastika.'[42]
But, just as for many nationalists the ending of partition ranked higher
than resisting fascism, for a large number of unionists the world conflict
could not distract their attention from the possible threat to the local
balance of power that wartime mobilization might bring. The sectarian
violence that had devastated Belfast between 1920 and 1922 had been
fuelled in part by loyalist resentment at what was perceived to be the
'peaceful penetration' of Ulster by Catholics from the South, who took
the jobs of Protestants who had volunteered for military service. The
bitter legacy of economic competition in the 1930s helped to encourage
a recrudescence of such fears during the early years of the war when
unemployment remained a problem. A direct appeal by the government
to those northern Catholics who were sympathetic to the Allied cause
might well have served to lessen Protestant reluctance to volunteer.
Tommy Henderson, the Independent Unionist MP for Shankill, an often
strident voice for the interests of this heartland of the Protestant working
class, became so frustrated with the low recruitment figures that he

demanded that Craigavon actively campaign in nationalist areas: 'tell them what the Roman Catholic countries had suffered at the hands of Hitler . . . he would be surprised at the good response.'[43] The government's answer was to put Basil Brooke in charge of a recruiting campaign. The Unionist politician most associated with the demand that Protestant employers take on only co-religionists was a less than inspired choice, and this was compounded by Brooke's decision to use the Unionist Party machine to organize the campaign.

With the end of the 'phoney war' and the formation of a new and more dynamic government in Britain, the contrast with what the official historian of the North's war effort called 'a sense of inertia . . . of fumbling uncertainty'[44] was stark. In May 1940 Edmond Warnock, a junior minister at Home Affairs, resigned from the government, denouncing its failure to mobilize the province for any of the demands of the war and accusing it of being 'in a state of lethargy, almost a coma'.[45] In June he was followed by another junior minister who echoed the views of those unionists who were sympathetic to the idea of an understanding with de Valera to ensure access to southern ports and airfields. Up until Dunkirk, support for the idea of North and South uniting within the empire as the only way of guaranteeing Britain's survival had been articulated only at the liberal fringe of the Unionist Party. Now it got the support of junior members of the government and at least one Westminster Unionist MP, Dr James Little, who declared he was prepared to stand by the side of 'any man, however much in other matters he might differ from me, who was willing to unite with me in defending the land of my birth against Nazi domination . . . we are all proud to be Irishmen and no land on the face of the earth do we love so well as this land.'[46]

Even that stalwart defender of the interests of border unionists, Basil Brooke, was racked by the conflicting pulls of parochial dominance and the call of an empire in peril. He had carried on his family's long tradition of military service, and of his three sons who enlisted, two were killed. A nephew of Sir Alan Brooke, Chief of the Imperial General Staff, he was an enthusiastic proponent of the North's total mobilization and of the priority of the world conflict over local considerations. Sounded out by an Independent member of the Dáil on his opinion of the sort of deal being broached with Dublin – to join the war in return for postwar unification – he claimed that such a proposal would split the cabinet but that he would vote in favour.[47]

Brooke, recognized even by the government's critics to be an energetic and effective Minister of Agriculture,[48] might have hoped to succeed

Craigavon. However, when the Prime Minister died in November 1940, the province's semidetached relation to the war effort was apparent in Andrews's unchallenged succession. Spender saw Andrews as totally incapable of rising to the challenge of war, mired as he was in the worst aspects of Craigavon's legacy: the obsessive concern to placate every parochial loyalist and Orange pressure group. The composition of his new cabinet did not reflect growing backbench pressure for radical change. Brooke was moved to Commerce, which he struggled to turn from a small and ineffective ministry, the butt of much criticism from those who held it responsible for the continuing high levels of unemployment, to the central directing core of wartime economic policy. The rest of the changes were an ineffective interchange of patently superannuated figures. The epitome of Andrews's leadership style was the promotion of Milne Barbour, the much criticized former Commerce minister, to Finance – the first example Spender could think of where a minister was promoted for incompetence. Brooke was replaced at Agriculture by Herbert Dixon, Lord Glentoran, the Chief Whip, whose hold on Andrews stemmed from his reputation as a fixer or, as one critic uncharitably put it, 'a notorious "twister"'.[49]

The first major indication that the change of leadership had done nothing to quell a rising tide of criticism of the regime's lack of energy and direction was the by-election caused by Craigavon's death. The Unionist Party lost North Down by a wide margin in a high poll to an Independent. A month later, in April 1941, the Belfast Blitz provided devastating evidence for its critics of the complacency and incompetence of the government. In the worst of the attacks, on the night of 15–16 April, over 800 were killed, the highest casualty rate in one night's bombing of any city in the UK. The total number of deaths from the four raids was 1,100, while over 56,000 of the city's houses, about half of its stock, were damaged, leaving 100,000 people temporarily homeless.[50] Although the origins of Belfast being the British city least physically and psychologically prepared for the Blitz lay in part in the advice from London in the early months of the war that Northern Ireland was unlikely to be attacked,[51] subsequent more pessimistic analysis had not produced any substantial improvement in the city's defences.

The government shared responsibility for the protection of the city with its Corporation, which demonstrated on a smaller scale the deadening and corrupting effects of untrammelled one-party rule, in this case extending back before partition. The abolition of proportional representation for local government elections, the main objective of which had been to reduce the number of councils controlled by Nationalists, severely damaged the electoral prospects of the NILP in Belfast. Here Labour's widely spread but thin support was under-represented in a simple majority system, unlike the Nationalists, whose support was heavily concentrated in a few largely Catholic wards.[52] In the last election for the Corporation before the war, eighteen of the Unionist Party's nineteen seats were obtained without a contest, as were the Nationalist Party's three, while the NILP, which had not contested any seats since 1937, had no councillors. The local Unionist political machine, the 'City Hall party', was largely oblivious to the possible effects of its conservative and complacent stewardship on an increasingly embattled government. Belfast's citizens had virtually no air-raid shelters and a fire brigade of only 230 full-time men, which the Corporation refused to expand even after the Luftwaffe had attacked cities in the north of England and Scotland. The indifference and neglect of the Corporation, particularly towards the poor and vulnerable, was further highlighted in June 1940 when a Home Affairs inquiry revealed extensive corruption and incompetence in the management of Whiteabbey Sanatorium, and another inquiry concluded that 'In respect of personal medical services, Belfast falls far short of what might be expected in a city of its size and importance.'[53]

The government's fear of conflict with the Belfast Unionist machine made it resist demands for the dissolution of the Corporation, but it did bring in commissioners to run the city for the duration of the war. Harry Midgley of the NILP had been prominent in the campaign that forced the inquiry into Whiteabbey, and he shook Andrews's government when he won a by-election in Willowfield, a largely Protestant constituency in East Belfast, in December 1941. Regarded as a safe Unionist seat, which the NILP had not contested before, Midgley's large margin of victory showed that Northern Ireland was not immune to the UK-wide shift to the left in public opinion that occurred during the early years of the war as a reaction to what was seen as the establishment's appeasement of fascism and consequent lack of an effective strategy for winning the war.[54] With the USSR an ally from June 1941, attacks on socialism disappeared from the speeches of Conservative and Unionist politicians, and as the state's role in economic and social life expanded massively, Andrews was warned by some of his brighter and frustrated junior ministers of the wide belief that 'the present socialistic policy of the (UK) government must continue if not be intensified when peace comes.'[55]

Much of the dissatisfaction with Andrews's government stemmed from the continuing existence of unemployment at a time when there was a labour shortage in the rest of the UK. When the war started there were 63,112 unemployed in Northern Ireland, 19.3 per cent of the insured population. The British unemployment figure was 8.3 per cent. By November 1940, while the British rate was 5.2 per cent, unemployment in the North had risen to 71,633, a rate of 21.3 per cent. The most important single factor in explaining this situation was one outside the government's control: the decline of the linen industry because of the loss of its major sources of flax in Russia, the Baltic states and Belgium as a result of the war. Unemployment in the industry, which employed 57,000 workers, one sixth of the insured population, increased from 11,261 at the outbreak of the war to 20,450 in November 1940.[56]

It was also the case that the lack of war contracts, about which the Belfast government complained, reflected a perception in the main supply departments that Northern Ireland suffered from higher production costs as a result of shortages of some types of skilled labour and from the extra transport costs involved for raw materials and finished products. Devolution itself had created major institutional impediments to an effective mobilization of the North's capital and labour resources. These were reflected in the administrative problems caused by the necessity of integrating the North's devolved structures with the new UK-wide system of regional Area Boards created by the Ministry of Supply. There was no direct liaison between the Ministries of Labour in Belfast and London. As Harold Wilson, a young Board of Trade civil servant, noted, 'So far as can be seen there is little or no economic co-ordination between Great Britain and Northern Ireland. Ulster is not represented on the Production Council, the Labour Supply Board, the Economic Policy Committee or Industrial Capacity Committee.' Although Wilson criticized the failure of Whitehall departments and the UK government to do more to integrate Northern Ireland into the war effort, his main strictures were aimed at the conservatism of local management, the uncooperative attitude of trade unions and the ineffectiveness of the Stormont administration. The result was, as he noted dispiritedly, that 'At the end of 15 months of war Ulster, so far from becoming an important centre of munitions production, has become a depressed area.'[57]

Yet within months of Wilson's reports there was evidence that the unemployment problem was well on the way to being resolved. By the time of the Belfast Blitz the unemployed total was reduced to 43,600, with a drop of over 40 per cent in male unemployment in the two previous months. Harland and Wolff, which had received less than its fair share of Admiralty contracts in the late 1930s,[58] was to make a major contribution to wartime output, building not only naval and merchant ships but also landing craft, tanks, anti-aircraft guns and searchlights. Employment in the yard, which stood at 10,500 at the outbreak of war, had risen to 23,500 by March 1941[59] and reached a wartime peak of 30,800 in December 1944.[60] Short and Harland's aircraft factories, whose workforce stood at 6,000 in 1939, employed 11,319 by 1941,[61] producing Stirling bombers and Sunderland flying boats. The engineering industry was increasingly employed on a range of work from aircraft fuselage production to shells, bombs and radar equipment. Linen's problems were lessened by contracts for parachutes, tents and uniforms. As the military authorities embarked on the building of army and navy bases and aerodromes across the province, much of the surplus labour in agriculture and the building trades was quickly absorbed. Added to this were the 23,000 men who enlisted and the 28,000 workers who went to Britain in the first two years of the war.[62]

The decrease in the unemployment figures did little to help the government's popularity. This was in part because much of the new employment was the product of the broader British mobilization, and critics claimed that things would have been even better but for the incompetent response of the local administration. Added to this was the increasingly hopeful if fractious atmosphere encouraged by the UK-wide shift to the left. Robert Greacen, one of the editors of the *Northman*, a new literary journal based in Belfast's Queen's University, described the 'thorough-going shake-up' that the war gave to such a conservative and inward-looking region: 'Go into our cafes and pubs, workshops and recreation centres and hear them speak of social conditions, of plans for post-war economic and physical reconstruction, talk knowingly of the Beveridge Report, of Britain's relations with the Soviet Union . . . and of the clean, decent world we are all hoping and working for.'[63] Long accustomed to seeing itself as a delicate flower wilting in an environment parched by the flames of bourgeois philistinism, sectarian division and provincial narrow-mindedness, the North's small literary intelligentsia was temporarily buoyed up with new, contrasting and ultimately chimerical visions of the future. These ranged from the poet John Hewitt's idea of Ulster regionalism as a common source of pride for Catholics and Protestants to socialisms with conflicting republican and Commonwealth loyalties.[64]

Whatever the limitations of this intellectual revival, its energy and optimism derived from the temporary dulling of the sectarian passions of the 1930s brought about by the material improvements and widening of horizons associated with the war. Even the Prime Minister was affected. Andrews, as President of the Ulster Unionist Labour Association, was critical of what he saw as Treasury sabotage of Northern Ireland's right to parity of public services with the rest of the UK. Although social conditions in housing, health and education had improved during the inter-war period, they still lagged behind those of Britain as a whole.[65] As Andrews pointed out to his cabinet, in areas such as mortality rates for expectant mothers and infants the gap had widened, something the NILP was concentrating on in its criticism of the government. To the dismay of Spender and the Treasury, the Prime Minister committed his government to an ambitious programme of post-war reconstruction. Responding to Treasury criticism that such a commitment went beyond Stormont's limited financial powers, Andrews explained to the Chancellor of the Exchequer that Northern Ireland could not be insulated from the British debate about the nature of post-war economic and social policy: 'In numerous public utterances of responsible people the minds of our people have been directed more than ever before towards what is called a "new order" or a "fair deal", the "scandal that poverty should exist" and the "horrors associated with the slums".'[66] Despite the horror that Andrews's approach provoked amongst some of his colleagues and a substantial sector of the Protestant middle class, he was successful in extracting a grudging acceptance from the Chancellor of the Exchequer that the North could incur extra expenditure to make up for 'leeway': its backwardness in infrastructure and social provision.[67] A Post-War Planning Committee was created in July 1942, and, although it was chaired by Brooke, who shared Spender's scepticism about Andrews's public commitments, it did mark the first faltering step in the government's initially reluctant acceptance of the welfare state. However, although the embrace of welfarism would be a crucial long-term factor in the strengthening of Unionist Party hegemony, it did little to shore up Andrews's decrepit administration. In January 1943 Jack Beattie of the NILP won the West Belfast seat at Westminster in a by-election with a 30 per cent slump in the Unionist vote,[68] and in April 1943, despite the fact that almost half the Unionist MPs at Stormont had government posts, a rebellion of backbenchers and junior ministers forced Andrews's resignation.

Class Conflict and Sectarianism

An important factor in Unionist Party dissatisfaction with Andrews was his perceived weakness in dealing with the increasing industrial militancy that had affected Belfast from 1941. During the war Northern

Ireland provided 10 per cent of the British total of working days lost through strikes while accounting for only 2 per cent of the UK's workforce.[69] Although some unionists were prepared to blame this on subversive immigrants from the South, who allegedly flooded the North to get jobs in the expanding war industries, there is more solid evidence that roots it in the recent industrial history of the region. Andrews's willingness to adopt a conciliatory approach to the workers reflected clear evidence of rigid, authoritarian and obstructive managerial attitudes, particularly in the shipyards and the aircraft factories. These stimulated the resurgence of a tradition of militancy that had lain dormant for two decades.

During the Great War a powerful unofficial shop stewards' movement had developed in Belfast's shipbuilding and engineering industries, and in the immediate post-war period the city had been convulsed by industrial militancy, culminating in a three-week general strike that shut down the city in January 1919. Deepening unemployment and the sectarian tensions associated with the intensifying conflict between the IRA and the British state had allowed loyalist militants to refocus Protestant working-class anger from employers to Catholics, who were said to have 'infiltrated' the North's industries, taking the jobs of loyalists who had enlisted. The result was the mass workplace expulsions of Catholics and socialists in July 1920 that severely weakened trade union organization in the city. Two subsequent decades of heavy unemployment had resulted in a situation of cowed workers and employers used to the exercise of unchallenged power. By the end of 1941 the war had produced a radical shift in the industrial balance of power. Employers and the official trade union movement had to come to terms with a new shop stewards' movement that used the alliance with the Soviet Union and the demands of industrial mobilization to carve out a role for itself in joint production committees, which the government encouraged as a way of maximizing production.[70]

For many workers, attitudes to the domestic war effort were coloured by memories of inter-war insecurity and hostility and distrust towards foremen and management. Ministers and officials in London complained of a lack of cooperation and goodwill, which seemed endemic in Northern Ireland's industrial relations. Harland and Wolff's productivity was lower than that of any British yard, and absenteeism was twice as high as that in the worst yards in the UK. A British official who visited Short and Harland's plants in late 1942 estimated that the firm was working at a mere 65 per cent efficiency and complained that 'any amount of people are drawing pay for loafing about'. The firm had an unenviable record for strikes, and it has been suggested that there and elsewhere industrial relations problems stemmed from the rapid recruitment 'from all and sundry'.[71] Despite tight RUC surveillance of industrial militants, it was none the less difficult to find suitable subversives. As a senior Stormont official explained to London about one major strike at Short and Harland, 'It is led by agitators whose motivation is sometimes doubtful though we cannot obtain proof of their subversive intention.'[72]

Part of the government's problem in finding scapegoats for the strikes was that many of those who would traditionally have been seen as subversives were members of the Communist Party. After the invasion of the USSR the party shifted from an anti-war position that had led to the jailing of some of its leading members to become the most vociferous champion of the subordination of sectional interests to the war effort. By 1943 the party had 1,000 members, the vast majority Protestant workers in key industries.[73] Andrews, who had helped found the Ulster Unionist Labour Association in 1918 to attack 'Bolshevist' influence in the Belfast labour movement, now publicly praised 'our gallant Russian allies who are fighting with such wonderful bravery in the common cause of freedom'.[74] Communists, who were active in the shop stewards' movement, did all they could in order to prevent strikes and denounced those that did take place.[75]

The government was also aware that workers had genuine grievances. Andrews explained to the Cabinet Committee on Manpower that the trade unions in Harland and Wolff had pointed out that the best way to deal with absenteeism at the shipyards was to do something about the primitive welfare facilities, particularly the lack of workers' canteens.[76] Management dismissal of any role for unions in schemes for improving productivity was common. The main cause of militancy was the use made by management of the wartime legal framework outlawing strikes. The Conditions of Employment and National Arbitration Order, introduced throughout the UK in August 1940, prohibited strikes and lockouts and created a National Arbitration Tribunal to deal with disputes. Workers and unions found the arbitration machinery excessively slow, and the result was a temptation to unilateral action. However, in Northern Ireland, employers, the police and the judiciary showed a markedly more repressive response to such action than their counterparts in the rest of the UK. Thus during the first two years the Order was in place 2,068 workers were prosecuted in Britain, while in Northern Ireland the figure was 2,271.[77]

As the war increased the power of labour, with trade union membership rising from 114,000 in 1941 to 147,000 in 1945,[78] tensions developed within unionism between the need to maintain harmonious relations among the main social classes in the Protestant community and the complaints of an industrial bourgeoisie and provincial middle class that was increasingly obsessed with the government's alleged capitulation to 'socialistic' trends imported from Britain. These tensions contributed powerfully to the dissatisfaction with Andrews. Brooke was dismayed at Andrews's approach to industrial unrest. The Prime Minister intervened to have fines imposed on workers for strike action reduced, despite the opposition of Brooke and Dawson Bates.[79] When the management of Short and Harland provoked a mass strike in October 1942 by sacking two shop stewards, Brooke was in favour of a hardline response, but Andrews chose a more emollient approach by setting up a court of inquiry, which, although it criticized the shop stewards, supported their reinstatement.[80] Churchill and Herbert Morrison, the Home Secretary, were critical of what they saw as a dangerous concession to an illegal strike,[81] but Andrews continued to exasperate London and infuriate Ulster's business class by refusing to use troops to move goods and raw materials from the Belfast docks during a carters' strike in March 1943.[82]

Within a month Andrews had gone, but if the middle class hoped for a hardening of approach from his successor they were to be disappointed. Brooke, who came to the premiership as a champion of industrial discipline, was soon forced to take a broader and more politicized view of industrial relations. In March 1944 a strike of engineers at Harland and Wolff for increased pay was supported by a sympathy action at Short and Harland. Despite instructions from union leaders in London to return to work, over 14,000 workers remained out for three weeks, severely disrupting essential war production; eventually the government had five leading shop stewards arrested. When the stewards were sentenced to three months' imprisonment, the industrial action spread to include dockers, who closed the port of Belfast.[83] Brooke had tried to persuade Churchill to treat the dispute exceptionally by having the wage claim dealt with quickly but had received no support from London.[84] Only Brooke's direct intervention to persuade the shop stewards that if they accepted bail an appeal would be assured of a sympathetic hearing, together with employers' offer of a pay rise, succeeded in getting the men back to work.[85]

The strike provided evidence of the way in which the government attempted to dissipate class tensions within the Protestant community by blaming unrest on those who wanted to exploit grievances to advance anti-partitionism. During the strike the RUC had visited the homes of leading shop stewards to find out, according to William Lowry, the Minister of Home Affairs, whether the shop stewards' movement 'was made up almost exclusively of Roman Catholics who were natives of Eire'.[86] Here Brooke's administration carried on with one of the most inglorious aspects of Andrews's legacy of Protestant populism. 'Éirean infiltration' had been a major concern of Andrews's government since the beginning of 1942, when some of its loyalist critics accused it of importing southern workers when northerners were still unemployed. The expansion of the North's industries in 1941 had acted as a magnet for the 7,000 Irish citizens who crossed the border that year. Of these, about 900 had been brought north by the Ministry of Labour to fill skilled jobs in engineering, shipbuilding and the construction industry for which there were no suitable local workers. Accused by the Independent Unionist MP for Shankill that his government was 'importing Fifth Columnists', Andrews immediately created a cabinet subcommittee to investigate the problem of 'infiltration' from Éire.[87]

The investigation concluded that there was no economic threat to northern workers, as most of the imported workers did work for which there was no adequate supply of local labour, and also that the temporary nature of their employment meant that they would be unable to qualify for unemployment benefit, which required residence for five years. It also dismissed security concerns as 'greatly exaggerated' and concluded that no special measures were necessary.[88] Despite this, Andrews's desire to deflect ultra-loyalist criticisms and Dawson Bates's obsession with republican threats to the war effort ensured that this was not the last word on the matter.

Bates, with Andrews's support, approached Herbert Morrison in March 1942 asking for new powers to control movement from the South. He focused on recent police raids that had produced evidence of IRA preparations for a renewed campaign.[89] The IRA's ambush of an RUC patrol in West Belfast, in which Constable Patrick Murphy was shot dead, may have lessened any doubts harboured at Westminster about the proposed legislation. Under the Residence in Northern Ireland Restriction Order introduced at Westminster in October 1942, all British subjects (a category into which, despite de Valera's new constitution, the Irish still fitted) not normally resident in Northern Ireland on 1 January 1940 were required to obtain a permit from the Ministry of Home Affairs if they wished to stay in Northern Ireland for longer than six weeks.

Permits were to be issued where the person was needed to fill a job vacancy for which there was no suitable local candidate.[90]

The existence of the new legislation simply intensified pressure on the government to be seen to defend the employment prospects of Protestants. Even Andrews's administration was prepared, on occasion, to withstand this pressure in the interests of the war effort. The cabinet supported the Minister of Labour when he permitted the importation of skilled quarry workers from the South who were urgently needed to produce the stone for building bases and air fields. But, as he pointed out, 'there will be protests against bringing men from Eire while there are still unemployed men on our register, no matter how unfit or unsuitable such unemployed men might be'. The cabinet decided that in this case the needs of the war effort should come before the defence of Protestant interests, particularly when it was pointed out to them that the local representatives of the British and American armed forces might inform their superiors that the government was putting narrow political interests before the anti-fascist struggle.[91]

Brooke, for all his criticisms of Andrews's failure to respond effectively to the demands of total war, showed himself only too willing to bring the most parochial sectarian grievances to the cabinet table. A complaint to the Prime Minister from a County Fermanagh Unionist about a Ministry of Agriculture veterinary inspector who was a southerner was brought to cabinet despite the fact the Permanent Secretary of the Ministry of Agriculture had defended the appointment, pointing out that the man was a distinguished graduate of University College Cork with exceptionally good qualifications in dairy science, which were much superior to those of northern candidates.[92]

Between the introduction of the legislation and September 1946, work permits were granted to 36,447 Éire citizens and to 21,881 workers from Britain. Permits were refused to 18 per cent of Éire applicants, compared to only 2 per cent of non-Éire applicants.[93] Brooke's strategy was to manipulate grass-roots pressure by its controlled indulgence. Thus the champions of a loyalist labour policy were apparently indulged while the demand of Protestant employers and farmers for badly needed labour from the South were largely satisfied, and the female members of the Protestant middle class were not denied access to their traditional source of maids and kitchen staff.

By 1944 the problem of unemployment had disappeared, but the cabinet was increasingly concerned with the spectre of a post-war crisis brought about by economic readjustment, the return of Protestants from the forces and an influx of southerners attracted by the new benefits of the welfare state. Ironically, the minister most perturbed by apocalyptic visions of a post-war invasion was Harry Midgley, the ex-NILP firebrand. He had resigned from the Labour Party in 1942 because he claimed it was increasingly dominated by anti-partitionists; he and his supporters set up a Commonwealth Labour Party. When Brooke formed his first government, he attempted to give it a more progressive tone by bringing in Midgley as Minister of Public Security. However, the deep reservations that many members of the Unionist Party had about the Beveridge Report were also reflected in substantial opposition to Midgley's role in government. His increasing fixation with the imminent deluge of southerners was an attempt to establish his loyalist credentials. By his exaggerated focus on the magnetic influence that the Beveridge proposals would have on citizens of Éire, he unintentionally stiffened the resistance of a substantial sector of the party to Stormont adopting the welfare state. The rejection of Beveridge on a class basis was amplified by fears of loss of ethnic dominance. The result was that the government fought the 1945 election on a strong anti-socialist platform, although it also stated that it would introduce whatever social reforms were made in the rest of the UK. This contradictory message contributed to a substantial Protestant working-class vote for the NILP and other left-of-centre parties. Labour parties of various shades won 32 per cent of the total Northern Ireland vote and five seats, while in the Belfast constituencies the 'non-Nationalist left', which included the NILP, the Commonwealth Labour Party and the Communist Party, won 40 per cent of the vote to the Unionists' 50 per cent.[94] While the electoral system ensured that the NILP won only two seats, the vote for the left helped to convince Brooke that his government would have to embrace the welfare state.

3. 'Minding Our Own Business': Éire during the Emergency

Defending Neutrality

De Valera, combining the positions of Taoiseach and Minister for External Affairs, proved skilled in exploiting the domestic political opportunities produced by international developments. During the 1930s, he used Irish membership of the League of Nations to portray Ireland as the vanguard of small nations threatened by the rapacious designs of bigger states and to provide a moral justification for Irish neutrality in any future world conflict. Neutrality during a major conflict in which Great Britain was involved was also a resounding statement of Irish independence and sovereignty, albeit in a truncated twenty-six-county form. Even before the return of the Treaty ports de Valera made it clear that neutrality would be his government's policy and that this would be the case even in the event of an end of partition. He also tried to reassure the British by asserting that he would resist any attempt by Germany to use Irish territory as a base for attacking Britain.[1]

The favourable terms of the 1938 Agreement and, above all, the return of the ports, which made neutrality feasible, were major ingredients in Fianna Fáil's electoral victory in 1938, with 52 per cent of the vote and seventy-two seats. Increasingly the party portrayed itself as the only effective guarantee of Éire's insulation from the horrors of war. Fine Gael was disorientated by de Valera's success in ending the economic war and in persuading the British to respect neutrality. Its support, which had picked up as the economic war began to bite, slumped seriously after the 1938 Agreement from 33 per cent and forty-three seats in that year's election to 23 per cent and thirty-two seats in 1944.[2]

De Valera was well aware of the formidable pressures that he would be under in the event of war and had been a strong supporter of Neville Chamberlain's appeasement policies, praising the Munich Agreement as 'the highest peak of human greatness'.[3] However, Hitler's occupation of Prague in March 1939 finally dispatched any lingering illusions that appeasement could contain Berlin's expansionist appetites and posed an unprecedented challenge to the very existence of the southern state. Although the return of the ports made neutrality possible, it by no means ensured that it could be successfully maintained. Dr Eduard Hempel, the German minister in Dublin, reported to Berlin in June 1939 that it was improbable that neutrality could survive an Anglo-German war, and that there was at least one cabinet minister who privately doubted the possibility of a continuing policy of neutrality.[4] De Valera had admitted the fragility of the policy when he had accepted that Ireland's role as an important supplier of food to the British market could lead, in the event of war between Britain and Germany, to attacks on Irish ports to destroy this trade and that 'if we were attacked our forces would be combined with the British forces for the defence of Ireland.'[5]

The decision to return the Treaty ports had reflected Chamberlain's belief that, whatever their strategic value to Britain in wartime, this would be negated by the southern state's lack of goodwill. Although the chiefs of staff supported the decision to return the ports, they pointed out that, in the event of a war with Germany, the non-availability of the Irish ports would seriously hamper naval operations.[6] They were also aware that the Irish state simply lacked the military capacity to defend its neutrality. When the war broke out, the country was almost defenceless, with an army of just 7,000 poorly equipped regulars, which, with reserves, provided a force of 20,000 upon mobilization.[7] The new Irish Marine Service, established in November 1939 to defend Irish territorial waters, consisted of two ex-fisheries patrol boats with six motor torpedo boats on order from Britain,[8] while the Air Corps was incapable of policing the skies over Dublin, let alone the country as a whole.[9]

On 2 September, the day after Germany invaded Poland, de Valera summoned the Dáil in order to introduce two bills: one was to amend the Constitution and the other an Emergency Powers Bill. The amendment to the Constitution extended the definition of the term 'time of war' to allow emergency legislation during an armed conflict in which the Irish state was not directly involved but that had created a national emergency affecting the vital interests of the state. This was the origin of the anodyne description of the Second World War as 'the Emergency' in Irish public discourse. De Valera made reference in the Dáil to those who mistakenly thought that it would be sufficient for neutrality to be declared for it to become a reality: in fact, it would need national determination to protect it 'at every stage'.[10] Yet, during the 'phoney war', the conservative priorities of the Department of Finance ensured that even the meagre forces available in September 1939 were reduced, and it took the German invasion of the Low Countries on 10 May 1940 to force the government to approve plans for an expansion of the army to

40,000 and the launch of a national recruiting drive in June.[11] After an initial surge of recruitment, spurred by a widespread but temporary fear of invasion, the Irish Army experienced great difficulty in reaching its target wartime strength. This reflected its low levels of pay, which compared unfavourably with those of the British armed forces and also with wages available for Irish labour in the factories, shipyards and building sites of Northern Ireland and Great Britain. As a result desertion was common.[12] It was not until the spring of 1943 that the Chief of Staff could report that his troops had passed from the stage of barrack-square training to being an 'effective and mobile field force'.[13] Even then the army lacked the most basic forms of equipment to support its role: it had almost no anti-aircraft defences, no armour worth the name, and was desperately short of artillery, anti-aircraft weapons, transport and munitions. Given this situation, the British intelligence estimate, made during the period of maximum German threat between the fall of France in May 1940 and the German attack on Russia in June 1941, that the Irish Army could have offered some form of organized resistance for between a week and ten days, was perhaps over-optimistic.[14]

The real defenders of Irish neutrality against a threat from Germany were the Royal Navy and the British forces in Northern Ireland, who would have been expected to cross the border to expel any invaders from the Third Reich. The officials of the Department of Finance had cited this reality in resisting demands for increased defence spending in the late 1930s. What J. J. Lee refers to as the state's 'astonishing achievement' in reducing public expenditure as a proportion of Gross Domestic Product between 1939 and 1945 indicates that the real burden of defending neutrality fell on the shoulders of the British.[15]

De Valera, the Nazis and the IRA

De Valera displayed considerable political skill in responding to the conflicting pressures from London and Berlin and in presenting what was a British-biased neutrality as an even-handed assertion of Irish independence and self-respect. Part of his success in this was due to the covert nature of the arrangements on intelligence and military cooperation with the UK. The Irish government was acutely aware of the danger of German exploitation of IRA activity against Northern Ireland or of a possible campaign in Britain. It was also under pressure from London because of British fears that 'fifth column' activities would be unchecked by the Irish security services.[16] The activities of a small group of German expatriates who were active Nazis had begun to concern Irish military intelligence in the late 1930s. The new state's desire to develop its indigenous resources, economic and cultural, had created openings for a small but significant influx of Germans. In 1926 a contract for the construction of the hydroelectric scheme on the River Shannon was given to the German firm of Siemens-Schuckert, which brought in a number of engineers and technicians, some of whom married and settled in Ireland. In 1938 the director of Siemens-Schuckert was one of the main Nazis in Dublin. German prominence in the fields of the archaeology and language of Celtic Ireland had also provided a bridgehead between the two countries, and the leading Nazi in Dublin, Dr Adolf Mahr, was the Director of the National Museum.[17] A German who acted as an adviser to the Turf Development Board also functioned as a Nazi intelligence agent, travelling the country and photographing railway stations, river bridges and reservoirs.[18] The most bizarre case was that of the German who headed the Irish Army's School of Music and who had sought permission from the Chief of Staff to set up a branch of the Nazi Party in Dublin.[19]

Shortly after the 1938 Agreement, and to give practical effect to his promises that Éire would not be a base for hostile activity against Britain, de Valera sent officers from the Irish Army and Joe Walshe, Secretary of the Department of External Affairs, to London to discuss defence and intelligence cooperation with the British. One result was that MI5 was asked to assist in the formation of a new counter-espionage service within the Irish Army. By the outbreak of war the two intelligence services were in regular correspondence on the activities of German agents, Irish Nazi sympathizers and IRA–German collaboration. Walshe was an admirer of Mussolini, and when the war began he favoured an Axis victory.[20] For him, cooperation with the British intelligence services served to quieten concern in London about the security threat of German intelligence operations in Ireland and lessen the possibility of a British invasion. However, the British, who had reservations about the capacity of the Irish counter-espionage service, were ultimately more impressed by the ruthlessness of de Valera's response to the IRA threat.

Although many IRA men had been won over to Fianna Fáil since 1932, through a mixture of patronage and de Valera's success in convincing them that he could achieve the destruction of the Treaty settlement nonviolently, a sizeable rump remained. Under the leadership of the resolute militarist Seán Russell, the IRA declared war on Britain in January 1939 and launched a bombing campaign in British cities that was to claim seven dead and almost 200 wounded by the end of the year. The leadership of the IRA was eager to enlist German assistance, deluding themselves that a victorious Nazism would respect Ireland's independence. Using the novelist Francis Stuart as an emissary, the IRA had opened up contacts with the Abwehr, the military-controlled German foreign intelligence service.[21] Although the dominant German policy towards Ireland was to ensure that its neutrality was preserved, twelve Abwehr agents did land in Éire between 1939 and 1943, aiming to make contact with the IRA and develop plans for joint action in the North.[22]

De Valera responded swiftly to this direct threat to his pledge that the territory of his state would not be used as a base for attacks against Britain. The Offences against the State Act, introduced in June 1939, allowed for the creation of special courts and increasing police powers to search, arrest and detain.[23] But when a number of imprisoned IRA men went on hunger strike, de Valera was reluctant to allow them to die, especially as one was a veteran of the 1916 Rising. Six were released, despite the misgivings of his Minister for Justice, Gerry Boland, who de Valera had appointed on the outbreak of war precisely because he was both tough and loyal.[24]

The IRA's response to this concession was an audacious raid on the Irish Army's ammunition stores in the Magazine Fort in Dublin's Phoenix Park, which removed explosives and over one million rounds of ammunition. Although the bulk of the material was recovered, the raid marked the end of any tendency to concession. An amendment to the Emergency Powers Act in January 1940 allowed the introduction of internment without trial. Over 500 were interned and another 600 committed under the Offences against the State Act during the war years.[25] With the IRA writing to newspapers, claiming grandiloquently that the 'Government of the Republic' would no longer tolerate censorship of its activities by de Valera's government, the public position of the government was expressed by Seán MacEntee, who warned the IRA that 'in a continental state such criminals would have a speedy court-martial and an equally expeditious execution.'[26] Service on the republican side during the revolutionary period would no longer be an insurance, as the government displayed the same ruthlessness that it had denounced when the British and Northern Ireland authorities executed IRA men.

One particularly stark example was the case of George Plant, executed in March 1942 for the killing of an alleged IRA informer. He had fought during the War of Independence, then on the anti-Treaty side during the Civil War, and while on the run had emigrated to the United States. He did not return to Ireland until 1940 and, as his defence put it, 'His prolonged absence from the country did not enable him to appraise the change of circumstances.' Many in Fianna Fáil, remembering their own recent past, were profoundly uneasy about the action taken against men like Plant.[27] Seán Lemass, who was close to breaking with the government on the issue, was reminded by his mother that Plant and others were doing precisely what he and others had done a quarter of a century earlier.[28]

Nevertheless, despite such conscience-wrestling and criticism from the grass-roots of the party, the government maintained unity. When the Special Criminal Court discharged Plant because the only evidence against him was that of retracted statements by the two other IRA men accused of the murder, he was re-arrested and tried by a military court, which sentenced him to death. Five other IRA men were executed during the war and another three were allowed to die on hunger strike. Despite the overt political conflict between the two Irish states, there was also covert cooperation against the IRA threat. A link between the RUC and the Garda was established soon after the outbreak of the war to exchange intelligence on IRA activities.[29] Little wonder that when the IRA took over a broadcasting station in Cork in April 1940, the core of its address to the populace was a denunciation of de Valera as 'Judas'.[30]

The good relations between the British and Irish intelligence services were an important element in a range of Irish activities that gave the operation of neutrality a degree of bias towards the Allies. These included the exchange of meteorological information; the relaying to the British of information gathered by the Irish coast-watching service on German planes, ships and submarines in or near Irish territory and waters; permission for the overflying of Irish airspace in northern Donegal by Allied aircraft for easier access to the Atlantic; and close cooperation between the military authorities North and South.[31]

These forms of covert cooperation led Maurice Moynihan, Secretary to de Valera's cabinet, to exclaim in May 1941, 'We could not do more if we were in the war.'[32] A British intelligence analysis of the impact of neutrality on the war effort tended to support Moynihan's view. Acknowledging the shipping losses incurred because of the lack of access to southern Irish ports, it argued that neutral Ireland was still of more value than a belligerent Ireland would have been. If Ireland had entered the war on the Allied side, the resultant conscription would have denied the British war effort the Irish servicemen and workers who did in fact cross the border or the Irish Sea. At the same time, given that a belligerent Ireland was judged not to be in a position to defend itself against a German attack, Britain would have had to supply its new ally with arms and men, both of which were scarce.[33]

Over 45,000 southern Irish men and women volunteered for the British forces during the war, compared to about 44,000 from the North. Even more important, however, were the 120,000 who went to work in Britain and Northern Ireland: 'So great was the need for this Irish labour before and during the Battle of Britain in 1940 that without it the airdromes, so desperately needed, could not have been built, and great as the need for Irish labour was then, it increased throughout the war as the calls on our manpower became great.'[34]

This relatively benign assessment of neutrality, written with the benefit of hindsight, should not be allowed to obscure the fact that in the period of maximum German threat, after the fall of Norway and Denmark and the attack on the Low Countries, there was deep concern in British government circles about Dublin's stance. It was reflected in Churchill's assertion in November 1940 that the denial of the ports was 'a most heavy and grievous burden . . . which should never have been placed on our shoulders'.[35] Denial of the ports to the Royal Navy, which reduced its capacity to provide convoy protection, was reckoned by the Admiralty to have cost 368 ships and 5,070 lives during the war.[36]

Such calculations challenge what the Cork-based historian Geoffrey Roberts has called 'the pragmatic pro-neutrality narrative', which still dominates academic and popular approaches to the issue in the Republic. According to this narrative, neutrality was a necessary policy, which benefited Ireland and the Allies alike.[37] But, as Roberts points out, during the early phase of the war, when it looked as if Germany might win, Irish cooperation with Britain was limited. RAF planes were prohibited from overflying Irish headlands, a ban that was later abolished; and in 1940 the Irish refused a British request for an agreement on trans-shipment facilities for British merchant shipping.[38] Moreover, the secret contributions of the Irish state were far outweighed by the tens of thousands of Irish men and women who on their own initiative volunteered for service in the British forces or became war workers in Britain. The Irish state's role here was one of turning a blind eye to Irish military volunteers and actively facilitating the mass migration of Irish labour, which, if it had remained at home, might have presented major social and political problems.[39]

Neutrality and Partition

It has been argued that the continuing strength of anti-British feeling in the political culture of the South made the neutrality policy the only conceivable one.[40] At the time, even liberal unionists in the North tended to see de Valera's options as strongly constrained by the effect of his party's strident anglophobia and irredentism in the period since 1932.[41] Sir John Maffey, the UK Representative in Dublin, observed: 'It is remarkable how even the "pro-British" group, men who have fought for the Crown and are anxious to be called up again . . . agree generally in supporting the policy of neutrality for Eire.'[42] The main opposition parties found it difficult to avoid tail-ending Fianna Fáil views of neutrality and security issues. De Valera created a consultative Conference on Defence in May 1940 in which Fine Gael and Labour had representatives. Although consultation was minimal, it very effectively neutered the opposition for the duration of the Emergency.[43]

On 16 June, for the first time since the Civil War, before an enormous crowd in the centre of Dublin, the leaders of all three parties stood together on a joint platform to launch a national recruiting campaign for the army and a new part-time Local Security Force. By 1941 this had 100,000 members, and the Irish correspondent of the pro-Commonwealth *Round Table* noted the unifying effects of the campaign to defend neutrality: 'Men who fought on opposite sides in the Civil War are now drilling and working together. British veterans of 1914 are serving in the local security force side by side with men who fought against the British.'[44] That James Dillon, the deputy leader of Fine Gael, was forced to resign from the party in February 1942, for arguing in the aftermath of the Japanese attack on Pearl Harbor that Ireland should, on moral grounds, ally itself with America,[45] has encouraged the view that there was no alternative.

Yet, in the summer of 1940 when the German threat to both Ireland and Britain was at its height and there was a real sense of fear and panic in official circles in Dublin, the leaders of Fine Gael urged de Valera to abandon neutrality in return for British action on partition. On 16 May, less than a week after Germany invaded the Low Countries, de Valera had a meeting with Sir John Maffey, at which he asked for Britain's assistance in the event of a German invasion.[46] The arrest in Dublin of an Irishman of German extraction, who had been one of the IRA's go-betweens with Germany and who had been concealing in his house a large amount of money, maps and other equipment belonging to a recently arrived German agent, increased Irish apprehension about Hitler's intentions. It encouraged an intensification of the process of constructing a covert set of intelligence and security arrangements with the British. Although de Valera's emissaries to London found that their offers of covert cooperation with the British war effort were positively received, they none the less had major problems persuading the British that arms and equipment should be provided to the Irish Army but that there could be no question of British troops being invited into Ireland until the Irish themselves had begun to resist the invaders.[47]

London's doubts about the military capacity of the Irish state, which were probably not assuaged by de Valera's boast that they were 'very good hedge fighters',[48] were shared by leading members of the main opposition party. Soon after the withdrawal of Allied forces from Dunkirk, de Valera received a Fine Gael memorandum arguing that the only way of preventing a German invasion was to provide a unified defence command for the whole island and invite in French and British troops. Aware of the danger of a nationalist backlash against such a decision, it suggested that the 'logical consequence' of the cross-border defence arrangements would be the 'subsequent impossibility of survival for the anachronism of Northern Ireland'.[49]

The Fine Gael approach was to be echoed in the British proposals that Neville Chamberlain's emissary, Malcolm MacDonald, discussed with de Valera in Dublin in the third week of June. The offer envisaged the South immediately joining the Allies and the setting up of an All-Ireland Defence Council in return for an immediate British declaration of acceptance of the principle of a united Ireland and the creation of a North–South body to work out the practical details of such a union.[50] De Valera's rejection of the proposal, which was rooted in his scepticism about the ability of any British government to deliver unionist acquiescence, has tended to be accepted as the only feasible response in the circumstances.[51] Certainly the vehemence of Craigavon's reaction when he was provided with the details of the British offer indicated a central difficulty with the British proposal.

Yet the Unionist position in June 1940 was more vulnerable than at any time since 1921. Craigavon's own leadership at such a time of crisis was itself increasingly subject to internal party criticism because of the regime's lack of preparedness for the challenge of wartime mobilization. The Unionist leadership was open to the charge of putting a sectarian 'little Ulsterism' before the interests of not just the British Empire but also of the 'Christian civilization' that was threatened by Nazi barbarism. Basil Brooke's subsequent recollection of the period highlighted the fear that they would be faced with an agonizing choice: 'I had an awful feeling that had we refused we would have been blamed for whatever disasters ensued.' Brooke's son claimed that at the time his father had told him that faced with the choice between 'western civilization' and Irish unification, he would have to accept the latter.[52]

There is also some evidence that public opinion in the South was less of a potential obstacle to an alliance with Britain than has been asserted. The British intelligence evaluation was that the return of the ports had increased goodwill towards Britain but that the attitude of the average Irishman was 'of indifference to either side, except in so far as the acts of either belligerent might affect his own or Irish interests generally'.[53] In a context in which a move to end neutrality was linked to a British commitment to unity, it might not have been beyond de Valera's considerable political skills to carry a majority of the southern electorate with him. Even the semi-official biography of de Valera notes that in those circumstances 'the whole atmosphere would have been so completely transformed that one can only speculate as to what path Ireland would or would not have chosen.'[54] However, although there is some evidence to suggest that in the summer of 1940 the country would have split two thirds to one-third in favour of participation on Britain's side, anti-British sentiment would have been much stronger within the ruling party. James Dillon, the lone figure in the Dáil who would by the end of 1941 openly reject neutrality, did not think that de Valera had a choice in June 1940, given that he would have split his party if he had jettisoned neutrality.[55]

The Unionist leadership was saved from having to consider such an excruciating choice by de Valera's preference for defending the integrity of the existing twenty-six-county state and the unity of Fianna Fáil over what might have been a historic opportunity to undermine partition. W. T. Cosgrave, the leader of Fine Gael, was wasting his time when, after de Valera's rejection of the British proposals, he continued to press privately for entry to the war on Britain's side using the prize of unity to attract the Fianna Fáil leader.[56] De Valera's own pronouncements on the issue had made it clear that the territorial completion of the national revolution would always take second place to the imperative of maintaining a broad coalition of 'national' forces and sentiment behind Fianna Fáil. Just as any trade concessions to northern manufacturers in 1938 had been ruled out by a combination of southern economic interests and Fianna

Fáil fundamentalists, de Valera had, in a memorable speech in the Senate in February 1939, asserted that he would not accept unity at the price of the project of restoring the Irish language.[57] Those in London or amongst the opposition in the Dáil who saw in the offer of unity, even if it had been more of a realistic possibility, a chance of ending neutrality misunderstood the deeply partitionist dynamics of Fianna Fáil rule.

Another important factor behind support for neutrality in 1940 was the widespread belief that Britain was going to lose the war, something that was not an unwelcome prospect to some. Hempel, the German minister in Dublin, reported to Berlin that his discussions with Joseph Walshe and Frederick Boland of the Department of External Affairs showed an Irish government concerned to ensure that Germany would support 'an entirely independent united Irish state' in the event of Britain's defeat, a position that displayed a wilful blindness to the record of Nazi treatment of small neutral countries on the continent.[58] Walshe's pro-German position – he declared to David Gray, the US envoy in Dublin, that 'no one outside of Great Britain believed that Great Britain was fighting for something worthwhile'[59] – was shared by the leader of Ireland's Catholics, Cardinal MacRory, Archbishop of Armagh. A northerner who saw partition as placing Britain on the same moral level as Nazism, he was believed by the Germans to favour an invasion to end partition.[60] In October 1941 he publicly supported the idea of a negotiated peace.[61] Such opinion was more extreme than that of most cabinet ministers and senior civil servants. De Valera's own inclinations may have been in favour of an Allied victory,[62] but the rigorous censorship regime did little to challenge the world-view of those who dismissed the war as a manifestation of inter-imperialist rivalry.

Such views were widespread at both elite and mass level. The *Round Table*'s pro-Allied Irish correspondent described public opinion as not pro-German 'but by no means enthusiastically pro-British . . . the popular view may perhaps be best summed up in the words of one old farmer, who on being asked to express his views on the war said "I hope England will be nearly beat."'[63] Arland Ussher, a southern Protestant who favoured neutrality, claimed that most southerners either took no interest in the war or had the sort of 'detached and comfortable interest with which one might take in a serial "thriller"'. His description of the views of 'most educated Irishmen' indicated an attitude of insular superiority: 'England they would tell you was a "liberal" or secularist state, Germany was a "pagan" state and there was no great difference between them.'[64]

Frank Aiken, as Minister for the Coordination of Defensive Measures, had responsibility for censorship. Commander of the Fourth Northern Division of the IRA at the time of the Treaty and Chief of Staff of the anti-Treaty IRA at the end of the Civil War, he was considered, even by some of his own colleagues, to be a bigot as well as deeply anti-British.[65] His rigidity had led to his being shifted from the Ministry of Defence in 1939. In his new ministry he did all within his considerable powers to ensure that the coverage of the war excluded any hint of a moral preference or any news of the nature of the Nazi regime that would trouble those who treated it as little worse than the 'Stormont dictatorship'. At times it appeared that Aiken was prepared to allow pro-Nazi propaganda. Thus the *Dundalk Examiner*, of which he was a shareholder, was permitted to publish an editorial praising the Nazi organization as 'the natural protector of the Catholic Church', while statements critical of the Nazis for the persecution of Catholics in Germany and Poland made by the Bishop of Münster and the Irish Bishop of Achonry were censored.[66] Aiken ensured that the sufferings of Stalingrad's population were kept from the pages of Ireland's newspapers lest they elicit pro-Soviet sentiment. Reports of atrocities from German-occupied Europe, starting with the first stories of Gestapo executions of 'mental defectives' and mass executions of Polish Jews in early 1941, were stopped. This was justified by Aiken on the grounds of the use of atrocity stories by Allied propaganda in the First World War and by his contention that the Soviet record was as bad as that of the Nazis.[67]

The leaders of Fine Gael and Irish Labour shared such sentiments. When Dillon spoke in the Dáil in favour of the unity of 'all Christian men' to repel the Nazi threat, his leader William Cosgrave repudiated his views, claiming that 'the British were not thinking of the Ten Commandments.'[68] Labour's William Norton berated Dillon for his pro-Allied line: 'when the propaganda machines of the belligerents were working overtime to mislead the people of the world it was good Irish policy to mind our own business.'[69] They thus contributed to the high moral tone of neutrality and unintentionally to de Valera's political dominance as the policy's champion. To forsake neutrality risked a major domestic convulsion that would have damaged Fianna Fáil more than Fine Gael. This may help explain why, even after the US entered the war, and the chances of a German invasion receded with other neutral states adopting pro-Allied shifts in policy, Ireland maintained the policy unaltered.[70] A sense of Irish superiority to two sets of morally equivalent belligerents, while it might have provided a source of psychological support for de Valera's neutrality policy, would contribute powerfully to the state's international isolation at the end of the war as well as deepening the sense of embittered alienation from the South amongst northern unionists. The moral myopia associated with the state's promotion of neutrality was most flagrantly exposed in de Valera's infamous visit to the German minister in Dublin to present his condolences on the death of Hitler.

Much of the recent discussion on neutrality has tended to reject the harsh judgement of F.S.L. Lyons, who used the metaphor of Plato's Cave to suggest that during the Emergency the Irish relegated themselves to a shadow world.[71] An account of Irish culture during the period has dismissed the allegation that the South remained 'insularly indifferent to the war and uninformed or incurious about its course'.[72] Yet the author, who was a schoolboy in Wexford during the war, relates that he was able to follow the North African campaign and the battle of Stalingrad only by listening to the BBC.

A similar point was made during the war by Sean O'Faolain, the novelist and commentator who in the 1940s provided an outlet for dissent and social criticism as editor of the *Bell*. Responding to charges from, amongst others, the American historian Henry Steele Commager that de Valera and the Irish people were ignorant of the war and blind to the moral issue at stake, he noted that 'British and American radio, news services, newspapers, periodicals and books' were all available in Ireland.[73] The problem with this debate was that the critics tended to focus not on the reality of everyday life in Ireland, where it was indeed possible to find out about the war from external sources, but on the official policies of the Irish state, which led to such absurdities as the banning of the import of a book on the persecution of the Catholic Church under the Third Reich.[74]

O'Faolain lamented some of the effects of neutrality: 'Our people, are, it would seem, self-absorbed to an amazing degree, so self-absorbed as to be cut off, in a way that one would hardly have thought possible in this modern world of constant inter-communication, from all detachment, critical sense, a sense of proportion and even a sense of humour.'[75] Neutrality from this perspective encouraged the most self-satisfied and parochial elements of Irish society and would pose a major problem of adjustment when the state wished to reintegrate itself into the wider world. It also deepened the division on the island and made the ending of partition even more unlikely than it had appeared in 1939. As O'Faolain put it, the different relation to the war North and South 'must increase the gap beyond bridging by creating two completely discordant modes of life'.[76] MI5's assessment of neutrality was stark: 'he [de Valera] provided the British people with an overwhelming reason for the maintenance of partition.'[77]

Social Conflict during the Emergency

Despite the strong national consensus in favour of neutrality and the government's rigorous use of censorship to marginalize dissenting opinions, the period was characterized by the emergence of considerable social and economic discontent, which for a time seemed to portend a radical shift in the nature of political opposition in the state with the Irish Labour Party displacing Fine Gael as the major anti-Fianna Fáil force.

Within the government there was acute concern that Britain's wartime priorities, not to mention resentment over neutrality, could have severely disruptive effects on the economy, which was dependent on the British market to take the vast bulk of its exports, and which imported much of the fuel, machinery and raw materials for its manufacturing industries from Britain. In the month of Dunkirk, de Valera met with Irish bankers to solicit assistance, pointing to the possibly subversive potential of the large pool of urban unemployed,[78] while in July 1940 Seán Lemass, who had been moved into a new Ministry of Supplies, tried to persuade the cabinet of the need for a strongly interventionist and progressive set of economic and social policies. These would be necessary, he argued, to deal with the inevitably very high level of unemployment in the event of the state's total economic isolation.[79] Luckily for the economic conservatives in the cabinet, for instance Seán MacEntee and the officials of the Department of Finance, who saw the Emergency as a golden opportunity for a national exercise in belt-tightening, British resentment at neutrality was not allowed to obstruct the important contribution of Irish farmers, economic migrants and recruits to the anti-fascist struggle.

The revival of the British economy after 1935 helped to ease the government's problems in delivering on promises of job creation. The changed international conditions threatened this convenient, if potentially politically embarrassing, way of disposing of the state's surplus labour force. It forced the Irish state into an unprecedented degree of cooperation with Britain, which challenged de Valera's ability to present neutrality as a policy that did not tilt to one or other of the belligerents. At the outbreak of the war the British had introduced the requirement of an identity card for all persons travelling to the UK. The Department of External Affairs cooperated in the running of the scheme, but in the aftermath of the evacuation of Dunkirk controls were tightened, and the government was faced with the choice of allowing such restrictions to disrupt seriously the flow of Irish workers to Britain or, for the first time, negotiating a framework by which the state would facilitate workers who wished to go to Britain. The resultant agreement of July 1941 ensured that well over 100,000 Irish migrants travelled to Britain during the war.[80]

The potentially disruptive effect of this exodus on the government's attempt to build a national consensus around neutrality was noted by the state's chief censor: 'stories picturing thousands of starving Irish workers flocking across to the bombed areas of England or to join the British forces . . . have simply got to be stopped if public morale is not to be hopelessly compromised.'[81] The small group of left-wing activists, largely from the Communist Party of Ireland, who had been struggling to organize the Dublin unemployed since 1939, did their utmost to point out the contradiction between neutrality and the government's covert migration policy. Prior to Hitler's invasion of the Soviet Union in June 1941, the CPI had denounced the war as an 'inter-imperialist' conflict rather than an anti-fascist one, and had been supportive of neutrality while criticizing de Valera for his repression of the 'anti-imperialist' IRA. Even before the Irish–British agreement to facilitate migration, these leftists were publicly denouncing official notices in the central Dublin Labour Exchange, asking the unemployed to volunteer for work in England.[82] Strict censorship of the press, police surveillance of meetings, and the internment and imprisonment of leading activists all helped to minimize public debate on the true nature of neutrality.

Police concern over leftist exploitation of the unemployed had disappeared by early 1942. In part this reflected the effectiveness of British construction sites and munitions factories in helping to drain the pool of unemployed, although there were still 70,000 in 1943.[83] It was also a result of the Communist Party's shift to an anti-neutrality policy after the Soviet Union entered the war on the Allied side. This brought about the liquidation of the party in the South, where its members entered the Irish Labour Party. Although the vigorous pro-war policies of the Communist Party in Northern Ireland could not be openly espoused in neutral Ireland, the former communists who had dominated the leadership of the unemployed agitation lost any interest in pointing out the contradictions between neutrality and the facilitation of economic migration to Britain.

Despite the best efforts of Aiken's censorship regime, Éire could not be totally insulated from what was happening across the Irish Sea or in Northern Ireland. British newspapers and magazines continued to circulate, though in reduced numbers. More importantly, many of the 52 per cent of households in large towns and cities and of the 13 per cent in rural areas that had radio sets listened in to the BBC.[84] The long history of emigration to Britain and the tens of thousands of men and women who went to work or enlist during the war meant that there was a cross-channel network of personal and familial links, which provided a constant flow of information about conditions on the other island. Closer to home there were no restrictions on North–South movement, and there was awareness of the rapidly improving economic conditions in Northern Ireland.[85]

Fianna Fáil's ability to present itself as a national movement that paid special attention to the needs of the working class, an image particularly cultivated by Seán Lemass, was severely challenged during the war. Lemass himself was replaced at Industry and Commerce by the acerbic and economically right-wing Seán MacEntee. Prior to the shift of positions, MacEntee had been Minister for Finance and had shared the view of its senior officials that the government's commitments to job creation and increased spending on social welfare were 'economically unsound'.[86] His last pre-war budget in May 1939 had increased direct and indirect taxation, and his successor, Seán T. O'Kelly, introduced an Emergency budget in November 1939 that further turned the screw and sparked a rash of strikes as workers attempted to get wage increases to compensate for the rise in the cost of living.[87] The government rallied behind MacEntee's advocacy of a repressive response. A strike by Dublin Corporation workers caused MacEntee to warn the workers that they were posing a revolutionary threat, and the government and the local bishop exerted themselves to help the Corporation resist the strikers.[88] Using the argument that exceptional circumstances demanded a move away from peacetime forms of industrial relations, MacEntee imposed a Standstill Order on Wages in May 1940 and outlawed strikes. Although the Order was relaxed somewhat in 1942, restrictions on union rights remained, and real wages dropped by 30 per cent between 1939 and 1943. While the cost of living rose by two thirds during the Emergency, wages increased by a third and pre-war real wage levels were not achieved again until 1949.[89]

Although supplies of some foodstuffs, such as potatoes, eggs and meat, were adequate, other staples, such as tea, butter and margarine, were scarce.[90] A combination of moral persuasion and compulsory tillage orders more than doubled wheat output between 1939 and 1944, leading to a darkening of the colour of bread and prompting one historian to comment sardonically, 'The furore over wheat revealed the Irish concept of hardship – how white would the bread be.'[91] Rationing of some commodities had existed from early in the war, but a general rationing scheme was not introduced until June 1942, and profiteering and black marketeering were rife. Coal imports, for which the country was totally dependent on Britain, fell to one third of the 1938–9 level by 1944–5. Rationing of coal was introduced in January 1941, but by September there was only one week's supply of domestic coal left in Dublin.[92] The government had launched a campaign to increase the tonnage of turf drawn from peat bogs as a substitute. This was organized by the state's Turf Development Board, though the turf produced was sold through private fuel merchants, some of whom had close relations with Fianna Fáil, leading to charges of both nepotism and profiteering.[93]

That the Emergency years were far from cosy for the poorest sections of Irish society was clear from the statistics of tuberculosis mortality. Between 1939 and 1941 mortality rates rose in both Irish states, but whereas in Northern Ireland tuberculosis mortality in 1945 had fallen below its 1939 level, it was still higher in the southern state in 1947 than it had been in 1939. While other indices of health sensitive to poverty fell rapidly from the middle of the war in Northern Ireland, in the South infant mortality, a sure guide to trends in living standards, rose during the Emergency. Greta Jones has argued that in the 1940s tuberculosis became symbolic of the failure of the Irish government to tackle social deprivation and injustice. Dublin, with its concentration of the poorest working-class families often living in overcrowded housing conditions, was at the core of the state's tuberculosis problem. In 1936–41 Dublin's population accounted for one fifth of the total population of the state but for one third of all deaths from tuberculosis.[94]

It was not simply the brutal realities of deteriorating conditions that produced increasing dissent but the perception that the government had forgotten its only very recent protestations of social radicalism and concern for the worst-off sectors of Irish society. In 1941 the dole in rural areas, the most important indicator of Fianna Fáil's social concern in the 1930s, was stopped. This reflected the rise in the demand for rural labour brought about by the compulsory tillage orders and the drive to expand turf production. The government also prohibited the emigration of men who were normally resident outside towns with a population over 5,000. In response one of those very rare creatures in rural Ireland, a female communist, addressing a large audience of unemployed labourers in Foynes, County Limerick, voiced an increasingly common anti-Fianna Fáil sentiment: 'They started off by passing acts helpful to the workers . . . but they had given way to the farmers and industrialists, the people who had the money.'[95]

The government had made some attempts to retrieve its 1930s image of social concern through a number of welfare reforms: free food and fuel for the poorest were introduced in 1941 and 1942, and unemployment benefits were increased in 1942. However, these did little to decrease dissatisfaction amongst the majority of workers, who faced a substantial increase in the cost of living at a time when the state not only froze wages but appeared to want to intervene decisively in a radical restructuring of the trade union movement.

Splitting the Labour Movement

Irish trade unionism had been divided for some time over the desire of the leadership of the largest union, the Irish Transport and General Workers' Union, for a 'rationalization' of the movement into far fewer industrial organizations, which would eliminate smaller unions and also diminish the influence of the British-based amalgamated unions that continued to organize in the South after independence. Lemass, as Minister for Industry and Commerce, had been strongly in favour of the ITGWU's ideas, in part because of his desire to give a streamlined union movement a role in a more corporatist form of economic policy-making, and also because he was opposed on nationalist grounds to so many Irish workers still being members of British-based unions.[96]

The General Secretary of the ITGWU, William O'Brien, was Lemass's main ally in the trade union movement. He instigated the decision of the Irish Trade Union Congress (ITUC) to set up a Commission of Inquiry into union structures in 1936. At that time the ITUC, which had unions affiliated from both sides of the border, represented 134,000 workers in forty-nine unions. While two of these had over 10,000 members each, seventeen had memberships of less than 500. Inter-union conflicts between craft and general unions, and Irish and British unions, certainly weakened the movement and meant there was a serious argument for radical reform.[97] O'Brien's pursuit of a rationalization into ten industrial unions may well have had the objective of strengthening weakly organized workers in rural areas and smaller towns to resist government and employer demands that they accept low wages as the price of a job.[98] However, many of his critics saw his proposals as being aimed at eliminating the British unions and absorbing the small unions into a much enlarged ITGWU. The Commission of Inquiry failed to agree, split as it was between Irish and British unions, and in 1939 a Council of Irish Unions was set up to promote O'Brienite ideas. It provided the union base of support for Seán MacEntee's Trade Union Bill, which was published in April 1941 and contributed powerfully to the subsequent disastrous split in the political and industrial wings of the labour movement.

The bill proposed that all unions had to obtain a licence to allow them to negotiate and lodge a financial deposit with the High Court. There was to be a tribunal with the power to grant one or more unions the sole right to negotiate for a category of workers where these represented a majority of the workers. Although officials from the Department of Industry and Commerce had consulted the ITUC executive and the Congress of Irish Unions (CIU) and received tacit support, the publication of the bill sparked off a substantial movement of opposition spearheaded by the Dublin Trades Council and the Irish Labour Party, which saw in the bill a powerful issue with which to amplify existing working-class dissatisfaction with the government's performance. On 22 June 1941, the day that Hitler launched Operation Barbarossa against the Soviet Union, the Trades Council organized the largest demonstration of working-class anti-government resolve since the formation of the state. The crowd cheered the ageing union firebrand, Jim Larkin, when he set alight a copy of the bill.[99]

Speakers at the meeting had bemoaned the fact that a city with such a substantial working class should not return one Labour Party representative to the Irish parliament. The combination of falling living standards and resentment over the wages freeze and the Trade Union Bill appeared to be set to change this. There was a large increase in Labour Party membership, with the number of branches rising from 174 in 1941 to 750 in 1943.[100] In the municipal elections in August 1942, the party became the largest group on the Dublin Corporation; and in the general election in 1943 the Labour vote was 15.7 per cent, a 10 per cent improvement on the previous election, and it gained eight new seats, for a total of seventeen.[101] Its vote in Dublin exceeded its national average for the first time, seeming to indicate that it could become more than a party of rural and small-town protest and actually challenge Fianna Fáil for the support of the capital's working class.[102]

Fianna Fáil, which had been at the receiving end of anti-communist allegations from the incumbent government in 1931 and 1932, was by 1943 not averse to using similar tactics against a growing Labour Party threat. It was helped by the bitter legacy of an intra-ITGWU dispute between William O'Brien and Jim Larkin.[103]

Larkin, who had won a North Dublin seat as an Independent Labour candidate in the 1937 election, had subsequently joined the Labour Party and attempted to get an official Labour nomination, but this was resisted by O'Brien and by the ITGWU, which had provided financial support for a number of TDs who were union members. Larkin's political radicalism had diminished substantially by the end of the 1930s, and he had severed any connection with communism.[104] The division in the union movement over the question of rationalization and the suspicion of many that O'Brien had given tacit support and encouragement to the MacEntee Trade Union Bill resulted in Larkin assuming a central role in opposition to the bill and subsequently in an increasingly bitter response from O'Brien and the ITGWU. In 1943 the Dublin Labour Party nominated Larkin as a Dáil candidate, and he was returned in the election of that year.

During the election campaign, which Fianna Fáil had fought under the conservative slogan 'Don't change horses when crossing the stream',[105] MacEntee had waged a lurid anti-communist campaign against Labour, alleging that the party had been infiltrated by a middle-class intelligentsia and, if that was not damning enough, adding that it was taking its orders from Moscow.[106] The decision of the Communist Party of Ireland to dissolve its small organization in the South in 1941 was accompanied by a direction to its former members to enter the Dublin Labour Party and work for an end to Irish neutrality. Former communists and other radicals, along with Larkin and his son, formed a new Central Branch of the Labour Party, which was soon closely monitored by the Special Branch, whose reports were the basis for MacEntee's campaign.[107] Lemass, who still hankered after an image as the leader of the left wing of Fianna Fáil, was less than happy with MacEntee's claims that the Labour Party was 'honeycombed with agents of the Comintern'.[108] He asked MacEntee to keep out of Labour strongholds during the campaign, fearing that a backlash against these lurid claims would make Labour voters reluctant to give second-preference votes to Fianna Fáil.

The 1943 election result was a severe setback for Fianna Fáil: the party's share of the vote dropped from 51.9 per cent in 1938 to 41.9 per cent, and it lost ten seats.[109] The blow was softened by the fact that Fine Gael also experienced a severe rebuff, with a drop of support from 33.3 per cent to 23.1 and a loss of thirteen seats. Its losses were in large part attributable to the party's support for neutrality, which eroded its difference with Fianna Fáil. Nevertheless, the discomfiture of Fianna Fáil's main rival could not hide the rise in support for Labour, particularly in Dublin, where it doubled its first-preference vote.

The sort of denunciations of communist infiltration that MacEntee had specialized in during the election campaign would appear in a new form when O'Brien's ITGWU disaffiliated from the Labour Party in January 1944 and five of its eight TDs split from the party to form a new National Labour Party (NLP). The ITGWU attacked the 'Larkinite and Communist Party elements' who, it was claimed, had taken over the Labour Party.[110] The split and the anti-communist assault put the leadership of the Labour Party on the defensive. It launched its own inquiry into communist involvement, which, although it resulted in the expulsion of a mere six members,[111] had allowed the terms of debate in the labour movement to be defined by the Catholic nationalist right. The report of the inquiry proclaimed that the party's programme 'is based on a set of principles in keeping with Christian doctrine and wholly at variance with the principles of atheistic communism'.[112] Labour's leader, William Norton, faced with a snap general election in May 1944, declared that the Labour Party 'proudly acknowledges the authority of the Catholic Church in all matters relating to public policy and public welfare.'[113] But, weakened and demoralized by the split, the Labour Party saw its vote sink to 9 per cent and eight seats, with the National Labour Party winning 3 per cent and four seats.[114]

The trade union movement subsequently succumbed to the long-standing tension between Irish and British unions. This was now further inflamed by the nationalist assault on the pro-Allied position adopted not just by Irish communists but by those unions with British headquarters and a strong base in Northern Ireland. Symptomatic of the assault was the publication by the National Labour Party of a pamphlet by Alfred O'Rahilly, President of University College Cork and a frequent contributor to the right-wing Catholic weekly the *Standard*, which had run a series of exposés of alleged communist infiltration of the Labour Party. O'Rahilly's *The Communist Front and the Attack on Irish Labour* widened the assault to include the influence of British-based unions and communists in the ITUC. In January 1944 the ITUC executive had declined an invitation to attend a world trade union conference on the war economy and reconstruction, which was to be hosted in London by the British TUC. When this decision was reversed, after a campaign by British-based unions, fifteen unions disaffiliated and created a Congress of Irish Unions, with the ITGWU at its core, in April 1945. This split (although the exact membership figures for each organization are disputed[115]) was a disastrous blow to the Irish left's hope that the South would experience the increasing shift to the left that was occurring in public opinion in Britain and even in Northern Ireland.

The Cold War started in Ireland before the defeat of fascism. The outpourings of the *Standard*, recycled in the pronouncements of the NLP and CIU, encouraged a strong public sentiment that there was only one global enemy of Irish faith and fatherland: the USSR. The theme of a communist conspiracy to destroy Irish neutrality through the manipulation of the labour movement had split that movement and removed a significant threat to Fianna Fáil. In the longer term it ensured that when the continuing social and economic dissatisfaction with the government manifested itself, it would not be in secular-class terms but through a new left-republican formation, which would deepen the political and ideological division on the island that neutrality had done so much to consolidate.

Éire and Beveridge

The Second World War was, for many of those on the Allied side, a struggle not simply for military victory but for a better society. In Britain it meant a commitment to a comprehensive welfare state and full employment. The initial reaction of de Valera's cabinet to the Churchill government's acceptance of the *Beveridge Report* in 1942 was one of vulgar political fear. It was felt that the Irish labour movement had been given a tremendous propaganda weapon by the British decision. Hugo Flinn, a parliamentary secretary to the Minister of Finance, set out the prospect in a letter to de Valera:

The publication of this report, its adoption by public opinion in England and the promise of the Six County Government to implement it if adopted at Westminster is a 'god send' for the Labour party and, properly worked, worth quite a few seats.

Every wildest claim made by them may be made to seem possible of accomplishment: 'if this can be done by England after a horribly costly war, what could not be done by a country that has remained at peace?'[116]

Flinn, a Cork man who had spent much of his life running the family fish business in England and who had no involvement in the independence struggle,[117] personified what Fianna Fáil's critics saw as its growing conservatism.[118]

Lemass was the only member of the government who favoured a radical response to the challenge of Beveridge. Authorized by the cabinet to prepare an analysis of the report, he was prepared to endorse publicly Beveridge's objective of overcoming the 'giants of want, disease, ignorance, squalor and idleness'.[119] He had by now reclaimed his former Department of Industry and Commerce, which he combined with Supply; this provided him with the institutional and policy-making clout to push government planning for the post-war period in a more social-democratic direction. He bombarded his colleagues with quotations from 'modern economic research', which usually meant Beveridge, Keynes or Nicholas Kaldor. His argument was that post-war Ireland should maintain many of the controls, particularly on labour, that had been introduced during the Emergency. These should be developed into a new set of relations between the state, employers and unions that aimed to achieve trade-offs between full employment, improvements in productivity and wage restraint.[120] Aware of the limited capacity of Irish capitalism to generate new jobs, he also proposed an ambitious set of post-war state-spending schemes in areas such as afforestation, drainage, fisheries, hospitals and housing.[121] The objective was full employment, and he argued that such arrangements would require the state to adopt a 'new kind of budget policy' that transcended the narrow accounting priorities of balancing the books.

Unsurprisingly, such notions were anathema to the Department of Finance, which saw them as 'bureaucratic control of the most oppressive and objectionable kind'. Lemass's economic theorists were dismissed as the 'Escapist school of economics'. The Finance view was that the Beveridge proposals were unaffordable for a country like Ireland, and the government needed to avoid any further commitments to social welfare improvements. The only sure way to deal with unemployment was through measures to improve the efficiency and productivity of Irish agriculture and to cut taxes.

De Valera, while not totally sharing this perspective, was uncomfortable with Lemass's radicalism. His inclination was to try to persuade the Irish people of the attractiveness of his own folksy vision of an Ireland that put spiritual values above vulgar material concerns and that should put up with economic problems as the price of being saved from the horrors of war. In a Dáil debate on unemployment in August 1940, he declared that a small country like Ireland should be content with 'frugal comfort' and that unemployment was a problem that defied solution.[122] His famous St Patrick's Day radio address in 1943 has, as Charles Townshend has noted, been frequently quoted 'more often in mockery than in admiration':[123]

The Ireland which we dreamed of would be the home of a people who valued material wealth only as the basis of right living, of a people who were satisfied with frugal comfort and devoted their leisure to things of the spirit – a land whose countryside would be bright with cosy homesteads, whose fields and villages would be joyous with the joy of industry, with the romping of sturdy children, the contests of athletic youths and the laughter of comely maidens, whose firesides would be the forums for serene old age.

This Rousseauesque vision of a land dominated by family farms and industry dispersed to small towns and villages, avoiding the extreme inequalities of fully fledged capitalism and the 'servile state' associated with socialism and communism, remained a powerful influence on Irish political life. As critics at the time and since have pointed out, de Valera failed to provide any realistic ideas about how this vision was to be realized at a time when many of the policies of his government actually undermined it.[124] But, whatever its lack of economic realism, the speech reflected a keen awareness of the threat to his party's support in the west of Ireland because of small-farmer discontent. This focused on what was seen as the government's failure to deliver on the constitution's commitment to 'settle as many families as possible on the land'. The threat from Clann na Talmhan was a real one, as the 1943 election demonstrated. It won 11 per cent of the vote and fourteen seats, but in parts of Fianna Fáil's western heartland, where its support had been highest in the 1930s, the vote for the Clann was almost double its national average, while there were big drops in support for de Valera's party.[125]

It was to this threat that the core sentiments of the St Patrick's Day speech were directed. So also was de Valera's resistance to pressure from Lemass, on this issue at least in alliance with the Department of Finance, that there be a fundamental re-examination of the commitment to further land redistribution and of the large number of smallholdings that would never be able to provide adequate support for their owners.[126] In this sense the sentimental ruralism of the speech had very real effects.

It also reflected de Valera's problem of integrating the realities of urban life and poverty into his vision of Ireland. During the 1943 election campaign he had declared that 'there is nobody in this country who is not getting proper food' and that 'every section of the community has had the careful regard of the government.'[127] The sizeable support for Labour in Dublin was a resounding response to this myopia, as was the increasingly active role played by individual Catholic bishops in dealing with or highlighting urban poverty.

The Catholic hierarchy and clergy, drawn in large part from the rural bourgeoisie, had traditionally been uncomprehending and unsympathetic to the conditions of the urban working class. However, since the publication in 1931 of Pope Pius XI's encyclical *Quadragesimo Anno*, with its promotion of corporatist ideas of social organization, there had been a belated development of a Catholic social movement in Ireland. At times combining corporatist ideas with open worship of Franco and Mussolini, it had provided what little intellectual backbone the Blueshirt movement possessed. But corporatist ideas also influenced some in Fianna Fáil and clerics close to the party.

John Charles McQuaid, who was appointed Archbishop of Dublin in 1940, played a central role in developing the Church's social involvement. A long-standing friend of de Valera, who had pressed his candidacy on the Vatican, McQuaid was a former headmaster of Blackrock College, an elite Catholic school run by the Holy Ghost Fathers. De Valera had taught there and his son was a pupil. McQuaid rapidly developed a high-profile role for the Church's charitable role in Dublin and made it clear that he was aware of the reality of those excluded from de Valera's vision. His first lenten pastoral in 1941, at a time when government ministers were taking a hard line against strikes, declared that 'The very widespread yearning for social peace is itself proof of the grave need for social reform.'[128] In April 1941 he created the Catholic Social Service Conference, which set out to coordinate and expand Catholic welfare work in the diocese and transformed the quality of social work in Dublin, providing up to 250,000 free meals a month.

It was this substructure of Church-organized and privately financed charity that de Valera was prepared to bank on as the practical alternative to Beveridge. For, although the work done by the Church could on one level be seen as a criticism of the inadequacies of the state, the Church itself was at the forefront of the ideological assault on the principles underlying the *Beveridge Report*. McQuaid was an opponent of the expansion of state welfare services[129] and within the cabinet he could rely on Seán MacEntee to scour British and Irish newspapers and journals for Catholic criticisms of Beveridge, particularly those that echoed the section of the Irish Constitution that guaranteed the family as bearing the primary responsibility for the education and welfare of its members. Beveridge threatened to make the state 'omnicompetent', according to one cleric who had recently been made the first Professor of Sociology at Maynooth, the national seminary.[130] Thus, even when clerics criticized the inadequacies of existing welfare services, they were careful to ensure that any proposed alternative relied on the development of their existing role and did not involve any expansion of the role of the state. Such criticism could be acutely embarrassing to the government, as when in 1944 Dr John Dignan, Bishop of Clonfert, produced a pamphlet on the existing health service in which he described the medical assistance service, on which a large section of the population depended for medical care, as tainted by 'destitution, pauperism and degradation'.[131] Yet it was the very Catholic social teaching underlying Dignan's critique that was used ideologically to bury Lemass's radical proposals and that greatly assisted in the political offensive against the upsurge of support for the Labour Party in 1943.

It was of course true that only the massive expansion in the functions and size of the state in wartime Britain made the post-war welfarism and Keynesian economic management possible. A radical such as Lemass faced an Irish situation in which, despite the large increase in state regulation of private economic activity, there was an actual shrinkage in the proportion of national income taken by the state during the Emergency.[132] The implementation of his policies would have brought the government into conflict not only with the traditionally conservative mercantile, financial and large-farmer interests, some of whom had begun to soften their anti de Valera positions in the late 1930s, but also with the new bourgeoisie that had grown up under protectionism. They would have solidified and expanded Fianna Fáil's support in what remained a large but minority constituency, the urban and rural working class. They might have won back support lost to Clann na Talmhan, but they would have unleashed the sort of distributional class warfare that de Valera had set up Fianna Fáil precisely to avoid. Neutrality and its ideological buttressing by anti-communism and Catholic social thought made a conservative response politically sustainable but left the state seriously unprepared for the challenges of the post-war world.

4. Stagnation: Ireland 1945–1959

Ireland's post-war history contrasts with that of most Western European states, where the war proved to be a watershed in social, economic and political terms. Neutrality and the isolation of the war years had served to consolidate a conservative nationalism based on protectionism, a strong Catholic moral community and irredentism in relation to Northern Ireland. The major political challenge to de Valera's government would come from those who charged it with forsaking the radical social republicanism of the 1930s and were thus demanding a reinvigoration of the autarkic and irredentist themes of classic de Valeraism rather than a change of course. It would take the shock of economic crisis and accelerated population loss in the mid 1950s to force a radical rethinking of isolationist economics and the adoption of a more realistic tone in the state's approach to the North.

Protectionism under Pressure

The main motivation for those in government prepared to consider the need for new policy directions was the fear of a destabilizing influx of workers who had gone to the UK during the war. This was a major concern for Lemass when he produced a substantial document on full employment for the cabinet's Economic Policy Committee in January 1945. In fact, the main challenge to the southern state in the next decade would not be the high levels of unemployment exacerbated by returned emigrants but an intensification of the wartime exodus to Britain. Data on net emigration indicate that over 30,000 people left Ireland annually in the immediate post-war period, and this figure rose to over 50,000 in the 1950s.[1] Irish nationalists had, since the Great Famine in the 1840s, defined emigration as the gravest symptom of British misrule. Political independence, land reform and state-sponsored economic development were supposed to lead to an end of the problem. In the year before Fianna Fáil first won power de Valera had claimed that the implementation of his party's development proposals could provide the means of existence for a population of 20 million.[2] Land redistribution, a shift from pasture to tillage and the development of indigenous industry, together with the closure or severe restriction of emigration opportunities in the 1930s, did see a lessening of the rate of population decline. But, as Kevin O'Shiel, a member of the Land Commission that was charged with land redistribution, put it in a memorandum on agrarian strategy for the cabinet in 1942, the 'dry rot' might be ceasing but there was little sign of a rural resurgence: 'In 1847 there were 6,700,000 of us in Eire's Twenty-Six Counties with 4,000,000 sheep and cattle and 3,129,000 acres of tillage. Today we are about 2,968,000 with 7,000,000 cattle and sheep and 1,845,000 acres of tillage.'[3] O'Shiel, like de Valera, was a firm believer in what he termed the 'national school', which viewed the land question as more than a simple matter of economics, in contrast to the 'big business' view, which prioritized efficiency and productivity, inevitably leading to larger holdings and a diminishing demand for labour. Land and the rural communities it supported formed the basis for the preservation of the nation's essential character as expressed in history, legends, folklore, customs and language. The objective of agrarian policy was not to maximize productivity but 'to make the land maintain as large a number of tradition-preserving cells as possible . . . as many families as possible on holdings large enough to assure them a fair measure of frugal comfort'. While these ideas were reflected in government policy and in de Valera's St Patrick's Day address in 1943, they were under increasing pressure from elements in the political and administrative elite.

The problem was clear, even to O'Shiel, who pointed out that of the 344,500 holdings in the state, at least 200,000 could be regarded as 'uneconomic', because the farmer could not support himself and his family at even a level of 'frugal livelihood'. A high percentage of these uneconomic holdings were in the 'congested districts' along the western seaboard from Donegal to Kerry. The west of Ireland, with its high concentration of native Irish speakers, had been at the core of the cultural definition of Irishness for de Valera and his party, and their agrarian policy had had real effects in maintaining the small-farm economy in the west. Part of O'Shiel's critique of existing policy was that the activities of the Land Commission had been largely concentrated in these areas, where vast tracts of land were bog, moor and mountainside and much of the remainder was land of very poor quality. Almost half of the land redistributed since the process began under the British had been in the western province of Connacht. However, if the government had acceded to his desire to extend land redistribution to the richer areas, it would have risked disrupting the all-important cattle trade with Britain, which depended on the large cattle farms long denounced by Fianna Fáil radicals as 'ranches', with their owners dubbed parasitic 'graziers'.

The attempt to alter the balance between tillage and pasture had been silently given up by the middle of the 1930s, when the centrality of the cattle trade in earning the surplus necessary for the importation of machinery and raw materials for the industrialization drive had been recognized in the Coal–Cattle Pact negotiated with Britain in 1935. De Valera admitted before the war that 'the flight from the land was a fact',[4] but this was the extent of his concessions to economic realism. The land redistribution programme was slowed down, and there would be no indulgence of O'Shiel's demand for something just short of 'a whole-sale obliteration of the big graziers'. But de Valera still wanted agrarian policy to pursue two essentially incompatible objectives: the maximiza-tion of food production and the retention of as many families on the land as possible.[5]

Lemass, who had asked his leader in vain for an indication of which objective he prioritized, went on to produce his own dramatic proposals for post-war agriculture in a long memorandum on full employment in 1945. He recommended the 'displacement' of the worst farmers, if neces-sary through state powers of compulsory purchase:

It is necessary to ensure that the Nation's resources of agricultural land are fully utilised. The rights of owners should not include the right to allow land to go derelict or to be utilised below its reasonable productive capacity. Only a limited number of families can be settled on the land, on economic holdings, and policy must be directed to ensuring that ownership will be confined to persons willing and capable of working them adequately.[6]

The radicalism of his approach to agriculture was anathema to most of his colleagues, combined as it was with a far-reaching set of proposals for Keynesian budgetary policy, a substantial expansion of the state's role in industrial development, a new system of economic planning involving the trade unions and a critical review of the workings of protectionism. It was predicated on the assumption of an economic and political crisis detonated by the return of the tens of thousands of men and women who had migrated to Britain during the war. Pressure for this sort of change was greatly reduced as it became apparent that wartime migrants were not returning. It was also the case that, despite wartime emigration, the 1946 census showed a population decline of only 0.4 per cent and that the bulk of this was accounted for by a sharp drop in the Protestant population.[7] A new census in 1951 was the first since 1841 to register an increase in population.[8] These apparently favourable demographic trends were accompanied by a post-war consumption boom as people tried to make up for the dearth of goods during the Emergency. Personal expenditure rose by almost a quarter between 1945 and 1950 and industrial output rose by two thirds.[9]

But beneath these short-term improvements the problems that had motivated Lemass's radicalism remained. The increased output of Irish industry was destined mainly for the domestic market, and even by the end of the 1950s exports of manufactured goods represented only a small percentage of total exports. Over 80 per cent of industrial firms in the Republic employed fewer than 50 persons and lacked the resources for research, improved production methods, and the development of export markets.[10] At the same time the Republic's dependence on imports for machinery and raw materials contributed, along with the demands of Irish consumers for a range of imported consumer goods, to recurrent balance-of-payments crises. A protected domestic market did provide the basis for some continued expansion, but the small size of the market put an inherent limitation on the capacity of Irish industry to absorb what became the largest rural exodus since the worst periods of population loss under British rule.

The 1940s saw a decisive shift in the attitude of many rural dwellers to life in the countryside. A commission appointed in 1948 to examine emigration and other population problems noted the unanimity of view expressed to them by those with direct experience of rural life: 'the relative loneliness, dullness and generally unattractive nature of life in many parts of rural Ireland, compared with the pattern of life in urban centres and with that in easily accessible places outside the country'.[11] The limited amount of industrial development since the 1930s, together with the much greater employment opportunities in Britain, broke whatever limited attraction subsistence living on the family farm had for tens of thousands of young men and women. The post-Famine dominance of the 'stem family' system of inheritance, where the land was passed intact to the eldest son, had produced a society with an extremely low marriage rate and a high age at marriage.[12] The social and sexual casualties of this system, particularly the younger sons and daughters without dowries to make them an attractive match and thus condemned to celibacy, now voted with their feet for the building sites, hospitals and hotels of post-war Britain. Agriculture had a total workforce of 580,000 in 1946; by 1951 this had dropped to 504,000, and by 1961 to 376,000.[13]

Fianna Fáil's post-war agrarian and industrial policies did little to address this exodus. The government's main priority in agricultural policy was to restore the relatively favourable terms for exports to Britain provided in the 1938 Trade Agreement. There had been a decrease of 35 per cent in agricultural exports to the UK from 1939 to 1946, which the Irish blamed on inadequate UK prices. After the war the scope for increased agricultural exports at satisfactory prices was further adversely affected by food rationing in Britain and increasing competition from cheap Commonwealth food.[14] Irish industry was also continuing to suffer from British reluctance to allow scarce supplies of coal and industrial raw materials to cross the Irish Sea. When de Valera opened negotiations with the British in September 1947, his priorities were the revival of the cattle trade to its pre-war level and countering resistance from the British to further industrialization in the South. The latter stemmed from Britain's economic weakness, which had led to the suspension of sterling convertibility against the dollar in August 1947. Ireland's external assets, which were held in sterling, had increased from £163 million in 1939 to £450 million in 1945, and the British Treasury was concerned lest too rapid a process of Irish industrialization ran these down as they were used to buy dollars to import machinery and raw materials. In response de Valera was insistent that 'it was the fixed policy of the Eire government to develop their own industries insofar as they were capable of doing so. Eire did not wish to remain a predominantly agricultural country [but one] whose economy would be based on the export of manufactured goods.'[15]

The Irish were successful in persuading the British to respect their right to pursue independent economic policies, but the price of a substantial coal allocation was the acceptance that, in the words of Patrick Smith, the Irish Minister for Agriculture, Éire's agricultural production had 'to fit in with the British programme'.[16] De Valera, who had boasted in the 1930s that Irish agriculture could do without the English market, was quoted in a British Treasury document as calling for the 'dovetailing of the two economies'.[17] The limit of his agrarian radicalism was a demand, conceded by the British, for the removal of the price differential between Irish fat cattle and animals fattened in Britain. Although the negotiations were interrupted by the 1948 general election, the Trade Agreement signed by the inter-party government in June 1948 was based on the elements largely agreed on by de Valera. While this meant that fewer cattle were exported to be fattened in England, thus increasing the value of cattle exports, it added little to the employment-generating capacity

of Irish agriculture at the same time as the agreement intensified dependence on the British market, which in the mid 1950s was taking 86 per
cent of Irish agricultural exports.[18]

If the more diversified and labour-intensive agriculture that had been
the aspiration of Fianna Fáil agrarian radicalism was now chimerical, it
only served to underline the limitations of the party's industrial strategy.
Lemass had, in 1945, hinted at the possibility of breaking with a key
tenet of economic nationalism when he informed the cabinet that 'While
it is desirable that all industries should be owned and controlled by Irish
nationals, there is less reason for insistence on national ownership of
export industries than of industries supplying only the home market.'[19]
It would be another twelve years before he was able to implement this
idea with the amendment of the Control of Manufacturers Acts of the
1930s to make substantial foreign investment possible. He was already
being attacked for being too sympathetic to foreign interests, and the
immediate post-war period, with the emergence of a radical social-
republican challenge to Fianna Fail, was not conducive to policy
innovation.[20] Yet, without a new source of employment generation based
on foreign capital developing the export capacity that indigenous industry
lacked, the other arm of potential industrial strategy was doomed by the
overwhelming resistance from the party's powerful allies amongst the
manufacturing bourgeoisie that had developed behind tariff walls.

Lemass, the main sponsor of protectionism in the 1930s, was well aware
by the end of the war of the inefficiencies and restrictive practices that
protectionism had permitted. Speaking to a group of businessmen in 1947,
he explained that protective tariffs and other import restrictions were
going to be much less important in the future.[21] He was attempting to
prepare the ground for his controversial Industrial Efficiency Bill, which
proposed to establish a new and powerful Prices Commission to inquire
into prices, prevent cartels and promote efficiency. Manufacturers would
be required to participate in 'development councils', including workers
and consumers, to promote efficiency, and recalcitrant industrialists were
to have their directors' fees stopped. Together with the establishment of
a Labour Court in 1946 as an instrument of industrial conciliation, the
bill was an attempt to promote the modernization of Irish industry in a
semi-corporatist fashion. In the bleak conditions of post-war Ireland, it
was visionary. Apart from the fierce resistance of some of Lemass's former
business allies, the major practical problem was that successful modernization would often have meant more rather than less unemployment.
Until the nettle of foreign capital was grasped, Lemass's modernizing

project provided no way out of the impasse created by a shrinking agriculture and a stagnant industrial sector.

The bill fell victim to Fianna Fáil's ejection from office after sixteen years in power. A large role in the defeat was played by the surge in support for a new party, Clann na Poblachta, whose main themes were an embarrassing reprise of the more radical republican sentiments expressed by de Valera and Lemass two decades previously.

The First Inter-party Government

Alvin Jackson has provocatively described the decade after 1948 as 'the heyday of Irish Butskellism . . . an era characterised by unrelenting party warfare but also by minimal ideological and policy distinctions'.[22] But the post-war consensus in Britain was constructed around the welfare state and a commitment to full employment achieved through Keynesian techniques of economic management. In stark contrast, what consensus emerged in Ireland was in this period centred on resistance to British welfarism on the basis of the social teachings of the Catholic Church and the prioritizing of the balance of payments over economic growth and employment creation.

In the immediate post-war period it became apparent that Fianna Fáil could not count for long on the gratitude of voters for being saved from the hazards of war. This was clear in 1945 from the results of the first election for the office of President, a post created under the 1937 Constitution and originally held with all-party agreement by the Protestant Gaelic revivalist Douglas Hyde. The Independent candidate Patrick McCartan polled an impressive 20 per cent of the vote. McCartan, who had a solid republican pedigree, was supported by disaffected IRA men, Labour and Clann na Talmhan. This quickly improvised coalition was to encourage the emergence of a more serious challenge to Fianna Fáil with the creation of Clann na Poblachta ('Party of the Republic') in July 1946.

The new party was yet another attempt to meld republicanism with left-of-centre politics, a project that could be traced back to the writings of James Connolly and that had its previous most significant manifestation in the Republican Congress in the 1930s. However, the leftism of the Clann owed much more to papal encyclicals than to the sort of Marxism that had influenced the republican radicals of the 1930s. Its leader, Seán MacBride, had briefly been Chief of Staff of the IRA in the 1930s. MacBride had been born into the republican aristocracy. His mother, Maud Gonne, was a lifelong activist in the nationalist cause, and his father, Major John MacBride, had been executed for his part in the Easter Rising. He had left the IRA arguing that de Valera's new constitution showed that full sovereignty and an end to partition could be achieved constitutionally. De Valera's robust response to the IRA during the war had been the prime cause of his disillusion with Fianna Fáil. A barrister, MacBride had spent the war years defending IRA men and came to public notice when he represented the family at the inquest of the former Chief of Staff of the IRA Seán McCaughey, who died on hunger strike in 1946.[23] Twenty-two of the twenty-seven members of the provisional executive of the Clann had been active members of the IRA at some stage in their lives, and for them the priority was to press on for the full republican objectives that de Valera was seen to have betrayed.

Yet MacBride's own experience of republican politics in the two decades after the Civil War had taught him that Fianna Fáil's rise to a hegemonic position in Irish politics depended on an ability to provide a left-of-centre social and economic programme as well as a radical nationalist agenda. It was therefore the Clann that did much to ensure that emigration was a major issue in electoral politics, using it to highlight the winners and losers in de Valera's Ireland: 'The nation is being weakened by the forced emigration of its youth. A small section has been enabled to accumulate enormous wealth while unemployment and low wages, coupled with an increasing cost of living, are the lot of the workers.'[24]

The party also proposed that the state assume responsibility for full employment based on a minimum wage related to the cost of living. Underlying such demands was MacBride's commitment to the economic ideas set out in the iconoclastic *Minority Report to the Commission of Inquiry into Banking, Currency and Credit* written by P. J. O'Loghlen. This had attacked the direction of economic policy followed by all governments since 1923. It doubted the ability of the private sector to generate sufficient employment and supported comprehensive government intervention in areas including industrial development, afforestation, land reclamation and a public housing drive. All this would be financed by severing the link with sterling and repatriating the sterling assets held by Irish nationals. O'Loghlen had cited papal encyclicals to support his arguments, and MacBride was careful to establish the Catholic credentials of his party's economic and social programme. He vigorously espoused the social welfare plan devised by Bishop Dignan of Clonfert, which had been rejected out of hand by MacEntee in 1944, and the Clann asserted, in a manner that would return to haunt it, that the family was the basic unit of society and that the state could not encroach on the fundamental responsibilities of the heads of families in the social and moral spheres.[25]

The radical tone of the Clann's economic and social programme made it attractive to a younger generation who had grown up after the Civil War and were less influenced by the party loyalties the conflict had generated in their parents. It was partly to appeal to this group that MacBride chose Noel Browne, a young doctor with a passionate commitment to the eradication of tuberculosis, as his Minister for Health. Noel Hartnett, the man responsible for recruiting Browne to the party, was typical of another important source of recruits and voters: disillusioned Fianna Fáil activists. The feeling that de Valera's government had turned its back on the central agrarian and cultural goals of the revolutionary generation had begun to be articulated in the party itself. Michael Joe Kennedy, a prominent Fianna Fáil TD, wrote to Frank Gallagher, director of the government information services, in December 1946 complaining that the agrarian and language policies of the party had been jettisoned:

The Land Commission has ceased to function . . . and two ministers [Land and Agriculture] are proclaiming . . . that there are too many people on the land. Our language policy is as dead as a dodo . . . We'll have English holiday camps in Gormanstown and beautiful international airports as your name is Frank Gallagher but the Irish Ireland programme will be watered down before Fianna Fáil leaves office.[26]

Hartnett had been a member of Fianna Fáil's national executive but had resigned in 1937 in protest at the decision to accept a £1,000 donation from a businessman.[27] Like that of the teachers, small businessmen and lawyers who dominated the executive of the Clann,[28] Hartnett's social philosophy was for a nostalgic return to what Richard Dunphy has described as the 'essentially petty-bourgeois ideology' of 1920s republicanism.[29] Fianna Fáil was accused of selling out to big business, bankers and graziers, and of betraying its working-class and small-farmer supporters. The Ireland that de Valera still admitted to dreaming about was the one that the Clann claimed could yet be created if the will was there: an Ireland of small farms and small- and medium-sized factories run by patriotic Irish capitalists with contented and healthy workers. Although the state was assigned a large role in the Clann's economic and social vision, charges of communism were deflated by the party's proclamation that it would put a priority on rehabilitating the moral fibre of the nation from the attacks of 'modern materialism' and other 'alien, artificial and unchristian concepts of life'.[30]

Conditions could hardly have been better for a challenge to Fianna Fáil. An excessively wet summer in 1946 followed by one of the coldest winters on record hit agriculture and domestic consumers badly. Things were made even worse by a serious energy crisis brought about by a major cutback in coal supplies from Britain. In consequence, transportation became chaotic, and the already marked shortage of raw materials was exacerbated, forcing many industries to close. The country ran a serious balance of payments deficit of over £25 million in 1947. Bread rationing was reintroduced in January 1947 as was soap rationing, and, critically, beer and porter supplies were drastically reduced. There was a widespread popular anger sparked by high prices (these had more than doubled during the war), a scarcity of goods and black-marketeering. A Lower Prices Council set up by Dublin Trades Council was able to bring out crowds of up to 100,000 and, in an unprecedented movement for such a patriarchal society, the Irish Housewives' Association set up a Women's Parliament where 300 delegates representing over 300,000 women made a range of demands, from that for the provision of hot dinners for all school children to the dottily xenophobic one for restrictions on the 'influx of tourists'.[31]

Lemass and the government appeared to turn their backs on earlier pro-trade union stances in the face of widespread pressure from workers wanting to reverse the decline in their living standards associated with the wartime wage standstill. A wave of strikes or threatened strikes hit the docks, buses, banks, insurance offices and the crucial flour-milling industry. But it was the government's victory over striking teachers that harmed it most politically and provided the Clann with a powerful new source of support. A pre-war wage demand, revived after the end of the wage freeze, was brusquely dismissed by Tom Derrig, the Minister for Education, and the government showed no inclination to use Lemass's recently established Labour Court as a possible means of arbitration. The strike by the teachers' union focused on Dublin, with teachers in the rest of the country being levied to support their striking colleagues. It lasted from March to October, when the teachers, defeated, returned to work. The government took a hard and uncompromising line. It spurned an offer by the Archbishop of Dublin, John Charles McQuaid, to mediate, and striking teachers who invaded the pitch during the All-Ireland football final were brutally dispersed by the police. The policy backfired and left a legacy of bitterness. Teachers were traditionally regarded as the backbone of Fianna Fáil, the organic intellectuals of the national revolution, essential for the realization of de Valera's commitment to the Irish language and culture. Many teachers left Fianna Fáil, and teachers became the organizational bedrock of the new party.

Three scandals involving allegation of corrupt practices by ministers, two of them implicating Lemass, contributed to the pervasive sense of malaise. Although only one junior minister was forced to resign and Lemass was cleared of all the charges, the Clann made effective use of the issue of 'political decadence' and won by-elections in Counties Dublin and Tipperary in the autumn of 1947. Worryingly for Fianna Fáil, not only had MacBride defeated Tommy Mullins, the high-profile National Secretary of the party in Dublin, but both the Clann victories had been helped by substantial vote transfers from Labour and Fine Gael candidates. De Valera attempted to pre-empt the new party's development by calling an early general election, in the knowledge that his Minister for Local Government, Seán MacEntee, had just carried out a quite radical revision of constituency boundaries designed to favour the larger parties. His strategy nearly succeeded. Dizzy with its by-election successes and with the totally unrealistic hope of challenging Fianna Fáil's dominance, the Clann put up candidates in every constituency, ninety-three in all, which was more than Fine Gael. With only rudimentary organization in most constituencies and many candidates new to electoral politics, if not to underground activity, the result was a major disappointment.

Despite nine extra Dáil seats being available, Fianna Fáil lost eight, giving it a total of sixty-eight, and its share of the poll dropped 7 per cent to 41.8 per cent, the same as in the bad year of 1943. Fine Gael's share of the vote dropped slightly to 19.8 per cent although it gained one seat, giving it a total of thirty-one. The two Labour parties' overall share of the vote was more or less unchanged with 8.7 per cent for Labour and 2.6 per cent for National Labour. However, the number of Labour seats rose by six, while National Labour gained one. Labour had benefited from the Clann's overambitious decision to put up candidates in every constituency. While many of these candidates were defeated, their vote transfers went disproportionately to Labour candidates. This helps to explain why the Clann got 2 per cent more of the national vote than the two Labour parties – 13.2 per cent – while winning nine fewer seats, for a total of ten. Clann na Talmhan, which lost support to MacBride's party, saw its vote halved to 5.6 per cent and won seven seats.[32]

Peter Mair has argued that Labour and the Clann faced a crucial choice: they could either allow Fianna Fáil to remain in office as a minority administration and allow themselves time to mobilize a radical alternative to the two main Civil War parties; or they could subordinate their differences in the interests of forming a broad anti-Fianna Fáil alliance, which would inevitably be dominated by Fine Gael.[33] Although some in the Labour Party and the Clann had favoured a 'Republican–Labour–Farmer' alliance against Fianna Fáil and Fine Gael, the failure of the Clann to make a major breakthrough ruled this out. Ironically, it was MacBride's own mistaken belief that the international situation was favourable to radical action on partition that made him eager to contemplate coalition with a party led by General Richard Mulcahy, a man whose role as commanding officer of the provisional government's military forces in the Civil War caused the strongly republican element in the Clann to regard him as a 'bloody murderer'.[34] Mulcahy had suggested a possible Fine Gael–Labour–Clann na Talmhan coalition during the 1944 election.[35] At the time Lemass had denounced this on the basis that Labour would end up as the tail-end of a Fine Gael coalition implementing 'anti-national policies'. While the first inter-party government would put an end to a decade of electoral decline for Fine Gael, it would do so partly on the basis of that party repudiating the less anglophobic and pro-Commonwealth themes of its discourse that Mulcahy had articulated in 1944.[36]

Many people expected the inter-party government to break up almost immediately. It was, after all, based on an uneasy and purely expedient alliance between the conservative Fine Gael, the sectional Clann na Talmhan, two antagonistic Labour groups and the untried Clann na Poblachta. How would, for example, the desire of William Norton, the Labour Tánaiste, for a generous social security scheme be reconciled with the determination of Patrick McGilligan, Fine Gael's Finance Minister, to keep a close eye on government expenditure? Nevertheless, the government lasted from February 1948 to May 1951 and had some considerable achievements, particularly in the area of social policy.

Mulcahy's easy acceptance of a Clann veto on his becoming Taoiseach and the filling of that position by John A. Costello, a barrister and former Attorney-General in his late fifties, eased the process of government formation. Costello had few of the resources for strong leadership. His personal style was more suited to the court room than to the political platform. He was not party leader, had no choice in who became a minister and had none of the patronage normally enjoyed by a Taoiseach. He therefore had in part to rely on his acknowledged skills as chairman of government meetings to deal with the numerous areas of potential inter-party conflict. He was helped by his good relations with MacBride, whom he had helped to persuade to take up constitutional politics through their common membership of the Law Library,[37] and was also on friendly terms with leaders of the Labour Party through family connections and common involvement on hospital boards. But most significant in limiting the scope for conflict was his government's willingness to borrow to finance capital expenditure and a shared set of Catholic and nationalist values.

Fine Gael's Patrick McGilligan was seen by the economic conservatives in Finance and the Central Bank as a safe Minister for Finance. His first budget took an axe to estimates prepared by Fianna Fáil, which had planned an increase in spending on food subsidies, rural electrification and the treatment of tuberculosis. His views on Norton's proposals to overhaul and extend the state's social welfare system were clear in some of his notes for the 1948 budget: 'Social services – levelling down . . . servile state . . . all taken by state to pay out pocket money.'[38] Despite this, some commentators have seen the introduction of a capital budget in 1950 as a triumph of Keynesianism.[39] But, as Brian Girvin has noted, the capital budget was not part of an overall strategy to facilitate growth in the economy, and there continued to be a commitment to a balanced budget.[40] McGilligan's central purpose remained the traditional Fine Gael one of lowering the rate of income tax.

The idea for the capital budget came from Patrick Lynch, a young Finance official who was seconded to the Department of the Taoiseach to act as Costello's personal economic adviser. He had discussed it with Alexis FitzGerald, an adviser to the Taoiseach who was also Costello's son-in-law.[41] It attracted Costello because it represented a *via media* between the conflicting economic and social views of McGilligan and MacBride. Although MacBride's ministerial domain was a non-economic one, his strongly developed economic views and his desire to promote the socially radical image of the Clann led him into direct conflict with Finance. He remained a strong proponent of the need for more state investment in areas such as land reclamation, afforestation, housing and health to be financed through the repatriation of sterling assets.

MacBride's department was also responsible for Ireland's participation in the European Recovery Programme: the Marshall Plan. Between May 1948 and May 1951 the country received £6 million in grants and £46 million in loans. This did something to ease intra-government conflicts over public expenditure issues, and its emollient effects were amplified by an unprecedented willingness to resort to borrowing: £65 million was borrowed through national loans between 1948 and 1950.[42] It was in this way that some of the major social achievements of the government were financed. There was a remarkable improvement in house building, particularly in the countryside. In 1945 it was estimated that 110,000 new houses were required to deal with the immediate need.[43] In 1947, 744 local authority houses had been completed. By 1950, through the effort of the National Labour Minister for Local Government, T. J. Murphy, the annual figure had risen to over 8,000. In the countryside the Minister for Agriculture, James Dillon, had used a large amount of the Marshall Aid to launch the Land Project, which aimed to reclaim four million acres through drainage and fertilization and, by providing new holdings and extra employment, did much to launch Fine Gael's electoral recovery in the 1950s.[44]

The Mother and Child Crisis

But the main social achievement of the government was in public health, where the Clann na Poblachta Minister for Health, Dr Noel Browne, gave a forceful political lead and urgency to the anti-tuberculosis campaign. There had been a sharp increase in the tuberculosis death rate during the war years, in contrast to that in Northern Ireland, which, after an initial rise, had declined by 1945. The southern Irish death rate from tuberculosis in 1945 was 124 per 100,000, compared to eighty in the north, seventy-nine in Scotland and sixty-two in England and Wales.[45] The government's response had been constrained by the dominant feeling that Ireland could not afford the sort of welfare state envisaged in the *Beveridge Report*, and also by the Catholic Church's resolute opposition to government intervention in these areas. The Church believed that the provision of social and medical benefits by the state undermined the integrity of the family. When the initiative for a more pro-active policy had been taken by non-governmental organizations and private individuals who set up an Anti-Tuberculosis League in 1942, this was sabotaged by Archbishop McQuaid, who saw it as a Trojan horse for the expansion of the powers of the state. A Red Cross investigation in 1943 pointed out that there were only 2,110 beds for tuberculosis patients, the majority in small voluntary and local authority institutions. This left a shortfall of 4,500 beds by current international standards of treatment. Growing dissatisfaction with sanatorium conditions and the treatment of patients had led to the Tuberculosis (Establishment of Sanatoria) Act in 1945 and the Public Health Act of 1947. Despite this, the number of beds for tuberculosis patients had increased to just 3,701 in 1948, with only a third of these in institutions that had access to the latest clinical and diagnostic facilities.

Browne had been recruited to the Clann by Noel Hartnett when the former was working at Newcastle Sanatorium. Browne's passion for the fight against tuberculosis came from bitter personal experience: his parents and three sisters had all been killed by the disease. He was educated in England, where he and his siblings had been forced to move after the death of his parents. He later studied medicine at Trinity College Dublin. Browne had contracted tuberculosis himself in 1940[46] and been treated in England, subsequently working in English hospitals before returning to Ireland in 1945. Having been treated and having worked in English sanatoria, he was scornful of the services available to tuberculosis sufferers in Ireland. He had played a central role in making the disease a major issue during the election campaign and was, to the chagrin of some of the older and more ideologically driven members of the party, chosen by MacBride to be the other Clann member of the government. In government he secured a remarkable expansion in anti-tuberculosis services. By the time he left office in 1951 the total number of beds had risen to 6,857. Expenditure on the disease increased almost fourfold between 1948 and 1953, the largest increase in any area of health and social services.[47] Just as the Clann had modernized political campaigning by the use of the cinema with its effective propaganda film *Our Country*, Browne's department ran a national tuberculosis-awareness campaign using posters, film and radio. He achieved all this by liquidating the assets of the Hospital Sweepstake Fund, which until then had been used stintingly to cover the working deficits of hospitals. Now Browne, despite the unease of McGilligan, used not only the fund's interest but also its capital to finance the department's ambitious programme.[48]

Browne's single-mindedness, crusading zeal, impatience with his more conservative colleagues and an inevitable amount of political naivety, given his relative youth and lack of political or administrative experience, led him to bear a disproportionate amount of the blame for the

Mother and Child Affair, which pitted the young minister against the leaders of the Catholic Church and rocked the government to its foundations. The origins of the crisis lay in Fianna Fáil's 1947 Health Act, which included provisions for a free health-care scheme for mothers and for children up to the age of sixteen. The hierarchy had written to de Valera expressing their disapproval of parts of the Act, but the response of the government was not tested as it was soon out of office. These communications carried on behind the scenes, concealed from the public at large and the incoming government.

When Browne decided, in 1950, to reactivate the provisions in the 1947 Act he was already out of favour with the hierarchy. They were unhappy with the trend towards greater state control of, and investment in, the health service, of which the anti-tuberculosis campaign was one manifestation.[49] Browne's medical training at Trinity College made him inevitably an object of suspicion. Trinity was regarded as a bastion of the Protestant Ascendancy, and any Catholic who attended it was at risk of contamination. The bishops had long made clear their disapproval of attendance by Catholics, who were urged to go to one of the three constituent colleges of the National University, which were thought 'sufficiently safe in regard to faith and morals'.[50] McQuaid had tightened the screw in 1944 with a ban on attendance unless he granted permission, which would be given only 'for grave and valid reasons'. Failure to heed the ban was a mortal sin and meant a refusal of the Sacraments.

The hierarchy's objections to the scheme were set out in a letter to Costello that denounced the measure as 'a ready-made instrument for future totalitarian aggression'. The right to provide for the health of children belonged to parents and the state's role was purely subsidiary: to help the 'indigent or neglectful' 10 per cent through some sort of means-tested benefit. Along with the threat to parental responsibility, the scheme's provisions for health education in regard to motherhood were seen as the thin end of a wedge that could lead to Trinity-educated doctors advising 'Catholic girls and women' on sex, chastity and marriage, which could include advice on birth-control.[51]

Browne, who was summoned to McQuaid's residence to be informed of the contents of the letter, appears to have accepted that the provision for education might have to be reconsidered, but he was not prepared to move on the question of a means test. What remains unclear is whether his subsequent quixotic attempt to persuade the hierarchy that the scheme was compatible with Catholic moral law, if not with the Church's social teachings, was a reflection of naivety or a disingenuous cover for a desire

to provoke a crisis in the Clann and government because of his dissatisfaction with MacBride's leadership.[52] However, there is little doubt
about his passionate commitment on the issue. In speeches in 1948 he
revealed that the death-rate of Irish infants in their first year of life during
the previous five-year period had been 55 per cent higher than in England
and Wales, and he was convinced that one of the reasons for the differential
was the absence of a national system of maternity education and care
for all mothers.[53] McQuaid offered him no comfort with a peremptory
declaration that Catholic social teaching meant 'Catholic moral teaching
in regard to things social'.[54] Browne published the details of the scheme
on 6 March 1951, and a month later McQuaid told Costello that the
hierarchy had rejected the scheme. The cabinet met the next day and,
with the exception of Browne, voted to drop the scheme and prepare
another one in conformity with Catholic social teaching. When Browne
did not resign immediately MacBride demanded that he do so, hastening
the decomposition of the Clann as its urban radical element departed
in disgust. The loss of Browne and another TD, Jack McQuillan, over
the affair accelerated the process by which the government's majority
had already begun to be whittled away; and when there were defections
from Clann na Talmhan over the price paid to farmers for milk, the
government was brought down in April.

What did the affair reveal about the relationship between Church and
state? According to J. J. Lee, 'Browne was probably his own worst enemy,
despite the competition from Costello, MacBride and McQuaid.'[55] The
most substantial history of the inter-party government agrees: 'much of
the blame for the crisis must rest on Browne himself.'[56] It is true that the
hierarchy was only one of the forces ranged against Browne. The Irish
Medical Association, which feared that the Mother and Child scheme
would undermine doctors' earnings from private practice, denounced it as
a form of socialized medicine and state control. Other members of the
government found Browne a very difficult colleague, and it has been
suggested that without the antagonism of these other forces the hierarchy's
intervention might not have been so decisive.[57] Yet the evidence of the
unalloyed and enthusiastic loyalty of Costello and his colleagues to the
Church is compelling. The message of 'respectful homage' sent by the new
government to Pope Pius XII spoke of their 'desire to repose at the feet
of Your Holiness the assurance of our filial loyalty and devotion as well as
our firm resolve to be guided in all our work by the teachings of Christ
and to strive for the attainment of social order in Ireland based on Christian
principles'. This out-deferred de Valera and prompted an unprecedented

protest from Maurice Moynihan, the secretary to the cabinet.[58]

MacBride, later an icon of the Irish republican left and the winner of both a Nobel and a Lenin Peace Prize, was a particularly depressing example of what Ronan Fanning has termed 'the near feudal deference' of the government to the hierarchy in general and the Archbishop of Dublin in particular.[59] As soon as he was elected to the Dáil, he hand-delivered a letter to the Archbishop's house paying his 'humble respects' and, like his future government, putting himself 'at your Grace's disposal . . . Both as a Catholic and a public representative I shall always welcome any advice which Your Grace may be good enough to give me.'[60] Later he would urge McQuaid to appoint an ecclesiastical adviser to the Irish delegation of the Council of Europe to advise on Catholic teaching on social, political and diplomatic questions. This invitation for the Church to be publicly involved in the formation of Irish foreign policy was ignored by the astute cleric, who preferred more opaque channels of influence.

That MacBride had been, however briefly, Chief of Staff of the IRA may have encouraged these abject overtures to prove his reliability. In the same way, a government including a party full of unrepentant republicans and some social radicals may have seen its profuse Catholicism as an insurance policy against Fianna Fáil's tendency to resort to 'red peril' scares when it suited. Yet there could be no doubting the deep, obedient Catholicism of Costello, who, like at least four other members of his government, was a member of the Catholic society the Knights of St Columbanus. Founded in 1922 to counter anti-Catholic discrimination by Freemasons and others, it was soon accused of organizing discrimination itself.[61]

Costello's willingness to sacrifice a colleague and put the future of his government at serious risk reflected not just personal religiosity and inter-party manoeuvring but a Church that was in a particularly peremptory mode. The post-war development of Irish Catholicism was divergent from that of most other European countries, where the Church's support for inter-war authoritarianism produced a liberal reaction. Instead, Ireland experienced a mood of increasing 'integralism': the desire to make it an even more totally Catholic state than it had yet become.[62] One factor in explaining this divergence was the neutrality that insulated the South from the social and moral upheaval produced by direct involvement in the war. Another was the fear of 'contamination' from across the Irish Sea as Britain embarked on a post-war embrace of the welfare state and 'socialistic' planning. One of the reasons that the hierarchy was so concerned about emigration was the high level of female emigrants attracted by the demand for nurses and domestic help in post-war Britain. The threat to the moral purity of these young women from life in 'heathen' England prompted some bishops, supported by Seán MacBride, to propose a ban on the emigration of women under twenty-one.[63] Other more realistic voices in the Church recognized that emigration continued to act as a safety valve by siphoning off many of the most thoughtful and energetic voices of potential criticism in Irish society, and the proposal was rejected.

For those who remained, the Church still maintained a strident and ever-watchful cordon sanitaire against the threat of communist ideological penetration. The Church's anti-socialism was nothing new: both Connolly and Larkin had had bruising encounters with it before partition. But the development of the Cold War gave the struggle against the 'reds' a fresh intensity. It mattered little that the Irish Communist Party, revived in 1948 as the Irish Workers' League, was tiny. The Irish bishops were determined to demonstrate that Ireland's Catholics were in the vanguard of the struggle against the communist threat.[64] During the Italian general election of 1948, Archbishop McQuaid appealed over Radio Éireann for funds to fight the communists, and within a month £20,000 had been collected.[65] The arrests and show trials of Catholic prelates in Eastern Europe produced a display of intense and affronted solidarity. A rally in Dublin in protest against the imprisonment of Cardinal Mindszenty of Hungary attracted 150,000 – considerably more than the same year's all-party anti-partition protest against the Ireland Act.

It would be wrong to assume that the Church's pretensions were uncritically accepted by all elements in Catholic Ireland. The failure of the CIU to hegemonize southern trade unionism was in itself an indication of one important group that resisted the integralist agenda. When Archbishop D'Alton of Armagh suggested that the trade union movement affiliate to the International Federation of Christian Trade Unions, a body consisting mainly of Catholic trade unions, his advice was heeded by the CIU but rejected almost unanimously by the ITUC.[66] The strong support given to Browne and the small number of TDs who supported him in the 1951 general election showed that, in Dublin at least, there was a certain amount of resistance to the Church's opposition to the health proposals, leading Dr D'Alton to complain that 'we are more deeply infected than we think with the virus of secularism and materialism.'[67] Yet the fact remained that there was little inclination within the political elite to risk a conflict with the hierarchy. As the Fine Gael

Minister for Justice, Seán MacEoin, put it, 'I don't want to get a belt of a crozier.'[68] At a time when electoral outcomes had a new element of unpredictability, neither the leaders of any potential coalition government nor those of Fianna Fáil had an interest in handing their opponents the role of the most demonstrably loyal sons of the Church.

De Valera had imposed a discipline of total silence on his party during the Dáil debate on Browne's resignation, saving for himself the sole dismissive line: 'I think we have heard enough.' When Fianna Fáil returned to power, its new Health Bill was not as ambitious as Noel Browne's. Mothers and infants were to be given free treatment, but infants were covered only up to the age of six weeks rather than sixteen years, and a means test of £600 was a central part of the scheme.[69] Initial clerical opposition was assuaged by de Valera's instruction to Lemass to ask McQuaid to suggest amendments to those sections of the draft legislation that the Church found obnoxious.[70] The implications of the Mother and Child Affair for the anti-partitionist project were severe, as the secretary of the Manchester branch of the Anti-Partition League pointed out in a letter to the *Irish Times*:

Let us look for a moment at the situation through 'Ulster' eyes, and we will see people enjoying the benefits of Britain's progressive National Health scheme, without the indignity of a means test. It does not strengthen their desire to unite with the South if by doing so these things would be taken from them because they conflicted with some 'Christian principle'.[71]

The Contradictions of Anti-partitionism

Fianna Fáil's failure to make progress on ending partition had been high on the agenda of those who formed Clann na Poblachta. Seán MacBride was convinced that the strategic needs of the US and Britain in the struggle with the USSR would make both powers more amenable to Irish demands. At the same time he was also aware of the economic, social and cultural divisions on the island that made the achievement of unity problematic – something that could not be brought about simply by producing a change of policy in London. During the general election campaign, while supporting the idea of opening up the Irish parliament to elected representatives from Northern Ireland, he also admitted that until social and economic standards in the South were at least as good as those in Northern Ireland, it would be impossible to expect even nationalists in the North to be interested in unity.[72] In government he supported the development of closer economic and cultural relations with the North, and, although his more grandiose scheme for a customs union along the lines of the proposed Benelux scheme came to nothing, a number of limited but important forms of cooperation with Stormont were agreed: a buyout of the bankrupt Great Northern Railway, drainage of Lough Erne and a joint fisheries commission for Lough Foyle. However, the potentialities for improving North–South relations inherent in such forms of functional cooperation were undermined by the decisions to declare a republic and to reject an invitation to join NATO.

Costello's coalition displayed a depressing continuity with de Valera's penchant for combining rhetorical anti-partitionism with a realpolitik that prioritized electoral competition in the South. Fine Gael had traditionally been the party that favoured close cooperation with Britain and the Commonwealth; indeed, during the war Mulcahy had made a strongly pro-Commonwealth speech advocating that Éire resume active membership when the hostilities were over.[73] During the election campaign Fine Gael was divided on the question of continuing Commonwealth links, for, while Mulcahy defended the legislative basis for Commonwealth membership, the External Relations Act, other prominent members supported its repeal. The External Relations Act of 1936 was one of two pieces of legislation rushed through the Dáil in response to the abdication of King Edward VIII. The Constitution Amendment Act had abolished the residual functions of the British monarch in the internal affairs of the Irish Free State but the External Relations Act had confirmed a continuing role for the King in external affairs: as long as the Free State remained a part of the Commonwealth, the King, as head of that association, had a role in diplomatic and consular appointments and international agreements. Although a purely symbolic role, it sat uneasily with the fact that under de Valera's constitution of 1937 Ireland had its own head of state. Britain's representative in Dublin, John Maffey (now Lord Rugby), was convinced that de Valera wanted to maintain the Act as a bridge to the North, but feared that the emergence of Clann na Poblachta might force him to propose its repeal in order to cover Fianna Fáil's flank from more extreme nationalist attacks.[74] In fact the repeal of the Act had not featured as a major issue during the campaign, and MacBride publicly accepted that the new government could not claim a mandate for repeal. That Costello would announce a decision to get rid of the Act within six months of the formation of his government said more about inter-party competition in the Free State than it did about his government's possession of a coherent set of policies on Anglo-Irish relations and Northern Ireland.

Costello took the initiative on the issue, and his main motivation seems to have been to pre-empt a Dáil private member's motion to repeal the Act from Peadar Cowan, a fractious former member of Clann na Poblachta who had been expelled from the party in June 1948 for opposing acceptance of Marshall Aid. Costello also feared a Fianna Fáil assault on the coalition's republican and anti-partitionist credentials as de Valera, on losing office, embarked on a tour of America, Australia and Britain to denounce the 'artificial division' of his country. More positively, there was the possibility that by taking the initiative in removing the last symbolic links with the Crown and the Commonwealth, Fine Gael would, once and for all, make it impossible for Fianna Fáil to question its 'national' credentials and break out of the downward spiral of election performances that had led Rugby to refer to the possible 'elimination of Fine Gale [*sic*]'.[75] Yet the relatively narrow range of considerations that led the Taoiseach unexpectedly to announce the end of the Act on a visit to Canada in September 1948 was evident not just from the annoyed surprise of his colleagues, who had not formally approved the decision, but from the government's outrage at what might have been foreseen as the likely British response – the Ireland Act of 1949, which consolidated Northern Ireland's position within the United Kingdom. The implications of the decision to leave the Commonwealth for the government's strongly pronounced policy on ending partition does not appear to have been seriously considered by either Costello or MacBride.

The only original thinking on partition in the government came from the Minister for Finance. Patrick McGilligan saw in the tensions of the Cold War a way in which the new republic could join NATO and also approach the Commonwealth about a mutual defence treaty. This, he argued, would help shift attitudes in the North and make a 'healthy reunion' a possibility. But, as Troy Davis has pointed out, the Finance Minister's radical memorandum, prepared for his Fine Gael cabinet colleagues, was at fundamental variance with Costello and MacBride's policy of making Irish defence cooperation with the Western powers contingent on unification.[76]

McGilligan's blueprint, which fully justified Patrick Lynch's description of his having the 'finest and most original mind',[77] could have done much to bridge the ideological divide on the island through a shared stake in the defence of 'Western civilization'. His colleagues' lack of interest reflected the fear of a break with MacBride and a premature end to a coalition that was restoring Fine Gael's credibility as a party of government. The result was a foreign policy that only served to convince those European and American politicians that paid any notice to MacBride's frequent foreign trips of Ireland's irredeemable parochialism.

MacBride was encouraged in his misreading of American attitudes to the strategic significance of Ireland's participation in the proposed NATO alliance by his friendship with George Garrett, who had been appointed American Minister Plenipotentiary to Ireland in 1947.[78] Unlike his predecessor, David Gray, who had become a fervent supporter of Ulster unionism and was cordially detested by de Valera, Garrett, 'a typical Hibernophile Irish American',[79] pushed for a radical change in US policy on the Ulster question. Arguing that a united Ireland would contribute strategically to Western defence measures, he suggested that Washington should persuade London to extend its 'enlightened policy' in India and other parts of the empire to Northern Ireland. The response of officials in the State Department to Garrett's proposals was critical and dismissive. The State Department's Director of European Affairs, John Hickerson, pointed out that the claim that a majority of Irishmen on both sides of the border wanted unity simply ignored the desires of a majority in Northern Ireland. He also disputed, on the basis of Ireland's wartime neutrality, Garrett's strategic argument:

If the Dublin Government were to gain control of Northern Ireland, facilities in that area might be denied us in the future, just as they have been denied . . . in the past. With the United Kingdom in control of Northern Ireland we have . . . every reason to count on the use of its bases . . . I am sure you will agree that this is a powerful argument for this Government's favouring the continued control of Northern Ireland by the United Kingdom.[80]

Despite this analysis, delivered in May 1948, which continued to be the basis of American policy throughout MacBride's tenure at External Affairs, he maintained what Seán MacEntee termed the 'sore thumb' approach to Ireland's foreign policy. While declaring that Ireland was in solidarity with the West in its struggle to contain communism, MacBride then added that the Irish desire to play a useful role on the international stage was nullified by the 'injustice' of the 'artificial division' of the country. When, in January 1949, the US government asked what the Irish reaction to an invitation to become a member of NATO would be, MacBride's rejection of membership justified itself in terms of the danger of a nationalist uprising against his government for 'selling out' the North. This approach caused severe disquiet not simply in Fine Gael but even in Fianna Fáil, where the appeal of an international crusade against 'atheistic materialism' to some extent counteracted the more solipsistic forms of anti-partitionism. It was on this issue, where the Church's virulent anti-communism made it sympathize with the NATO project, that MacBride failed to display his usual eagerness to please Archbishop McQuaid.

The suspicion remained that, for all the emphasis MacBride and Costello placed on the partition issue, the real focus of their attention was not the 'occupied six counties' but the brooding presence of de Valera. Surely, as some critics at the time pointed out, echoing McGilligan's internal memorandum for Fine Gael, NATO membership with the UK would have increased the pressure on the Stormont administration to at least cooperate more closely with Dublin. Instead, as R. P. Mortished, a former Labour Party politician and now Chairman of the Labour Court, put it, the government's attitude 'on the problem of the defence of Christian Civilisation against Soviet Communism was completely negative and futilely isolationist'.[81] While it is possible that MacBride's passionate nationalism blinded him to these considerations, it seems more likely that his major motivation was the urge to cede no ground that de Valera could have used electorally. It was also the case that he faced an intransigent republican rump in his own party that could not stomach collaboration with Britain even if it was aimed at Stalin.

As part of his determination that Fianna Fáil would not exploit the freedom of opposition to embarrass the government on its northern policy, MacBride had proposed an all-party committee on partition. This became a reality during the heated exchanges between Belfast and Dublin provoked by the repeal of the External Relations Act. Responding to Brooke's calling of a Stormont election to register loyalist unity in the face of this challenge, Costello invited the leaders of all parties in the Dáil to a meeting in Dublin's Mansion House to consider ways of helping anti-partition candidates in the northern elections. The meeting's main result, a collection to be held outside Catholic churches throughout the South on 30 January 1949, was hailed by MacBride as 'the first real sign of unity in the national sense since 1921'.[82] Unionists were predictably delighted with this manifestation of southern Catholic-nationalist intent to 'interfere' and used it to great effect in wiping out the NILP.

The effect of official anti-partitionism in solidifying unionist resistance to change might have been of lesser import if there had been any indication that the campaign was having an impact in London, which was,

after all, supposedly the real source of the division of the island. Instead
Costello and MacBride were faced with the Ireland Act and in response
cranked up the ideological assault on the North. The Mansion House
Committee was kept in existence to produce a stream of anti-partitionist
propaganda under the direction of Frank Gallagher, who had been for
many years de Valera's principal assistant in press and propaganda affairs.
MacBride's motivation for transferring responsibility for anti-partition
propaganda from his ministry to an all-party committee heavily influenced
by a Fianna Fáil traditionalist may have stemmed from his strong suspicion of the allegedly pro-British sympathies of some officials in Iveagh
House. Frederick Boland, who was Secretary of the Department of
External Affairs when MacBride was appointed, later claimed that his
minister's first words to him were a request for a list of all the British
agents working in the department.[83] Boland, a pragmatic nationalist,
found working for MacBride an uncongenial experience and moved to
the position of Irish Ambassador in London in 1950. His subsequent
memoranda and those of Conor Cruise O'Brien, whom MacBride had
promoted to a new post of Information Officer, provide some early
evidence of a growing awareness of the futility of the Irish state's official
policy on the North.

O'Brien, who claims that he was already weary of 'the usual anti-
partition rubbish',[84] had an opportunity to dissect its shortcomings when
he had to respond to a full-frontal assault on the Mansion House
Committee by the ex-Free State cabinet minister Ernest Blythe. A member
of that rare breed of northern Protestants who supported Gaelic and sepa-
ratist ideals and was imprisoned during the 1916 Rising, Blythe had
produced a devastatingly critical analysis of the anti-partition campaign.
O'Brien summarized his arguments in a memorandum for Boland:

1 The British will not coerce the North to join us. The maximum
   which we can achieve by our propaganda would be to get British
   troops to leave Northern Ireland.
2 If the British do leave, the North will fight. Mr Blythe believes that
   because of their industry and probable British aid they would be likely
   to win.
3 Guerrilla activity in the North would be a pretext for pogroms and
   the mass expulsion of the Nationalist population.
4 In these conditions our propaganda campaign abroad, however well
   conducted, cannot lead to effective action and serves only to increase
   contention between ourselves and the Unionists.

5 There is therefore no prospect of bringing in the North except by
   peaceful persuasion. This would be a long-term job of 20 to 50 years.[85]

Blythe's own proposals centred on a pledge from the Irish government
that they would not coerce the North, coupled with support for initiatives to increase cooperation in the social and cultural sphere as a means
of lessening unionist suspicions. He also urged northern nationalists to
end policies of non-recognition and to participate actively in the public
life of the state. O'Brien criticized the 'unreality' of some of these proposals
but accepted that there was a good deal of strength in Blythe's basic
contention: 'that the hard core of the Ulster Unionists will only be made
harder by direct attacks, threats and propaganda campaigns'.

O'Brien added one concern that had not featured in Blythe's critique
by suggesting that unionists should be assured that in a united Ireland
there would be no question of Irish laws on divorce and censorship
being extended to them. This reference to what he called 'their very real
fears of Catholic coercion and domination' would soon be reflected in
a revived emphasis on the religious dimension in unionist arguments
even before the Mother and Child débâcle. It was sparked by the statistics on religious denominations in the *Interim Report of the Irish Census*
of 1946, which showed a sharp decline of 13 per cent in the state's
Protestant population during the previous decade. Speeches by Unionist
politicians increasingly focused on what one referred to as an inexorable
tendency to 'the complete and utter extinction of the Protestant population south of the border'.[86]

There could be no doubting the embarrassment caused to the anti-
partition movement by such figures. The government's response was to
prepare statistics on the position of Protestants in the economic and
public life of the state. Thus Protestants who represented 5.7 per cent of
the total population of the state were 26 per cent of those who owned
farms of over 2,000 acres, 25 per cent of male professionals, 45 per cent
of bank officials and 32 per cent of all industrial employees. Given that
this reflected a pre-partition Protestant pre-eminence in such fields, the
statistics were not particularly reassuring, since they demonstrated little
about how the minority felt about the direction of public policy since
1922. It seemed to echo the loyalist argument in the North that if things
were as bad as nationalists claimed, why had the Catholic population of
the state increased since partition? As a leading government statistician
pointed out, the figures for the decline in the southern Protestant population reflected that non-Catholics had emigrated at a markedly higher

rate than Catholics in the decade. This was due to 'pull' factors: 'this class, relatively well-educated . . . could make a living here but they could do much better for themselves abroad in an environment that suits them.'[87]

While the pull of higher wages and salaries in Britain was one dimension of the problem, it remained that many had gone to serve in the Forces, and an 'environment that suits them' was an oblique reference to the reality of low-intensity unhappiness with what many southern Protestants saw as the anti-British and confessional nature of the Irish state. In 1950 Protestant concerns were reinforced by the Tilson judgment, in which the High Court in Dublin ruled that a Protestant husband who had signed the declaration required by the Catholic Church in mixed marriages that the children would be brought up as Catholics had to cede custody of his children to his estranged wife.[88] The strict censorship of publications, particularly the banning of anything that dealt with artificial methods of contraception, was a long-standing grievance, while compulsory Irish in schools aroused much Protestant resentment.[89] It was also noticeable that in the official response to unionist criticisms, the bulk of statistical material on employment related to the private sector. The claim was made that in government service and the judiciary Protestants were well represented, although the only example given was that they were two of the eleven members of the Supreme and High Courts. There was no response to the unionists who pointed out that in the three border counties of Donegal, Cavan and Monaghan, with a Protestant population of nearly 15 per cent, there were virtually no Protestants on the public payroll.[90]

Unionist concerns were obviously exacerbated by the Mother and Child Affair. More significant for the anti-partition campaign were the reverberations of the affair in Britain. The Unionist Party's publicity department produced 10,000 copies of a pamphlet, 'Southern Ireland: Church or State?', which was largely a reproduction of the correspondence between Browne, Costello and the hierarchy, together with extracts from the Dáil debate on the affair. Copies were sent to every member of the British Houses of Parliament, to US Senators and members of the House of Representatives, and to legislators in Canada, Australia and New Zealand.[91] The pamphlet had been preceded by one on the Tilson case, and the propaganda offensive appears to have had some effects in Britain, where it undermined support for the anti-partitionist cause in the Labour Party. Boland, who was now Irish Ambassador in London, reported on one key Labour figure affected by it when he recorded a visit of Aneurin Bevan, the former Minister of Health in Attlee's government, to the Irish Embassy. Bevan was a member of the 'Friends of Ireland' group of Labour MPs and was accompanied by Hugh Delargy, the group's secretary. Bevan's criticism of the Stormont regime, Boland noted, was based not on the 'moral aspects' of the argument for Irish unity but on his anti-Toryism and 'the rage he feels that partition gives the Tories nine seats in the House to which they are not entitled'. His attitude to Ireland was, the ambassador complained, those of a 'typical Britisher', particularly on the legitimacy of unionists' religious and economic concerns:

He is almost fanatically anti-Catholic. He has the idea that the Church exercises a constant and irresistible pressure on the government of the 26 Counties and he quotes the Dr Browne episode freely as proof of his belief, adding that he was on the point of sending a public message of support to Dr Browne at the height of the crisis when Hugh Delargy dissuaded him from the idea. He is also given to arguing with some vehemence that we ourselves have made the task of ending partition infinitely more difficult by our neutrality in the war and our subsequent repeal of the External Relations Act . . . he constantly harps on the comparison between the social services in the 6 Counties and in the rest of Ireland, asking how we expect, with our standards of welfare benefits, to attract a people already enjoying the best social services in the world.[92]

Boland attached a perhaps inflated role to the publication of a book on the Catholic Church in America by the anti-Catholic writer Paul Blanshard. Blanshard subsequently visited Ireland, and his book *The Irish and Catholic Power* was published in 1954 with a foreword by the Ulster Unionist MP H. Montgomery Hyde. Boland was also concerned by British newspapers' coverage of the intolerant treatment of Protestant Churches in Spain and Latin America. Suspicion of the Catholic Church was, he claimed, 'the only point upon which the Tory outlook of the Church of England and the theoretical socialism of the *New Statesman* and the *Tribune* agree'.[93] If the dormant embers of anti-Catholicism in British national identity were being rekindled, it could only damage the Irish state's ideological assault on the North.

When some of those frustrated by the evident failure of the official anti-partition campaign resorted to traditional physical-force methods, the result was the virtual collapse of the campaign in Britain. Delargy, whose loyalty to the Bevanite left was greater than his commitment to Irish nationalism, became increasingly alienated from his former allies. The nadir of traditional forms of anti-partitionism appeared to have been reached with the launch of the IRA campaign in 1956. A few months later Delargy confessed to Brookeborough that he 'was satisfied that we were right and he had told Eire that he would have nothing to do with them'.[94] But before any shift in policy towards the North could take place, a fundamental reassessment of the economic direction of the Irish state would have to be forced on a reluctant political elite.

The Economics of National Survival

The 1950s have been described by the economic historian Cormac Ó Gráda as 'a miserable decade for the Irish economy'.[95] Real national income stagnated between 1950 and 1958. Agriculture, which still employed 40 per cent of the workforce in 1951,[96] experienced a decline of almost a quarter in the numbers employed during the decade.[97] This reflected a sharp drop in the small-farm sector, which was drained by the opening up of employment opportunities in Britain and was not associated with any improvement in productivity. Net agricultural output rose by only 7 per cent in the periods 1950–52 and 1958–60, reflecting the continuing dominance of Irish agriculture by the demands of the British market.[98] Britain was still taking almost 90 per cent of Irish agricultural exports at the end of the 1950s,[99] but the advantages that Irish ministers believed the 1948 Trade Agreement would bring had not been realized. The dependence on Britain tied the Irish economy into what, at a time of unprecedented economic growth in the international economy, was the tortoise of Western Europe. The position was worsened by the British system of farm deficiency payments, which depressed prices on the British market.

The record of Irish industry was equally depressing. Industrial output expanded at what Liam Kennedy refers to as a 'miserable' 1.3 per cent per annum.[100] A large part of the blame for this can be attributed to an outdated protectionist regime. Brian Girvin has attempted a limited defence of the strategy, pointing out that the number of those employed in manufacturing industry expanded from 119,000 in 1950 to 134,000 in 1960.[101] For all that unionists would boast of the economic superiority of Northern Ireland, growth in the manufacturing sector in the North during the 1950s was inferior to that of the South. But, as Tom Garvin has noted, 'Ireland was the fastest of the slowcoaches, but also, fatally started at the lowest level of economic activity . . . to put it bluntly and sadly, Ireland started the period poor and ended it slightly less poor.'[102]

The problem of unemployment was concentrated on agriculture and the construction industry, which were hit by highly deflationary budgets in 1952 and 1956 and by the conservative policies followed by successive Ministers for Finance throughout the decade. The 15,000 job increase in manufacturing did little to compensate for the haemorrhage from agriculture, which employed 504,000 in 1951 and 376,000 in 1961, or for the loss of 25,000 construction jobs in the same period.[103] Therefore, although the protected industrial sector did more than hold its own, it remains the case, as Girvin admits, that the Irish state lacked a 'domestic engine of growth' that would have allowed it to take advantage of the general buoyancy of the international economy. Stormont was able to ease the pain associated with the decline of traditional industries by policies geared to the attraction of foreign capital and by substantial increases in public expenditure, courtesy of assistance from the British Treasury. However, south of the border the issue of foreign capital raised the ideological hackles of many in Fianna Fáil, while the strong influence of pre-Keynesian thinking in the Department of Finance acted as a major deflationary influence for most of the decade.

Lemass's willingness to press for radical revisions of policy on protectionism and the possible use of foreign capital in the late 1940s vanished for most of the next decade as he concentrated on the immediate political task of attacking those who had replaced Fianna Fáil in government. When his successor as Minister for Industry and Commerce, the Fine Gael politician Daniel Morrissey, established the Industrial Development Authority (IDA) in 1948, it seemed a posthumous victory for the Lemass approach to industrial policy. The IDA was given authority to encourage new industry and to expand and modernize that already existing. It was also empowered to examine the effects of protection and applications for tariffs. However, Lemass was bitterly critical of the IDA and promised to abolish it when he returned to power. Although there were potential structural problems involved in the relationship between the IDA and the Department of Industry and Commerce, which had lost most industrial policy functions to the new body, his opposition to it stemmed primarily from a desire to mend his fences with Fianna Fáil's allies in the industrial bourgeoisie following their hostile reaction to his earlier Industrial Efficiency Bill.[104] It also reflected the broader Fianna Fáil concern to undermine the nationalist credentials of the inter-party government in the economic field as on the partition question.

Not only did Lemass have to forget his earlier critical approach to Irish industry, but his strong expansionist and Keynesian instincts were subordinated to Seán MacEntee's electioneering attacks on the profligacy of the inter-party government. Back in government as Minister for Finance in 1951, MacEntee was confronted by a major balance of payments crisis caused by the rapid increase in imported consumer goods after years of austerity, the deterioration in the terms of trade caused by the devaluation of sterling in 1949 and the general post-Korean War economic crisis. MacEntee, who later used the term 'monetarist' to describe his approach, responded with the harshest budget in the history of the state. He announced another shilling in the pound on income tax; increases in the price of petrol, tobacco, spirits and beer; and impending increases in the price of the working-class staples of butter, bread, tea and sugar.

The reaction was sharp. A Labour Party rally in Dublin, to protest against the severity of the budget, was followed by disturbances in which a number of people were injured. Unemployment, which had stood at 36,000 when the inter-party government left office in July 1951, had risen to 57,000 two years later.[105] In the spring of that year a Dublin Unemployed Association was created and it embarrassed the government with sit-down protests in the city centre. Lemass, who had explained the increase in the Fianna Fáil vote in the 1951 election by the party's winning over of a larger slice of the working class,[106] was dismayed by such developments. The fervid anti-communism of the period undermined opposition to the government: the collapse of the Unemployed Association was in part brought about by a sustained campaign in the press emphasizing the alleged role of communists within it.[107] But anti-communism was not a sufficient basis to compensate for MacEntee's slap in the face to Fianna Fáil's working-class supporters. Even de Valera's usual tendency to acquiesce in the conservative prescriptions of the Department of Finance went temporarily into abeyance, and he asked his cabinet for proposals to stimulate employment.[108] This provided Lemass with the backing he needed to counter-attack and get support for some increase in state investment to stimulate the economy. A National Development Fund was created to finance road improvements and other infrastructural works; and an Undeveloped Areas Act, aimed at decentralizing industrial development away from the eastern seaboard towards the west in general and the Gaeltacht areas in particular, was passed in 1952.[109]

But the amount of resources involved was small and the attempt to get industries to establish in the west futile, given the major obstacles that the Control of Manufacturers legislation placed in the way of foreign investment anywhere in Ireland. Lemass's radicalism had not deserted him, but he still faced formidable resistance from fiscal conservatives in government and from a large sector of Irish industry that was opposed to any reconsideration of protectionism and to any hint that the state would adopt a more positive view of foreign capital. Yet the weakness of the Irish economy was starkly evident. A report by American experts, commissioned by the government in 1952 to investigate the export potential of existing industries, had confirmed that Irish industry was largely lethargic, inefficient and unready for competition in the world market. Lemass showed a willingness to discourage the more outrageous forms of protectionist feather-bedding in a Restrictive Practices Act of 1953 designed to eliminate price-fixing, and in January 1954 announced that he had asked the IDA to review the whole policy of protection. He also returned to a potentially explosive issue: the possibility of a break with the central tenet of Sinn Féin economic philosophy, namely Irish ownership of Irish resources.

On 1 May 1953 Lemass declared, 'We welcome foreign capital coming into Irish industrial development when it brings with it new opportunities for expansion and new industrial techniques.'[110] He attempted to counter the inevitable misgivings of party activists by emphasizing that foreign capital did not mean *British* capital. However, the fact remained that for republican ideologues foreign capital was a far more explosive issue than protectionism. Protectionism was only a means to an end: the building up of a native Irish industry. In theory at least it would be possible to abandon protectionism and maintain Irish control of Irish industry. The introduction of foreign capital on a large scale ended the dream once and for all. It was one thing to grumble about the inefficiency and low profit margins of protected industry; it was quite another to reject a fundamental thesis of Irish republicanism. At this time Lemass's embrace of foreign capital was only a very partial and, as it turned out, temporary one. It would take another election defeat and a subsequent economic and demographic crisis to force through an acceptance of foreign capital along with state investment as the twin growth engines that would lift the economy out of its mid-1950s slough.

Lemass's former good relations with the trade union movement had been damaged by MacEntee's deflationary policies, and as moves got under way in October 1953 to overcome the eight-year split in the trade union movement the importance of reconstructing his 'special relationship' with union leaders was underlined. Yet, rather than confront the forces of conservatism within his government, de Valera decided to mobilize the traditional rural and small-town support, particularly in the west and south-west. After by-election defeats in Cork city and Louth in March 1954 he dissolved the Dáil, and the campaign that followed was notable for the degree to which economic issues dominated the agenda. Costello succeeded in putting Fianna Fáil on the defensive by committing a Fine Gael-led government to a mildly inflationary programme of tax cuts, increased food subsidies and higher social benefits. Lemass's own expansionary instincts were submerged by MacEntee's traditionalist broadside against Fine Gael's 'irresponsibility', and he was reduced to lame attacks on Fine Gael's alleged lack of commitment to protecting Irish industry. The result was de Valera's second electoral defeat. Fianna Fáil dropped from seventy-two to sixty-five seats, while Fine Gael continued its post-1948 rise, from forty-five to fifty seats. A beneficiary of MacEntee's economic dominance was the reunited Irish Labour Party, which moved from sixteen to nineteen seats. The lesson was clear: on the two occasions, 1948 and 1954, when Fianna Fáil approached the electorate with an essentially orthodox economic record, it had been rejected. The failure of strategy in electoral terms would give Lemass a golden opportunity to identify Fianna Fáil with economic expansionism.

The second inter-party government was made up of Fine Gael, Labour and Clann na Talmhan, with Clann na Poblachta's three TDs supporting but not participating in government. Its first budget in May 1955 increased old-age pensions and other welfare benefits. However, the mildly ameliorative effects of the budget were soon obliterated by increasing evidence that the economy was moving rapidly out of control. A balance of payments deficit of £5.5 million in 1954 had rocketed to £35.6 million by the end of 1955. This was in part fuelled by a consumer boom arising from a successful union campaign for a national wage increase but also by a drop in cattle and processed-food exports to the UK, where demand had been hit by a credit squeeze and a deflationary budget.[111]

Gerard Sweetman, McGilligan's replacement as Minister for Finance, reacted with a series of vigorous measures. In March 1956 he imposed special import levies on sixty-eight classes of commodities and introduced new taxes on a wide range of consumer goods. The screw was tightened further in July with a widening of the range of import levies and further increases in indirect taxation. Costello, aware of the stress that these measures were putting on Labour's participation in government, tried to lighten the gloom by important new departures in the area of foreign investment. In October 1956 he announced a plan for national development that had at its core a special incentive to encourage exports by a

50 per cent remission of tax on profits derived from increased exports. Already his government had incurred traditionalist criticism by accepting the proposal of an Anglo-American oil combine to build an oil refinery in Cork Harbour. And when the Labour leader and Minister for Industry and Commerce, William Norton, toured Europe and the US to seek foreign capital, Lemass rediscovered the virtues of Sinn Féin economics and de Valera denounced the government for not 'keeping Ireland for the Irish'.[112]

Given Lemass's own shifting views on protectionism and foreign capital, such criticisms were not in themselves particularly damaging. What destroyed the coalition was the increasing sense of national crisis generated by the publication of the preliminary report of the census of 1956. This disclosed that the population, at 2,894,822, was the lowest ever recorded for the state, having declined by 65,771 since 1951. Although the natural increase between 1951 and 1956 was greater than during any period since 1881, the net emigration, at 200,394, was also higher. The year of the fortieth anniversary of the foundational event of the Irish state, the Easter Rising, was one in which the *Irish Times* could editorialize, in response to the census figures, 'If the trend disclosed . . . continues unchecked, Ireland will die – not in the remote unpredictable future, but quite soon.'

Fine Gael and the government as a whole were severely divided over how to respond to the crisis. Costello and Norton had not favoured Sweetman's strategy, and Norton was placed under particular pressure by the growing discontent in his party and in the trade union movement. But it was the withdrawal of support by Seán MacBride and the other two Clann na Poblachta representatives that brought the government down in January 1957. The motion of no confidence, although it was motivated in part by anger at the arrest of IRA men by the Irish police, focused on the government's failure to devise an effective long-term economic policy. There was some basis for the Fianna Fáil jibe that a multi-party government could not provide the coherence of principle and strategy necessary to respond to such a profound economic challenge. It was also the case that out of power it would have mercilessly harried the government if it had taken radical measures. Only Fianna Fáil, with its skill in portraying itself as the true inheritor of 1916, was in a position to revise fundamentally the economic nostrums of the national revolution.

It was the aggressively Keynesian themes of Lemass that dominated the Fianna Fáil election campaign. Its main press appeal was headed 'This is the issue: how to put our men and machines to work.'[113] The resultant triumph for the party – a gain of thirteen seats from sixty-five to seventy-eight and its highest ever share of the poll at 53 per cent[114] – meant that Lemass's position as Tánaiste and heir apparent to de Valera had been made impregnable. He was able to insist that MacEntee be moved from Finance to Health and be replaced by one of his closest political allies, Jim Ryan.[115] However, the main immediate beneficiaries of the expansionary ethos that Lemass had given to the election campaign were the party old guard. The result was a sharp contrast to the North, where a *Times* special correspondent noted that while Brookeborough's cabinet was filled with 'vigorous and youngish men', de Valera's government was 'remarkable' for the continuing representation of the revolutionary generation:

Four of his twelve colleagues served, as he did, in the Easter Rising. This is almost exactly in time and approximately in spirit, as though about half Mr Macmillan's government wore the Mons Star. Three others of the thirteen took part in the 'War of Independence'. The hold on the republic of this ageing group of men is far stronger than that of the coalition which preceded it.[116]

De Valera, seventy-four and almost blind when he became Taoiseach for the last time, would not hand over to Lemass for another two years, much to his deputy's increasing frustration. But, although the changes in economic policy came more slowly than Lemass wanted, there was no doubting that new directions were being plotted.

One indication was the important role played by the dynamic and intellectually formidable Secretary of the Department of Finance, T. K. Whitaker. Whitaker had been recommended for the top position in Finance in 1956 by the economically traditionalist Gerard Sweetman, who may have been impressed by Whitaker's analysis of the unsatisfactory performance of the Irish economy, which he explained by a low level of investment caused by a too rapid expansion of personal and state expenditure in the post-war period. He was particularly critical of high levels of state expenditure in areas of 'social' investment such as housing. He was also dismissive of the application of Keynesian ideas to Ireland.[117] There was an implicit target in this section of the analysis: the 'Clery's Ballroom speech', a strongly Keynesian manifesto delivered by Lemass to the Fianna Fáil organization in Dublin on 1 October 1955. This manifesto was an adaptation of the 1954 Vanoni Plan for post-war reconstruction in Italy.[118] In it Lemass attacked the view, still dear to the hearts of Finance officials, 'that the sole object of government policy should be to keep public expenditure at the lowest possible level'.[119] Its centrepiece was a proposal to create 100,000 jobs in five years through a major programme of public expenditure.

For the first two years of the new government Jim Ryan's budgets reflected the traditional Finance view. There were cuts in the public capital programme with severe deflationary effects. Whitaker was aware that Lemass's imminent shift to the Taoiseach's position would demand more from his department than the assertion of traditional arguments. The previous government's decision to set up a Capital Investment Advisory Committee without reference to Finance had come as a shock, and there was a fear that Lemass's growing ascendancy would result in either Industry and Commerce or the Department of the Taoiseach seizing the initiative in economic policy.[120] Therefore, when Whitaker asked Ryan for authorization to work out an integrated programme of national development for the next five or ten years, he was aiming as much at maintaining Finance's hegemony in the policy process as at addressing what he admitted was a mood of national despondency.

What has subsequently been recognized as the Lemass–Whitaker partnership in forging a new course out of the 1950s stagnation needs to be seen as a much more ambivalent and tension-filled relationship. Whitaker's report, subsequently published as *Economic Development*, was delivered to the government in May 1958. As Brian Girvin has noted, the report's influence on subsequent economic success may have been exaggerated.[121] There was much in it that reflected the traditional policy style and approach of the Department of Finance and some at least would have made painful reading for Lemass, particularly the jibe at 'setting up fanciful employment targets'. There was an emphasis on the primacy of export-oriented agriculture, something that Lemass rejected as an approach because it failed to comprehend that industry was the only possible engine of future growth. A major aim of the report was to restrict demand, and here it resulted in a continuation of the deflationary impact of budgetary policy. Only in advocating an easing of the restrictions on foreign investment in Ireland, a move towards freer trade and, at least formally, the need for a development perspective to be at the centre of state policy was it compatible with Lemass's views.

There were some distinct differences between *Economic Development* and the White Paper *Programme for Economic Expansion*, published in November 1958. The *Programme* set out a growth target of 2 per cent a year in the 1959–63 period and specified a five-year investment programme. There was also more emphasis on industry, and some of Whitaker's suggested cuts in areas such as farm price subsidies and the rural electrification programme were not implemented.[122] Whatever positive psychological impact the very notion of a plan for economic expansion may have had on actual economic performance was insufficient to counteract the rather minimalist nature of the proposed government expenditure. Despite the government's projection of it as a £220 million Five Year Plan, there was only £53 million in actual new expenditure, the rest being composed of pre-Whitaker commitments.

The crucial event for the inauguration of the expansion of the 1960s was not the publication of either document but Lemass's election as Taoiseach by the Dáil on 23 June 1959 after the ailing de Valera had been persuaded to retire. It soon became clear that Lemass would dominate economic policy formation and give the *Programme* a much more expansionary slant than Whitaker was happy with. No longer would the balance of payments be fetishized: the Organization of European Economic Cooperation was informed that the next balance of payments crisis would be met through the depletion of reserves rather than by deflationary measures. At the same time the proposals for government expenditure in the *Programme* were substantially exceeded after 1959, to the chagrin of such champions of financial orthodoxy as the Central Bank.

The relationship between the adoption of economic programming and the economic success of the 1960s is still a matter of debate for scholars, but the dominant tendency is one of scepticism.[123] Certainly the public expenditure and budgetary components of *Economic Development* and the *Programme* would not in themselves have caused the jump from an average annual growth rate of 1 per cent between 1950 and 1958 to a 4 per cent annual average between 1959 and 1973.[124] It was the broader political dimension of the 'watershed' documents that was crucial. As Tom Garvin has put it, 'It took the economic and social crisis of the mid 1950s to force through a fundamental rethinking of Irish economic policies.'[125] The notion of a critical moment in the life of the nation demanding radical new measures made it easier for Lemass to justify the reversal of policy involved in the Industrial Development Act of 1958, which made the first serious breach in the Control of Manufactures Acts. This, together with the existing provision for tax relief on profits from exports, laid the basis for the transformation in Ireland's external trade that would occur in the next decade as manufactured goods replaced cattle and other agricultural products as the largest

category in Irish exports. But Lemass was aware that further liberalization of the Irish economy would be demanded in the context of the
broader European tendency towards free trade. In particular, protectionism
would have to be phased out. This, he realized, could be politically
difficult, given the strong threat to the jobs of many workers, often Fianna
Fáil supporters, in the protected industries. To make change more acceptable, the strongly Keynesian perspectives he had first set out in 1945
needed to be maintained. As a result, public policy and the political
climate in Ireland were to move further to the left than at any time
since the formation of the state.

5. Modernization and Resistance: Northern Ireland 1945–1963

Ulster Unionism and British Socialism

Despite the British Labour Party's traditional sympathy with Irish nationalism, the strategic importance of Northern Ireland during the war had impressed itself upon leading members of the Attlee government. Although Baron Chuter-Ede, the Home Secretary, surprised and annoyed some of his officials by referring to Brooke's administration as 'remnants of the old ascendancy class . . . very frightened of the catholics and of the world trend to the left',[1] he soon became a strong defender of Stormont against the interventionist demands of the substantial backbench 'Friends of Ireland' group. The key pro-Stormont minister in London was Herbert Morrison. Like many in the Labour Party, Morrison had been unsympathetic to unionism, but the war transformed his attitude. As Home Secretary he had regularly visited Belfast and in a speech in 1943 praised the loyalty of the North, contrasting this with Irish neutrality and declaring that it was bound to have a permanent effect on the attitude of the British people to the two Irish states.[2] Although he had no direct involvement in Irish policy after the war, as Lord President and Leader of the House of Commons his views were influential on other senior members of the government, particularly Attlee and Lord Addison, the Dominions Secretary. In 1946, after a private visit to Ireland during which he had met de Valera and Lemass, Morrison wrote a memorandum for the cabinet in which he advocated total support for partition whatever the consequences for Britain's relationship with Éire. On the same trip he had also gone North, where he was privately dismissive of de Valera's regime: 'Éire was in a bad way . . . the Government had no real human sympathy for the people.' He impressed on his unionist hosts the need to cultivate Chuter-Ede and emphasized that the Attlee government did not intend to continue with nationalization beyond electricity, gas and transport, praising Brooke's government for 'behaving like moderate socialists'.[3] However, the pragmatic approach adopted by Brooke in his dealings with Labour had been assailed from the start by those who, like one senior Stormont official, denounced the direction of Brooke's government between 1945 and 1950 as 'the path of the fellow-travellers to the Socialist State'.[4]

For some in the government and party, the division of powers set out in the Government of Ireland Act, which had assumed a laissez-faire world, had been superseded by the pro-Keynesian policy consensus at Westminster. This meant, according to Sir Roland Nugent, the Minister of Commerce, that Britain, even when the Conservatives returned to power, would accept a large amount of government planning and direction. While this was perhaps appropriate for a largely urban and industrial society, such policies were alien to Northern Ireland, where the importance of small-scale agriculture and medium-sized family firms produced a strongly individualist culture. The only way to avoid a major constitutional crisis that would play into the hands of anti-partitionists was to negotiate a much larger degree of independence in the form of the dominion status enjoyed by Australia and Canada.[5]

Nugent's vision of a largely independent Ulster liberating local agriculture and industry from 'socialistic bureaucracy' and with lower rates of direct taxation had at least one major problem. As the only working-class member of the cabinet, William Grant, the Minister of Health and Local Government, pointed out: 'Any suggestion that our party had deserted its Unionist principles for Conservatism, or as our enemies would say, reactionary Toryism, would almost certainly result in the loss of a substantial portion of our Unionist–Labour support.'[6] That support for dominion status had by 1947 become significant within the party reflected the dominance within it of the urban and rural middle class. This group was prone to complain that the North, rather than being a net beneficiary of the post-war welfare settlement, was being over-taxed to support a range of benefits that would only serve to undermine the 'sturdy individualism' of the province's workers. The war years had seen a large increase in the taxation generated in Northern Ireland, a combination of increased income produced by economic expansion and increases in tax rates. In 1939–40 income tax raised in Northern Ireland amounted to £4,485 million, and by 1944–5 it had risen to £18,711 million, while customs and excise revenue had quadrupled. As a result of these buoyant revenues the Imperial Contribution, Northern Ireland's share of the cost of the UK's defence and foreign policy, had soared from £1.3 million in 1939 to £36 million in 1945.[7] At the core of the support for dominion status was the longing of the province's bourgeoisie and farming class for a reactionary utopia, an effectively independent state with low taxes and minimal social services.

Brooke's increasingly hard and dismissive tone towards dominion status reflected economic, political and constitutional considerations. He was influenced by the major financial benefits that flowed to the Northern Ireland Exchequer through a series of agreements negotiated with the Treasury from 1946. These ensured that the key principles of 'parity' and 'step by step' were maintained at a time when the range of services and benefits was being extended radically. The agreements covered National Insurance (including unemployment, sickness, maternity and retirement benefits) and social services (which dealt with non-contributory entitlements including national assistance, family allowances, old age pensions and health). Essentially they allowed for the transfer of resources to Northern Ireland when it could not pay for the cost of these services out of its own tax revenues. There was also provision for the Ministry of Finance to divert revenue from the Imperial Contribution to a new capital-purposes fund to support industrial development and other projects. It was made clear to Brooke and his ministers that the price of these favourable financial arrangements was closer Treasury control of the North's budgetary process.

The economics of the dominion status case simply disregarded the fact that Northern Ireland could not maintain her post-war standards of social services on her own income, even ignoring the questions of the cost of defence and law and order. Farmers might whinge about having to pay National Insurance contributions for their labourers, yet if the province became a dominion they would also lose the benefits of price guarantees for their produce, which represented a payment from the British Exchequer of £13 million in 1948. Brooke pointed this out to a Tyrone landowner who had written to him demanding that the premier 'cease to follow England along her socialist road to ruin'.[8]

Brooke had to take the possibility of defections of Protestant workers seriously. Even some of the leading proponents of dominion status in the cabinet accepted that it was not an option if it involved any deterioration in working-class living standards, a fairly damning concession to political realism. Brooke spelled out the danger to a party rally in Larne:

The government is strongly supported by the votes of the working class, who cherish their heritage in the Union and to whom any tendency towards separation from Britain is anathema . . . The backbone of Unionism is the Unionist Labour Party. Are those men going to be satisfied if we reject the social services and other benefits we have by going step by step with Britain?[9]

Brooke was convinced that any move to change radically the framework of the Government of Ireland Act would reopen the Irish question at

Westminster, and 'once that Act is open for fundamental amendment, Westminster would, some would say gladly, seek to merge Northern Ireland with Éire rather than grant greater independence to Northern Ireland.'[10] This exaggerated the amount of anti-partitionist sentiment in the higher reaches of the British state. More typical would have been the reflections of a senior Home Office official on the danger that 'if Éire workers continue to flood North there will in some future election be a Nationalist majority and a Government that wants to break with the United Kingdom and join with Éire.' The experience of the war, which showed the vital importance of British control of the coast and ports of Northern Ireland, meant that such a prospect 'may raise grave strategic problems'.[11] This sort of thinking determined the civil service advice to the Attlee cabinet after the Free State's withdrawal from the Commonwealth in 1948 that 'it will never be to Great Britain's advantage that Northern Ireland should form a territory outside His Majesty's jurisdiction. Indeed it would seem unlikely that Great Britain would ever be able to agree to this even if the people of Northern Ireland desired it.'[12] The government did not go as far as this, but in the Ireland Act of 1949 there was a significant strengthening of the Unionist position by the assurance that Northern Ireland would not cease to be part of the UK without the consent of the provincial parliament.

By 1948 the Prime Minister had won the economic and political arguments not only within the cabinet but also within the parliamentary party, where the leading proponent of dominion status, the MP for South Tyrone, W. F. McCoy, had the support of just two other MPs. There remained much unease at the general direction of government policy in the party at constituency level, particularly in rural areas and in the border counties. Here the conservatism of farmers was allied with a broader fear of the disruptive effects of welfarism on the local class and sectarian balance of power. One prominent Unionist in Londonderry supported dominion status as a means by which the government could ensure that the only immigrants from the South were members of its Protestant minority. In this way the extra labour needed if the city was to expand would not undermine Protestant control of its government.[13] The welfare state and the associated drive by Stormont to build up alternative sources of employment created much turbulence within unionism, and it implicitly raised major questions about the future direction of the state. McCoy's supporters were aghast not simply at the possibility of a deluge from the South but also at evidence that some working-class unionists were becoming less deferential. As one female party activist complained to the MP, 'things had

come to a pretty pass' when McCoy's services were declined at the opening
of an Orange fête in Dungannon because of his support for policies that
were perceived to threaten a recently opened factory. The local Orangemen
were apparently all pro-Labour.[14] For many rural and border unionists,
Brooke's support for the welfare state and new industrial development
policies was a slap in the face for 'loyal farmers' who, as one wife of a
Tyrone landowner put it, 'are more valuable voters than the factory workers,
whose politics may be inclined to be Red or Green!'[15]

Although Brooke gave no strategic ground to the government's critics,
he did make a number of tactical concessions. British schemes were
modified for local conditions. The legislation to create a new public
housing body, the Northern Ireland Housing Trust, bitterly attacked at
the Ulster Unionist Council in 1946, departed from the British pattern
by providing subsidies for private builders.[16] A Statistics of Trade Bill,
similar to one introduced in the rest of the UK to provide government
with a range of information from the private sector, including value and
ownership of fixed capital, created waves of apoplexy in chambers of
commerce and Unionist associations and was watered down.[17] Fears of
'Eirean infiltration' were assuaged by persuading the British government
to accept the replacement of the wartime system of residence permits
with a new Safeguarding of Employment Act in 1947. This demanded
that anyone who was not born in Northern Ireland or could not fulfil
stringent residency requirements had to obtain a work permit from the
Ministry of Labour. There was also a residency requirement of five years
for eligibility for welfare benefits, something not required in the rest of
the UK. The central concerns of the unionists in border areas had been
addressed in Stormont's rejection of the British Local Government
Franchise Act, which extended the franchise to all citizens over twenty-
one. Disenfranchisement of many working-class Protestants was considered
a small price to be paid if ruling 'loyal' minorities were to be defended
against the nationalist majorities. The pressures from sections of unionism
most prone to see the post-war world as full of threat damaged Brooke's
limited attempts to improve relations with the minority community.

Brookeborough's Regime and Catholics

The conventional wisdom about Sir Basil Brooke's two decades in power
is that a major opportunity for change was missed. Sabine Wichert
expresses it well: 'For the first time Unionism was in a position to use

the chances of post-war changes to improve life in the province substantially and thereby, however indirectly, make a positive case for Stormont rule.'[18] Instead, under the leadership of a rigid and sectarian Prime Minister, it was a period of social and economic change but political stagnation. More recently released archival material shows a more complex picture. It is reflected in a subtle analysis of a major conflict within Unionism in the early 1950s made by an Irish government official:

There is a definite cleavage of opinion between those like Lord Brookeborough and Mr Brian Maginess who believe that the best way of preserving partition . . . is to pursue 'moderate' policies designed to pacify the minority and impress opinion abroad, and those Unionists like Mr Minford, Mr Norman Porter and Mr Harry Midgley who consider that the only sure course lies in an uncompromising adherence to Orange and Protestant principles.[19]

The analysis had been prompted by the poor performance of the Unionist Party in the 1953 Stormont election: it had lost two seats and been attacked by the Independent Unionists, who had accused the Prime Minister of appeasing Catholics and nationalists. This backlash was a response to an attempt by the Prime Minister, supported by the more liberal elements in his cabinet, to tone down the more stridently sectarian aspects that the Stormont regime had acquired in the 1930s and make a direct appeal to the minority to accept partition for the economic and social benefits it delivered.

The motivation behind this shift was a dual one. The Prime Minister believed that changed national and international circumstances demanded a more emollient public face from Ulster Unionism. As Brookeborough's nationalist critics were aware, not only would future British governments have more leverage with Stormont because of the increased financial dependence attendant on integration into the welfare state, but the new US-dominated 'Free World' was ideologically committed to principles of democracy and freedom from discrimination that could easily be integrated into the traditional anti-partitionist repertoire. After 1945 Brooke's diaries reflect his concern to educate an often recalcitrant party in the new realities: 'I told them that the Convention on Human Rights compelled us to be fair and I insisted that I was not going to be responsible for discrimination.'[20] Much had changed from the days when he had boasted of not having a Catholic about the place.

There was more to this than concern with the province's image in the rest of the UK. Like his few liberal colleagues, he appears to have accepted that a combination of circumstances made a more inclusive form of unionism a possibility. The modernizers believed that the benefits of the welfare state had encouraged a pragmatic acceptance within the Catholic community that partition, now a quarter of a century old, was the inescapable framework within which they must work out their future. Such pragmatism was increasingly encouraged by the travails of the southern economy. Brian Maginess, the Minister of Home Affairs and the most optimistic interpreter of post-war trends, told the Prime Minister that 'the number of Roman Catholics who are gradually coming to have faith in us, our permanent constitutional position and our fair administration, would appear to be increasing considerably.'[21] Brooke publicly echoed the analysis, proclaiming during the 1951 general election campaign that 'even in Nationalist areas electors are beginning to realise that life in British Ulster is to be preferred to existence in a Gaelic republic.'[22]

The sharp disparity between social conditions North and South created by Northern Ireland's integration into the British welfare state was undeniable, and while Unionists made much of it in their propaganda war with Dublin, there was a genuine, if myopic, hope that such material advantages would lessen Catholic alienation from the state. At the first post-war Orange Order celebrations Brooke referred to the new system of family allowances as one indication of the government's 'progressive policy', which he claimed was aimed at benefiting 'all sections of the community'.[23] From family allowances, where five shillings a week was provided for each child after the first, in comparison to two shillings and sixpence for each child after the first two in the South, to unemployment benefit, where a single man got twenty-four shillings in the North and fifteen shillings in the South and a married couple forty shillings in the North and twenty-two shillings in the South, and with equally significant differences in sickness benefits and pensions, the welfare advantages of northern citizenship were clear.[24] Within three years of the end of the war the North was also enjoying a comprehensive health service, free at the point of delivery, which, as F.S.L. Lyons pointed out, was so much better than what existed in the South that little comparison was possible.[25] The Education Act of 1947 began the process of developing mass secondary education in the province, which resulted in the number of secondary school students increasing from less than 20,000 in 1945 to 104,000 by the time Brookeborough resigned.[26] It increased the capital grants for voluntary (i.e., Catholic) schools from 50 per cent to 65 per cent. It was complemented by the provision of grants for university students, which contributed to a more than doubling of the number of students at Queen's University in the twenty years after 1945.[27]

Housing was another area where there was substantial progress. According to a government survey carried out in 1943, 100,000 of the province's houses, almost a third, had to be replaced rapidly and, in order to deal fully with substandard and overcrowded dwellings, another 100,000 new houses would be needed.[28] The Housing Act of 1945 provided for the first time for a large expansion of subsidized local authority housing, breaking with the pre-war policies that had relied on private enterprise for the bulk of new housing. Aware of the obstacles that a combination of sectarianism and a concern for minimizing rate bills might have on a housing drive based solely on local authorities, the government had created the Northern Ireland Housing Trust with powers to clear slums and build and let houses throughout Northern Ireland. There was a substantial increase in the provision of housing after 1945: by 1961, 95,326 new houses had been built, compared with 50,000 in the whole inter-war period.[29] More than half, 56,000, were provided by either local authorities or the Housing Trust. From the outset, to the chagrin of many Unionist councillors, Housing Trust allocations were based on a points system and the system was free of allegations of discriminatory intent. Even in the much more contentious area of local authority housing, the record of a small number of Unionist-controlled authorities west of the River Bann has, because of their role in sparking the civil rights movement in the 1960s, been allowed to convey an overly black picture of the housing situation in the post-war period. Councils such as those of Dungannon, Omagh and Armagh, which built few houses for Catholics, were not typical. Recent academic studies of the question have tended to emphasize that there were no complaints against the majority of local authorities, and the veteran Nationalist MP, Cahir Healy, actually praised local authorities in Belfast, Antrim and Down for their fairness in allocating houses.[30] On the eve of the dissolution of the Stormont parliament, Catholics, who comprised 26 per cent of households in Northern Ireland, occupied 31 per cent of local authority households.[31] However, any improvements in the provision of public housing, and in access to such housing by Catholics, have to be set against the widespread charges of discrimination that dominated local government politics. These flowed from two features of Northern Ireland's system of local government. The first was that in twelve of the seventy-three local authorities, including the city of Derry and the county councils of Fermanagh and Tyrone, the Unionist Party controlled the councils, despite Catholics being a majority of the population. This was brought about by electoral gerrymandering, which had been a grievance since the local government boundaries were redrawn in the early 1920s. The second related to the local government franchise. This emerged as a major political issue after the 1945 Labour government abolished the house-holder franchise in the rest of the UK, while the Unionists retained it in Northern Ireland. The business vote, which allowed owners of busi-ness premises more than one vote in local elections, was also retained in Northern Ireland. Although this was fundamentally a piece of class discrimination – the largest group disenfranchised were working-class Protestants – it had clear sectarian implications, given that Catholics were generally less prosperous than Protestants. The franchise issue would eventually destroy all attempts to modernize and ameliorate the regime.

Even in the most contentious area of policing and public order there were signs of an attempt to soften the harder edges of the regime. Brian Maginess began to withdraw many of the regulations made under the Special Powers Act and in 1950 came to cabinet with a proposal to repeal the Act in its entirety.[32] Both he and Brooke supported the policy of the Inspector-General of the RUC that, unless there was a substantial threat to public order, nationalist parades should not be interfered with. Worse from the point of view of more traditionalist unionists, Maginess supported the police when they put limits on Orange parades, most dramatically in his ban of an Orange march along the predominantly nationalist Longstone Road in County Down in 1952.[33]

The universalistic implications of British welfarism and the more liberal and inclusive type of unionism associated with it brought an inevitable reaction. For many unionists, particularly in the border areas, they flew in the face of the post-war resurgence of anti-partitionist politics within the North, supported as it was by a much more aggressive international campaign by the inter-party government in the South after 1948. Despite the province's less than sterling contribution on the volunteering and industrial fronts during the war, nationalist resistance to conscription and the South's neutrality fed a strong current of resentful indignation that the minority should receive any benefits from the post-war settlement. The sentiments expressed by the Unionist MP Dehra Parker in an address to County Derry Orangemen were commonplace: 'These people who are protected under our laws are turning around and biting the hand that feeds them and are trying to blacken Ulster's good name at home and abroad.'[34]

The Orange Order, whose membership had declined during the depressed conditions of the inter-war period and that had forgone its traditional parades during the war, reasserted itself as a major force within unionism after 1945. The post-war expansion in state services and expenditures provided the Order with a whole range of new opportunities to pressurize party and government to ensure the proper defence of Orange and Protestant interests. The 1947 Education Act was seen by many Orangemen as a major concession to the Catholic Church, and the Order waged a rearguard action against the implementation of the Act and for the replacement of the Minister of Education, Colonel Samuel Hall-Thompson. When the Minister further enraged the unionist right and the Order by proposing in 1949 that the state should pay the employer's portion of Catholic teachers' National Insurance contributions, Orange pressure was so great that the Prime Minister had to attend a meeting of its supreme authority, the Grand Lodge of Ireland, to explain the government's position. He attempted to convince the leaders of the Order that the government had to be fair to all sections of the people and that 'they would still have a large minority in Northern Ireland and if they were treated unfairly as an "oppressed people" it would create a bad impression in England.' His listeners were reluctant to accept such conciliatory ideas, for, as one reverend gentleman from County Antrim put it, 'Not a single Roman Catholic was dissatisfied with the bill. They were getting butter on their bread and they wanted more butter.'[35] Brooke was able to save the bill only by sacrificing Hall-Thompson, whom he persuaded to resign and be replaced by the Labour renegade Harry Midgley, who had joined the Unionist Party in 1947. Midgley, embittered by the role the Catholic Church had played in his election defeat in the 1930s when he had been a champion of the Spanish Republic against the Church's hero Francisco Franco, had become evangelical in his opposition to 'concessions' to the Catholic school system.

The resignation of Hall-Thompson is illustrative of the need for a more nuanced reading of the relationship between the Order and the Unionist regime. The conventional view is one of an 'Orange state' in which the Order had direct representation at the party's ruling Ulster Unionist Council, and the vast bulk of Unionist activists and almost all MPs and cabinet members were members. This, it is assumed, had a determining effect on a range of government policies. In fact, while Orange pressure almost always evoked a government response, it was not always one that satisfied Orange militants.

The Prime Minister expected the leadership of the Order to take heed of the imperative of maintaining unionist unity and of not giving nationalists easy propaganda material. Thus, although he lost his Minister of Education, the legislation was unaffected, and Midgley's desire to claw back the increase in grants to Catholic schools in the 1947 Act was frustrated. It has been argued that Midgley's prejudices did have significant effects in ensuring that the Catholic sector got fewer resources than it might have from the large increase in government expenditure on education in the 1950s.[36] His ministry's estimates rose from less than £4 million in 1946 to more than £12 million in 1957. In the new sector of secondary intermediate schools, by 1957–8 there were 28,000 places in state (Protestant) schools and only 5,000 places in the voluntary (Catholic) sector. There were places for more than half the Protestant primary-school leavers but for less than a fifth of the potential demand from Catholic primary schools, although these contained 44 per cent of the primary-school population.[37] This was, in part at least, the price that Catholics paid for their Church's determination to maintain untrammelled control of its schools. Yet, as Unionists pointed out, the 65 per cent capital grant was higher than what was available in the rest of the UK, and a recent history of Ulster Catholics by a Jesuit referred to the provisions as generous.[38] Nevertheless, a yet more generous policy might have paid political dividends.

Where Midgley's views did seriously affect policy and provide the Catholic Church with justifiable cause for complaint was in the concession to the governing committees of schools within the wholly funded sector of the right to supervise denominational religious instruction and to assess teachers on 'faith and morals'. This substantially increased the influence of the Protestant clergy in the state sector. It was also the case that the often protracted process of getting planning approval for the building of new Catholic schools at times reflected strong grass-roots Orange pressure against what one Belfast lodge referred to as 'this subsidy of Popery and Nationalism which are the enemies of our Ulster heritage'.[39]

The strongest pressure against any 'appeasement' policies came not from the Orange Order, which was internally divided on the issue, but from an upsurge of Protestant fundamentalism in the late 1940s and early 1950s. This was the period when a young evangelical preacher, Ian Paisley, first emerged as a scourge of those in government and the leadership of the Orange Order, who were allegedly making concessions to 'Popery' and Irish nationalism. The initial focus of attack was the 1947 Education Act, which Paisley denounced for 'subsidising Romanism'.[40] This was linked to claims that Brooke's government was acquiescing in an invasion of southern Catholics getting jobs and buying up land in border areas. Sectarian animosities were intensified by developments in the South, where the influence of the Catholic Church on public policy was highlighted by the Mother and Child Affair in 1951, and by the preliminary report of the Irish census of 1946, which showed a decline of 13 per cent in the Protestant population in the 1936–46 period.[41] In Northern Ireland the Bishop of Derry, Dr Neil Farren, made his own contribution to community relations when he referred to Catholics being 'contaminated' by going into non-Catholic halls for dances.[42]

Protestant and Orange dissatisfaction with the government's education policy was surpassed in intensity by an increasingly hysterical chorus of complaint about 'soft' public-order policy. Maginess's attempts to implement a more balanced approach, which culminated in the banning of the Orange march on the Longstone Road in 1952, produced a fierce reaction from the Order and from within the party at all levels. Reaction had intensified as a result of sectarian confrontations over the enthusiastic displays of the Union flag occasioned by the coronation of Queen Elizabeth II in June 1953. Some loyalists had insisted on the display of the flag on houses and businesses in the heart of predominantly Catholic and nationalist areas like the Falls Road, and the RUC had been able to prevent riots only by persuading the loyalists to remove the flags.[43] For the government's loyalist critics this amounted to a cowardly ceding of public space to nationalism. Their disquiet was magnified when nationalists in the predominantly Catholic village of Dungiven, in County Londonderry, prevented a Coronation Day march by an Orange band.[44]

The government's alleged 'appeasement' policy was the main element in the campaign of the group of Independent Unionists who made substantial inroads into the Unionist Party vote in the 1953 election. Paisley's brand of Protestant fundamentalism was influential during the election that saw Hall-Thompson defeated by Norman Porter, an ally of Paisley who was the editor of the *Ulster Protestant*, a monthly paper fixated on the government's 'subsidies to Popery'. Brookeborough's response was a substantial tack to the right. Brian Maginess was shifted from Home Affairs and was never again a substantial figure in the government. In deference to loyalist fundamentalists, and against the advice of the Inspector-General of the RUC, a Flags and Emblems Act was passed in 1954. This obliged the police to protect the display of the Union flag anywhere in Northern Ireland and empowered them to remove any other flag or emblem whose display threatened a breach of the peace.

The latter provision would be used by loyalist ultras to demand that the RUC remove the Irish Tricolour even when it was being displayed in a predominantly nationalist area.[45]

There was increasing evidence of a reluctance on the Prime Minister's part to challenge the demands and prejudices of his more extreme supporters. He was prepared to support a Family Allowances Bill in 1956, which, while increasing allowances in line with Britain, proposed to abolish payments for the fourth and subsequent children. The bill reflected the fear, particularly strong in border areas, that a higher Catholic birth-rate would lead to a Catholic majority by the end of the century. Brookeborough reconsidered only when some of the Unionist MPs at Westminster pointed out that even their Tory allies would criticize what would be seen as a blatant piece of discriminatory legislation.[46] Behind the scenes he exerted himself in the interests of those Derry unionists who were afraid that if the government's industrial development policies were successful, the new industries would employ too many 'disloyalists'.[47] The Prime Minister's intervention appears to have been decisive in ensuring that the US multinational DuPont, which was planning a major investment in the city, appointed the secretary of the Derry Unionist Association as its personnel officer.[48] Although the appointment did not prevent DuPont becoming a large employer of Catholics, it was an indication of Brookeborough's firm belief that he had to show a continuing responsiveness to the most reactionary voices in the party. These depressing concessions to sectarian pressures were not uninfluenced by increasing signs of a resurgence of republican militarism, which culminated in the launching of a full-scale campaign against the northern state in December 1956.

Even without pressure from Protestant fundamentalists and the IRA, there were strict limits to the more inclusive form of unionism proposed by Brookeborough and Maginess. It did little to address nationalist grievances about discrimination in the employment practices of central and local government. The charge of 'vicious sectarian discrimination'[49] ignored important dimensions of the problem: lower levels of educational attainment and the attitude of suspicious hostility adopted by some Catholics to those of their co-religionists who joined the civil service or the police.[50] It also ignored the fact that at manual labour and clerical level Catholics generally received their proportionate share of public employment. Yet there could be no denying the stark under-representation of the minority in the higher ranks of the civil service, local government and the judiciary.

While discrimination was not solely responsible, it undoubtedly played a role. Brookeborough's conception of fairness seems to have entailed a belief that Catholics should have a proportionate share of the total number of public service jobs while leaving Protestant dominance of key positions unchallenged. In 1956, amidst Orange concern about Catholics employed in Belfast law courts, he asked Brian Maginess, the Attorney-General, to get figures that he hoped would soothe his critics: 'Brian showed that in the higher grades the proportion of Unionists was very high indeed and in the lower grades not worse than three to one. I said we had to be fair in giving employment but we need not go further than that.'[51] While he accepted that Catholics had a right to their share of the positions as law clerks, he was determined that there should be no more than one Catholic amongst the senior judiciary. A Catholic had been appointed to the Supreme Court in 1949, giving the minority one out of forty senior positions in the higher courts. When the Lord Chief Justice nominated a Catholic QC for a High Court judgeship in 1956, Brookeborough told him he would oppose it: 'I did not like the idea of another Nationalist on the bench.'[52] The man concerned, Cyril Nicholson, was a prominent opponent of republican violence and a proponent of a more positive engagement by Catholics with the state.

The undoubted material improvements of the post-war period – real income per head rose by one third during the 1950s – did not diminish Catholic resentment over actual or alleged discrimination in private employment. Although a largely political explanation of the Catholic economic disadvantage emphasizing the role of the 'Orange state' has been disputed by scholars,[53] the facts of Catholic disadvantage are undisputed. There was Protestant over-representation in skilled, supervisory and managerial positions and massive predominance in industries like shipbuilding, engineering and aircraft production, which provided well-paid and relatively secure employment. Catholics were over-represented amongst the unskilled and the unemployed and crowded into industries such as construction and transport, where wages were lower and employment more insecure.[54] In workplaces such as the shipyard there were strong Orange and loyalist influences on hiring, although they were countered to some degree by trade union organization. Perhaps even more important than overt pressure was the pervasive influence of kin and neighbourhood in a society with high levels of residential segregation on what was a largely informal recruiting mechanism.

Longer-term structural factors disadvantaged Catholics in the industrial heartland; they produced a clear east–west gradient in unemployment and living standards as well. The core of the industrial economy of the province remained the greater Belfast area. The government was accused of favouring majority Protestant areas like Belfast and the east of the province in its industrial development policies and neglecting the western periphery where Catholics were in a majority.[55] In fact, the Stormont regime did show some concern for high levels of unemployment in Londonderry, Strabane and other largely nationalist towns, particularly after a visiting British Labour Party delegation in 1954 warned of the potential for civil unrest and potential subversion.[56] However, the Ministry of Commerce officials involved in the government's programme of advanced factory building had major problems interesting potential investors in what were perceived to be remote areas that, although they had high percentage rates of unemployment, lacked large pools of the skilled and experienced labour that incoming industrialists often demanded. Although Belfast had the lowest rate of unemployment in the North, it also possessed the largest pool of unemployed skilled labour, and this, together with its port, meant that many new industries simply refused to look elsewhere. As the Minister of Commerce explained to the cabinet in 1956, 'we are not in as strong a position as to be able to turn away industry that is prepared to come to Belfast or not at all.'[57]

Although the charge of malign neglect of the west will not hold up, there was undoubtedly a tendency to pay more attention to the large concentrations of unemployed Protestants in the east, whose dissatisfaction could mean a loss of electoral support. There was also the complacent assumption that unemployed Catholics would remain quiescent because they had a realistic grasp of conditions in the South. When, in 1954, R. A. Butler, the Tory Chancellor of the Exchequer, questioned Stormont about the British Labour Party claim that high unemployment could lead to 'serious political trouble' in places like Derry and Newry, Brian Maginess dismissed the idea as 'complete nonsense . . . so long as these people continue to enjoy Northern Ireland rates of unemployment benefit or national assistance . . . we have no fear of any kind of trouble.'[58]

The fear of senior Derry Unionists that new industries would undermine their control of the city by bringing in an unmanageable influx of Catholic workers had an inhibiting effect on attracting new industries. Teddy Jones, MP for the city of Londonderry constituency, was the main messenger boy for the city's Unionist hierarchy. His lobbying ensured that these fears were discussed at the highest level of the state, where a cabinet subcommittee was set up to try to ensure that industrial development was made compatible with continuing Unionist control of the city. Brookeborough exerted himself to ensure that government departments and the Housing Trust did all they could to address the problem.[59]

Apart from its effect on employment, the local Unionist power structure also impacted on the city's housing. To maintain the situation of 1961, whereby Derry was 67 per cent Catholic but still under Unionist control, it was necessary that new housing for Catholics be concentrated in the south ward, where two thirds of the city's Catholics lived.[60] The need to maintain the gerrymandered system meant not simply a reluctance to house Catholics in the other two wards on the part of Derry corporation but also severe restraints on where the Northern Ireland Housing Trust could build. The result was a substantial amount of overcrowding and a long waiting list, largely Catholic, for public housing.[61]

The Derry situation epitomized the dynamics of the regime's sectarianism, which was more about the central government's complicity in a limited number of flagrantly unjust situations than Stormont being an activist 'Orange state'. There were limits to Brookeborough's willingness to indulge Jones and his friends in the north-west. When he received a letter from the MP opposing any further industrial development in Derry, the perversity of this caused the Prime Minister to exclaim, 'No government can stand idly by and allow possible industries not to develop.'[62] Derry Unionists did not prevent the Stormont government supporting investment in the city in the late 1950s or Brookeborough's vigorous lobbying of London to prevent the closure of the Navy's anti-submarine training base at Eglinton, near Derry, in 1958.[63] But the existence of a local authority with such deep hostility to development had serious effects on the government's industrial development policy. By the beginning of the 1960s Derry had a potentially explosive combination of unemployment and housing shortage, both of which could be given a plausible political explanation in terms of a hard-faced Unionist elite.

'An Invertebrate Collectivity': The Dilemmas of Northern Nationalism

The reaction of the leaders of nationalism to Labour's Westminster victory in 1945 was the predictable obverse of loyalist apprehension. Attaching an exaggerated importance to Labour's already frayed tradition of supporting a united Ireland and to the formation of the backbench pressure group 'The Friends of Ireland' at Westminster, the ten Nationalist

MPs elected to Stormont in 1945 promoted a new organization, the
Anti-Partition League (APL), whose purpose was to energize and unify
nationalism within Northern Ireland and press London to reopen the
partition question. The role of the US as the dominant power in the
non-communist world and Britain's economic and strategic dependence
on America were seen as giving a new opportunity for Irish-American
lobbying of Washington. Expectations of progress from London were
soon dashed as the Attlee government's pro-Union sentiment became
obvious. By 1947 the APL was denouncing Labour as the enemy and
beginning to consider the possibility of attempting to organize the Irish
vote in Britain to punish Attlee at the next election.

The Nationalist MPs returned to Stormont in 1945 were largely drawn
from the Catholic rural and small-town middle class – farmers, lawyers,
journalists, auctioneers and publicans – from the west and south of the
province.[64] Belfast nationalism had never recovered from the death of
Joe Devlin and his combination of pragmatic nationalism and pro-Labour
views. The city returned one Nationalist MP in 1945, the barrister T. J.
Campbell, who soon shocked the party by accepting a county court
judgeship. The Nationalists were subsequently never to hold a Belfast
seat, and their local government base in the city had almost vanished by
the early 1950s. They were pushed aside not by the more militant nationalism of Sinn Féin but by organizations labelling themselves socialist
republican and, after a split in the NILP in 1949, by Irish Labour. The
Nationalists' lack of appeal to the Catholic working class in Belfast was
not unrelated to their strong denunciation of the welfare state, which it
was proclaimed might be suitable to an industrial nation like Britain but
was 'wholly unsuitable to an area such as the Six Counties which is
predominantly agrarian and underpopulated'. Echoing the Unionist
right's arguments, they alleged that the 'extravagant scale' of benefits
provided by the welfare state and the National Health Service would
reduce the 'people' to bankruptcy.[65]

The Nationalists' conservatism was a northern manifestation of the
Catholic Church's opposition to the welfare state for its allegedly 'totalitarian' dangers. It reflected the strong Catholic faith of Nationalist MPs
and the central role that the clergy played in their primitive electoral
machine. Despite the formation of the APL the Nationalists failed to
develop a modern party organization. They concentrated on those areas
where Catholics were in a majority. Six of their ten MPs were returned
without a contest in 1945. The only real activity was carried on by regis-
tration committees dedicated to ensuring that all eligible Catholics were

registered to vote and as many as possible of the 'other side' had their eligibility challenged. Candidates were chosen at conventions often presided over by a priest and composed of delegates selected at after-mass meetings. As Conor Cruise O'Brien, then an official of the Department of External Affairs, noted, 'The nature of the structure at parish level plays into the hands of those who regard the nationalists in the Six Counties as a purely sectarian organization.'[66]

O'Brien acerbically commented that the APL 'can hardly be called an organization at all; it is an invertebrate collectivity. It has an allegiance but no policy.' Although Nationalist hopes in radical action from the Labour government were quickly disappointed, they were replaced by what would prove to be an equally empty faith in the new inter-party government in Dublin. Seán MacBride, as Minister for External Affairs, had promised to provide a right of audience in the Dáil for northern Nationalist MPs and to nominate leading northerners to the Senate.[67] This seemed to offer Nationalists a form of institutional involvement in the southern state after more than two decades of much resented neglect. However, the proposal was too much for MacBride's colleagues, and it was vetoed by Costello. Nevertheless, before disillusion could set in, the torpid waters of northern nationalism were churned up by the decision to repeal the External Relations Act and declare a republic.

The President of the APL and the leader of the Nationalist MPs at Stormont, James McSparran, a barrister who was MP for Mourne, saw the purpose of attending Stormont and Westminster as highlighting the iniquities of Unionist rule – not to elicit reform but rather to embarrass the British government sufficiently to make it willing to reopen the parti-tion issue. Rather predictably, the adoption of a much more rhetorically republican tone by the Irish government dealt a shattering blow to such hopes. The Ireland Act, by strengthening the Unionists' constitutional guarantee, produced a strong emotional reaction in the South that served only to underline the futility of constitutional anti-partitionism. The creation of the all-party Anti-Partition Campaign and its raising of funds for Nationalist candidates in the 1949 Stormont election by a collection outside Catholic churches throughout the island helped to ensure that the election was fought in the most viciously sectarian environment since the 1930s.

The inter-party government's rhetorical breach in the wall of northern nationalist isolation had an energizing effect, particularly in border areas like Derry, where Eddie McAteer, the leading APL politician in the city, attempted to give a new activist edge to anti-partitionist politics. In the pamphlet *Irish Action* he suggested a nationalist campaign of obstruction against Stormont involving a refusal to deal with such bodies as the Inland Revenue and the Post Office.[68] More realistic was his determination to exploit Derry Catholics' still-raw resentment over the gerrymandering of the city's government. This resentment was amplified by the determination of Unionists to define the centre of the city, enclosed within its plantation walls, as a loyalist public space. The upsurge of nationalist self-confidence in 1948 led to a proposal for a large anti-partition demonstration in Derry, which was banned under the Special Powers Act. McAteer became active in challenging future bans on nationalist parades within the city centre. The local Catholic bishop, Dr Farren, was opposed to what he regarded as 'anti-partitionist stunts', but McAteer saw in the inevitable conflicts with the police a means of maintaining a sharp sense of Catholic grievance and counteracting the integrative effects of the welfare state.[69]

When the return of de Valera to power in 1951 brought a shift towards a softer line on the North and an attempt to build up practical links in areas such as cross-border cooperation on transport and electricity production, the response from the APL was hostile. McAteer denounced the 'fraternization' policy as shoring up partition, and when officials of the South's Electricity Supply Board were invited to meet their northern counterparts at a lunch in Derry the event was boycotted by the APL. A frustrated Conor Cruise O'Brien, charged with liaising with the APL, noted the criticisms but added 'they did not have any alternative policy to propose . . . their main interest was in the local situation in Derry and in how it could be exploited for the discomfiture of Unionists rather than in any general strategy on partition.'[70]

The IRA's 1956 Campaign

McAteer's interest in more militant tactics reflected an awareness that as the sound and fury of southern-sponsored anti-partitionism dissipated in failure, it would leave the APL dangerously vulnerable to republican exploitation of the disenchantment with constitutionalism amongst a younger generation of nationalists. MacBride's presence in government had contributed to a decline in police activity against the IRA in the Republic and enabled it to regroup and be in a better position to benefit from the rise and decline of official anti-partitionist fervour. The IRA calculated that as long as violence was directed at the northern state, popular sympathy for 'the boys' would weaken the southern state's capacity to act against them, and a military council was created in 1951 to plan a full-scale campaign.[71] Although the Ebrington Territorial Army Base in Derry was raided for arms in 1951, the return of de Valera to power appears to have weakened IRA capacity to operate in the North. The next, and much more spectacular, raid, on Gough Army Barracks in Armagh did not take place until June 1954, when a new inter-party government was in power.

Out of office, MacBride had done his best to encourage republican militancy by going North to speak in favour of the IRA dissident Liam Kelly, who won the Mid Tyrone seat in the 1953 Stormont election. Kelly, who was expelled from the IRA for unauthorized 'operations', went on to establish a party, Fianna Uladh ('Soldiers of Ulster'), and a military organization, Saor Uladh ('free Ulster'). He followed MacBride in arguing that republicans should accept the legitimacy of the Republic and direct their energies solely against Stormont. This made him popular beyond the republican hard core. Cahir Healy, whose Westminster seat for Fermanagh and South Tyrone was vulnerable to republican challenge, bewailed the support given to Kelly in the South, particularly by the Fianna Fáil-supporting *Irish Press*, whose editor believed, despite the policy of de Valera, that only force would get rid of the border.[72]

MacBride, who was supporting the new coalition from the back-benches, managed to get Kelly nominated for the Senate. At a time when the Senator was serving a year's imprisonment for seditious statements during the election, MacBride's action helped to strengthen republican self-confidence, already boosted by the Armagh raid. Although McAteer had been enthusiastic about the effects of the raid in 'keeping up morale amongst a population which had been cowed and defeated',[73] many of his colleagues in the APL were dismayed by the signs that disillusion with constitutional politics was feeding into increasing sympathy for those prepared to use physical force. Brookeborough's concession on the Flags and Emblems Act gave the republicans a major propaganda victory when, on Kelly's release in August 1954, the RUC's attempt to prevent the flying of the Irish flag by a crowd of 10,000 that had gathered to welcome him in his home village of Pomeroy caused a major riot.[74]

In an evaluation of opinion in the wake of the Armagh raid, Conor Cruise O'Brien noted that while the event was 'greeted with universal approbation and even glee by all Nationalists in the Six Counties', many of those who applauded did so 'in a more or less "sporting" spirit without reflecting on the consequences of the actions or the logical conclusion of the policy behind them'. Bloodshed would alienate support for the IRA.[75] There was bloodshed during the next IRA arms raid, a botched attack on Omagh Army Barracks in October 1955. Five soldiers were wounded, two of them seriously. However, the absence of deaths amongst what even the Taoiseach referred to as 'forces of occupation', and the fact that the eight young men arrested, all southerners, were sentenced to long prison terms, ensured that moral and prudential qualms were submerged by waves of sympathy for what was widely perceived to be a group of brave young idealists.[76]

Sinn Féin was quick to exploit this popular mood and the APL's divided and demoralized state by putting up candidates, some of them serving time for the Omagh raid, for all the North's Westminster constituencies in the general election of May 1955. The result was a clear propaganda coup. It won Fermanagh and South Tyrone and Mid Ulster, where two of the imprisoned Omagh raiders were elected, and was able to boast of amassing the largest anti-partitionist vote ever: a total of 152,310 votes. Yet, as its APL critics bitterly but justly pointed out, this was a hollow victory. The size of the vote reflected the fact that the majority of seats had previously not been contested. As a result of Sinn Féin's intervention, Jack Beattie of the Irish Labour Party lost West Belfast to a Unionist and the other two Nationalist seats at Westminster were lost to Unionists after the disqualification of the two Sinn Féin MPs. Nor could Sinn Féin use its vote as a popular sanction for future IRA violence, as its candidates had insisted that they were not asking people to vote for the use of force.[77]

Nevertheless, the apparent surge in republican political fortunes did quicken the pace of IRA preparations for a northern offensive. The IRA leadership was also anxious to pre-empt a rival campaign by Kelly after Saor Uladh attacked a police barracks in Roslea in Fermanagh in November 1955. 'Operation Harvest' was launched in December 1956. From the start its focus was on the border counties where, it was hoped, local IRA units assisted by 'flying columns' from the South would destroy communications links with the rest of the province, destroy RUC barracks and, with the at least tacit support of local nationalists, create 'liberated zones' free of Stormont control. Whether this was envisaged as a prelude to a general nationalist uprising, perhaps provoked by a heavy-handed government response, or simply as a dramatic event that would force Britain to re-open the partition question is not clear.

The largely southern leadership of the IRA had a weak grasp of northern realities. Seán Cronin, the ex-Irish soldier who was IRA Chief of Staff and the strategist behind Operation Harvest, had some aware-ness of the dangers of IRA actions triggering the sort of sectarian violence that had occurred in the 1920s and in 1935. For this reason, and despite the complaints of northern IRA men, there were to be no attacks on the part-time and locally based B Specials.[78] Although the RUC was defined as a legitimate target, initially IRA attacks took the form of frontal assaults on police barracks by IRA members wearing surplus US and British Army uniforms. The most famous attack of the campaign, on Brookeborough RUC station in January 1957, in which the IRA's main martyrs of the campaign, Sean South and Feargal O'Hanlon, were killed, typified this approach. Whatever the military futility and political obtuseness of this type of attack, its capacity to ignite sectarian animosi-ties was less than the more classically terrorist attacks on police personnel by booby-traps and ambushes carried out by local IRA men in civilian dress. Although the RUC death toll was comparatively light at six, as the campaign failed to maintain its initial momentum and relied increasingly on local resources, it shifted to tactics more likely to provoke a violent loyalist response.[79]

That such attacks did not provoke a loyalist backlash was in large part owing to the fact that the campaign was clearly a failure and had not affected Belfast. Although Cronin has claimed that Belfast was excluded from his plan in order to avoid sectarian confrontation,[80] it does not appear that this was known by the Belfast IRA, which had drawn up plans for attacks on targets ranging from RUC stations and the homes of policemen to contractors who did work for the security forces.[81] RUC intelligence on the Belfast IRA was good, and the arrest, just before the campaign started, of one of their leading members in possession of impor-tant Belfast battalion documents was followed by a series of arrests that put the city's organization out of business for the rest of the campaign.[82]

Although the campaign was not called off until February 1962, its failure had been evident much earlier. Republicans had overestimated the degree of nationalist alienation from the Stormont regime and failed to understand that initial sympathy for what were often seen as brave but misguided idealists would not extend to the killing of policemen along with the attendant risks of loyalist retaliation. Condemnations of the campaign by Cardinal D'Alton, the head of the Catholic Church in Ireland, and by the Taoiseach did not impress the members of the RUC Special Branch, who thought they would not have the slightest effect on the IRA.[83] It was also the case that some of the local clergy in Fermanagh and Tyrone had strong republican sympathies. The defeated

APL MP for Mid Ulster was bitterly critical of the clergy of the constituency, some of whom had openly supported Sinn Féin, while others had instructed local convents not to vote and refused the APL the use of parochial halls during the 1955 campaign.[84] Liam Kelly's closest advisers were two local priests.[85] However, as the campaign continued, denunciations of IRA membership or support made by the local bishop and the clergy in Tyrone and Fermanagh were seen as having more effect.[86] Much more important in determining the attitude of the vast bulk of nationalists to the campaign was the evidence from its earliest days that it was little more than a series of pinpricks against the formidable security apparatus of the northern state. The RUC, with the aid of 13,000 Specials, the British Army and the introduction of internment, had little problem in ensuring that the idea of 'liberated zones' proved as illusory as the IRA appeal to the Protestants of Ulster to support Irish unity.[87] MacBride's support for the inter-party government did not prevent the coalition taking immediate action against the IRA, and when de Valera returned to power he did not hesitate to introduce internment. The result was clear from the RUC's figures for major incidents, which fell from 138 in 1957 to eighty in 1958 and nineteen in 1959.[88]

Sinn Féin's vote in the 1959 Westminster election slumped by over a half compared with 1955, but there was little sign that the setback to militant republicanism would do anything to lift the APL out of its organizational and intellectual torpor. The success of the NILP in the 1958 elections served to underline the ineffectuality of the Nationalist MPs at Stormont. An attempt by some of the less inert MPs, together with Irish Labour and Republican MPs to dissolve the party and replace it with a new formation, was only narrowly defeated.[89] The apparent collapse of the physical-force tradition and the growing dissatisfaction of a section of the Catholic middle class with the ineffectual negativism of the APL opened up the possibility of a more engaged and participationist type of nationalism. Unfortunately for the future of the North, the Unionist Party's increasing problems with its core support group, the Protestant working class, prevented a more positive engagement with these changes.

Economic Change and Unionist Politics

Despite the Brookeborough government's aggressively optimistic view of the economy in public, it had a much darker private assessment. For most of the period from 1945 to the early 1960s the major political foe of the regime was seen to be Irish nationalism. In its response to the anti-partitionist campaign it was easy for the government to point out the economic and social advantages that the Union brought to all the citizens of Northern Ireland. The British and American journalists who had arrived in Ireland to cover the IRA campaign were given the following riposte to nationalist tales of a northern minority thirsting for unity: 'In agriculture, in the social services, in education, in industrial development and in our standard of living, we are streets ahead of Éire and are strengthening our lead every day.'[90] The government's problem was that precisely because the majority of the electorate did not expect or desire to be part of an all-Ireland state, their frame of reference was British, not Irish. Wages and unemployment levels in the rest of the UK were the standards against which Stormont's economic record would be judged.

This was not a record of unadulterated failure. The government had to deal with an economy that suffered from remoteness, higher transport costs, and a lack of domestic supplies of raw materials and fuel for industry. Its narrow range of staple industries had overcome these disadvantages, but all of them faced major problems in the post-war period. In 1950 the province's economic structure was dominated by three industries: ship-building and engineering, linen and agriculture. By the beginning of the 1960s agriculture still employed 14 per cent of the province's labour force, compared with 4 per cent in the rest of the UK. It was the area's largest employer of labour, although its workforce had declined from 101,000 in 1945 to 73,000 in 1960. This was the inevitable result of mechanization (there were 850 tractors in 1939 and 30,000 in 1960) and the elimination of smaller, uneconomic holdings, which the government encouraged. The result was an 80 per cent increase in output by 1960.[91] There were also improvements in productivity in linen as it faced competition from low-cost, ex-colonial producers and the expansion of the synthetic fibre industry. Substantial amounts of state support for modernization were given through a Re-equipment of Industry Act introduced in 1950. Such modernization entailed a substantial amount of rationalization and concentration of production and the inevitable closing of plants and shedding of labour. Between 1954 and 1964 the number of jobs in plants employing twenty-five workers or more (the bulk of the industry) fell from 56,414 to 33,957.[92]

Unlike linen, shipbuilding had maintained its role as the region's pre-eminent employer of skilled male labour up to the end of the 1950s. In 1950 more than one tenth of the North's manufacturing jobs and one fifth of those in Belfast were in Harland and Wolff. Employing 21,000 in four yards on the Queen's Island, it was the largest single shipbuilding complex in the world. Until 1955 its major problem was a steel shortage due to the rearmament programme. Subsequently, as with the rest of British shipbuilding, it came under increasing pressure from more productive continental and Japanese yards. By 1960 the yard was still employing over 22,000 workers and the unemployment rate amongst shipyard workers was just 2.5 per cent, a third of what it was in British centres such as Tyneside and the Clyde. But, at a time when world shipbuilding capacity was double what was required, the cabinet's employment committee was anticipating between 5,000 and 8,000 redundancies.[93] The crisis in shipbuilding turned out to be much worse: employment was slashed by 40 per cent, or 11,500 jobs, between 1961 and 1964. It would coincide with fears of job losses in aircraft production at Short and Harland, whose workforce had fluctuated significantly in the post-war period and stood at 6,900 in 1962.[94] It was not part of either of the two main groups into which the British government planned to rationalize aircraft production, and its future appeared increasingly precarious. The problems created for Brookeborough's government by the decline of the staple industries were intensified by the province's demography. A birth-rate that was much higher than anywhere else in the UK fed through into a natural increase of 15,000 per annum throughout the 1950s.[95]

Pressure on the job-creating capacity of the economy was to an extent relieved by the direct and indirect effects of government policy. Although its contemporary critics and some later commentators have criticized Brookeborough's administration for passivity, there is considerable evidence of a long-standing concern to counter the anticipated decline of traditional industries by a strategy of diversification based on the attraction of external investment. In 1944 the government had decided that inter-war legislation aimed at attracting new industry was inadequate and replaced it with the Industries Development Act, which aimed to attract British, American and European firms by providing desirable packages, including advance factories, newly built factory premises at low rents, the necessary infrastructure and grants of up to one third of capital cost, which could be exceeded for 'desirable' projects.[96] This legislation put the North in a favourable position compared to British regions suffering similar problems, which, under the 1945 Distribution of Industry Act, were subject to rigorous Treasury control. No advance factories were built in Britain between 1947 and 1959.[97]

By 1961 almost 48,000 new jobs had been created, an average of 2,500 per annum for the 1950s. New employment was also created by the substantial expansion of the public sector, particularly in the areas of health and education. Higher incomes were reflected in an expansion in the distributive trades. The total number of insured employees in the province increased from 438,000 in 1950 to 449,000 in 1960, broadly in line with the trend in the rest of the UK.[98] However, despite these positive developments, unemployment in the province never fell below 5 per cent and averaged 7.4 per cent for the decade, four times the UK average and, more significantly, higher than the figures for other regional black spots such as Merseyside and Scotland.[99] The position would have been even worse had it not been that net migration was running at 9,000 per annum.[100]

Brookeborough, although already sixty-two in 1950 and subject to recurrent bouts of illness after an operation for a stomach ulcer in 1955, was initially quite effective in extracting extra resources from Westminster to mitigate the problem. He mercilessly exploited metropolitan gratitude for the North's wartime role and the more fundamental consideration that it was still of strategic value to the UK, given Irish neutrality. British annoyance at Dublin's anti-partition campaign also helped. In 1949, when unemployment in Northern Ireland was at 6.5 per cent, Attlee had written to his Home Secretary noting how much worse the situation was there in comparison with the rest of the UK and adding, 'It is, of course, of considerable political importance that we should do all we can to ensure full employment in Northern Ireland.'[101]

When the unemployment figure rose to a peak of 11 per cent in 1952 as a result of an international slump in textiles that hit linen badly, Brookeborough descended on Churchill and his ministers demanding a range of special measures. Although the Treasury and Board of Trade resisted, the Home Office stressed the political and strategic importance of helping 'Sir Basil':

The problem of unemployment in Northern Ireland was fundamentally different from that in this country because political considerations were involved which did not arise here. The adjacent Republic was politically hostile and there was in Northern Ireland a large dissident minority. Large numbers of unemployed constituted a potential source of serious civil disturbance, which might even lead in the long run to civil war.[102]

Brookeborough went home with extra Admiralty orders for ships, subcontract work for Short and Harland, and new textile orders from the Ministry of Defence. He also extracted the setting up of a joint committee of British and Stormont officials to investigate possible long-term solutions to the problem. There was strong resistance from the Treasury and other Westminster departments to many of the proposals that the Stormont officials put forward, particularly the remittance of employers' National Insurance contributions, but eventually a subsidy for the industrial use of coal and support for the creation, in 1955, of a Northern Ireland Development Council chaired by Lord Chandos were conceded.[103]

More important than these essentially palliative measures was the acceptance by the Treasury of the principle of 'parity plus'. It could be argued that this principle was implicit in the post-war agreements that underlay the extension of welfarism to the province, but the formal statement of the new principles underlying the financial relationship between Belfast and London strengthened Brookeborough's hand. In 1954 the Treasury representatives on the Joint Exchequer Board accepted not simply parity of social services and standards but the necessity to incur special expenditure to make up a substantial leeway on such services and amenities as housing, schools and hospitals. Crucially, it accepted the need for special expenditure to offset the economic disadvantage suffered by Northern Ireland by reason of geographical remoteness.[104] The result was in evidence by the end of the decade. In 1960 capital expenditure on hospitals in Northern Ireland over the previous five years was 12 per cent of the UK total at a time when the North's share of the population was 2.5 per cent. The share of the university building programme was 4.6 per cent; of roads, 5.3 per cent; and of housing, 3.6 per cent.[105] The success of Brookeborough and his officials in pushing the North's case for special treatment was reflected in the decline of the Imperial Contribution, which hovered between £17 and £20 million at the beginning of the 1950s but by 1961 had fallen to £8.7 million at a time when the annual subvention from Westminster had reached £44.8 million.[106]

If, despite this, the Prime Minister was under increasing political pressure on the unemployment question, it was in part because of rising popular expectations. The government's constant emphasis on how much better economic and social conditions were in the North compared to the Republic cut little ice with many of its trade union supporters, who were, like 80 per cent of northern trade unionists, in British-based unions and whose fundamental economic, social, and cultural frames of reference were set by developments in the rest of the UK. The regime was the victim of its own propaganda, which, in response to the dominion status lobby, had emphasized Stormont's distinct powers and its relative autonomy from Westminster. This played into the hands of the NILP, whose solution to the unemployment problem was a more activist government.

The fundamental problem was that Stormont's demands for special treatment were regarded in London as having been quite substantially indulged by the mid 1950s; and not even the onset of the IRA assault softened this attitude. To add to Brookeborough's problems, the UK investment boom of 1954–5 and what the Treasury perceived as inflationary pressures and a threat to the balance of payments led to a credit squeeze and interest rate rise. This had a severe impact on the linen industry in Belfast at the same time as UK firms were reluctant to consider new investments in the province. Unemployment, which stood at 6 per cent in June 1956, rose to 10 per cent in the same month in 1958.

The NILP had positioned itself skilfully to benefit from the government's problems. It had been devastated in the 1949 Stormont elections because of its internal divisions on the border, which allowed Unionists to depict it as a crypto-republican party. Its response was to take a pro-Union position, which led to the loss of its anti-partitionist elements, who then went on to set up branches of the Irish Labour Party in West Belfast, Derry and Newry.[107] Its leading members lost few opportunities to denounce the 'Franco state' in the South and to support the government in the use of internment and the Special Powers Act against the IRA. It also benefited from a critique of government economic policy in *The Economic Survey of Northern Ireland*, by two Queen's University economists, published in 1957. This had been commissioned by the Minister of Commerce in 1947 and delivered to his successor in 1955. Its publication had been delayed by the government for fear that it would buttress the NILP's attack, although the Minister of Commerce, Lord Glentoran, was able to quote an *Economist* review that described the *Survey* as giving 'a picture of the remarkable adaptation of the Northern Irish economy to the pace set by British economic progress – the adaptation of a hardy plant to an unpromising soil'.[108]

What the NILP extracted from the *Survey* was the idea that the various aids given to industry had not had a sufficient pay-off in terms of jobs created. This was linked to the accusation of a nepotistic link between the government, the Unionist Parliamentary Party and local industrialists, in particular those involved in linen production. In the 1950s twelve of the fourteen Unionist MPs for Belfast constituencies had links with traditional industry as proprietors or managing directors.[109] It was

certainly the case that pressure from local manufacturers, who feared that
the Industries Development Act would bring in new firms that would
compete for labour and force them to pay higher wages, had led to the
introduction of the Re-equipment of Industry Bill in 1950, which
compensated local firms by providing grants for new equipment and
modernization. When the uptake on this was judged insufficient, a new
and even more generous scheme, the Capital Grants to Industry Act, was
introduced in 1954. Although modernization almost inevitably implied
job losses, there was a widespread belief, shared by Terence O'Neill, who
was Minister of Finance at the end of the 1950s, that the 'linen lords'
were only interested in using government aid to buy up rivals and shut
them down.[110]

   Class-based tensions within the Unionist electoral bloc were nothing
new, but they were given increased potency by a relaxation of communal
tension in Belfast, where the collapse of the Nationalist Party and the
absence of any significant IRA activity made it easier for Protestant workers
to consider voting Labour. As early as the 1953 Stormont election, the
Unionist Party headquarters at Glengall Street was bemoaning the fact
that 'Our Party is losing the support of the lower paid income group and
the artisans to the NILP.' The lack of any working-class Unionist MPs
and the domination of Belfast Unionist representation by the local bourgeoisie were seen as important in encouraging defections. Whatever reserve
of working-class deference still existed was weakened by social change,
as the heartlands of proletarian Unionism began to lose population to
new housing estates in which the party had failed to establish a presence.
Most significantly, Glengall Street noted that 'the "Big Drum" which has
heretofore dominated Unionist politics' had lost its energizing power for
at least a section of the working class.[111] In the 1958 election the NILP
won four new seats in Belfast. Although two of these seats, in Oldpark
and Pottinger, had a sizeable Catholic working-class population, the other
two, Victoria and Woodvale, were solidly Protestant. The lesson was spelt
out in a ministerial discussion of unemployment:

The maintenance of a Unionist government at Stormont depends to an
increasing degree on the success or otherwise of its economic policy.
Particularly in the city of Belfast voters are considering such matters as unemployment when deciding how to cast their vote and unless success is
achieved in reducing the present total of unemployment . . . the Unionist
Party cannot hope to retain the allegiance of the working class population.[112]

With the strong prospect of serious redundancies in shipbuilding and the aircraft industry, an air of desperation descended on Brookeborough's ministers. The usually cautious O'Neill was so exercised by the threat that these redundancies 'would kill us off' that he may have reduced his colleagues to stunned silence by a proposal to drain Lough Neagh, the largest expanse of inland water in the British Isles, to create a new 'county Neagh' – this would be leased out in hundred-acre farms and have a new town at its centre.[113] The redundancies, when they came, were almost as bad as feared, and they exhausted Brookeborough's declining capacity to bring back good economic news from London. Early in 1961 Harland and Wolff announced that 8,000 men would be paid off in the summer, and later in the year Short and Harland declared that, because of lack of orders, there was a real danger of closure, threatening another 7,000 jobs. The year also saw the closure of the largest linen mill in Belfast, which employed 1,700 and had received a substantial amount of government assistance.[114]

Although the NILP did not win any new seats in the 1962 election, its share of the vote rose to 26 per cent from 16 per cent in 1958. It had fielded more candidates, but there was evidence, accepted by Unionist headquarters, that it had consolidated its position in Belfast, where its total vote in the sixteen constituencies it contested was 58,811 while the Unionist vote in the same constituencies was 69,069.[115] The inroads made by the NILP into the core working-class constituency of Unionism was recognized by Sir George Clark, Imperial Grand Master of the Orange Order, in a post-election speech in which he accepted that the election showed that the government needed a greater sense of urgency in dealing with unemployment. He also admitted that the Order contained 'a great many Labour men who, while wearing a sash, nevertheless had a different political outlook', adding that he had no quarrel with such members.[116] Clark and some other leading Unionists recognized that the NILP had to be fought on its chosen terrain and that 'banging the drum' would be insufficient.

The problem was that Brookeborough, who was seventy-two when the 1960s began, increasingly appeared to have hung on to power too long, particularly when de Valera stepped down in 1959. Although Lemass was already sixty when he became Taoiseach, his promotion of a radical shift in the state's economic policies and the launch of the first economic development programme undermined the more complacent Unionist assumption about southern 'backwardness' and strengthened the critics of Brookeborough's lack of a long-term strategy for the northern economy. His semidetached style of government, which had allowed him plenty of time for running his estate in Fermanagh, the indulgence of his beloved fishing and shooting, and occasional long winter cruises in sunnier climates, was increasingly seen as dangerously anachronistic. He became the butt of an effective NILP campaign against a 'part-time' and 'amateur' government. The death of the talented and moderate Maynard Sinclair in the *Princess Victoria* ferry disaster in 1953 had removed his most likely successor, while the marginalization of Brian Maginess, who left the cabinet to become Attorney-General in 1956, meant that the government had no member who would have been a substantial enough figure to suggest an earlier exit to the Prime Minister. Four decades of power had inevitably bred complacency. The large number of uncontested seats produced many backbenchers whose only imperative was to satisfy the parochial and often sectarian pressures from their constituencies. The sectarian tone of Unionist politics had deterred a substantial section of the Protestant middle class from political involvement and drained the already shallow pool of ability from which Unionism could draw.[117]

Brookeborough had successfully weathered the arrival in power of Labour and the onset of the welfare state. Unionism now faced new threats on both the economic and political fronts that were beyond him. His success in extracting resources in the 1950s had reflected his ability to argue that the security interests of the UK as a whole would be threatened by economic decline in Northern Ireland and the possible political unrest it would stimulate. His charm and strong familial links with the metropolitan elite had helped Ulster's case at Westminster. By the end of the decade, with signs of the IRA's defeat and a new and apparently more pragmatic nationalism in the South, British governments had less reason to be concerned about the political and security implications of the North's unemployment figures. At the same time, Brookeborough's old allies were passing from the scene, and he was increasingly perceived in London as a conservative obstacle to the modernization of the province's politics and better relations with Dublin.

In 1961 he had been able to extract a joint-study group of Stormont and Westminster officials chaired by Sir Robert Hall to look once again at unemployment. The Northern Ireland members suggested that the Treasury provide an employment subsidy to all manufacturing concerns in Northern Ireland, but the idea was summarily dismissed.[118] When the *Hall Report* was published in October 1962, making it clear that there was a marked reluctance to grant more special assistance to bail Stormont out of a local political crisis, Brookeborough was finished. His successor would replace demands for short-term palliatives with ambitious plans for regional planning and modernization. Unfortunately, the energy and ingenuity that were used to transform thinking on economic policy were not extended to the area of community relations.

6. Expansion: Ireland 1959–1973

Free Trade and Programming

An analysis of Anglo-Irish economic relations prepared by British officials in 1960 depicted Lemass's succession to de Valera as a political watershed:

With the ending of Mr De Valera's lengthy dominance of the Irish political scene and the emergence of Mr Lemass, himself a businessman, at the head of a more business-like administration, the political atmosphere in the South is changing. The spirit of 1916 and 1922 is on the wane. While it is too much to expect that any political leader in the Republic would ever abandon the hope that Partition will one day cease, Mr Lemass has been realistic enough to admit that this must be a long term objective.

It was much less optimistic about the Republic's economic prospects:

Their efforts to diversify their economy by the development of secondary industry have had only limited success. They depend, and are likely to continue to depend for as far ahead as can be seen, on selling their agricultural goods to the United Kingdom, but their prospects of expanding their market here are very poor . . . it is impossible to be optimistic about the Republic's economic future.[1]

What has subsequently become seen as the 'Lemass–Whitaker watershed' in the economic history of the Republic was also less than obvious to most of the state's citizens at the time. During a symposium on Whitaker's *Economic Development*, one economist pointed out that, outside of a small circle in Dublin, the impact of the document's publication had been extremely limited. It had done little to lift the mood of despondency and loss of confidence that had settled on the nation.[2] Trade unionists criticized Whitaker for his refusal to put job creation as the primary objective of the development programme. Certainly there was little to spark popular enthusiasm in *Economic Development*. It was no selling point to inform the public that the implementation of the programme would lead to a doubling of national income after thirty-five years.[3] Although it was soon evident to informed observers that the repeal of restrictions on foreign investment was bringing a rapid influx of capital from the US and Europe, there was little sign that the new mood of optimism amongst sections of the political, industrial and financial elite was perco-lating down to the broader population.

Lemass's reconsideration of the economic nationalist regime was threat-ening for employers and workers in the many sections of Irish industry that would find it difficult to compete with imports if there were a substantial reduction in the protective tariffs they enjoyed. Yet Lemass was aware that the creation of the European Economic Community and Britain's attitude to it would have profound implications for the Republic. Britain initially attempted to organize a rival group of countries to the EEC within a European Free Trade Area (EFTA). This threatened the privileged access of Irish agricultural exports to the British market, and in response in 1959 Lemass had opened negotiations with Harold Macmillan's government to try to achieve a radical revision of the frame-work governing Anglo-Irish trade. In return for the extension of the British system of price support to Irish farmers, he offered the removal of tariff barriers against British goods. However, pressure from British farmers and the Northern Ireland government blocked his proposals.

This did nothing to blunt the drive to liberalize the Irish economy, for it was soon apparent that Britain was reconsidering its attitude to the EEC, which meant Ireland had no option but to follow. As Lemass had explained to British officials in 1960, he 'did not believe that small countries could stand alone and the Republic had no alternative but to link her economy with that of the United Kingdom'.[4] With 90 per cent of its agricultural exports and 70 per cent of its exports of manufactured goods going to the UK, it would have been impossible for the Republic to consider joining the EEC if Britain had maintained its original scep-tical position. In July 1961 Lemass announced that if Britain applied to join, Ireland would apply too. It was being made clear to Irish industry that the days of a protected home market were numbered.

Resistance came from both the Federation of Irish Industry (FII) and Lemass's old department. Officials at Industry and Commerce argued that many of the 65,000 workers in the main protected industries would be vulnerable and that tariffs would have to be maintained for at least another decade.[5] However, some industrialists accepted that a phasing out of tariffs was inevitable. In 1960 Lemass had told the FII that it should study the problems that different sections of industry would face with freer trade. The organization had employed Garret FitzGerald, a young economics lecturer and financial journalist, to carry out a pilot study of the highly protected woollen and worsted industry. His report concluded that, unless there were drastic improvements in efficiency and marketing, the industry would face serious difficulties under free trade conditions and many firms would disappear.[6] This survey encouraged the government to create the Committee on Industrial Organization (CIO) in 1961. Composed initially of representatives of industry, officials and independent experts, it was extended to include workers' representatives and became the first of a number of tripartite institutions that Lemass was to use very successfully to build a national consensus around themes of economic modernization, growth and planning.

The CIO surveyed twenty-two industries employing about half of the total manufacturing workforce in the Republic. Its report painted a depressing picture. While there were some sectors that hoped to hold their own in a free trade situation, many more (including footwear, knitwear, wool, shirts, paper, steel and electrical equipment) expected considerable losses and the possibility of going out of business.[7] Lemass's response was that only systematic tariff reduction would provide the necessary drive and discipline to ensure improvements in efficiency and an expansion of exports. Although this harsh message was somewhat softened by the fact that the government committed itself to a phased reduction, starting with across-the-board cuts of 10 per cent in 1963 and 1964, there was no concealing that by the end of the decade, or soon after, Irish industry would have to sink or swim in a free trade environment. But fundamental to pacifying industry and possible doubters in his own party was the clear commitment that liberalization did not mean laissez-faire. An Industrial Reorganization Branch was created in Industry and Commerce, and substantial amounts of financial and technical assistance were to be provided for those industries that demonstrated a commitment and a capacity to change.

De Gaulle's veto on Britain's application in 1963 did not ease the pressure for change. Lemass returned to his earlier objective of a free trade agreement with Britain as a transitional measure towards eventual EEC membership. Although the Conservative government remained unsympathetic, the return of Labour in October 1964 was seen in Dublin as propitious. This initial optimism suffered a blow when, owing to a balance of payments crisis, the British imposed a 15 per cent levy on all imports with the exception of food and raw materials. However, Lemass skilfully used Wilson's desire for a breakthrough in Anglo-Irish relations to reopen the trade question, and on 14 December 1965 the Anglo-Irish Free Trade Agreement was signed in London.

The Agreement seemed to some traditional nationalists a gross betrayal of Fianna Fáil's founding principles. In the Dáil, Seán Treacy, a Labour TD from the republican heartland of County Kerry, attacked Fianna Fáil for reneging on its principles: '[they] have perpetrated an act of union with Britain more final, binding and irrevocable than the Charter of Henry II or the Act of Union.'[8] There was also opposition within the Department of External Affairs, which had produced a paper on the political implications of the Agreement arguing that 'the resulting concentration of our trade "eggs" in one basket would inevitably have an inhibiting effect on our freedom of action in the political field and would expose us to greater political pressure by Britain.'[9]

Lemass displayed both his underlying radical purpose and his finely honed political skills in jettisoning economic nationalism. He contributed powerfully to a recasting of Irish nationalist discourse, which has been well summed up by Peter Mair:

Whereas in the earlier period the national interest had been seen to demand political, cultural and economic isolation, in the later period it came to imply the achievement of material prosperity. Independence *per se* was no longer sufficient, rather economic and social self-respect were necessary . . . Nationalism remained a key motif, but by the 1960s the success of the nationalist endeavour was to be measured in wealth and economic growth rather than in cultural or territorial integrity.[10]

Soon after becoming Taoiseach, Lemass had defined the supreme national task as 'to consolidate the economic foundation of our political independence . . . it should be no exaggeration to say that our survival as an independent state depended on our success.'[11] Economic success became the supreme national value because only through it could national unity be restored. While his approach to Ulster unionism and the northern state could be refreshingly revisionist, he did not hesitate to use anti-partitionism as a means of giving a nationalist veneer to policies that could have appeared heretical to traditional Fianna Fáil supporters. Economic success in the Republic would remove one of the main unionist objections to unification:

There are people today in the north-east of the country who say that we are here paying an uneconomic price for our freedom. We have got to prove them wrong. We have got to demonstrate that we can bring about a higher level of achievement and greater progress with freedom than without it.[12]

By 1961, with the first clear evidence of the success of the new policies, Lemass was publicly contrasting the 'dynamism' of the South with
the North's growing unemployment problem and Brookeborough's resort
to begging missions to London:

We are proving that there are better ways of dealing with the country's
problems than by sending deputations to plead for help from others. The
bread of charity is never very filling. I am convinced that the success of our
economic programme can be a decisive factor in bringing about the change
of outlook which the North requires and the discarding of all the old falla-
cies and prejudices on which partition has rested.[13]

Traditional territorial nationalism was also used to disarm the criticisms
of tariff reductions that came from large sections of Irish industry. In
advance of any free trade agreement with Britain, Lemass offered tariff
reductions to northern manufacturers, to the chagrin of their counterparts in the Republic. When delegations of angry southern industrialists
met Jack Lynch, the Minister for Industry and Commerce, they were
rebuffed and told that the reductions 'would be a considerable help in
reducing suspicion and advancing national unity'.[14]

The shift in nationalist discourse was impelled by harsh economic realities, but it was soon rooted in economic success. By December 1962 a
delighted Lemass could boast in the Dáil that 'in many industrial occupations [there was] a scarcity of workers and in many areas full employment
had been realised.'[15] The performance of the Republic's economy for the
next decade would continue to justify his early optimism. During the
period 1959–72 manufacturing output increased by 5.9 per cent per
annum, as compared with an overall growth rate of just under 4 per cent.
Employment in manufacturing rose from 169,000 to 212,000. The pattern
of the export trade showed a marked change: in 1960 industrial goods
represented only one third of total exports, but by 1972 this share had
risen to 55 per cent. An important source of change was the influx of
foreign capital attracted by the government's relaxation of controls, its
commitment to join the EEC, its generous tax allowances, and other
inducements and wages that were low by American and West European
levels. By 1973 new foreign-owned firms employed some 40,000 workers,
or one fifth of the manufacturing workforce in the Republic.[16]

Economic historians sceptical of the role played by *Economic
Development* and the *First Programme for Economic Expansion* have
pointed out that during the 1960s international trade was buoyant, the

terms of trade moved in Ireland's favour, and the doubling of the British rate of growth between 1959 and 1963 had a locomotive effect on the Irish economy.[17] It is also true that moves to open up the economy and attract foreign capital had been initiated by the two inter-party governments. Yet, it is difficult to deny the elements of decisiveness and coherence that Lemass gave to the process of reintegrating the Republic into the international economy. Perhaps even more important was his determination that Ireland's development strategy would not be based on a liberal model but would take a semi-corporatist form involving partnership between the state, trade unions and employers.

The reunification of the trade union movement in the Irish Congress of Trade Unions in 1959 encouraged Lemass to return to some of the themes of social partnership that he had first raised during the Emergency. Some of his own close associates were critical of his allegedly benign and uncritical attitude towards organized labour. In fact, his approach towards the Irish trade union movement, whatever its limitations as an economic strategy, was very much a vital political resource. It enabled him to re-establish Fianna Fáil's image as a broadly progressive force, something that had been severely damaged by its uninspiring performance in government and opposition during the 1950s. Gone was de Valera's emphasis on the virtue of frugality: as Lemass told delegates to the 1959 Ard-Fheis, 'We used to say that we preferred freedom in a hair shirt to the fleshpots of serfdom, but that is not a choice we have to make. I believe in the beneficial force of disciplined nationalism.'[18]

Although there had been no trade union involvement in the formulation of the *First Programme*, the leader of the largest union in the country, the Irish Transport and General Workers' Union, praised the government for 'its imagination, initiative, enthusiasm and tendency to long term planning which has attracted many new industries to the country'.[19] The executive of ICTU was pleased to be wooed by Lemass through involvement in the CIO, in trade union advisory councils set up to consider problems of industrial adaptation to free trade, and, from 1963, in a new tripartite forum of unions, employers and government, the National Industrial Economic Council (NIEC), chaired by T. K. Whitaker.[20]

A central purpose of Irish corporatism, as of its European counterparts, was to control wage demands that could threaten Irish industry's competitiveness. In the period 1960–64 unit wage costs rose by 17 per cent in the Republic, compared to 7 per cent in Britain.[21] Trade union leaders were expected, in return for a consultative role in economic policy-making and the promise of real economic and social gains for

their members, to deliver wage discipline. From this perspective Irish
corporatism failed. The removal of the fear of unemployment led to a
new confidence amongst rank-and-file trade unionists who were determined to press for higher wages and shorter hours. There was a sharp
upturn in industrial conflict: in 1964 Ireland topped the world league
in man-hours lost through strikes.[22] Lemass's frustration with what he
complained was the 'lack of cohesion and authority in the trade union
movement'[23] had initially encouraged an attempt to impose discipline.
A White Paper, *Closing the Gap*, published in February 1963, proposed
that the Employer–Labour Conference produce binding guidelines for
wage increases and a pay freeze in the public sector. The sharp response
from the ICTU, which withdrew its representatives from all government-
sponsored bodies including the CIO and the Employer–Labour
Conference, produced a rapid retreat, and the rest of Lemass's premiership would see little application of the stick but much of the carrot in
the government's approach to the unions. He was soon to declare that
national policy should take a 'shift to the left' and promised more government measures to ensure the translation of economic progress into
improved social conditions in areas such as education, health and state
benefits. This was more than rhetoric: social spending by government,
which had declined from 14.8 per cent of GNP in 1952 to 13.7 per
cent in 1962, rose to 16.6 per cent in 1966.[24] Lemass was also involved
in the negotiations that led to the first national wage agreement in 1964,
which some of his critics in the party regarded as too generous.

The political pay-off for Lemass's identification with economic
programming and his positive relationship with the leadership of the
trade union movement was seen in the 1965 general election. In his first
election as Taoiseach in 1961 it had been too early for the gains of the
new policies to be registered and, with a low turnout reflecting what
J. J. Lee calls 'uncertain public morale', Fianna Fáil's vote dropped from
48.3 to 43.8 per cent and its number of seats from seventy-eight to
seventy, leaving Lemass to lead a minority government.[25] However, in
the 1965 election its share of the vote rose to 47.4 per cent and its
number of seats to seventy-two, at a time when it faced the most
significant challenge from the Labour Party since 1943. It was the first
time in Fianna Fáil's history that it gained votes as an incumbent government after a full term of office.

But if the political achievement of Lemass was clear by the time of
his retirement in 1966, his economic legacy was more ambiguous. Those
who, like Whitaker, had doubts about his nudging of public policy to

the left seemed to draw increasing support from the evidence that economic growth was accompanied by strikes, wage inflation and increasingly large balance of payments deficits. Economic programming itself was being thrown into question by the widening gap between forecasts and results. The *First Programme* had avoided setting specific targets; the *Second Programme*, launched in 1963, did commit itself to more precise objectives, including a net increase in employment of 81,000 by 1970 and a reduction of net emigration to 10,000 a year by the same date. While the forecasts for industrial growth were fulfilled, the continuing problems of agriculture meant unemployment remained higher than expected, and emigration, which had fallen in the early 1960s, rose again in 1965 to over 20,000 and did not fall below 15,000 for any year between 1963 and 1967.[26] Government expenditure also rose faster than planned. As a result of these major discrepancies the *Second Programme* was brought to a premature conclusion and replaced by a (supposedly more realistic) *Third Programme* to cover the period 1969–72. Given the rapid economic transformations that the Republic was undergoing in the 1960s and its more open relation to the international economy, the whole programming project had an air of unreality about it. Yet, at its heart was Lemass's search for a development project based on class collaboration rather than on conflict. This would leave a lasting imprint on public policy in the South.

Lemass and Northern Ireland

Lemass's reputation as a supreme iconoclast, as a radical force making an often reluctant party substitute reality for fantasy, has been seen as exemplified in his policy towards Northern Ireland. Indeed, J. J. Lee has argued that he was the first Taoiseach actually to have a northern policy.[27] The core of this policy was constructive engagement with Stormont, and its symbolic highpoint was his meeting with Terence O'Neill at Stormont on 12 January 1965, the first such meeting since 1922. However, there were important elements of continuity with his predecessor's approach to Northern Ireland.

It is true that, as Jonathan Bardon states, Lemass abandoned the overt irredentism of previous governments.[28] However, some of what have been seen as his innovations – for example, the idea that northerners could be attracted only by a higher standard of living in the Republic – had already been articulated by de Valera, who had many other subtle

and even heretical views on the subject. Despite the traditional nationalist fixation on Britain's primary responsibility for ending partition, de
Valera as he approached retirement had shifted the focus, telling a group
of American journalists in 1957, 'The solution of the partition question
was strictly an Irish problem, one that must be worked out between
Irish people in the north and south. It must be achieved on a satisfactory basis for both sides.'[29] This directly anticipated one of the central
themes in Lemass's discourse on Northern Ireland. In his Ard-Fheis speech
in 1957 de Valera also raised the notion of functional cooperation that
would dominate Lemass's approach: 'the proper way to try to solve the
problem of partition was to endeavour to have as close relations as possible
with the people of the Six Counties and get them to combine with us
in matters of common concern.'[30]

If Lemass produced little that was new in the way of ideas on Northern
Ireland, his premiership was notable for a serious attempt to implement
those that de Valera had articulated but had done little about for fear
of annoying the more republican section of the party – above all his
veteran Minister for External Affairs, Frank Aiken. His more active
approach to Northern Ireland was in part a reflection of his long immer-
sion in economic and industrial policy, which made him prone to see
the radical policy reversals of the late 1950s as creating the material basis
for political accommodation. It has been already noted how he used
the supreme importance attached to Irish unity in Fianna Fáil's traditional ideology to sell EEC membership to the party. However, there
can be no doubting the genuineness of his belief that the dismantling
of customs barriers associated with the European project would have
major political spillover effects: 'In the long term economic considerations influence and determine political arrangements. The identity of
economic interest in the two areas into which Ireland is now divided
will, in time, bring about political unity.'[31] Although he was also prepared
to recognize that the division on the island was more than a tariff barrier
– 'it represents a spiritual cleavage which has its origins deep in our
history' – there could be no doubting his belief that religious and cultural
divisions were increasingly anachronistic survivals that would be
displaced by economic modernization. His own private religious agnos-
ticism and his renowned lack of interest in the Irish language and the
other cultural accoutrements of Irish identity,[32] so important to de
Valera, caused him to underestimate the power of more primordial voices
in both nationalism and loyalism.

His optimism was partly based on the positive response that some northern manufacturers had given to his proposal for a North–South free trade agreement. Despite the rejection of the proposal by Brookeborough,[33] a number of northern businesses ignored Stormont and approached the Ministry of Industry and Commerce in Dublin directly to negotiate reductions. Eventually Brookeborough was forced to modify his line and declare publicly that he would not stand in the way of manufacturers who sought better treatment from Dublin.[34] Lemass was impressed with this Ulster bourgeois pragmatism and tried to encourage it as much as possible, asking the state airline, Aer Lingus, to consider ordering aircraft from Short Brothers and Harland, and Irish Shipping to encourage Harland and Wolff to tender for vessels it needed.[35] The optimism that pervaded his approach to the North was based partly on the apparent contrast between the difficult conditions facing the province's staple industries in the early 1960s and the first signs of economic expansion in the South. The publication of the *Hall Report* and its rejection of what he referred to as 'begging missions seeking British subsidies' were seen as prompting 'enlightened opinion' in Northern Ireland to reconsider the value of the continued division of the island.[36]

But, as some contemporary critics pointed out, there was a fundamental contradiction in Lemass's approach to the North. This was evident in the first major statement he made on Northern Ireland when he participated in an Oxford Union debate on partition on 15 October 1959. The speech certainly impressed some in the British political elite with its support for 'the growth of a practical system of co-operation between the two areas even in advance of any political arrangement' and the argument that 'quite apart from any views one may hold about the eventual reunification of Ireland, is it not commonsense that the two existing communities in our small island should seek every opportunity of working together in practical matters for their mutual and common good?' He had also warned that 'we cannot expect speedy results: the barriers of fear and suspicion in the minds of partitionists are too strong to be demolished quickly.'[37] Yet he also made it clear that, although he believed the fundamental barriers to unity were internal ones, the British government could and should undo its historic responsibility for partition by declaring that it would like to see partition ended 'by agreement among the Irish'. Pressure on the British to declare in favour of the Irish nationalist project could only undermine the real efforts that were made to foster practical schemes of cooperation with Stormont.

While Brookeborough was in power and insisting on the Republic's

full constitutional recognition of Northern Ireland as a condition of
any North–South cooperation, there could be little progress. Terence
O'Neill initially maintained the same position but was under some
pressure from the Conservative government to respond to Lemass's
overtures.[38] With even the former Secretary to the Northern Ireland
cabinet, Sir Robert Gransden, saying in private that he thought the
demand for constitutional recognition 'completely unrealistic',[39] Lemass
went some way to accommodate O'Neill. He used a Fianna Fáil dinner
in Tralee to make his most important speech on partition. In it he
declared that he recognized that 'the government and parliament there
exist with the support of a majority in the Six County area' and
insisted that 'the solution of the problem of partition is one to be
found in Ireland by Irishmen.'[40] Although he also referred to Northern
Ireland as an 'artificial area', the speech represented a significant shift.
As Robert Savage has noted, Lemass's recognition of the government
and parliament of Northern Ireland 'was a significant gesture to
Unionists and an extraordinary statement for a Fianna Fáil leader to
make'.[41]

O'Neill gave a guarded welcome, describing the speech as 'not without
courage', but cautioned that 'As long as every gesture of friendship and
every possible co-operation was subordinate to a long-term undermining
of the constitutional position, so long would they have to moderate with
a good deal of caution their wish for co-operation with their neigh-
bours.'[42] Lemass's response was to ask his ministers for proposals for an
Irish agenda at civil service level on cross-border cooperation, thus putting
aside the demand for a summit with all the difficulties that that could
create for O'Neill.[43] The implication of all this was what the Secretary
to the Department of the Taoiseach called a 'new departure' in the policy
on partition, which would have at its core two elements: 'to disregard
London as a factor in maintaining partition' and 'to concentrate on the
Parliament and people in the Six Counties'.[44] However, the likelihood
of a positive response from O'Neill was undermined by a number of
speeches Lemass made on a visit to the US less than a month later. In
an address to the National Press Club in Washington, he called on the
British government to issue a statement that it would welcome an opportunity to end partition 'when Irishmen wanted to get rid of it'.[45] Later,
at the United Nations, he repeated the request and added that 'he believed
that the circumstances of partition were also under review in Britain.'[46]

So on the one hand Lemass pursued North–South cooperation, while
on the other he challenged the legitimacy and permanence of the state

with which he was proposing to cooperate. These conflicting strands of his position reflected the substantial resistance from the more nationalistic elements within Fianna Fáil to 'concessions' to the Stormont regime. His Minister for External Affairs, Frank Aiken, was a bastion of traditional anti-partitionism and, given his closeness to de Valera, a possible focus of resistance to any new direction on northern policy. It was Aiken who insisted on seeing the North as an imperialist vestige that Britain should look at in the context of its post-war decolonization process.[47] Lemass's policy of discouraging the civil service and the Republic's radio and television services from referring to Northern Ireland as 'The Six Counties' was not popular with some of his colleagues,[48] and his officials reported some political resistance from ministers to his proposals for North–South discussions at a civil service level.[49] Too radical a shift on Northern Ireland policy could have had severe political repercussions within a minority Fianna Fáil government at a time when he was proposing a radical reversal of economic nationalism. The result was that when O'Neill decided to meet Lemass it was more in response to pressure from Harold Wilson than to any positive inducement from Dublin.

But if Lemass's northern policy only partially accommodated unionist concerns, it did even less for Stormont's minority. The Taoiseach regarded northern nationalism as being as conservative and sectarian as the regime it opposed. In a speech to students at Queen's University after he retired, Lemass attributed a part of the responsibility for the North's problems to the 'narrow attitudes' of the Nationalist Party,[50] and in a subsequent interview he commented of northern nationalists that 'for them the day partition ended would be the day they would get their foot on the throat of the Orangemen.'[51] The sort of trips made by Conor Cruise O'Brien in the early 1950s to meet northern nationalists had been discontinued as the official anti-partition campaign had waned. By 1960 there had not been a visit to Northern Ireland by an official from External Affairs for over four years. Eddie McAteer complained that Dáil deputies had more contact with parliamentarians abroad than with nationalists in Stormont.[52] The attempt to develop functional cooperation with Stormont discouraged visits that unionists might see as destabilizing, and a request from External Affairs for a resumption of visits 'if only to show the Six-County people that we are still with them' seems to have been ignored.[53]

What little interest Lemass had in northern nationalism seems to have focused on any signs of fresh thinking, particularly those associated with the formation of National Unity, a new grouping of younger nationalists critical of the Nationalist Party, in 1959. He used Erskine Childers, a Protestant and the son of one of the first republicans executed during the Civil War, as his most direct link with developments in the North. This in itself was revealing, as he regarded Childers as a lightweight and after inheriting him as Minister for Lands demoted him twice within the space of two years.[54] Nevertheless, Childers's advice could only have encouraged the Taoiseach to continue with his focus on improving relations with Stormont while largely ignoring the concerns of the minority. After a visit to Belfast in March 1961 Childers wrote to Lemass of the 'utter breakdown of the Nationalist Party' and went on to give an analysis of the discrimination issue that was at stark variance with the traditional nationalist perspective:

Discrimination is decreasing, although it still exists. We hear of the local authorities who show discrimination in the allocation of houses, but there are quite a number who are not guilty of this practice, about whom we hear nothing. Discrimination in industry varies enormously. Some of the new English and American industries permit no discrimination whatsoever; in some cases they have been suborned by local pressure. In the case of the older industries, a few are absolutely fair and square in their attitude. Others employ numbers according to the population in the district to make sure that no Catholic men ever become foremen. In fairness to managements in some industries, it would be the men themselves who would create the trouble and who exercise pressure through the shop stewards regardless of what the managers think.[55]

Within the Department of External Affairs there was little stomach for attempts by northern nationalists to raise the discrimination issue. Much of the material that had been used during the anti-partition campaign was out of date, but when McAteer approached the Department with material for a new pamphlet the response was dismissive. A senior official was scathing:

I must assume that the facts and figures it mentions are correct. But I ask myself what is the purpose of the pamphlet? There is no need to tell Irish Nationalists. They have been given the facts over and over again in previous anti-partition propaganda. If the pamphlet is directed at a non-Irish audience I very much doubt if it will get farther than their waste-paper baskets. I am afraid it is regrettable but true that very little, if any, interest in the problems of the Northern Ireland minority is taken outside Ireland.[56]

As the first stirrings of the civil rights movement emerged in Northern Ireland, Dublin was if anything even less concerned with the discrimination issue than was London. After the summit with O'Neill, Lemass's priority was the consolidation of new links with the northern regime in areas such as trade and tourism. It was made plain to McAteer that he should not look to Dublin but lead his party into a more constructive relationship with the northern state, and it was as a result of this pressure that the Nationalist Party at last agreed to become the official opposition at Stormont. The long-term significance of this approach was brutally spelt out by a Dublin official in response to demands from some in the Nationalist Party for support: 'The alternative to taking any action at the present time must inevitably be that the gap between the Nationalists in the North and the people here will grow wider. This development will of course force the Nationalists to adopt policies which are fully in keeping with their status in the Six Counties.'[57] The next few years would see the frustration of this southern desire for the minority to sort out its relationship with Stormont under its own steam, while those who had had deep reservations about the Lemass approach tried to use the northern crisis to overthrow the whole edifice of partition.

Politics and Social Change in the 1960s

John Horgan has described the 1960s as 'socially turbulent years',[58] and Kieran Allen has claimed that the Republic was significantly affected by the wave of political and cultural radicalization associated with the anti-Vietnam war movement and the student uprisings of 1968.[59] While in any international framework of comparison this might seem an exaggeration, there is no question that, after the stagnation of the previous decade, the governments in the Republic faced an unprecedented range of traditional and new demands. Industrial militancy, while not a new phenomenon, did develop an intensity that led to the decade being labelled a period of 'unparalleled turbulence in Irish industrial relations'.[60] The multiplicity of trade unions made any national agreement negotiated between the ICTU and employers difficult to enforce at a time when many groups of workers were keen to use improved economic conditions to extract the maximum that the market could bear. A sectional concern with the defence of pay relativities was an important source of militancy, and there was also considerable tension between groups of rank-and-file trade unionists and national leaderships regarded as too inclined to compromise with employers and the state.

The authoritarian streak in Fianna Fáil's relation to the unions, first evident during the Emergency, reappeared when in 1965 a breakaway union of telephonists began to picket telephone exchanges to support a demand for recognition. Lemass lambasted these 'anti-state activities', and strikers were jailed for breaching a government injunction against picketing. When their comrades attempted to protest outside the Dáil, the government did not hesitate to use the Offences against the State Act to ban such activities. In 1966 a strike by fitters in the state Electricity Supply Board (ESB) was met by legislation outlawing strike action in the industry and providing for heavy fines against both unions and individual strikers. This produced a major confrontation in 1968, when the legislation was used to jail more than fifty strikers in a dispute over pay.[61] The culmination of this period of unrestrained wage bargaining was the maintenance craftsmen's strike in early 1969, which lasted for six weeks and was a source of unprecedented bitterness not simply between workers and employers but between the strikers and other unions and the leaders of the ICTU.

Some on the Irish left interpreted this industrial militancy as a potential threat to capitalist rule.[62] This inflated its political significance. Just as in Northern Ireland militant trade union consciousness was quite compatible with traditional political affiliations, a Gallup survey found that only 37 per cent of trade unionists supported Labour.[63] However, there was some spillover from industrial militancy into politics. Specifically, there was a substantial increase in the size and self-confidence of the Irish Labour Party. As Emmet O'Connor has noted, William Norton, who resigned as leader in 1960, had come to personify 'the achingly, conservative, clientelist style of Labour deputies'.[64] The dispiriting experience of the second inter-party government had left Labour, after the 1957 election, with 9 per cent of the vote and twelve Dáil deputies. Its only secure electoral base was amongst agricultural labourers and other rural workers in small towns and villages in Munster and Leinster. It had only one seat in Dublin.[65] Like Norton, most of its deputies were trade union officials whose main focus was on their union business and their constituencies. Conservative, Catholic and fiercely anti-intellectual, they showed little interest in or concern about the national profile of the party or the need to seek new bases of support.

Norton's successor, Brendan Corish, had a background that was typical of the rural and familial basis of much of the Labour support at the time. He had won his Wexford constituency in a by-election caused by the death of his father and during the 1950s had shown little sign of a desire to swim against the stream, declaring in 1953 'I am an Irishman second; I am a Catholic first' and defending those involved in the Fethard-on-Sea boycott of Protestants in 1957.[66] However, as Labour leader he displayed some capacity to transcend his background. He encouraged the party to adopt a go-it-alone electoral strategy, rejecting future participation in a coalition government. The shift in Labour's ideological image was done in a gingerly fashion, with Corish explaining that Labour's socialism was a 'Christian' variety, and it would be towards the end of the decade before he dared to proclaim that 'the Seventies will be Socialist.' Yet there was evidence that, in the Dublin area in particular, Labour was trying hard to attract socially conscious sections of the middle class and a new generation of intellectuals and radicals through a more leftist profile.

Corish was heavily influenced by the new secretary of the party, Brendan Halligan.[67] Halligan's key strategic idea was that Labour should force the two larger parties to coalesce by itself adopting a distinctive left-wing identity. Arguing that the two main parties had lost their *raison d'être* as the generation formed by 1916 and the Civil War faded from the scene, he identified a historic opportunity for the Labour Party to realign the political system along a more 'normal' left/right cleavage. Halligan was also at the centre of efforts to modernize the party. There was a serious effort to expand the number of branches: Labour in 1964 had only 248 branches, as compared with over 1,700 for Fianna Fáil and 600 for Fine Gael. By 1969 the party had 500 branches nationally and the number in Dublin had risen from twenty-nine to eighty-three.[68] The party's traditional image as an appendage of the trade union movement was also undermined by the recruitment of a number of prominent intellectuals, such as the Trinity academics Justin Keating and David Thornley, and with the return to Ireland, after a high-profile diplomatic and academic career, of Conor Cruise O'Brien. By the time of the 1969 election only a fifth of Labour candidates were trade union officials, while the largest category was 'professionals' – in the 1961 election only one Labour candidate had been from this category.[69]

In the first two elections under Corish's leadership, Labour made steady progress, with 11.6 per cent of the national vote and sixteen seats in 1961 and 15.4 per cent and twenty-two seats in 1965. Corish and his young advisers became convinced that the rapidity of economic and social change in the Republic made a major breakthrough a real possibility. The 1969 'New Republic' manifesto captured the mood of optimism:

The politics of the old Republic are over. The choice is no longer between two identical parties, divided only by the tragedy of history. The choice is now between the old Republic of bitterness, stagnation and failure, represented by the two Civil War parties, and the New Republic of opportunity, change and hope, represented by the Labour Party.[70]

Expectations were high, and there was talk of a possible Labour government. In fact, the result of the election was a shattering disappointment and marked the end of the go-it-alone policy. Labour's share of the vote increased to 17 per cent, but this reflected a substantial increase in the number of candidates from forty-four in 1965 to ninety-nine in 1969. Overall the party lost four seats, with gains in greater Dublin being overshadowed by disastrous results in traditional rural bastions.

Labour's optimism had had some basis, but its main defect lay in an overly unilinear view of the process of economic and social modernization in Ireland that ignored the continuing strength of rural and small-town Catholic traditionalism. Its activists blamed a 'red smear' campaign carried on by Fianna Fáil. There had certainly been such a campaign, with Labour being accused of wanting to introduce 'Cuban socialism' in Ireland. Visions of Labour imposing collective farms on the small farmers of Kerry and other areas may well have lost some Labour TDs crucial votes. More significant would have been the Catholic Church's long-standing identification of 'socialism' with atheism and its associated immoralities. One Fianna Fáil candidate in Mayo, not content with the totally unfounded claim that Labour in power would legislate for abortion and divorce, added, 'it would be great for the fellow who wanted a second wife every night.'[71] But the problem with the 'red smear' argument was that many of the party's own rural TDs were also dismayed at the radical noises coming from Dublin and did all they could to dissociate themselves from the party's national campaign, fighting the election on purely local issues and their record of constituency service. In a society in transition Labour's new-found radicalism would have disconcerted many of its traditional supporters no matter what Fianna Fáil chose to allege about it.

While a radicalized Labour Party was vulnerable in many constituencies – according to the 1971 census only 52 per cent of the Republic's population lived in towns with a population of 1,500 or more – it did have a substantial potential base of support in Dublin. Conor Cruise O'Brien, as a cosmopolitan intellectual, a divorcé who had remarried, and a supporter of the Republic establishing diplomatic links with Cuba, was the epitome of Labour's threat to traditional Catholic values. Yet, standing for the first time in Dublin North-east, he came second to Charles Haughey, the leading Fianna Fáil TD in the constituency.[72] The imperviousness of a sizeable section of Dublin's electorate to a traditionalist message can be explained by a number of factors. Although government policy aimed at dispersing industrial development away from the east coast and the Dublin area in particular, in the early 1970s just under a half of the total manufacturing employment was still in the greater Dublin area.[73] Economic expansion encouraged the self-confidence associated with union militancy, which strained Fianna Fáil's relation with sections of the working class to the benefit of Labour, and this was given concentrated expression in Dublin. It was also the case that a substantial amount of the new public sector employment, which expanded significantly in the 1960s, was located in Dublin. The decade saw the beginning of a long-term process of expansion of white-collar unionization and militancy in the public sector.

Expansion also lessened the pressure to emigrate and, as this had affected younger workers disproportionately, it increased the size of that section of the working class less prone than their parents to accept clerical direction.[74] Although by international standards the Republic in the 1960s was still an intensely Catholic country, there was some evidence of change. A 1962 survey into the attitudes of Dublin Catholics towards religion and clerical authority carried out for the ultra-orthodox Archbishop of Dublin, John Charles McQuaid, revealed sharp differences between those who had completed secondary education and the rest. Whereas an extraordinary 88 per cent of the sample endorsed the proposition that the Church was the greatest source of good in the country, an almost equally massive 83 per cent of the educated group disagreed with it.[75] In the early 1960s less than 20 per cent of schoolchildren went on to complete secondary education. By the end of the 1970s this had risen to just under 50 per cent.[76] This rise in participation in secondary education and an associated expansion of higher education did much to produce what Tom Garvin has called the 'post-Catholic and à la carte Catholic' segment of the population.[77]

In the early 1960s Lemass and other members of the political elite displayed a continuing willingness to indulge clerical pressure. A proposal from the Director of the National Library for a book-sharing arrangement with Trinity College, aimed at avoiding duplication and cutting costs, was submitted by Lemass to McQuaid for his opinion and dropped as soon as McQuaid opposed it. Similarly, an attempt by the Minister for Education to extend nationally an experiment in comprehensive schools begun in the western and border counties was threatened with opposition by McQuaid until he was reassured that they would be denominational, non-coeducational and managed by the parish priest.[78] But as the decade progressed there were some signs of a less deferential attitude. In part this reflected the more liberal environment encouraged by Pope John XXIII and the Second Vatican Council, which had opened in Rome in October 1962. Vatican II, with its emphasis on improving relations with the Protestant Churches and on a more demotic Catholicism, served to highlight the conservative, not to say reactionary, position of the Irish hierarchy and of McQuaid in particular.

Much of the change was an inevitable consequence of the radical turn in economic policy that was made at the end of the 1950s. The emphasis in *Economic Development* on the need for efficiency, competitiveness and quality raised major questions over the sustainability of the state's continued acquiescence in an educational system whose whole ethos was so heavily influenced by the non-material values of the Catholic Church. As late as 1962 the annual report of the Council of Education, the official advisory body representing teachers and the Catholic school authorities, was arguing that the principal objective of education was the religious and moral development of the child and that the aim of science teaching in secondary school 'is cultural rather than practical'.[79] It also dismissed the idea of universal secondary education as utopian. With the exception of a separate system of vocational schools providing technical education, secondary schools charged fees until the late 1960s. The result of this approach was evident in the stark contrast with Northern Ireland. While secondary school enrolments had doubled in the South between 1945 and 1963, there had been a more than fivefold increase in the North.[80]

Lemass and his Minister for Education, Patrick Hillery, initiated reform with the appointment of a small expert body, chaired by the economist Patrick Lynch, which produced the seminal *Investment in Education* report in 1965. Its chosen focuses – on the relation between the education system and the country's manpower requirements and the participation rates of different socio-economic groups – were an implicit challenge to the status quo and the Church's heavy investment in it. The state's increasing involvement in promoting change, which culminated in the introduction of free secondary education by Hillery's successor, Donogh O'Malley, in 1967, was one significant indication of the decline of the Church's hegemony in an area where its dominance had been hitherto uncontested.

Another such area was the censorship of books and films. Here the government's emphasis on Ireland's new openness to investment and trade and its desire to be a participant in the European project made it less willing to tolerate the widespread image of the Republic as existing in a backward, priest-ridden time warp. The strict censorship of films and books under legislation passed in the 1920s and concerned with anything 'subversive of public morality' and 'indecent or obscene' had been encountering increasing domestic criticism from the small Irish intelligentsia in the 1950s. The five-member Censorship of Publications Board had been reconstructed in 1957 in order to ensure a more liberal composition. However, the fact remained that previous decisions had resulted in many of the major literary works of the twentieth century being banned, including most of the best works of contemporary Irish writers.[81] Brian Lenihan, who became Minister for Justice in 1964, liberalized film censorship by the simple expedient of licensing films for viewing by persons above a certain age, and, in 1967, introduced legislation that provided for the unbanning of books after twelve years. The result was the release of over 5,000 titles. While the liberalism of the Irish censors still had very narrow limits, and novels that would be major literary successes in Britain in the 1960s like *The Country Girls* by Edna O'Brien and *The Dark* by John McGahern continued to be banned, it was increasingly the censors and not the authors and publishers who were on the defensive.

A far more potent threat to traditional values than the appearance of Steinbeck or Sartre in bookshops in Dublin, Cork and Galway was the arrival of television. From the early 1950s it had been possible to receive programmes from Britain and Northern Ireland in the border counties and along the east coast. A report prepared for the government in 1956 had estimated that 7,000 homes in the Republic had televisions. It warned about the dangers of cultural pollution, given that British programmes were 'governed by ideas that are wholly alien to the ordinary Irish home'. Particular exception was taken to the 'frank' treatment of sex and the emphasis on the royal family and the 'British way of life'.[82] A major motivation behind the setting up of an Irish television service in 1961 was therefore a traditionally nationalist and Catholic one. However, the strong opposition of Whitaker and the Department of Finance to a publicly funded service meant that the state broadcaster, RTÉ, was financed by advertising, and the dynamics of competition with the BBC and Ulster Television soon exerted more influence on production values than did moral protectionism.

By the end of 1962 there were 93,000 television licences in the state, and by 1970 the figure had soared to 438,000.[83] The relative inexperience of staff and the cost of making programmes meant that there was a substantial reliance on imports from Britain and the US. Combined with the influence of British television along the east coast and despite the aims of those who set it up, Irish television became a powerful force for the Anglo-Americanization of Irish popular culture. It also encouraged a more critical public discourse and a new openness to discussion of such issues as contraception and divorce on programmes including the phenomenally successful *Late Late Show*. Following trends in Britain there was a less cautious and deferential style in the handling of current affairs. In both countries the decade saw the emergence of political satire and a more daring and mocking mood that spread out from television to the staid preserve of radio and the print media. Lemass, who had seen in television a potent means of propagating the gospel of modernizing nationalism, was soon disturbed by programmes that, as he saw it, focused too much on the defects and shortcomings of the Republic. He intervened privately and occasionally in public to try to curb unruly broadcasters, but with little effect. Increasingly it became clear to all but the most obdurately reactionary politicians and clergy that the rules by which they exercised power and authority were being remade and that the mere invocation of the value of traditional forms of life and thought would be insufficient to defend them.

Factions in Fianna Fáil

Although television undoubtedly encouraged the long-term process of liberalization of Irish society, its capacity to bring almost instantaneous images of the flaring up of violence in Derry and Belfast in August 1969 into living rooms throughout the South provided a powerful impetus to a wave of territorial nationalism that seemed for a brief period to threaten the stability of the state. The northern eruption had all the more impact because of the effects it had on a governing party that was already showing signs of an unprecedented degree of internal division.

Lemass's approach to the leadership of party and government had differed starkly from that of de Valera. Whereas the latter had tended to deal with divisions through a process of avoidance or such extended discussion that unity was effected through boring dissidents into submission, Lemass's style was brusque and peremptory. The change of style was reflective of the much more radical and activist content of his government's programme of economic liberalization and modernization, which left less time to consider questions of party management at a time when some of Lemass's new departures were bound to cause internal conflict. The pursuit of a free trade agreement with Britain and the end of restrictions on foreign capital raised the hackles of the champions of protectionist economics in the party. The policy of détente with the Stormont regime was also deeply unsettling for those still loyal to the idea of it as an unjust Orange junta. Lemass's engagement with the leaders of Irish trade unionism annoyed sections of the party suspicious of what was perceived as an anti-rural and anti-farmer bias and produced the first cabinet resignation on a policy question in the party's history when his Minister for Agriculture, Patrick Smith, left the government in protest at its alleged capitulation to 'trade union tyranny'.[84]

On top of radical policy reversals, Fianna Fáil had entered the process of transition to a party leadership no longer sanctified by its participation in the Irish Revolution of 1916–23. Lemass had begun the process of organizational renewal following the defeat in the 1954 election, bringing in a potential replacement cadre for the 1916 generation. Some of these, including George Colley and Eoin Ryan, were the sons of the founding members of Fianna Fáil, while others, such as Brian Lenihan and Charles Haughey, were sons of republicans who had taken the Free State side during the Civil War. Together with Neil Blaney and Kevin Boland, they had revitalized the tired and complacent Fianna Fáil electoral machine. Haughey, Lenihan and the brilliant but undisciplined and alcoholic Donogh O'Malley were fervent supporters of Lemassian economics. This was probably sufficient in itself to arouse the suspicion and hostility of those, like Seán MacEntee and Frank Aiken, who had long harboured doubts about the compatibility of the Lemass project with traditional republican values. However, it was the flamboyant lifestyle of the group labelled the *Camorra* by James Dillon, the leader of Fine Gael, that caused most unease.[85] As the prosperity associated with economic expansion manifested itself in building and redevelopment programmes, property values rocketed, as did the fortunes of those unscrupulous enough to use their insider knowledge to buy land that they knew was destined for development.

Haughey, who had entered the Dáil as TD for Dublin North-east in 1957 and been appointed Minister for Justice at the age of thirty in 1961, was at the centre of rumours and allegations about what an opponent would later call 'low standards in high places'. Although the son-in-law of Lemass, his rapid promotion was a reflection of his undoubted abilities. Peter Berry, the formidable Secretary of the Department of Justice, declared him the best minister he had ever served.[86] But it was his connections with the worlds of business and property development, and his increasingly ostentatious lifestyle, that drew the most gossip. Haughey had bought his first racehorse in 1962 and by the end of the decade owned a number of them as well as a farm and one of the Blasket Islands off the Kerry coast, which became his holiday retreat. In 1969 he bought Abbeville in Kinsealy, County Dublin, an eighteenth-century mansion that had served as the summer home of several Lord-Lieutenants of Ireland, and with it a 250-acre estate.[87] Some senior members of Fianna Fáil shared Gerry Boland's view that Haughey 'would yet drag down the Party in the mire'.[88] Others such as Frank Aiken saw Haughey as the epitome of the 'materialistic' and 'de-nationalizing' effects of Lemass's leadership and wanted a successor who was truer to traditional republican values and not associated with what a survey of the decade referred to as 'an unsavoury get-rich-quick cabal . . . [with] the sleek Mercedes and mohair suits'.[89]

Lemass was subsequently criticized by MacEntee and other Fianna Fáil veterans for failing to provide for a smooth succession.[90] This criticism tended to ignore the degree to which the post-1966 divisions in the party had their origins in inevitable tensions generated by the policy departures of the late 1950s. Fianna Fáil's traditional depiction of itself as a national movement rather than as a mere political organization had as its corollary a strong emphasis on maintaining an outward show of disciplined unity, and many in the party found the idea of a succession race deeply unsettling. But if there had to be a contest, there was at least a reassuring absence of any conflict of ideas. No candidate issued a statement of principles or publicly identified himself with any policy positions. Of the two original front-runners, Haughey and George Colley, the *Irish Times* commented that while Haughey was 'the modern man, essentially pragmatic and business-minded', Colley was a 'chip off the traditionalist block'.[91] The central attraction of Colley to the party elders who supported him was that he was seen as hostile to what was perceived as Haughey's ruthless materialism. In fact, on central economic policy issues and on Northern Ireland there was no recorded difference of opinion between the two. Despite this, Lemass's original attempt to get either Dr Patrick Hillery or Jack Lynch interested in the succession may have reflected his fear that a Haughey/Colley contest would allow those traditionalists defeated in such key areas as free trade and Northern Ireland to stage a comeback.

Although Lynch had originally resisted Lemass's overtures, the decision of Neil Blaney to intervene in the contest brought further, and this time successful, pressure from the Taoiseach. A TD for the border constituency of Donegal, Blaney had little time for policies of *rapprochement* with Stormont, and Lemass was aghast when he became a candidate. Jack Lynch had entered the Dáil as a TD for Cork in 1948 at the age of thirty-one and had been appointed Minister for Education by de Valera when Fianna Fáil returned to power in 1957. Under Lemass he had been centrally associated with the new directions in economic policy, first as Minister for Industry and Commerce and from 1965 as Minister for Finance, where he had developed a very good personal relationship with T. K. Whitaker. He was a strong supporter of Lemass's overtures to O'Neill but lacked the protective shield of a revolutionary pedigree, although this was compensated for to some degree by his record of prowess in Gaelic games, where he had the unique achievement of winning six senior All-Ireland hurling championships in succession.[92] Promoted by Lemass as a unity candidate, Lynch was accepted on those terms by both Blaney and Haughey, who withdrew from the contest, and he easily defeated Colley by fifty-nine votes to nineteen in the election by the Fianna Fáil parliamentary party on 9 November 1966.

Lynch's initial reluctance to stand led the other candidates for the leadership to view him as a caretaker until the party got a leader more in tune with its traditions. Lynch's low-key style, a strong desire for consensus and his apparent lack of strong views on most issues led to the early years of his government being characterized by conservatism, lack of control over the cabinet and the loss of the momentum of the Lemass years. Symptomatic was the Taca episode. Taca (Irish for 'support') was a party organization created in 1966 with the object of raising money from the business community. Lemass had been involved in his own discreet fund-raising efforts in his later years, setting up a committee with John Reihill of the coal-importing family as chairman.[93] However, Taca, of which Haughey and Blaney were the foremost supporters, was a more brazen affair. Supporters were invited to join by making an annual payment of £100 per year towards the party's electoral fund, while the interest was used to fund dinners at which members of Taca could mix with cabinet ministers.[94]

Taca was seen by critics of Fianna Fáil as proof of the corruption of its founding principles, with Máirín de Búrca of Sinn Féin claiming that 'the selfless idealism of Easter Week has become the self-seeking degeneracy of Taca.'[95] Within the party Colley, who had not given up his leadership ambitions, openly criticized Taca and demanded that the party return to its original tradition of seeking 'justice for all sections of the community but with special concern for the small man, the small farmer, the urban working man and the clerk'.[96] The Taca episode may well have contributed to the depth of the government's defeat in the October 1968 referendum on a proposal to replace proportional representation with a simple majority system. That this was the first time since 1932 that the party had failed to get more than 40 per cent in a national poll and that many TDs and Senators had not campaigned for the change gave rise to much speculation about the future of Lynch's leadership.[97]

Fianna Fáil's victory in the 1969 election did much to shore up Lynch, in the short term at least. He won in partnership with Haughey, whom he had made director of elections. Choosing to deal with his most formidable potential leadership opponent by a strategy of generous accommodation, he had made him Minister for Finance and tolerated Taca until internal criticism led to its being phased out in 1968. The 1969 campaign combined Haughey and Blaney's brutal anti-communist assault on Labour with Lynch's low-key but effective series of visits to convents to deliver the same message. The campaign was noteworthy as the first in which a leader's telegenic qualities had an effect. For whatever reservations some of his colleagues and the party grass-roots had about Lynch's lack of decisiveness, his soft-spoken, 'honest Jack' image on television was successful with the electorate.[98] Relations between Lynch and Haughey were warm during the campaign, but within months of victory developments in Northern Ireland would open up a chasm between them.

The Arms Crisis

Soon after the outbreak of major disorder in Derry and Belfast in August 1969, a senior Irish official recalled a journalist's caustic comment that 'our mass media and general public opinion only discovered the Six

Counties on October 5 1968.'[99] There is little evidence that the political and administrative class was much better prepared. In retirement Lemass had become a member of the Dáil Committee on the Constitution, which he had initiated when still Taoiseach. Its report in 1967 was characterized by a realism that some Fianna Fáil fundamentalists found disturbing. It argued that, so far from looking provisional, partition had 'hardened to a degree which only the vaguest of optimists can think of as temporary',[100] and suggested that Article 3 of the Constitution, which laid legal claim to Northern Ireland, should be reformulated in less 'polemical' terms as an aspiration. Although Lynch sympathized with this approach, the strength of opposition within party and government dictated that nothing was done. When T. K. Whitaker, in his final year as Secretary to the Department of Finance, wrote to Charles Haughey, his minister, arguing the advantages of a recasting of Articles 2 and 3 in improving relations with unionists, Haughey's response was vehemently republican, emphasizing that there was no moral objection to the use of force but only a practical one.[101]

For those like Lynch and Whitaker who wished to maintain Lemass's approach and for whom unity would come through North–South *rapprochement* assisted by some gentle prodding from London, the civil rights movement was a new, unpredictable and not entirely welcome development. Lemass was initially dismissive, claiming that 'two or three wet days will finish things'.[102] While the British state, however reluctantly, was substantially increasing its involvement in Northern Ireland, the Irish government's approach was somnambulistic. As O'Neill's administration buckled in the spring of 1969, the Irish cabinet had its only discussion of Northern Ireland before the disastrous events of August. Frank Aiken was sent to New York to speak to the Secretary-General of the United Nations but, as he explained to the British Ambassador in Dublin, the purpose of the UN initiative was a temperature-lowering exercise on both sides of the border.[103]

As northern temperatures stubbornly continued to rise, those who had favoured a moderate line could only watch with increasing dismay. Whitaker, who had moved from Finance to become Governor of the Central Bank, continued to impress on his former minister the need for moderation and responsibility. Echoing the views of those on the right of unionism, he cautioned that Dublin should avoid playing into the hands of the 'extremists who are manipulating the civil rights movement and who wish to stir up trouble and disorder'. His hope that the Irish government could appeal to the civil rights movement for a period of restraint with an end to all street protests was ignored, as was his advice that it should 'do nothing to inflame the situation further, but aim to impress and encourage the moderates on both sides'.[104]

On 13 August, the day after an Apprentice Boys parade had ignited 'The Battle of the Bogside', Lynch attempted to get cabinet approval for an address to the nation that he proposed to make on RTÉ that evening. A substantial section of his government, led by Haughey, Blaney and Kevin Boland, the Minister for Local Government, regarded the draft as too mild and forced a major revision. In his broadcast Lynch, claiming that the Stormont government was no longer in control, opposed the introduction of British troops and called for the introduction of a UN peacekeeping force. With equal futility he requested the British government to enter into negotiations on the constitutional future of Northern Ireland. He announced that the Irish Army was to open field hospitals for victims along the border and, in lines that would encourage nationalist hopes of more direct intervention and loyalist paranoia, he declared: 'The Irish government can no longer stand by and see innocent people injured and perhaps worse.'[105] Both Blaney and Boland favoured sending Irish troops across the border into Derry and Newry, but the majority of their colleagues recoiled in horror from this lunatic counsel, precipitating Boland's unpublicized temporary resignation from the government. The Planning Board of the Irish Defence Forces stated that the army had 'no capability of embarking on a unilateral military operation of any kind' and that all it could do was provide military training for northern nationalists in the Republic and supply arms, ammunition and equipment to nationalist elements within Northern Ireland.[106] Even this was recognized to have the danger of assisting 'subversive organisations': 'care would have to be taken to ensure that training would not be given or weapons supplied to organisations whose motives would not be in the best interests of the state.'[107] But if the invasion option was rejected, Lynch appears to have been powerless to prevent some of his ministers from sponsoring what became a serious attempt to subvert partition by forming an alliance with those northern republicans who were to become the nucleus of the Provisional IRA.

Haughey was to play a central and, to many who had observed his previous political career, surprising role in what became known as the Arms Crisis. While Blaney and Boland's visceral anti-partitionism was not in question, many had doubts about Haughey's, seeing in his involvement little more than an opportunistic use of the North in a bid to topple and replace Lynch. His public utterances had hitherto displayed no more than the conventional republicanism to be expected from any prominent member of Fianna Fáil. When he was appointed Minister for Justice in 1961, he had pinpointed the crushing of the IRA as his main objective and had reactivated the Special Criminal Court to achieve it.[108] He had, as Minister for Agriculture after the first O'Neill–Lemass summit, met with Harry West, his northern counterpart, and been a powerful advocate of the advantages of the Anglo-Irish Free Trade Agreement.[109] However, his private response to Whitaker's revisionist ideas on the North suggests there was more to his role than opportunism. The British Ambassador, who met him in October 1969, came away convinced of his 'passion for unity' after Haughey told him that there was nothing he would not sacrifice for unity, including the position of the Catholic Church and Irish neutrality.[110] His father and mother came from Swatragh in County Tyrone, and both had been active in the republican movement during the War of Independence.[111] Three decades after the crisis Haughey would refer to his family being 'deeply embedded in the Northern Ireland situation'.[112] In fact, his connections were with a part of Northern Ireland, mid Tyrone, which had a strongly republican tradition. It was for this area that the dissident IRA man Liam Kelly was returned to Stormont in the 1950s. Insofar as his northern connections influenced Haughey, they were unlikely to have encouraged moderation. His father had fought on the pro-Treaty side during the Civil War – something for which Frank Aiken had never forgiven him – and this influenced Aiken's apparent detestation of his son.[113] This 'Free-Stater' stain on his pedigree may have encouraged a compensatory lurch into an alliance with Blaney and Boland. For Haughey, the events of August 1969 produced a powerful confluence of ideological affinity and political ambition.

Exploiting the febrile atmosphere of mid August, he and his allies seized temporary control of the government's response to northern events. As Minister for Finance he was given the responsibility by the cabinet for a relief fund of £100,000 for victims of the unrest. He was, along with Blaney, part of a new cabinet subcommittee given the task of liaising with northern nationalists to promote 'a united cohesive force of anti-unionists and anti-partitionists'.[114] Over the next few months he and Blaney would establish links, both directly and through a network of Irish military intelligence officers and other government employees seconded to work in Northern Ireland, with some of the most militant elements of northern nationalism.

In response to the August events, a special section had been created in the Government Information Bureau aimed at improving liaison with nationalist opinion in Northern Ireland and putting the Irish case internationally. George Colley was given charge of this operation, which was largely staffed by public relations officers seconded from bodies such as Bord Bainne, the Irish Milk Marketing Board. Some of those employed would play key roles in linking Haughey and Blaney with those traditional republicans in Derry and Belfast who were most vociferous in their criticisms of Cathal Goulding, Chief of Staff of the IRA, for leaving Catholics undefended. Part of the £100,000 that Haughey assigned to the Northern Relief Fund thus found its way into the financing of a new virulently anti-partitionist and anti-Goulding newspaper, *The Voice of the North*, which began publication in October. It was edited by Seamus Brady, a former speech-writer for Blaney, who was until September 1969 an employee of the Government Information Bureau. His successor as editor was Hugh Kennedy, an employee of Bord Bainne, who had become Press Officer of the Central Citizens' Defence Committee in Belfast in the immediate aftermath of the August violence.[115] Both men and Captain James Kelly, an Irish Army intelligence officer, were active in promising northern republicans support as long as they cut their links with the 'communists' who controlled the IRA.

In August prominent Northern politicians, including Paddy Devlin of the NILP and Paddy Kennedy of Gerry Fitt's Republican Labour Party, arrived in Dublin to demand that, if the government would not send troops, it should at least provide Catholics with the weapons to defend themselves.[116] Captain Kelly visited Fitt's home in early September to hear the politician exclaim: 'It's not next month we need arms. It's now.'[117] Lynch refused to meet Devlin and his colleagues; Haughey and Blaney did, and both were determined to obtain arms for the North. The purpose of these weapons was made clear in Captain Kelly's report to his superior, Colonel Michael Hefferon, the Director of Irish Army Intelligence, on 23 August: 'It would seem to be now necessary to harness all opinion in the state in a concerted drive towards achieving the aim of reunification. Unfortunately, this would mean accepting the possibility of armed action of some sort as the ultimate solution.'[118]

There were failed attempts to buy weapons in London, in which Haughey's brother Padraig was involved, and in the US. Eventually Captain Kelly was able to make an arrangement with a German arms dealer, and 500 pistols and approximately 180,000 rounds of ammunition were set to be flown from Vienna to Dublin on 21 April 1970.[119] It was Haughey's failure to arrange clearance for the arms at Dublin

Airport, when his former Secretary at the Department of Justice, Peter Berry, made it clear the guns would be seized by the Irish Special Branch, that precipitated the Irish state's most serious crisis since its formation. By this time the dangers inherent in the Blaney–Haughey line were increasingly apparent. In early February 1970 delegations of northern nationalists had come south to meet Lynch and other ministers about their fears of imminent loyalist attacks. The Chief of Staff was instructed to 'prepare and train the Army for incursions into Northern Ireland if and when such a course becomes necessary'. Arrangements were to be made for arms, ammunition and respirators to be ready for distribution to Catholics in the North who had to defend themselves.[120] In April, after Blaney told the Chief of Staff that attacks on the minority were imminent and that the British security forces would be withdrawn, 500 rifles, 80,000 rounds of ammunition and 3,000 respirators were moved north to be near the border with Northern Ireland. Irish military intelligence subsequently discovered that Blaney's story had no foundation, and the weapons were returned to their original stores. By this time Captain Kelly's superiors were alarmed at his activities. In October, Garda Special Branch had observed a meeting in Bailieborough, County Cavan, which Kelly had arranged with the assistance of £500 from Haughey's Distress Fund. It was attended by leading IRA figures.[121] Military intelligence observed that Kelly failed to keep in regular contact with Dublin and was 'openly consorting with illegal groups'. His 'emotional reaction' to events in the North meant that he was now judged to be incapable 'of that cool behaviour so necessary in an Intelligence Officer'.[122]

Although Lynch was informed of the plot by Berry, he attempted to contain its reverberations by accepting denials of involvement from both Blaney and Haughey. It was only when news about the failed importation was leaked to the Fine Gael leader, Liam Cosgrave, that Lynch was forced to act. On 5 May he demanded the resignation of the two ministers, and, when they refused, he sacked them. He had already forced the resignation of his weak and incompetent Minister for Justice, Micheál Ó Moráin. Boland resigned in protest at the firings, and so in one day Lynch had lost three senior ministers. Blaney and Haughey were subsequently arrested and charged with an attempt to import guns illegally into the state. The charges against Blaney were dismissed in a Dublin district court, but Haughey, along with Captain Kelly, a Belgian-born businessman and a Belfast republican, was brought to trial at the High Court. They were all eventually acquitted in October, the jury possibly finding it difficult to accept that the arms importation did not have at least covert government sanction.

Although Lynch has been subject to criticism for not moving against the conspirators earlier, his defenders would suggest that he had played a subtle game, allowing Blaney and Haughey sufficient rope with which to hang themselves. His achievement, given the precariousness of his position, has been well summed up by Garret FitzGerald:

His handling of the Arms Crisis was very difficult for him: he was dealing with people who had deeper roots in the party than he had. His success in overcoming that difficulty and stabilising the Government and in marginalising those who had adventurous ideas about the North was of crucial importance to the stability of the state and of the island as a whole.[123]

On his acquittal Haughey demanded Lynch's resignation, but the Taoiseach was able to use party members' overwhelming desire to maintain unity and stay in government against the much weaker mobilizing capacity of anti-partitionism. Such was the power of the imperative of party over 'national' unity that both Blaney and Haughey voted with the government against an Opposition motion of no confidence.[124] Not since 1940 and de Valera's rejection of the British offer of unity in exchange for an end to neutrality had the primacy of twenty-six-county nationalism been so apparent. Public sympathy for the Catholic victims of northern violence was still strong, but it did not extend to support for those who appeared ready to contemplate direct involvement in arming one side in a potential sectarian civil war. An opinion poll carried out just after Haughey's dismissal showed that 72 per cent of the electorate supported Lynch's decision, while a staggering 89 per cent of those who had voted for Fianna Fáil in the last election still supported him as their preferred choice as Taoiseach.[125]

Haughey avoided any public confrontation with Lynch's stand on the North after August 1969, as the Taoiseach relied increasingly on the advice he was getting from T. K. Whitaker and also from senior officials in External Affairs. In a letter to Lynch, Whitaker referred disparagingly to the 'teenage hooliganism and anarchy' in Derry and Belfast during the worst of the August violence and warned against the 'terrible temptation to be opportunist – to cash in on political emotionalism – at a time like this'.[126] It was Whitaker who provided most of the text of a speech given by Lynch at Tralee on 20 September that firmly restated the most positive aspects of Lemass's conciliatory approach to Northern Ireland, emphasizing that the policy of seeking unity through agreement was of its nature a long-term one.[127]

This approach was also apparent in a major assessment of the Irish state's Northern Ireland policy produced by the Department of External Affairs in November 1969. It emphasized that the government's basic approach should remain that of seeking reunification 'by peaceful means through co-operation and consent between Irishmen. The use of force should be dismissed publicly as frequently as may appear necessary.' The fact that the Republic was a 'confessional society' was recognized as an obstacle to unity. As a consequence, reforms to take account of the concerns of northern Protestants on such issues as divorce and birth-control and also in education and the role of the Irish language should be considered. Lemass's legacy of functional cooperation with Stormont needed to be maintained and enhanced despite 'such temporary cooling of relations as has happened recently'. Most significant of all for the subsequent development of Anglo-Irish relations, it advocated the 'maximum discreet contact with Whitehall' at both official and ministerial level.[128]

By early 1970, as tensions in the North abated, Patrick Hillery, Minister for External Affairs, was being secretly briefed at the Foreign Office in Whitehall that 'a lot of steam had gone out of the situation' and that the only troublemakers were 'professional agitators' with little popular support.[129] Even when the Ballymurphy riots in April challenged this Panglossian view, Eamonn Gallagher, the most senior Irish official liaising directly with northern nationalists, was unsympathetic to those involved, fearing that new disturbances in Ulster might help the Tories in the forthcoming British general election.[130] At a time when the British were impressing on Dublin the capacity of the army to ensure that Catholics anywhere in Northern Ireland were safe from the threat of another pogrom, and with the B Specials disbanded and the RUC disarmed, Blaney and Boland's open championing of the possible use of force to bring about unity appeared increasingly extremist. Lynch's moderation would remain unchallenged until the introduction of internment and Bloody Sunday unleashed another wave of irredentist emotion.

The emergence of the Provisional IRA and its offensive in the North did much to tarnish the image of an 'oppressed people' awaiting salvation from the South. Fear of contagion from violence 'up there' became widespread. Lynch's new Minister for Justice, Desmond O'Malley, soon demonstrated a zeal to repress any subversive spillovers from the North. In December 1970 he announced that the government was considering the introduction of internment to deal with 'a secret armed conspiracy' that allegedly planned kidnappings, armed robberies and murders – all activities in which the Provisional IRA was soon to be involved. In May 1971 the Offences against the State Act was activated to create a 'special criminal court' of three judges sitting without a jury, and in November a further amendment to the Act allowed the indictment of those suspected of membership of an illegal organization on the word of a senior police officer.[131] The response of 'honest Jack' to the IRA threat appears to have done him no significant electoral damage, for in the 1973 election Fianna Fáil actually increased its share of the poll, but lost the election because a pre-election pact between Labour and Fine Gael meant an improvement in vote transfers between their supporters, which led to the combined opposition returning more TDs.

In his address to Fianna Fáil's Ard-Fheis in January 1970, Jack Lynch provided a convincing and passionate rebuttal of Blaney's claim in a famous tirade at Letterkenny in December 1969 that Fianna Fáil had never taken a decision to rule out the use of force to bring about unity. Echoing Lemass's Tralee speech of 1963, he informed the delegates that 'like it or not, we have to acknowledge that two-thirds of the one and a half million people who make up the population of the six counties wish to be associated with the United Kingdom.' The 'plain truth' was that the southern state did not have the capacity to impose a solution by force, and, even if it had, 'would we want to adopt the role of an occupying conqueror over the million or so six county citizens who at present support partition?'[132]

Around the same time Lynch had met three leading northern nationalists, including Paddy Doherty, who was playing a key role in running the Bogside behind the barricades, and Seán Keenan, the founder of the Provisionals in Derry. Lynch not only refused Keenan's request for weapons but made it clear that 'if we were given a gift of Northern Ireland tomorrow we could not accept it.' This was primarily because the Republic could not afford to support the level of social services enjoyed by the province's citizens and at the same time bring up standards in the South to the same level. The three left convinced that 'that man has no interest in getting involved in Northern Ireland.'[133]

Lynch had defeated the republican hawks within the party because their activities were perceived to threaten the security of the southern state. While Boland, who left Fianna Fáil to found a pure republican party, and Blaney, who was expelled, would remain marginalized as one-issue politicians, Haughey stayed in the party, sure of the support of its traditionalist wing, but by now well educated in the limited power of anti-partitionism in southern politics. Anti-partitionism would remain a largely unquestioned element of the national consensus and a powerful component of the internal political culture of Fianna Fáil. Yet, throughout the 1970s, opinion polls would not rank it high on the list of voters' priorities. The violence and intractability of the northern conflict ensured that unity remained a low-intensity aspiration. Haughey would be able to use the 'whiff of cordite' associated with the Arms Crisis as a valuable resource in his ultimate displacement of Lynch, but it was the failure of the latter's economic policies, not his Northern Ireland policy, that would prove decisive.

7. Terence O'Neill and the Crisis of the Unionist State

Liberal Unionism: Opportunities and Enemies

The problems facing those who wanted a more accommodating unionism had been made clear in 1959 in a much publicized row over the question of whether Catholics could become members of the Unionist Party. The slump in Sinn Féin's vote in the 1959 general election – it dropped by almost 60 per cent, from 152,000 in 1955 to 63,000 – was accompanied by an increase in the Unionist Party vote in the eight constituencies where there was a straight fight with Sinn Féin, and there was evidence that this was a product of some Catholics voting Unionist.[1] The previous year at a Catholic social study conference at Garron Tower in north Antrim a number of the participants had argued that the way to obtain social justice for their community was to become more positively engaged in public life. The former Minister of Home Affairs and *bête noire* of loyalist militants, Brian Maginess, who was now Attorney-General, saw in these developments a good reason to go public with a plea for a more inclusive unionism. At a Young Unionist weekend school in Portstewart he spoke of the need to treat political opponents 'not as enemies but as fellow members of the community' and attacked those who made abusive references to the religious beliefs of others, a reference not simply to the increasing public profile of Ian Paisley but to the sectarian utterances of some members of his own party.[2]

However, it was the response of Sir Clarence Graham, Chairman of the Standing Committee of the Ulster Unionist Council, to a question about possible Catholic membership of the party that produced most reaction. His support for Catholics becoming parliamentary candidates enraged a substantial section of the government and party.[3] Brookeborough privately recognized that Catholic membership might indeed come about but was critical of Graham and Maginess for raising it in public, as this would 'only delay matters'.[4] His bruising experience with Protestant populism in the early 1950s had left him determined to give no further hostages to the right. The result was a government immobilized by fear of schism and unable to respond to a real opportunity to develop a better relationship with the minority community. Sir George

Clark, Grand Master of the Grand Orange Lodge of Ireland, proclaimed that the Order would never accept Catholics as members of the Unionist Party.[5] Privately he apologized to the Prime Minister for the hardline tone but explained it by the need to placate Orangemen annoyed by Graham's remarks and by a government ban on a proposed Orange march through Dungiven. He was also concerned about the growing influence of Paisley in the Order.[6]

Paisley had been able to increase his support amongst loyalists worried by the IRA campaign and concerned about looming redundancies in the shipyards and the aircraft factories. An organization called Ulster Protestant Action had some limited success in recruiting in workplaces by demanding that any redundancies were not suffered by loyalists.[7] Such sectarian pressures had echoes in mainstream unionism. During the 1961 Belfast municipal elections the St George's ward Unionist Association produced a leaflet stating that its three candidates 'employ over 70 people, and have never employed a Roman Catholic'. In the same year a prominent Unionist, Robert Babington, told the Ulster Unionist Labour Association that the party should keep registers of unemployed loyalists from which employers would be invited to pick workers.[8]

Yet closet liberals in the cabinet might have taken some encouragement from a number of developments in the early 1960s. There was evidence of a more pragmatic and democratic nationalism taking root in sections of the Catholic middle class, particularly the expanding numbers of university graduates who had benefited from the 1947 Education Act. National Unity had been set up in Belfast at the end of 1959 to give voice to those dissatisfied with the ineffectuality of traditional forms of nationalist and republican politics and to argue that any move towards unity had to have the consent of a majority in Northern Ireland.[9] The ecumenical movement and the pontificate of John XXIII helped to smooth the edges of inter-Church conflict. There was also some evidence that, in the greater Belfast area at least, there was a thawing in the communal cold war.

In their pioneering study of community relations published in 1962, Barritt and Carter noted that Catholics would now venture into the Protestant heartland of Sandy Row in search of work and had no fears about shopping on the Shankill Road, a judgement later confirmed in Gerry Adams's autobiographical account of growing up in Belfast in the early 1960s.[10] The Belfast correspondent of the *Irish Times* commented on the growing moderation of ordinary people:'It is something composed of simple human feeling, a wish to live in peace, an unwillingness to hate irrationally, a recognition that Ireland's conflicts are small ones in today's world.'[11] This was evident in politics. Despite the advocacy of a sectarian approach to dealing with unemployment by Ulster Protestant Action and some Unionist politicians, even William Douglas, the crusty apparatchik who was Secretary of the Unionist Party, recognized that the challenge from the NILP in the 1962 election would have to be met on economic and social issues and that banging the tribal drum was no longer sufficient.[12]

Attitudinal change was in part a reflection of important social developments. The post-war improvement in living standards meant that the arrival of the 'consumer society', while not displacing traditional fixations, drained them of some of their emotional centrality. The move of significant numbers of Belfast's traditional working-class communities into new housing estates or to surrounding towns and villages such as Newtownabbey, Castlereagh, Dunmurry and Lisburn, where many of the new industries were established on green-field sites, weakened traditional allegiances to the Unionist Party.[13] The arrival of television helped to expand the horizons of a still intensely parochial society. The BBC had brought television to Northern Ireland in 1953, broadcasting from a small temporary transmitter in Belfast. A powerful new transmitter was built in Belfast in 1955, and the number of television sets in the North rose from 3,000 in 1953 to over 38,000 by 1956. The arrival of independent television provided a major stimulus to the market for sets.[14]

Traditionally the senior officials of the BBC in Belfast had been close to the viewpoint of the government, but in the 1950s the Director-General, Sir William Haley, had encouraged the local Controller to extend the areas for discussion and to bring differing viewpoints into civilized contention.[15] One result was *Your Questions*, a local version of the popular radio series *Any Questions*. First broadcast in 1954, it was produced by the Protestant socialist John Boyd and its regular contributers included Jack Sayers, editor of the *Belfast Telegraph*, the liberal nationalist J. J. Campbell, the Oxford-educated NILP activist Charles Brett and the Queen's University historian J. C. Beckett, all of whom were proponents of the need for the political renovation of the North through a more constructive engagement between nationalism and unionism.[16] However, the response of some leading members of the government to even such mild innovation was one of suspicious hostility. The up-and-coming Unionist politician Brian Faulkner was at the forefront, with his condemnations of the BBC for its alleged anti-government bias. For Faulkner, as for a sizeable section of the cabinet and parliamentary party, someone like Sayers was too liberal to be an acceptable unionist representative and Beckett's links with southern historians made his supposed neutrality suspect.[17]

When the *Tonight* programme sent Alan Whicker to Belfast in 1958, there was an outpouring of unionist rage when Whicker informed viewers in the rest of the UK that in Northern Ireland policemen carried revolvers, pubs were open from morning to night, and betting shops had been legalized and carried on a brisk business. The Regional Controller apologized to the Northern Ireland public, and *Tonight* did not show any of the remaining films.[18] Making allowance for some understandable annoyance at the programme's failure to deal with the ongoing, if declining, IRA campaign, there remained something disproportionate in the response. This brittle defensiveness that affected a substantial section of the unionist community was a warning to those who would make too much of the first signs of the blunting of traditional antagonisms.

There was a geographical dimension to unionist divisions. Barritt and Carter noted that, while more tolerant feelings had become manifest in Belfast, the situation in rural areas, especially those near the border, was different. Here the IRA campaign had polarized the communities: 'the political and national issues have become more prominent and have brought a new hardness to attitudes.'[19] Unionists in border areas were also dealing with a nationalism that showed fewer signs of the questioning and flexibility that had begun to appear in the east of the province. The *Belfast Newsletter*, a traditionalist counterweight to Sayers's *Telegraph*, warned of the dangers of mellowing unionist attitudes:

For Unionists in Belfast and its hinterland the border issue is at a discount, and many there think that they can forget about it altogether. But it is the one thing that matters in Nationalist held areas and is probably the big issue that matters among Nationalists of all persuasions throughout Ulster. Forgetting about the border is something that is expected of Unionists but not of Nationalists.[20]

It was to Brian Faulkner that those unionists who were most unsettled by the vision of men like Maginess turned for leadership. Faulkner, who had entered Stormont as MP for East Down in 1949, became the dominant voice of the right in the government when Brookeborough promoted him from Chief Whip to Minister of Home Affairs in 1959. He had worked in his father's shirt-manufacturing concern during the war and, worried that his lack of war service might hurt his progress in the Unionist Party, cultivated an activist pro-Orange image as compensation.[21]

He demanded an inquiry when Brian Maginess banned the Orange parade along the predominantly nationalist Longstone Road in 1952, and when the ban was lifted in 1955 led a march of 15,000 Orangemen along the road, guarded by hundreds of RUC men in full riot gear.[22] Faulkner had also criticized the government for not defending the right of an Orange band to march in the largely Catholic village of Dungiven in 1953. After the same band provoked a riot and a subsequent Catholic boycott of Protestant shops in July 1958, the following year's march was banned by Colonel Ken Topping, Maginess's successor at Home Affairs. Although previously identified as one of the cabinet's more reactionary figures,[23] Topping was now execrated by the Orange lodges and was replaced by Faulkner, who allowed the band and 10,000 Orangemen to march through Dungiven in July 1960, sparking off two nights of rioting.[24]

Ambitious, energetic and very able, Faulkner was positioning himself to succeed Brookeborough. His assault on liberalism in the party endeared him to many grass-roots unionists, particularly outside Belfast. His industrial experience also led him to believe that the modernizers in the party were out of touch with working-class loyalists. As early as 1959 he warned those who saw the fall in support for Sinn Féin as indicative of a shift in the minority's attitude to the state that traditional nationalism was not a spent force but a 'volcano smoking harmlessly enough until the day when it flares up to engulf all those who live unsuspecting on its slopes'.[25] In the cabinet he was in the vanguard of those who saw Lemass's proposals for practical cooperation between North and South as simply a more insidious form of anti-partitionism. Even the harmless Irish Association, composed of the great and the good and aimed at improved understanding between the citizens of the two states, was denounced by him as having an Irish nationalist agenda.[26] Connolly Gage, a former Unionist Party MP at Westminster, put the common liberal view of Faulkner when he argued that his succession to Brookeborough would be a 'disaster': 'it might put us in the South African category with knobs on.'[27]

But it was the Minister of Finance, Terence O'Neill, who succeeded Brookeborough as Prime Minister on 25 March 1963. Following the Conservative Party tradition, the new leader 'emerged' after consultations between the Governor, Lord Wakehurst, Brookeborough and the Unionist Chief Whip, William Craig. A straw poll carried out by Craig amongst the Unionist MPs at Stormont gave O'Neill a comfortable lead over his two main rivals, Faulkner and J. L. O. Andrews, son of the former premier and a genial and affable Minister of Commerce.[28] However, it was widely believed in the party that O'Neill's 'superior' social standing weighed heavily in the Governor's decision.

He was the son of the Conservative MP and Orangeman Arthur Bruce O'Neill, the first Westminster MP to die at the front in the First World War. His mother was the daughter of Lord Crewe, a member of Asquith's cabinet, and he was brought up in London in his mother's liberal circle. Educated at Eton, he drifted through several stock-exchange jobs before military service in the Irish Guards during the Second World War. Although he was not a landowner himself, his family's secure membership of the social elite in County Antrim, where his uncle was a Westminster MP, had made it relatively easy to acquire the nomination for the Stormont constituency of Bannside in 1946. From his earliest days at Stormont he felt that his social standing, military credentials and metropolitan upbringing made him worthy of a place in Brookeborough's inner circle.[29] He first entered the government as a junior minister in 1948 and became Minister of Finance in 1956. Beneath the languid demeanour and the aristocratic drawl was what one of his closest civil service allies called a 'constructive ruthlessness'.[30] He made little attempt to disguise his low opinion of the quality of the average Unionist MP and of many of his cabinet colleagues. His aloof style, Brookeborough's failure to recommend him as his successor and the lack of any direct role for members of the parliamentary party in his selection gave his critics a powerful argument about the new premier's lack of popular legitimacy.

'Stealing Labour's Thunder'

For the first two years of his premiership O'Neill's priority was to respond to the NILP's charge that the regime was incapable of dealing with the problem of unemployment because of its reactionary ideology and its antiquated and amateurish style of government. Here he was able to make a distinctive break with the approach of his predecessor. As Minister of Finance, his difficult relationship with his permanent secretary, Sir Douglas Harkness, stemmed in part from a belief that Harkness was too compliant with the demands of the Treasury and not robust enough in pressing the province's case for extra resources.[31] He had as a result got more directly involved in relations with Treasury officials than had been the case previously. Part of his approach involved dining with them at the London St James's Club; but there was also an increasingly clear line on financial relations with London to support his charm offensive. In essence it involved a shift away from Brookeborough's emphasis on the North's special circumstances and ad hoc responses to short-term crises of the local economy, and towards portraying Northern Ireland as a relatively backward region of the UK whose modernization would contribute to the economic health of the kingdom as a whole.

Depression in many of Britain's heavy industries at the end of the 1950s had increased unemployment in the regions at the same time as there was evidence of 'over-heating' in the south-east, which was pushing up wages and threatening the balance of payments. The result was an increasing interest in developing a regional policy that would direct investment to those parts of Britain where resources were underemployed. Regional expansion could thus be seen as a contribution to a higher rate of national economic growth and became part of the 1960s vogue for national planning. Regional planning initiatives in Scotland and Wales were associated with new investments in 'growth centres', new towns and motorways.[32]

A long-standing conflict between the Stormont government and the Belfast Corporation over the latter's desire to have the city's boundary extended provided the basis for a largely civil service-based initiative that allowed the province to plug profitably into these national initiatives. Brookeborough's cabinet had resisted the boundary extension because of a fear that it might increase the number of Nationalist seats, but eventually had to concede a request from the Corporation for a survey of the Belfast area by an independent consultant. Sir Robert Matthew, an eminent planner, was engaged, and his report, published just before Brookeborough's resignation, was a much more ambitious document than its title implied. By dealing with the question of Belfast's boundary within the context of the future development of infrastructure in the province as a whole, it was a blueprint for a massive increase in public investment. It suggested the creation of a new town between Lurgan and Portadown, the development of a number of 'growth centres', and a major improvement in the transport system with a new motorway and road network.[33]

The *Matthew Report* would be the basis for O'Neill's subsequent success in extracting significantly more resources from the Treasury than his predecessor. However, at the time of Brookeborough's resignation the full implications of the report were far from apparent, and O'Neill's succession was not linked to the promulgation of a distinctive philosophy on either the economy or community relations. At the same time there were some hints of what was to come. As Minister of Finance he had spoken of the need for the province to be more proactive in developing solutions to its economic problems, and this might have been interpreted as an implicit criticism of Brookeborough's importuning London for more subsidies for local industry. Given that the challenge from the NILP had been in part based on the criticism of the government for being too ready to feather-bed local industrialists, O'Neill had a distinct advantage over Faulkner, who was a strident defender of the local bourgeoisie.

In his first speech to the Ulster Unionist Council, O'Neill defined his government's task as being 'to transform the face of Ulster'.[34] This transformation would be based not on directly addressing Catholic demands for reform but on a new approach to the economic and social modernization of the province. He referred to the *Matthew Report* as a way in which 'Northern Ireland could capture the imagination of the world'.[35] This would be as a region that had turned its back on its historic conflicts and united in the pursuit of full employment and higher living standards. His view of the modernization proposals in the *Matthew Report* and in the subsequent Wilson plan for economic development was that they would make such issues as discrimination and gerrymandering redundant: 'As for the divisions in our society, I sometimes wonder whether we do much good by so frequently talking about them. There are so many things which should unite all Ulster people. If we emphasize these things, the divisions will seem less significant.'[36]

Such an approach seemed dangerously superficial to liberal Unionists like Sayers, but they in their turn ignored the major political imperative under which any leader of the Unionist Party had to labour. This was to maximize support for the party in the Protestant electorate, given that very few Catholics would vote Unionist in the foreseeable future. Brookeborough had lost support in the party because he appeared to be unable to stem losses to the NILP in the greater Belfast area. Winning back this support was the immediate priority for O'Neill. The consolidation of the Unionist bloc in the east of the province was a prerequisite for the pursuit of reforms in community relations, as these, if they were to address some of the major complaints of the minority community, would inevitably lead to serious internal party conflict in Tyrone, Fermanagh and Londonderry. The problem for O'Neill was that, although this approach was successful in dealing with the NILP, it unintentionally sharpened community antagonisms.

Plans for economic expansion inevitably had sectarian implications, given the religious and political geography of the region. The fact that the *Matthew Report*'s designated 'growth centres' were concentrated in the east of the region did little to discourage the traditional nationalist complaint about discrimination against Catholic-majority areas in the west and south of Northern Ireland. When O'Neill announced the creation of an inter-departmental inquiry into the possible scope of economic planning in October 1963, the economic consultant chosen was the Oxford-trained Ulsterman Thomas Wilson, a committed unionist who was Professor of Economics at Glasgow University. Wilson's report, with an accompanying White Paper, was published in February 1965. It set out an ambitious target of 65,000 new jobs and 64,000 new houses by 1970 and proved decisive in O'Neill's campaign against the NILP.[37] However, Wilson's view on where new industries should locate followed Matthew's suggestions and emphasized the difficulties of getting British and foreign industrialists interested in the peripheral parts of what seemed to them 'a discouragingly remote area on the very fringe of Europe'.[38] This was a bleak message for towns such as Derry, Strabane and Enniskillen, and intensified the perception amongst nationalists that the focus of O'Neill's development plans was on the unionist communities in the east, symbolized above all by the location of the new town between the predominantly Protestant towns of Lurgan and Portadown.

Although there was no suggestion that Wilson was influenced by political or sectarian considerations, this was not to be the case with the report of the Lockwood Committee on Higher Education, which had been considering the case for a second university in the province. There was a potential base for this in Magee College in Derry, but the report suggested that the best choice would be the largely Protestant town of Coleraine in County Londonderry. While many Derry Protestants participated in the protest campaign against the proposal, it was the fixation of the hierarchy of the city's Unionist Party on avoiding any significant economic and social development that would upset the sectarian balance that proved determinant.[39] Even the 'liberal' O'Neill was not immune to the corrosive influence of the sectarian myopia of some Derry Unionists, wondering how, if such a development took place, it would be 'possible to insure against a radical increase in R.C. Papes?'[40] The triumph of parochial sectarianism did much to disillusion those Catholics and liberal nationalists who had looked to O'Neill for change. It came on top of the resignation of Geoffery Copcutt, the Englishman who had been appointed head of the design team for the new town that Matthew had recommended. Copcutt embarrassed the government with a public statement urging a special development plan for Derry and supporting its case for the new university. He also described the administration as a 'crisis-ridden regime, too busy looking over its shoulder to look outwards'.[41] The government's subsequent decision to name the town 'Craigavon' appeared to vindicate this judgement and seemed a world away from O'Neill's optimistic rhetoric about transforming the face of Ulster.

For O'Neill, these decisions were the price to be paid for the maintenance of party unity at a time when he was modernizing not only economic and social policies but also the style and structure of his government. Initially the necessity for continuity and party unity meant that his rivals for the leadership had key positions in his government, with Jack Andrews at Finance and Faulkner at Commerce. However, he sought to bypass the cabinet and centralize the initiative in policy-making in a small group of senior and trusted official advisers centred on his Private Secretary, Jim Malley, and two key Northern Ireland civil service allies: the cabinet secretary, Cecil Bateman, and his private secretary, Ken Bloomfield.

His modernization project also resulted in a major change in the structure of government: the creation of a new Ministry of Development. Such a ministry had been recommended in the *Matthew Report*, but the fact that it would involve the removal of planning powers from local authorities had ensured opposition from within party and cabinet. In response, O'Neill reshuffled his cabinet in July 1964, when most of his colleagues were on holiday. Although the shifts in personnel were not radical, the most significant being Jack Andrews's departure from the government, there was a realignment of cabinet responsibilities, with the concentration of power over planning, transport, roads, local government and housing in the Ministry of Health and Local Government. William Craig, who as Chief Whip at the time of Brookeborough's resignation had been an important supporter of O'Neill, moved from Home Affairs to be the new Minister of Health and Local Government.[42] Finally, in January 1965, O'Neill was able to boast to Harold Wilson of the first important alteration to the structure of devolved government since its inception, with the creation of a Ministry of Development and the transformation of Health and Local Government into Health and Social Services.[43]

The new ministry had as its task the development of a 'master plan' for Northern Ireland and was the centrepiece of O'Neill's strategy for dealing with the challenge from the NILP. As such it would prove extremely effective. However, the disruptive effects of these reforms on local Unionist structures of power and patronage, together with his increasingly presidential style of government, produced a reaction within the party. This was manifest as early as the annual Ulster Unionist Council meeting in April 1965, where a resolution attacking the 'dictatorial manner' of recent government planning proposals was passed, as was one attacking encroachments upon the powers of county councils. Worryingly for the Prime Minister, the fissure that had opened up between central government and local Unionist power structures was complemented by evidence of geographical and political contentions as well.

The debate on the *Lockwood Report* had produced unprecedented alliances at Stormont, with only two Unionist MPs speaking in favour. The government was able to ensure victory only by making the vote on the report an issue of confidence.[44] Many Unionist MPs, and not only those in the west of the province, felt that O'Neill was prepared to allow the peripheral areas to stagnate and decline in pursuit of the defence of Unionism in the greater Belfast area. As Minister of Finance, O'Neill had set up a committee to investigate the loss-making railways run by the Ulster Transport Authority, and when the *Benson Report* was published in July 1963 it recommended substantial line closures, including Derry's two rail links to Belfast. Although one line was eventually reprieved, the *Benson Report* was a major factor in the formation of a 'Unionist Council of the West' by prominent Unionists in Derry, Tyrone and Fermanagh to campaign against neglect by the centre.[45] There was also increasing evidence that those who attacked O'Neill's aloof style, his centralizing of power and his neglect of the outlying parts of the province saw him as too willing to accommodate the traditional enemies of Ulster.

O'Neill's decision to end decades of the cold war with Dublin by inviting Seán Lemass to meet him in Belfast in January 1965 was not revealed to his cabinet colleagues until the Taoiseach had arrived at Stormont. Driven by a desire to placate pressure from London for improved relations with the South, O'Neill did not even bother to call a meeting of the Unionist MPs to explain his thinking on the issue.[46] The focus of the meeting was on low-key areas of possible common interest such as tourism and trade promotion, and the joint statement issued afterwards declared that the talks had not touched on 'constitutional or political questions'.[47] However, Lemass's inability to resist the temptation to portray it as a portent of more substantial constitutional changes[48] helped those, still in a minority in the parliamentary Unionist Party, who attacked O'Neill for weakening the union by talking to the Prime Minister of a hostile state.[49]

The increasing evidence of divisions in the party meant that O'Neill's success in what he termed 'stealing Labour's thunder'[50] paid fewer political dividends than he had hoped. The Unionist Party fought the 1965 Stormont election with a manifesto entitled 'Forward Ulster to Target 1970!' Labour's advance was firmly reversed, with a 7 per cent swing to the Unionist Party in the contested constituencies and the loss of two Labour seats in Woodvale and Victoria. David Bleakley, the defeated Labour MP for Victoria, put his defeat down to the success of O'Neill's rhetoric of planning and job creation: 'for my voters Labour appeared to have lost its *raison d'être*.'[51] But if O'Neill's determination to defeat the NILP had been largely successful, the price was the opening up of divisions in his party that made it even more difficult to deal with reforms demanded by the minority.

O'Neillism and Discrimination

An unintended effect of O'Neill's commitment to the modernization of the North was a new mood of increasingly impatient expectation on the part of Catholics that the regime would address the issue of discrimination. Yet the dismal truth about O'Neill was that he displayed not the slightest inclination to do anything on this issue. Even his major ally in the press, Jack Sayers, was forced to deliver a critical review of O'Neill's first year in office: 'It is indicative of government reluctance to admit that grievances exist and to forestall political attack that the National Assistance Board, the Housing Trust and the newly appointed Lockwood committee are without Catholic members.'[52] Already there were signs of disillusionment amongst those middle-class Catholics who wanted a more positive relationship with the state. J.J. Campbell, a lecturer at St Joseph's Teacher Training College, and Brian McGuigan, a prominent Catholic lawyer, published three letters they sent to O'Neill between August 1963 and March 1964, after the Prime Minister failed to reply to any of them. They had expressed some disappointment that he had not responded to increasing evidence of goodwill from the Catholic community with appointments to bodies such as the Economic Council and the Lockwood Committee.[53] For O'Neill the blame for the maintenance of sectarian divisions lay with the hierarchy of the Catholic Church and its insistence on segregated education. He also claimed that attempts to appoint Catholics had been turned down by those approached.[54] In fact, there is little evidence of any serious effort to attract suitable Catholic candidates. Despite the post-war expansion in the size of the Catholic middle class, appointments to public bodies reflected the existence of what an NILP critic called 'the old boy network: since influential Protestants usually have never met their opposite numbers and indeed do not even know their names, the network to which ministers and senior officials belong fails to come up with the right answer.'[55]

But there was more to it than the complacent ignorance bred by decades of social and cultural segregation. While not reflecting an active discriminatory intent, it was in part a product of what Barritt and Carter described as a feeling of superiority amongst Protestants, which they explained in part as a relic of the former Protestant Ascendancy but also as a result of 'the present day fact that a Catholic is more likely to be unskilled and poor than a Protestant'.[56] Thus, as Charles Brett noted, the usual excuse was made that 'it's hard to find a suitable person'. But when such feelings of social superiority were confronted with lists of suitable Catholics that had been submitted to the cabinet secretariat[57] and still no action was forthcoming, even such a stalwart of the regime as the *Belfast Newsletter* criticized the timidity and bad faith of O'Neill's government. When in March 1965 John Taylor, a leading Young Unionist and a member of the Executive of the Ulster Unionist Council, told a National Council of Civil Liberties conference that discrimination was confined to private firms, a *Newsletter* leader set him straight and challenged the Prime Minister to address Catholic complaints directly:

There are local authorities which cannot show clean hands and they are not in all cases Unionist . . . Discrimination breeds discrimination but in a community which is predominantly Protestant and which has such distasteful slogans as 'a Protestant parliament for a Protestant people' to live down the lead must come from the majority party and the government it forms.

Captain O'Neill, by the initiative he has shown in his summit talks with Mr Lemass, has created the proper atmosphere for a new approach to community problems inside Northern Ireland. The need now is for the government to follow up the signal success it has attained in external relations by similar conciliatory moves inside the province which will persuade Roman Catholics to play their full part in the affairs of the country.[58]

But the core of O'Neill's approach had been articulated by Taylor when he focused on the image of O'Neill's 'new Ulster': 'In the social and economic programmes now being outlined there is neither place nor time for discrimination.'[59] Even if the new town project and the *Lockwood Report* had not provided room for serious doubt on this claim, there remained the fact that O'Neillism offered economic growth in exchange for collective amnesia on the part of the Catholic community about past and present grievances. Behind this bland appeal to shared material interests there was a steely resolve to do nothing that would add to the strains that his anti-NILP strategy was placing on Unionist Party unity. The result was a failure to grasp a very brief historical moment when timely and rather minimalist concessions might have tied the Nationalist Party and the Catholic middle class into a more positive, if still subordinate, relationship to the Unionist state.

The Origins of the Civil Rights Movement

The most radical shift in nationalist strategy since partition originated in a local campaign against the housing policy of Dungannon Urban District Council by a group of young Catholic housewives who claimed they were living in cramped and unsanitary conditions because of the council's policy of discrimination in favour of Protestants. The Homeless Citizens' League, which they established with the help of two local doctors, Conn and Patricia McCluskey, in May 1963, adopted novel tactics such as protests at council meetings, lobbying of Stormont and squatting.[60] As alleged discrimination in the allocation of public housing was to be the central precipitating factor in the civil rights movement, it is important to emphasize the very localized nature of this and other central civil rights issues. As the most systematic and judicious of the analyses of the issue puts it,

A group of local authorities in the west of the province provide a startlingly high proportion of the total number of complaints. All the accusations of gerrymandering, practically all the complaints about housing and regional policy, and a disproportionate amount of the charges about private and public employment come from this area.[61]

The overall record on housing in Northern Ireland after 1945 was not a discreditable one. Between June 1944 and December 1964, 45,920 council houses were built; the Northern Ireland Housing Trust erected 28,513; and 3,102 were built by other public bodies. This was a reasonable achievement when compared with the 100,000 new dwellings that the 1943 Northern Ireland Housing Survey showed were needed.[62] Allegations of wholesale discrimination against Catholics in the allocation of housing simply do not stand up to serious scrutiny. This can be seen in the 1971 census of population taken in the dying months of the Stormont regime. In that year there were 148,000 local authority dwellings in Northern Ireland, of which between 45,000 and 55,000 were occupied by Catholic families (depending on what is assumed about the religion of those who declined to answer the religion question in the census). Catholics had a disproportionately large share of local authority housing – even allowing for the lower average incomes of the Catholic community – comprising 26.1 per cent of households but occupying 30.7 per cent of local authority households.[63]

However, misallocation where it did occur could be crude and blatant and was usually associated with situations where the two communities were closely balanced numerically or where an actual Protestant and Unionist minority controlled a local authority through the manipulation of electoral boundaries. In Dungannon there was a slight Catholic majority in the population but control of the council was firmly in Unionist hands through boundary manipulation.[64] Although much of the council's housing efforts went into slum clearance, from which Catholics benefited substantially since they were disproportionately affected by slum housing, there had been a marked reluctance to allocate houses to new Catholic families. The result was that in 1963 there were upwards of 300 families on the housing waiting list, some for as long as twelve years; and not one new Catholic family had been allocated a permanent house for thirty-four years, though a few houses had been allocated to comfortably-off Protestants.[65]

While such malpractices were confined to a small number of local authorities, their capacity to embarrass the regime was aided by its complacent tendency to dismiss complaints as part of the failed anti-partitionist agenda. This simply refused to recognize the radical shift in the tactics of protest associated with the Dungannon agitation, which from the beginning sought to increase its potency by drawing on media images of the ongoing struggle for black civil rights in the US. Just as blacks claimed equality and justice as part of their constitutional birthright and were prepared to use a range of tactics from 'sit-ins' at segregated lunch counters to mass marches to force action from the federal government, now Catholics were urged to turn to Westminster, to demand not British withdrawal but rather a new form of British involvement in Northern Ireland.

The McCluskeys along with other Catholic professionals signalled the new departure with the establishment of a Campaign for Social Justice (CSJ) on 17 January 1964. The campaign was a self-conscious break with the approach of the Nationalist Party. As Conn McCluskey explained to Eddie McAteer, the time had come to 'concentrate on getting our rights and trying to overcome gerrymandering ... to mention the border just puts the Unionists' backs up and some other poor devils lose their chance of a house or a job.'[66] The CSJ now turned to British politicians particularly within the Labour Party, with a captivatingly simple argument: 'we lived in a part of the UK where the British remit ran, we should seek the ordinary rights of British citizens which were so obviously denied us.'[67]

The leader of the Labour Party, Harold Wilson, had written to Patricia McCluskey in July 1964 'deploring' religious and other kinds of discrimination and supporting the NILP's proposals for new and impartial procedures for the allocation of public housing and a tribunal to deal with cases of alleged discrimination in public appointments.[68] In a second letter in September he pledged that a Labour government would do everything in its power to deal with infringements of justice in Northern Ireland. However, he also pointed out that this would be 'no easy task' and claimed that the most immediate way of getting progress would be to vote for NILP candidates in the forthcoming general election. As Bob Purdie has pointed out, 'Making the will-o'-the-wisp of an NILP electoral breakthrough a precondition for action by a Labour government was a safe way of putting off any action whatsoever.'[69]

Wilson's Huyton constituency had a large number of voters of Irish extraction, and such grand gestures as his decision to have the remains of Roger Casement, executed for treason in 1916, returned to Ireland convinced many unionists that he was sympathetic to Irish nationalism. Yet in his first years in power Wilson did little to pressurize O'Neill on the discrimination issue. He and his Home Secretary, Frank Soskice, relied on the advice of senior Home Office officials traditionally sympathetic to the Stormont government:

Section 75 of the 1920 Act certainly provides technical authority for the United Kingdom parliament to impose legislation on Northern Ireland against the wishes of that government, but the consequences of such an act could only be a disastrous rupture between the two governments. Allegations of religious discrimination against Roman Catholics in Northern Ireland have a very long history. The commonest allegations are of gerrymandering in local government, favouritism in the making of appointments and bias in the allocation of houses by local authorities. There is no question that all these matters are squarely the area of 'peace, order and good government' for which the Northern Ireland government has full responsibility.[70]

Rather than give any public indication of concern about the Stormont regime, Soskice used the one and only visit by a Labour Home Secretary to the province between 1964 and August 1969 to declare of O'Neill's administration: 'From England we watch it, we admire it and we rejoice in it.'[71]

Part of the reason for Wilson's lack of action was O'Neill's own success in impressing on London that he was serious about change by his meeting with Lemass in January 1965. There was also the advice from the security services that, despite the end of the IRA campaign in 1962, the organization was preparing for a new assault. An alarmist report from the Special Branch in New Scotland Yard in November 1964, although discounting the likelihood of an imminent campaign, estimated that there were 3,000 men who had received some degree of training in the use of arms and explosives, of whom it was estimated that several hundred were sufficiently well trained to undertake active operations.[72] As O'Neill kept stressing to London the problems he faced in getting his cabinet and party colleagues to accept change, this report of an added threat by republicans may well have encouraged sympathy for an administration facing such conflicting challenges.

However, much more important factors were Labour's narrow parliamentary majority of three and the UK's difficult economic situation, which dominated Wilson's concerns for the seventeen months of his first administration. Sir Oliver Wright, his Private Secretary at the time, subsequently commented, 'I cannot remember in my time in Number 10 . . . that Ireland ever really rated very high in Wilson's preoccupation.'[73] Other priorities and the tendency of the Home Office to defend the constitutional status quo encouraged Wilson to give the benefit of the doubt to O'Neill's modernizing intentions. However, his own clear sympathy for improved relations with Dublin,[74] and his increasing frustration with the support that Ulster Unionist MPs gave to the Conservative opposition in Westminster, alarmed O'Neill and was conducive to growing Labour backbench interest in a more interventionist posture towards Northern Ireland affairs.

The formation of the Campaign for Democracy in Ulster (CDU) in early 1965 by a group of Labour Party activists with strong left-wing republican influence provided an increasingly effective Westminster echo of the Campaign for Social Justice's anti-Stormont crusade. The CDU focused on Section 75 of the Government of Ireland Act with its assertion of the ultimate supremacy of the Westminster parliament over 'all persons, matters and things' in Northern Ireland. This, it claimed, should allow for the appointment of a Royal Commission to investigate charges of discrimination and, if necessary, direct intervention by the British government to establish full civil rights for Catholics.[75]

The CDU soon had the support of around one hundred Labour MPs,[76] and after the general election of March 1966 Wilson's attitude towards O'Neill showed some indication of a toughening. Labour now had a majority of ninety-seven and CDU pressure was intensified by the return of Gerry Fitt as Republican Labour MP for West Belfast. This tough and shrewd former merchant seaman used his maiden speech to launch a passionate onslaught on the 'injustice' of the Stormont regime, ignoring the convention that domestic Northern Ireland affairs were not discussed at Westminster. At their first meeting after the election Wilson told O'Neill of the pressure he was under from the CDU and urged O'Neill to make 'a real effort . . . to meet some of the grievances which had been expressed; otherwise Westminster would be forced to act.'[77] O'Neill emphasized the fraught conditions in Northern Ireland that had followed the large republican celebrations of the fiftieth anniversary of the Easter Rising and the growing Paisleyite backlash and pleaded for breathing space before taking the reform process forward. The Home Secretary, Roy Jenkins, warned that any backsliding on reform would lead to direct rule, but Wilson did express his continuing support for O'Neill and when he met the Irish Prime Minister in December he asked Jack Lynch to understand O'Neill's 'problem': 'if he went ahead with reform too quickly he could face problems from within his own party.'[78]

When O'Neill returned to London in January 1967 he and his colleagues William Craig, Minister of Home Affairs, and Brian Faulkner got a rougher ride. Wilson again emphasized the pressure he was under from 150 Labour MPs, many of them from the 1966 intake: 'a new and irreverent generation who were challenging everything'. These MPs were already questioning the financial assistance given to Stormont by the British Exchequer and would ask why Northern Ireland should continue to be subsidized 'to operate a franchise system that no British government would consider for any independent Commonwealth state'. Jenkins claimed that pressure for reform in Derry was bound to grow. O'Neill's response was minimalist. He indicated his government's willingness to set up a statutory boundary commission to review all Stormont constituencies and to abolish the business vote in local elections. Craig used a forthcoming review of local government structures to procrastinate on the issue of universal suffrage in local government.[79]

But it was soon obvious that, while Wilson and Jenkins might be frustrated with Stormont's prevarication, they accepted O'Neill's argument that any attempt to push him too far would split his government and perhaps spark a Protestant uprising, forcing direct rule. For all Wilson and Jenkins's willingness to threaten intervention and direct rule, there could be little doubting their profound reluctance to be sucked into the 'Irish bog'. When Eddie McAteer wrote to Jenkins at the end of 1967 complaining of lack of progress on nationalist complaints, he got the standard brush-off: the matters in dispute were 'wholly within the constitutional ambit of the Parliament and Government of Northern Ireland'. He was advised to seek direct discussions with O'Neill.[80] The lack of movement by O'Neill combined with the increased debate on discrimination issues at Westminster encouraged those within the opposition who favoured more robust ways of publicizing their grievances.

Radicalization: Northern Ireland's 1960s

The Northern Ireland Civil Rights Association (NICRA) was to play a central role in the intensifying crisis of the unionist state from October 1968. Founded in February 1967, NICRA was subsequently alleged by William Craig to be a front for republicans and communists with a hidden anti-partitionist agenda. It was the case that republicans and some trade unionists with Communist Party affiliations dominated the executive committee of NICRA and that the leadership of the republican movement had decided to commit much of the energy of its northern members to the development of the civil rights movement. After the calling off of the 1956–62 campaign, the new Chief of Staff of the IRA, the republican socialist Cathal Goulding, had shifted the focus of the movement towards social agitation and left-wing politics. The Wolfe Tone Society, founded in 1963 and named after the Protestant leader of the United Irish insurrection of 1798, was created as part of Goulding's strategy of building a coalition of 'progressive and nationally-minded forces'. It was at a meeting of the Wolfe Tone Society in the house of a leading republican in Maghera, County Tyrone, in August 1966 that the decision to create NICRA was made.

Yet the view of NICRA and the subsequent development of the civil rights movement as a republican–leftist conspiracy is oversimplified. First, the priority of Goulding was to build the republican movement as a radical 'anti-imperialist' alternative to the Irish Labour Party: the focus of republican strategy was the South. Second, in Northern Ireland the priority was the reform of the Northern Ireland state, not its abolition. Pressure on Stormont from within Northern Ireland and from Westminster would, Goulding believed, force reforms on a reluctant Unionist Party that would split apart under the strain, thus freeing sections of the Protestant working class for 'progressive' politics and ultimately for republicanism. There was much that was naive in the approach of Goulding and his leftist advisers on the North. In particular they consistently underestimated the strength of Paisleyism. However, for all their inadequacies, the Goulding group did realize that any armed assault on the northern state risked a major sectarian conflagration. Third, it was most unlikely that the mass mobilization of the Catholic community that occurred after October 1968 could have been the work of such a small group, no matter how dedicated. The IRA in Belfast comprised a mere twenty-four members in 1962, and this number had grown to a less than formidable 120 by 1969.[81]

A less conspiratorial explanation of the growth of the civil rights movement was provided in the report of the Cameron Commission set up by O'Neill to investigate the violence that broke out in October 1968. The report argued that the determining factor in the unrest was the emergence in the 1960s of a 'much larger Catholic middle class . . . which is less ready to acquiesce in the situation of assumed (or established) inferiority and discrimination than was the case in the past'.[82] This stratum was created by the extension of secondary and higher education to working-class Catholics after 1945. Children of the British welfare state, they were less interested in the national question than in the fact that post-war expansion had disproportionately benefited Protestants.

There had indeed been a major expansion of the Catholic middle class under Stormont. The proportion of Catholics in professional and managerial occupations more than doubled between the censuses of 1911 and 1971, and this was clearly linked to the substantial expansion of the education, welfare and health services after 1945. Yet this stratum remained a narrow one, and the much broader appeal of the civil rights movement remains to be explained. What provoked mass support was a unique and very temporary fusion of 1960s ultra-leftism with a much more rooted sense of ethnic exclusion and oppression, which saw the movement, however inchoately, as an opportunity for striking a blow not simply at structures of discrimination but at the fundamentals of the northern state itself. Civil rights appealed precisely because it seemed to have the capacity to transcend the passivity that was a product of the failure of the two dominant traditions in Catholic politics: constitutional anti-partitionism and physical-force republicanism.

Hemmed in by the rhetoric of O'Neill and Lemass and responding to the pressure of criticisms from such groups as National Unity and the Campaign for Social Justice, the Nationalist Party unenthusiastically shuffled towards modernity. In November 1964 it produced its first ever general policy statement, with McAteer declaring that 'The Party is now anxious to step into the twentieth century.' However, this proved premature as many of the MPs resisted the idea of a modern party structure.[83] The first annual conference of the party did not occur until December 1965, and by then some of its younger members were pushing for a more radical realignment that would bring in the republican labour tradition in Belfast and for the adoption of 'left of centre' policies.[84] Fitt's return to Westminster and his high profile and good relations with many CDU MPs increasingly made him, rather than McAteer, seem the spokesman for Northern Ireland's nationalists. Fitt's main publicity coup was the tour of three CDU MPs on a fact-finding mission across the province in April 1967. Yet, while the visit may temporarily have raised hopes of Labour intervention, there was little indication that this was even on the horizon when 1968 began. For all their activities, the CSJ, CDU and NICRA had remarkably little to show in the way of results. The first year and a half of NICRA's existence was, according to the best scholarly account, 'a period of general ineffectuality'.[85]

But, if there was little to show in the way of action by O'Neill or Wilson, there had been a noticeable loss of political and moral authority on the part of the Nationalist political leadership. Increasingly attacked as ineffectual 'Green Tories' by a coalition of Nationalist modernizers, republicans and young leftist members of the NILP, Nationalist Party notables like McAteer were ignored even when their warnings about the dangers of street politics were to be proved prescient. McAteer's own experience of the polarizing effect of contested marches in Derry in the early 1950s may have contributed to his unease with the radical tactics suggested by Austin Currie, a young Queen's University graduate who won the Stormont constituency of East Tyrone in 1964. Currie supported the squatting of homeless Catholic families in houses owned by Dungannon Rural District Council and told a student audience at Magee

College in Derry that what was needed was 'more squatting, more acts of civil disobedience, more emphasis on "other means" and less on traditional political methods'.[86]

Nationalist leaders' reluctance to go down this road reflected social conservatism and the knowledge that their republican critics were better placed to exploit the housing issue at a local level. But there was also a deeper comprehension of the underlying sectarian geography of town and countryside in Ulster and of the danger that a more confrontational strategy would produce not reform but major communal conflict. Younger nationalist modernizers, socialist republicans and an increasingly influential group of leftist students all had a typically 1960s contempt for middle-aged politicians and what were seen as antiquated Orange and Green traditions. Yet the first civil rights march showed that, despite the non-sectarian language of the march organizers, many of the marchers and their opponents defined 'civil rights' in terms of traditional aspirations and antagonisms. The executive of NICRA had not initiated the march, from Coalisland to Dungannon, on 24 August 1968; the idea had come from Currie, who had recently grabbed the headlines by squatting in a vacant house in Caledon, County Tyrone, to highlight a particularly obtuse decision by Dungannon Rural District Council to award a house to a young, single Protestant woman.[87]

The NICRA leaders were divided on the wisdom of taking their demands on to the streets. The veteran Belfast communist Betty Sinclair opposed the whole idea of marches, and it was only local pressure from the leaders of the CSJ and republicans that ensured NICRA support for the march. Both the Inspector-General of the RUC and Bernadette Devlin, the young Queen's University student from Cookstown, County Tyrone, who would have brief media fame as the 'La Pasionaria' of the civil rights movement, agreed that, despite the marchers singing 'We Shall Overcome', the anthem of the black civil rights movement in the US, the march's dynamic was robustly nationalist. The 2,000 or so marchers were accompanied by bands that played traditional nationalist and republican tunes, and when the RUC prevented the march reaching the centre of Dungannon, where local unionists and Paisley supporters had organized a counter-demonstration, they were denounced as 'black bastards' by Gerry Fitt while Currie attacked O'Neill and 'the Orange bigots behind him'.[88]

The Inspector-General of the RUC described the march as 'a republican parade rather than a civil rights march' and criticized NICRA for allowing its platforms to be used by 'extremists and trouble-makers'. In fact, the leadership of the IRA was as keen as northern communists such as Betty Sinclair to prevent conflict with the RUC and loyalists, and the prominent role that republicans played in stewarding the march reflected this concern. However, as Bernadette Devlin subsequently pointed out, there was a naivety in the NICRA executive's belief that their own non-sectarian reformist intent gave them the right to march where they wanted in Northern Ireland. Coalisland was 'ninety per cent republican',[89] and Protestant and unionist perceptions of the civil rights movement were increasingly that it was just a new way for nationalists to undermine the state.

The crisis of the Unionist regime was not the execution of some 'republican-communist' conspiracy to destroy the state under the guise of civil rights. Like all significant historical events, it was brought about by a combination of factors. Amongst the most crucial were O'Neill's reluctance to move quickly on reforms because of divisions within his cabinet and party, Wilson's desire to 'leave it to O'Neill' rather than risk a confrontation with Stormont, and the Nationalist Party's loss of direction. Nationalist disarray ushered in a period of fluidity and competition in Catholic politics that allowed relatively small groups of local militants to exert a powerful influence on events.

This would have particularly momentous results in Derry. Here the Derry Housing Action Committee (DHAC), a coalition of leftist republicans and the Trotskyist-influenced Derry Labour Party led by the charismatic activist Eamonn McCann, had already initiated a civil disobedience campaign against the Corporation's housing policies. In the aftermath of the Coalisland–Dungannon march, the DHAC asked NICRA to march in Derry. McCann and his comrades proposed a march that would enter the historic walled centre of the city, where previous attempts to organize nationalist parades had been banned. Although the leadership of NICRA went along with this plan on the basis that theirs was not a nationalist march but one for civil rights within the UK, there were severe misgivings about the potential for confrontation and violence. This was especially the case as the day chosen for the march was one on which the Protestant Apprentice Boys had an annual initiation ceremony attended by members from all over the North. William Craig banned the Apprentice Boys' parade and excluded the civil rights march from the predominantly Protestant Waterside, where it was supposed to start, and from the centre of the city. Although McAteer advised a postponement, as did Conn McCluskey of the Campaign for Social Justice, the leadership of NICRA was divided and a small but determined group of Derry radicals prevailed.

Although to the organizers' disappointment only 400 turned up for the start of the march in Duke Street,[90] the RUC's response and the presence of television cameras ensured that it would have an unprecedented effect in politically energizing the Catholic community throughout Northern Ireland. Gerry Fitt had brought three Labour MPs from England and local republicans ensured that the MPs and McAteer were pushed up against the RUC line blocking the march's route to the city centre. Although the Cameron Commission found that Fitt's conduct was 'reckless, and wholly irresponsible in a person occupying his public positions',[91] the RUC response to relatively low-level verbal abuse and jostling was to baton both him and McAteer. Nationalist MPs had been batoned in the 1950s, but, as one of the regime's most formidable opponents has noted, 'there had been no TV then and meanwhile expectations had changed.'[92] A group of student radicals from Belfast, who had arrived late, were able to complete the RUC's disgrace by throwing their placards and banners at the police, who responded by assaulting the politicians at the front of the march. They then baton-charged the rest of the demonstrators.

The television footage of RUC violence brought an abrupt end to Wilson's policy of 'leaving it to Terence'. The next civil rights march in Derry, on 16 October, saw over 15,000 marchers sweep into the city centre, swamping RUC lines by force of numbers. The small group of activist students, grouped around the Young Socialist Alliance at Queen's University, exploited the RUC's overreaction, and Craig's crude defence of it, to become the self-styled 'vanguard' of an unprecedented mobilization of what had hitherto been one of the most docile campuses in Western Europe. Its leading figure was Michael Farrell, a formidable debater influenced by both republican socialism and Trotskyism. Craig's ban on a student protest march about the Derry events led to the formation of People's Democracy (PD), a mass-based student organization with Farrell's militants styling themselves as its hard core.

Influenced by the upsurge of student radicalism in Europe and the US, and particularly by the 'May Events' in France, PD militants saw in the burgeoning civil rights marches the possibility of the North's own revolutionary situation. Although some were genuine, if naive, in their belief that their commitment to a socialist project equally dismissive of unionism and nationalism could appeal to the Protestant working class, others such as Farrell were prepared to settle for a solely Catholic insurgency dressed up in the Leninist notion that an uprising of Derry's Catholic proletariat would create a situation of 'dual power'.[93] With a sharp sense of the impact that Catholic mobilization and intensifying pressure from London was having in dividing and demoralizing the Unionist regime, the student radicals gave little thought to what would result if they succeeded in bringing down O'Neill. Adopting a crude Trotskyist approach that was contemptuous of 'mere' reforms aimed at 'buying off' the just rage of the masses, the radicals in the PD were to prove disastrously successful in undermining the real support for O'Neill's reformism that still existed despite the events of October.

Disintegration

In a memorandum for his cabinet colleagues, O'Neill set out the agonizing choices likely to face them in the aftermath of the Derry events:

Can any of us truthfully say . . . that the minority has no grievance calling for a remedy? Believe me, I realise the appalling political difficulties we face. The first reaction of our own people to the antics of Fitt and Currie and the abuse of the world's Press is to retreat into old hard-line attitudes. But if this is all we can offer we face a period when we govern Ulster by police power alone . . . concessions . . . could well be the wisest course. We would have a very hard job to sell such concessions to our people, but in this critical moment may this not be our duty? We may even have to make a bitter choice between losing Londonderry and losing Ulster.[94]

Anticipating a demand for universal suffrage in local government elections from Wilson, O'Neill was faced with total inflexibility from his Minister of Home Affairs. Initially an ally of O'Neill, who regarded him as bright and progressive when he made him one of the youngest-ever Unionist cabinet ministers, Craig proved disastrous in Home Affairs. Blunt and outspoken, he had been used as O'Neill's 'battering ram' against local Unionist resistance to his original attempts to modernize government and party. However, as Minister of Home Affairs he made it clear that for him modernization did not extend to any indulgence of the civil rights agenda. Over-impressed by Special Branch reports on communist and republican involvement in NICRA, he publicly denounced its supposed ulterior agenda. He was also an early and strident voice against 'Westminster dictation'. O'Neill could have dealt with Craig's resistance – he did sack him in December – but Craig's obduracy was reinforced by the much more substantial figure of Brian

Faulkner. Although Faulkner did not oppose franchise reform in principle,[95] he was at one with Craig in demanding that O'Neill stand up to pressure from Wilson.

At a Downing Street meeting on 4 November with Wilson and James Callaghan, who had replaced Roy Jenkins as Home Secretary, Craig refused to be moved by the Prime Minister's strongly expressed desire for the quick introduction of one-man-one-vote. He and Faulkner were also unsettled by Wilson's criticism of the police behaviour in Derry and his recommendation of an inquiry.[96] O'Neill tried to convince his government that Wilson would not be satisfied without franchise reform and that the UK government was not bluffing, but the cabinet could not agree on the core issue, with Faulkner declaring that he was not prepared 'to yield to financial or economic duress'.[97] In the short term it was Craig and Faulkner who were vindicated in their assessment of the British Prime Minister as a paper tiger. For, despite a direct threat from Wilson to impose universal adult suffrage if Stormont did not introduce it, when O'Neill informed him that it was not politically possible, he and Callaghan capitulated.[98]

A five-point reform package was announced on 21 November: the introduction of a points system for the allocation of public housing; the appointment of an ombudsman for Northern Ireland; the abolition of the business vote in local government elections; a review of the Special Powers Act; and the replacement of the Londonderry Corporation by an appointed Development Commission. O'Neill feared that without a commitment to one-man-one-vote it would be impossible to satisfy the UK government or restrain the civil rights movement, and he would soon be vindicated.[99] The longer franchise reform was delayed, the more debilitating were the effects on O'Neill's position. On the one hand it encouraged more civil rights marches, while on the other it strengthened the impression amongst the unionist grass-roots that the government was reeling ineffectively before internal and external pressures. Even before the Londonderry events, the Unionist Party headquarters was receiving increasing numbers of letters complaining about the adverse media coverage of the situation in Northern Ireland and the government's failure to counter it effectively.[100] For a sizeable section of the party's grass-roots, if Catholics did have real grievances, then the extent of them was being grossly exaggerated by the civil rights movement, a movement that was perceived to be simply a more effective and dangerous incarnation of the traditional nationalist enemy. O'Neill was seen as running a government that was more responsive to its opponents than to its supporters. A report on discussions with grass-roots members in September 1968 revealed the extent of the problem:

The ordinary loyalist no longer believes that the Unionist Party is an effective influence on the course of events . . . There is a feeling in many associations that those at the top of the Party are reaching out over the heads of the people who put them there. There was criticism that much of the legislation 'does not help Unionists and favours non-Unionists'.[101]

With William Craig publicly condemning the civil rights movement as 'bogus', blaming the Catholic Church's teaching on birth-control for any Catholic disadvantage in housing and employment, and warning Westminster that 'interference' would be resisted,[102] O'Neill made one last, desperate effort in a broadcast on local television on 9 December. He declared that 'Ulster stands at a crossroads' and appealed to the civil rights movement to 'take the heat out of the situation', claiming that his government was totally committed to a reforming process. To unionists he emphasized the financial and economic support from Britain and attacked 'Protestant Sinn Feiners' who would not listen 'when they are told that Ulster's income is £200 million a year but that we can spend £300 million – only because Britain pays the balance'. He said that Wilson's declared willingness to act over their heads if adequate reforms were not forthcoming would be fully within the terms of Section 75 of the Government of Ireland Act. Most significantly, he tried to drain the local government franchise of the exaggerated importance it had assumed for many loyalists by pointing out that the adoption of the civil rights agenda would not lose the Unionist Party a single seat at Stormont.[103]

The response was encouraging. 'I Back O'Neill' coupons printed in the *Belfast Telegraph* were signed and returned by 150,000 supporters within days, and NICRA announced that there would be a moratorium on marches until the middle of January. When Craig made another defiant speech vowing to resist any British interference, O'Neill sacked him. Then on 12 December the Unionist Parliamentary Party supported a vote of confidence in the Prime Minister by twenty-eight to four abstentions. Yet O'Neill still had to win the argument for one-man-one-vote in his own cabinet, and he knew that the party in the three western counties of the province was solidly against any change. Some leading Unionists in the west were convinced that O'Neill had decided to sacrifice them in order to consolidate the Unionist cause in the greater Belfast area.[104] If O'Neill had decided to save Unionist control of

Northern Ireland by sacrificing Unionist local domination in Derry and other peripheral areas, he needed a period of calm on the streets. While the leadership of NICRA was prepared to concede this, his ultra-left critics in the PD were not.

Concerned that the civil rights movement would come to a stop because its leadership was prepared to accept O'Neill's 'miserable reforms',[105] Michael Farrell and his couple of dozen supporters in the Young Socialist Alliance promoted the idea of a 'Long March' from Belfast to Derry. Modelled on the Selma–Montgomery march in Alabama in 1966, it aimed to force British intervention and reopen the Irish question. A mass meeting of the PD at Queen's had rejected the idea in early December, aware as many were of the probability of attacks on the march as it passed through strongly loyalist areas. However, using the New Left commitment to direct democracy for a more traditionally Leninist purpose, Farrell's supporters convened another meeting at the end of term when most students had gone home and got the decision reversed. Criticized by the mainstream leaders of the civil rights movement and with the support of only a few dozen students, the march set off on 1 January accompanied by eighty policemen. O'Neill had rejected loyalist demands to ban it but did remarkably little to ensure that it was adequately protected. The marchers were harried by loyalists at various places along the route, while local republicans guarded them at night. On the final day of the march, when its size had grown from forty people to several hundred, it was attacked by 200 loyalists, some of whom were identified as off-duty B Specials, at Burntollet Bridge near Derry. Farrell had predicted that if the marchers were subject to a serious attack there would be an uprising in Derry, and he was proved correct.[106] When the marchers arrived in the centre of the city, after another attack by loyalists in the Waterside, they unleashed a wave of anti-RUC rioting that transformed the situation and strengthened the hostility of many Catholics to the state. It marks the pivotal point at which the civil rights phase of the 'Troubles' ended and the conflict began to focus on more ancient disputes over national and religious identities.

O'Neill saw the Derry violence as the end of his hopes of gradual reform from above and was dissuaded from resigning only by pressure from Wilson and Edward Heath, the Leader of the Opposition.[107] If the march had not taken place, he might at last have been forced to grasp the nettle of franchise reform. With Craig gone the only substantial voice of opposition would have been Faulkner. But Faulkner had made clear in cabinet that he had an open mind on the issue but was opposed to

being seen to act under Westminster pressure. The strengthening of
O'Neill's position after the 'Crossroads' speech and the favourable response
of NICRA would have allowed him to present a change of policy as an
expression of his government's own reformist intent. The 'Long March'
destroyed this possibility. John Hume, who had emerged as the leader of
more moderate opinion in Derry, now declared that the 'truce' on
marching was over and that there would be a return to militant action.[108]

O'Neill pleaded with his cabinet to see that a simply repressive response
would fail. Anticipating pressure from Wilson and Callaghan, he argued
for an independent public inquiry into the disturbances and for acceptance of universal suffrage in local government: 'in resisting this molehill
of reform we are allowing a mountain to fall upon us.'[109] Rebuffed on
the central suffrage issue, he was able to extract support for the decision
to set up a commission of inquiry into the recent disturbances to be
headed by the Scottish judge Lord Cameron. A week later, on 23 January,
Faulkner, who had opposed the idea of an inquiry in cabinet, resigned,
declaring that the decision to set up the commission was an 'abdication
of authority': the Prime Minister should have persuaded the party of the
need for a change of policy on the franchise issue. Yet, as O'Neill pointed
out at the last discussion of the franchise issue in the parliamentary party
in November 1968, change had been opposed by the 'vast majority'.[110]
Perhaps if Faulkner had come out earlier in support of reform this opposition could have been significantly reduced. O'Neill's anger at his
colleague's late conversion was understandable. His decision to call a
general election in February, a course of action that he had specifically
rejected in the 'Crossroads' broadcast, reflected this anger as well as
increasing desperation.

For the first time in its history the Unionist Party entered an election campaign divided. The existence of at least twelve MPs who were
now openly calling for his resignation led O'Neill to impose a loyalty
pledge on all candidates, who had to support a reformist manifesto. The
ultra-democratic structure of the Unionist Party, which left the choice
of election candidates to individual constituency associations, resulted in
the Prime Minister supporting 'unofficial' candidates against 'official'
candidates from the right. Thirty-nine Unionists were returned: twenty-
four 'official' Unionists and three 'unofficial' Unionists who supported
O'Neill; ten 'official Unionists' who opposed the Prime Minister; and
two undecided. Support for O'Neill was greatest in suburban constituencies in the greater Belfast area, while anti-O'Neillism was strongest in
the border counties and in working-class Belfast constituencies.[111]

O'Neill had gambled on a comprehensive vote of confidence and a repudiation of his critics, but the result, as a key aide has subsequently admitted, was 'muddied and inconclusive'.[112] All twelve of his Unionist critics were returned, and in his own Bannside constituency he was returned on a vote of 7,745, with Ian Paisley polling 6,331 and the PD leader Michael Farrell 2,310. With the parliamentary party split and a narrow majority of support in the Ulster Unionist Council, O'Neill eventually delivered one-man-one-vote on 22 April, although only after a very narrow vote. The resignation of the Minister of Agriculture, James Chichester-Clark, in protest at the timing of the decision was a final and stunning blow, the effect of which was amplified by bomb attacks on Belfast's water supply. Blamed on republicans, these were in fact an attempt by loyalist paramilitaries to create an atmosphere of crisis.

O'Neill resigned on 28 April and within a week a deeply divided parliamentary party chose Chichester-Clark over Brian Faulkner by a narrow majority of seventeen to sixteen. Although the government had finally conceded the core demand of the civil rights movement, developments since 1 January had shifted the conflict on to a different level, where what was at issue was the relationship between the police and an increasingly militant section of the Catholic working class. Derry would be the focus of this new and increasingly violent phase. The riots that had followed the arrival of the 'Long March' prefigured what was to come. Hours of rioting in the city centre were followed by the collapse of discipline amongst sections of the RUC, some of them drunk, who attacked people and property on the fringes of the Bogside, the city's oldest concentration of Catholic housing. Barricades were erected, and traditionalist republicans began to carve out a role in 'citizens' defence' committees.[113] By the spring of 1969 confrontations between a hard core of unemployed Derry youth and the police had become regular events. Derry's violence had also an increasingly sectarian dimension as Catholic youths clashed with members of the small Protestant working class that lived on the predominantly Catholic west side of the River Foyle.

O'Neill's divided and pressurized government had introduced a Public Order Bill in March 1969 outlawing many of the tactics used in the civil rights campaign. Protests against this culminated in a major confrontation between Catholic crowds, the RUC and loyalists in the centre of Derry on 19 April, which developed into three days of rioting. RUC men pursuing a group of rioters entered a house in the Bogside and assaulted several members of the household, including the father, Samuel Devenny, who died from his injuries in July. The April riots completed the process by which in Derry the issue of 'civil rights' had given way entirely to that of 'defence', and that of 'discrimination' to complaints about the RUC.[114] The riots also had an impact on other parts of Northern Ireland, where NICRA and the PD organized solidarity demonstrations. Many of these ended in rioting, which was particularly severe on the Falls Road. With a weak and divided government and an Opposition whose demands focused no longer on reforms but on the security apparatuses of the state, the Stormont regime had passed the point of no return.

8. Northern Ireland from Insurrection to the Anglo-Irish Agreement

The British State and the Birth of the Provisional IRA

By the spring of 1969 the violence in Londonderry was producing reverberations in Belfast. The city's IRA commander, Billy McMillen, a loyal supporter of Cathal Goulding's shift to the left, was under increasing criticism from a number of formidable traditionalist figures. These accused the leadership of neglecting the IRA's military role and leaving Catholics vulnerable to attack. McMillen had maintained a residual military role for the hundred or so volunteers who had to share twenty-four weapons between them.[1] Any major outbreak of communal violence was bound to overwhelm such paltry resources, and McMillen was conscious of Goulding's determination that the IRA should not be drawn into sectarian warfare.

In April 1969 anti-RUC riots in the Ardoyne district of North Belfast had increased pressure on McMillen to prepare the IRA for 'defensive' action, and on 12 July IRA members were mobilized during clashes between Orange marchers and Catholics living in the inappropriately named Unity Walk flats complex at the bottom of the Shankill Road. In the same month, in an oration during the reinterment of two IRA men executed in England in 1940, Jimmy Steele, a Belfast IRA veteran, launched a bitter attack on Goulding's leadership. Although he was suspended from the movement, the speech became a rallying point for those who were soon to emerge as the leaders of the Provisional IRA. The traditional march by the Apprentice Boys in Derry on 12 August was to give them their opportunity.

After the April clashes with the RUC the influence of the more moderate leaders of the civil rights movement in Derry had gone into precipitous decline. In July, soon after the death of Samuel Devenny, popularly believed to be a direct result of his beating by the RUC in April, the 'middle-aged, middle class and middle of the road'[2] Derry Citizens' Action Committee was superseded by the Derry Citizens' Defence Association (DCDA). This was dominated by local republicans, and Seán Keenan was its chairman. But, as Eamonn McCann, the Derry Trotskyist, noted, events were increasingly determined by 'the hooligans':

the unemployed youth of the Bogside whose energy and aggression had done much to power the early civil rights movement but who were now set on a major confrontation with the police and loyalist marchers.[3] Although the DCDA had met with leaders of the Apprentice Boys and promised to provide effective stewarding on the day of the march, it put much more energy into preparing for the defence of the Bogside. Barricades were erected in anticipation of an RUC and loyalist 'invasion', heaps of stones were piled at strategic points, and over the four days that culminated in the march a local dairy lost 43,000 bottles as large numbers of petrol bombs were prepared.[4] The DCDA made little more than a token effort to prevent the march being stoned, and for more than two hours a police cordon shielding marchers was subject to a constant hail of missiles before launching the series of baton charges that began 'The Battle of the Bogside'. An attempt by the RUC to follow the rioters into the Bogside was repulsed with barricades, bricks and a rain of petrol bombs from the top of a block of high-rise flats, and by 13 August 'Free Derry' had effectively seceded from the northern state.

With NICRA calling marches and demonstrations to relieve Derry nationalists by stretching the limited manpower of the 3,000-strong RUC, Chichester-Clark's government was told by Callaghan and his Home Office advisers that it must exhaust all the resources under its control, including the 8,500 B Specials, before a request for army assistance would be contemplated.[5] The result was disastrous. Robert Porter, the liberal Unionist whom O'Neill had appointed to Home Affairs shortly before his resignation, was told by the Home Office that he could allow the RUC to use a new weapon, CS gas, against rioters. Over two days, huge amounts were used, and the Bogside became blanketed with gas.[6] This served simply to stiffen resistance, as did the television broadcast by the Taoiseach, Jack Lynch, on the evening of 13 August, in which he declared that his government could 'no longer stand by and see innocent people injured and perhaps worse'. By the next morning the RUC commander in Derry told Chichester-Clark that his men were exhausted and incapable even of holding the centre of the city.[7] Stormont then ordered a general mobilization of the B Specials. The Specials, who had been conceived as a counter-terrorist force, had no training in crowd control or dealing with rioters. After forty-eight hours of rioting, with the RUC depleted by casualties and exhausted and with the prospect of a murderous confrontation between Derry Catholics and the Specials, Wilson and Callaghan agreed to the dispatch of troops.

In Belfast, where there had been attacks on RUC stations and some rioting on 13 August, the Lynch broadcast and the mobilization of the Specials contributed powerfully to the worst outbreak of communal violence since the 1920s. It centred on the streets that linked the Falls and Shankill Roads. While Catholics erected barricades on the Falls Road, crowds of Protestants, amongst whom were members of the recently mobilized Specials, gathered on the Shankill. The Derry conflagration was the subject of two conflicting and destructive ethnic myths in Belfast. For Catholics it was a case of the Bogside residents being besieged by bloodthirsty RUC men and loyalists, while for Protestants, including many members of the RUC and Specials, the Bogside was in a state of IRA-sponsored insurrection. Both communities feared that their ethnic nightmare was about to become a reality in Belfast and acted accordingly.

Overreaction by the police led to the use of armoured cars mounted with machine-guns to disperse rioters. Protestant mobs pushing down towards the Falls Road petrol-bombed Catholic houses as they proceeded. In these confrontations and in similar ones in the Ardoyne area over 150 houses were destroyed. Seven people were killed including a nine-year-old Catholic boy, Patrick Rooney, who was asleep in his bedroom when he was struck by a stray RUC bullet. The small number of IRA members with a few handguns and a Thompson sub-machine gun could do little to prevent the carnage. They were equally powerless the next day when, before British troops could be effectively deployed in the city's trouble spots, Protestants launched an attack on the Clonard district, a small Catholic enclave near the Shankill Road, after rumours that there were IRA snipers on the roof of Clonard Monastery. Gerald McAuley, a member of the Fianna, the IRA's youth wing, was shot dead, and a whole Catholic street, Bombay Street, was razed. The burning of Bombay Street would become integrated into the founding mythology of the Provisional IRA, in which it was depicted as the inevitable consequence of the defenceless state of Belfast Catholics that resulted from the misguided policies of the 'Marxist' leadership in Dublin.[8]

British troops were on the streets of Belfast and Derry for the first time since 1935, but Wilson and Callaghan, who had both threatened to introduce direct rule if troops were sent in, now backtracked. For, although direct rule had been on the British cabinet's agenda since the early months of 1969, there was an undercurrent of horror at the possibility of such a deepening of involvement. As early as February 1969 Callaghan had told the cabinet that direct rule was a 'serious option', although he added that independence for the North might be a 'preferable alternative'.[9] The truth was that, although direct rule was held like a sword of Damocles over the heads of Chichester-Clark and his colleagues, neither Wilson nor Callaghan had the stomach for it. In part this reflected an understandable desire not to be drawn into what was seen as the bog of Irish politics, but it also reflected a fear of a Protestant backlash. Sir Harold Black, the Northern Ireland Cabinet Secretary, warned senior Whitehall figures that in the event of direct rule, 'there would be a frightening reaction by the Protestant community which would make anything that had happened up to now seem like child's play.'[10] The warning seemed to have the desired effect.

But if the British government recoiled from direct rule, it also made clear that Stormont could continue to exist only as a client regime under constant supervision at both ministerial and official levels. Called to Downing Street on 19 August, Chichester-Clark pre-emptively emasculated his government by proposing to give the army's GOC in Northern Ireland supremacy over the RUC and Specials in security matters. Although the declaration issued after the meeting affirmed Northern Ireland's constitutional status, it had an implicitly critical tone, affirming that 'every citizen in Northern Ireland is entitled to the same equality of treatment and freedom from discrimination as obtains in the rest of the United Kingdom irrespective of political views or religion.'[11] Two senior civil servants were sent from Whitehall to work within the Stormont Cabinet Office and the Ministry of Home Affairs, and Chichester-Clark accepted a British proposal for a committee of inquiry into policing, to be chaired by Sir John Hunt. The humiliation of the Stormont regime was complete when, in a subsequent television interview, Wilson indicated that the Specials were finished.

Callaghan's arrival for his first visit to the North deepened the impression of a new Westminster overlordship. Joint working groups of officials from Belfast and London were to examine how far Stormont's existing practices and commitments would ensure fair allocation of houses and public employment, and promote good community relations. Greeted as a conquering hero when he entered the Bogside, which, like large sections of Catholic West Belfast, was a 'no-go' area for the RUC and the British Army, he had a much less positive reception on the Shankill Road.

This system of direct rule by proxy enraged the unionist right and eventually unleashed a downward spiral of loyalist reaction and republican assertiveness. Lord Hunt's committee reported on 9 October, recommending that the RUC become an unarmed civilian force and the B Specials be disbanded to be replaced by the Ulster Defence Regiment, a locally recruited part-time military force under the control of the British Army. In response, loyalists rioted for two nights on the Shankill Road, and shot and killed the first RUC man to die as a result of political violence since the IRA's 1950s campaign. Ian Paisley's attacks on Chichester-Clark, whom he portrayed as Callaghan's submissive poodle, were increasingly influential in the Protestant community.

Although Callaghan had privately declared his desire 'to do down the Unionists',[12] he and his colleagues were soon convinced that there was no alternative but to support Chichester-Clark. Oliver Wright, a senior diplomat who had been Wilson's emissary to Rhodesia, was now sent to oversee the implementation of the reforms and 'put some stiffening into the administration'.[13] Although Unionist ministers feared that he would listen only to their critics,[14] his reports to Downing Street were surprisingly sympathetic to the good intentions of Chichester-Clark and his colleagues, if not to their abilities: 'They were not evil men bent on maintaining power at all costs. They were decent, but bewildered men, out of their depth in the face of the magnitude of their problem.'[15] Wright was critical of the recently published *Cameron Report* into the 1968 disturbances because it displayed so little understanding of Protestant fears: 'not only the loss of political power within his own community, but his absorption into the larger society of Southern Ireland – alien in smell, backward in development and inferior in politics'. His central conclusion, one followed by Wilson's administration until it lost office, was that 'our central purpose should be to support the Northern Ireland government, both to keep the problem of Ulster at arm's length and because they alone can accomplish our joint aims by reasonably peaceful means.'[16] However, Wright was well aware of the pressure which Chichester-Clark's government was under from its own supporters, who increasingly complained that it was a puppet regime implementing pro-Catholic reforms under pressure from Wilson and Callaghan:

Her Majesty's Government is not allowing the Northern Ireland Government to do what they want to do: to issue statements about a timetable for proper action against the Catholic barricades and the extremists who seem to call the tune behind them. The result is that the Northern Ireland Government feel that the Catholics are getting away with it and they themselves are reduced more and more to the role of puppets . . . If and when we take over, and it will be a minor miracle if we don't have to, we shall, on present indications, have a pretty unfriendly majority party and majority community to deal with.[17]

Despite this, by the beginning of 1970 there was a facile optimism in the British cabinet and Whitehall that was reflected in an *Irish Times* investigation into the new relationship between Stormont and Westminster: 'The British view is that the Northern Ireland problem "has been licked".'[18] At a meeting in the Foreign and Commonwealth Office in London in February, Wright informed Patrick Hillery, the Irish Minister for External Affairs, that 'a lot of steam had gone out of demonstrations' and that the only ones making trouble were 'professional anarchists'. Irish fears about the growing support for Paisley, whose Protestant Unionist Party had recently won two council seats in Belfast, were dismissed with the claim that Chichester-Clark had a 'moderate and united Unionist Party' behind him and that the prospect was one of 'steady improvement in the situation'.[19] This ignored the reverberations from the violence of the previous summer in which thousands of people, most of them Catholics, had lost their homes. There was a dangerous new sharpness to sectarian tensions in Belfast from which both Paisley's Protestant populism and the infant Provisional IRA were already benefiting.

Traditionalist republicans had asserted themselves in the wake of the August violence. By September they had forced the Belfast IRA command to break its links with the national leadership, and by the end of the year the nucleus of an alternative republican movement had emerged, leaving Goulding's supporters to define themselves as the Official IRA. When in December an IRA convention voted in favour of ending the policy of abstention from the Dáil, Goulding's critics seceded and created a Provisional Army Council. In January 1970 the political wing of the movement, Sinn Féin, also split. While the largely southern leadership of the Provisionals – men including the new Chief of Staff Seán MacStiofáin and Ruairí Ó Brádaigh – were driven by a fundamentalist commitment to the main tenets of republican ideology, many of their new supporters in the North were motivated by a mixture of ethnic rage against loyalists and the RUC and the increasingly fraught relations between the British Army and sections of Belfast's Catholic working class.

Although the violence of August had created a reservoir of fear, resentment and anger that the Provisionals could exploit, recent research has pointed to slow and limited growth of the organization until the spring of 1970. The first 'general army convention' of the Provisional IRA was attended by just thirty-four people.[20] For many of the young Catholics who approached veteran republicans to get trained in the use of arms, the enemy was not the British soldiers, who were enjoying a brief honeymoon period as the saviours of their communities, but loyalists and the RUC. Republicans such as Joe Cahill and the young Gerry Adams were aghast at the behaviour of Falls Road housewives who gave cups of tea to soldiers while their daughters attended discos organized by the army. But as early as September 1969 Callaghan himself had admitted to his cabinet colleague Anthony Crosland that British troops were no longer popular: 'He had anticipated the honeymoon period wouldn't last very long and it hadn't.'[21] British soldiers soon found themselves in the unenviable position of policing major sectarian confrontations and acting as the first line of defence of a Unionist government under intense pressure from the loyalist right.

Republicans had long denounced Stormont as a 'police state'. However, the dominant characteristic of the RUC's response to the civil unrest after October 1968 had been its weakness and ineffectuality. In contrast, the army, whose presence had grown from the pre-Troubles garrison of 2,000 to 7,500 by September 1969,[22] responded to rioting with often overwhelming force. The loyalists who rioted on the Shankill Road after the publication of the *Hunt Report* were the first to experience the difference. Two were shot dead and more than sixty injured, with a police surgeon commenting that the injuries were the worst he had ever seen after a riot.[23] Given the atmosphere of intense sectarian animosity and potential confrontation that existed in the 'shatter-zones' of North and West Belfast, it was inevitable that the army's brutal and often indiscriminate response would be meted out to Catholics as well.

The first major conflict between Catholics and the army occurred in April 1970 after an Orange parade near the Ballymurphy estate in West Belfast, which was by then home to many of those displaced by the August violence.[24] The Ballymurphy riots were accompanied by the expulsion of Protestant families from the nearby New Barnsley estate. Further confrontations in West and East Belfast precipitated by Orange parades in June led to the first significant military actions by the Provisionals. IRA men defending the small Catholic enclave of the Short Strand in East Belfast shot dead two Protestants, while republicans killed three Protestants in clashes on the Crumlin Road. The brutal sectarian headcount of five Protestants to one Catholic killed established the Provisionals' ghetto credibility over that of the more squeamish Official IRA, which had remained loyal to Goulding. The Provisionals experienced their first major influx of recruits since the previous August and accelerated their plans for moving from a largely defensive to an aggressive posture.[25] A bombing campaign that had begun in Belfast in March 1970 was intensified in the autumn.

The growth of the Provisionals was encouraged by the combination of a Unionist government that was hostage to the right and by a new Conservative administration that republicans could portray as crudely pro-Unionist in sympathy. Ian Paisley and a supporter had been returned to Stormont in two by-elections held in April, Paisley taking particular relish from a victory in O'Neill's former constituency of Bannside. Paisley went on to win the Westminster seat of North Antrim in the June general election. Callaghan was later to blame 'the far more relaxed and less focused regime' of Reginald Maudling, his successor as Home Secretary, for allowing the situation to deteriorate radically.[26] This too conveniently ignored the profoundly destabilizing effects of the policy of direct rule by proxy, which Wilson and he had bequeathed to Heath and Maudling. But it is true that while Callaghan and Wilson were inclined to be cautious, Maudling and Heath were disposed to give the army its head. Maudling's own character has been described as 'brilliant if a little lazy'.[27] His strong aversion to the North's warring factions – 'these bloody people'[28] as he referred to them – may have encouraged Sir Ian Freeland, the GOC in Northern Ireland, to a more aggressive approach than he would have adopted under Callaghan. It was Freeland who, without consulting Chichester-Clark's government, made the decision to impose a curfew on the Lower Falls area in July after a search for arms had provoked rioting. For two days 3,000 troops supported by armour and helicopters conducted a massive house search while saturating the area in CS gas and taking on both the Official IRA, who controlled the Lower Falls, and the Provisionals in gun battles in which five people were killed.[29]

A triumphalist tour of the area by the Stormont Minister of Information, who was a son of Lord Brookeborough, contributed to the politically disastrous results of this military operation, which marked the turning point in the relations between the army and the city's Catholic working class.[30] By the end of the summer the Provisionals had launched a bombing campaign against government buildings and commercial targets and were organizing the importation of weapons from the US. Their strategy was aimed at provoking a more repressive response from Stormont, including internment, which they correctly calculated would fail and lead to direct rule. Republican theology saw Britain as the enemy, and the Provisionals did all in their power to reduce the conflict in Northern Ireland to one between the British state and the 'Irish people' without the complication of Stormont. They would be spectacularly successful in pushing the contradictions of direct rule by proxy to their limit and in bringing down Stormont, but the price would be a low-intensity sectarian civil war.

Republican violence exacerbated the problems that Chichester-Clark was experiencing in his attempts to maintain the momentum of a reform programme against a substantial section of his own party and the Unionist grass-roots. The decisions, post-August 1969, to create a Central Housing Authority and appoint a review body on local government reform chaired by Sir Patrick Macrory, were bitterly resented, particularly in the west of Northern Ireland where they were seen as 'handing over half the Province to a one third minority.'[31] To the consternation of many party members, Brian Faulkner, who as Minister of Development was in the forefront of reform, defended the need for a Central Housing Authority by pointing to the deficiencies in the North's housing stock: 'half the houses were over 50 years old, 35 per cent were over 80 years old, there were 100,000 houses that should be replaced as quickly as possible.' The usual governmental defence of its 'progressive record' gave way to the admission that 'Our housing programme since the War has been badly behind the rest of the United Kingdom.'[32]

When the *Macrory Report* was published in June 1970, it recommended the centralization of major services such as health and education in a small number of area boards and the reduction of the number of councils from seventy-three to twenty-six. Disgruntled Unionists in border areas formed the West Ulster Unionist Council, led by Harry West and other prominent Unionist and Orange opponents of reform. The concerns of border Unionists were amplified by a more general discontent with the government's security policies, where it was alleged that a weakened and demoralized RUC and the newly created Ulster Defence Regiment were failing to counter growing lawlessness and subversion. In March 1970 five of the most prominent dissidents, including Craig and West, voted against the police bill that was implementing the Hunt recommendations and were expelled from the parliamentary party.[33] Chichester-Clark's refusal to reinstate them infuriated many in the party's grass-roots, as did the regime's failure to impose authority on the 'no-go' areas. Such criticisms intensified when on July 23 the government imposed a six-month ban on parades. In September the usually supportive Executive Committee of the Ulster Unionist Council passed a resolution of no confidence in the government's security policies.

The Belfast IRA killed their first unarmed RUC men in August 1970 but did not manage to kill a British soldier until February 1971. In March the particularly brutal murder of three young off-duty soldiers by Ardoyne Provisionals precipitated Chichester-Clark's resignation when Heath refused his request for a toughening of security policy, including a military occupation of 'no-go' areas in Derry. Brian Faulkner, who easily defeated William Craig in the election to succeed Chichester-Clark, set out to restore the morale of his divided party by a determined reassertion of Stormont's role in security policy. Taking over the Home Affairs portfolio, he pressurized Heath and the new GOC, General Sir Harry Tuzo, to move from a containment policy to one of actively re-establishing the 'rule of law' in all parts of Northern Ireland.[34] He complemented this with an attempt to court moderate nationalists by offering a new system of powerful backbench committees at Stormont, some of which would be chaired by the opposition.

The IRA greeted Faulkner's accession with an intensification of its campaign. In Derry, where the Provisionals were still weak and where no shots had yet been fired, the RUC had been able to resume patrols in Bogside and Creggan.[35] With Seán MacStiofáin complaining about lack of activity in Derry, the Provisional IRA in the city deliberately and abruptly escalated their activities against the army in early July.[36] They began to use the routine confrontations between the city's young unemployed rioters and the army as a cover for sniping and the throwing of gelignite bombs. Within days the army shot and killed two Catholic youths, and all Nationalist MPs withdrew from Stormont in protest.

In the year to July 1971, fifty-five people had died violently, and there had been 300 explosions. Then the Provisionals launched their heaviest campaign of bombing in Belfast, with ten explosions along the route of the 12 July Orange parades and some 'spectaculars', including the total destruction of a new printing plant for the *Daily Mirror*.[37] According to Faulkner, these summer bombings tipped the scales in favour of internment: 'I took the decision . . . no one objected.'[38] In fact, when he went to Downing Street on 5 August to get the approval of Heath and his colleagues, it was pointed out to him that neither the Chief of the General Staff nor the GOC believed internment was necessary from a strictly military point of view and the 'national and international implications' of such a serious step were stressed. Heath made the point that if internment were tried and failed, the only further option was direct rule.[39]

Launched at 4.15 a.m. on 9 August, 'Operation Demetrius' pulled in 337 of the 520 republicans on RUC Special Branch and Military

Intelligence lists. These lists turned out to be grossly inadequate: they relied on outdated information about pre-1969 republicanism, which meant that, while middle-aged veterans of earlier campaigns were arrested together with many Officials, many of the new recruits to the Provisionals were untouched.[40] Not one loyalist was interned, adding to the outrage in the Catholic community. Most damaging politically were the claims, later officially verified, that internees had been brutalized during arrest and interrogation and, in particular, that eleven men had been singled out for 'in-depth' interrogation. This involved being deprived of sleep, food and drink and forced to stand hooded and spread-eagled against a wall while subjected to high-pitched sound from a 'noise-machine'.[41]

Though the RUC and the army were satisfied that internment had damaged the Provisionals in Belfast, there was little evidence of this on the streets, where violence intensified dramatically. The reverse was true, in that internment had provided a major boost to Provisional recruitment. In 1971 prior to internment there had been thirty-four deaths; within two days of its introduction seventeen people had died, and by the end of the year 140 more.[42] By the beginning of October, Heath was complaining that the crisis in Northern Ireland was threatening to jeopardize the success of the government's economic and defence policies and its approach to Europe. Despite this, he still gave priority to the defeat of the IRA by military means whatever this meant in terms of alienation of the minority and bad relations with Dublin.[43] However, other senior ministers and officials favoured an approach that kept the option of a united Ireland open. The consensus that emerged was that Faulkner should be pressed to consider a radical political initiative that would involve bringing 'non-militant republican Catholics' into the government, while the issue of internal reform would be separated from that of creeping reunification by the periodic holding of referendums on the border. Faulkner rebuffed the pressure, telling Heath that he could not contemplate serving in government with republicans − amongst whom he included politicians such as John Hume and Gerry Fitt. He was too mindful of previous British failure to deliver on threats of direct rule and placed too much faith in ritualistic statements by British ministers ruling it out. In fact, a belief that direct rule was likely had formed at the highest level of the British state by the autumn of 1971. The principal reason was the communal polarization generated by internment and an increasing inclination to reach out to the nationalist community by a radical break that would undermine support for the

Provisionals. Suspension of Stormont had therefore become likely even before the tragedy of Bloody Sunday.

In Derry the GOC had come to an agreement with leaders of moderate Catholic opinion in August 1971 that the army would lower its profile in order to allow the 'extremists' to be marginalized. By the end of the year it was obvious that the wager on moderation had failed: 'At present neither the RUC nor the military have control of the Bogside and Creggan areas, law and order are not being effectively maintained and the Security Forces now face an entirely hostile Catholic community numbering 33,000 in these two areas alone.'[44] This had allowed both sections of the IRA in the city large zones for rest and recuperation, from which they had emerged as the most formidable military challenge in the North. The large numbers of nationalist youth, 'Derry Young Hooligans' as the military commanders in the city referred to them, also used the 'no-go' areas as bases for incursions into the city centre, which was being decimated by the effects of rioting, arson and Provisional bombs. By the end of the year, faced with an increasingly rampant level of 'Young Hooligan' activity, which the IRA often used as a means of luring soldiers into situations where they were vulnerable to snipers or nail-bombs, there was a feeling amongst some senior military commanders that a more aggressive posture was necessary. This was the background to the events of Bloody Sunday, 30 January 1972, when, after rioting that had developed in the wake of a banned civil rights march, members of the Parachute regiment, whose deployment in Derry had been questioned by local police and army commanders because of their reputation for gung-ho brutality, opened fire, killing thirteen civilians.

The material released to the Saville Inquiry into Bloody Sunday, set up in 1997 by the British Prime Minister, Tony Blair, provides no evidence that the killings were the result of a policy decision by either the Faulkner or Heath cabinets. Instead there was a clearly defined local dialectic leading to the disaster. Major-General Ford, the Commander of Land Forces who was responsible for day-to-day operational decisions in Northern Ireland, had come to the conclusion that a 'softly-softly' approach to the Bogside and Creggan had placed an increasingly intolerable strain on his men as they faced strong and self-confident aggression from 'Derry Young Hooligans' and from the local IRA. He was contemptuous of the moderate advice coming from the local RUC commander, a Catholic. Afraid that the city centre itself was in danger of becoming a 'no-go' area, Ford had come to believe that only the shooting of identified 'ringleaders' would stop the rot.[45]

The Heath cabinet had no desire to push events in Derry to such a brutal conclusion, as a minute of the cabinet discussion shows:

As to Londonderry, a military operation to impose law and order would require seven battalions . . . It would be a major operation, necessarily involving civilian casualties, and thereby hardening even further the attitude of the Roman Catholic population.

Heath's own summing-up of the situation on 11 January was that a military operation to 'reimpose law and order' in Derry might become inevitable, but it should not be undertaken until there was a successful political initiative.[46] The British political and military establishment may have been prepared to contemplate civilian deaths in Derry during an operation against the IRA in the Bogside and Creggan, but only when they believed that the political conditions were right. This would entail a major political initiative and one was not yet on the horizon when Bloody Sunday occurred. Less than a week before, the Chief of the General Staff, Sir Michael Carver, on a visit to the province, had defined the 'IRA propaganda machine' as the main enemy.[47] The actions of the First Parachute Regiment on 30 January provided that machine with sufficient fuel to guarantee years of effective work.

Direct Rule and the Fragmentation of Unionism

The Derry killings unleashed a wave of angry protest in the South that culminated in the burning of the British embassy in Dublin after it had been attacked by a crowd of more than 20,000. Amidst a torrent of international criticism and with growing unease amongst his own colleagues and Tory backbenchers, Heath summoned Faulkner to Downing Street to discuss the possibility of a political initiative. Faulkner was confronted with a series of ideas, including repartition, a periodic border poll, a broadening of his government to include members of the recently formed moderate-nationalist Social Democratic Labour Party (SDLP) and the transfer of all Stormont's security powers to Westminster.[48] On 3 March, as newspapers carried a number of speculative articles on the imminence of direct rule, Faulkner read out a telegram from Heath to the annual meeting of the Ulster Unionist Council. In it, Heath had described the stories as 'pure speculation'. Kenneth Bloomfield noted that Faulkner 'should have been more wary of that elastic form of words'.[49] Even at a cabinet meeting the day before the crucial Downing Street meeting on 22 March, Faulkner told his colleagues that 'consultation rather than announcement of decisions was what was in Mr Heath's mind – indeed he thought it would be unrealistic after weeks of independent study for him to be expected to accept any new ideas on the strength of a one-day meeting.' Harry West was the only minister who is recorded as regarding Faulkner as 'over-optimistic': 'preparations should be made for either of two extreme situations – an anti-climax causing major trouble by Republican supporters or such radical solutions being imposed on the Government that it would have to seriously consider its position collectively and individually.'[50] It was West who was proved correct. At their meeting the following day Heath spelt out the realities as perceived in London:

At present there were 17 Battalions in Northern Ireland; the Army presence had existed for two and a half years and it was now becoming apparent that while the Army could deal with the IRA up to a point . . . there could be no purely military solution. The drain on United Kingdom resources was very considerable and there had been massive interference with the British Government's international commitments.

The United Kingdom Government had a situation where they had a responsibility and the blame for what happened as regards internment and on the security front but were without real power: this was a very unsatisfactory situation which was accentuated by the growing financial dependence of Northern Ireland.[51]

A military solution would mean an 'escalation of force, whereas what was needed was a de-escalation . . . to swing the Catholic community away from those who were using force'. A political initiative was needed, and the British government did not consider that Faulkner's proposals were 'sufficient to give the permanent, active and guaranteed role to the minority'. No specific proposals were put forward by the British, but they suggested the need to phase out internment and added that in order to do this it was necessary for Westminster to take over responsibility for law and order.[52]

Faulkner recounted his response: 'I was shaken and horrified, and felt completely betrayed.' The next day he set out the British proposals to the cabinet and admitted that he had been proved wrong about Heath's intentions. The cabinet's almost unanimous decision was to resign rather than to stay on as a 'bunch of marionettes'.[53] But as the

Unionist government accepted its peaceful expropriation, it remained to be seen how the unionist community would react and what the implications would be for the leaders of the UUP.

Unionism was driven towards a bitter and fevered fragmentation by the twin threats of Provisional violence and British intervention. Deaths from the conflict had risen from fourteen in 1969 to 174 in 1971. The first three months of 1972 produced eighty-seven more, and that year would be the worst in three decades of violence with 470 deaths, 14 per cent of all those killed in Northern Ireland between 1969 and 1998. Other indices of sharply escalating violence were a rise in the number of shootings from seventy-three in 1969 to 1,756 in 1971 and of explosions from nine to 1,022 in the same period.[54] On 20 March the Provisionals made their most destructive and indiscriminate contribution to the tool-kit of terrorism with the first use of a car-bomb in a devastating explosion in Belfast's Donegall Street. Claimed to be a blow at 'the colonial economic structure'[55] and the British ruling class, this Provisional bomb killed six people, most of them members of the crew of a bin-lorry.[56] With the IRA declaring that 1972 would be the 'Year of Victory' and Harold Wilson being prepared to meet leading Provisionals in Dublin and declare his support for their inclusion in all-party talks in the event of an IRA ceasefire, many unionists scented betrayal, fearing that Wilson was a surrogate for Heath, who would do anything to extricate his government from the Irish quagmire.[57]

This was the environment in which support for both radical constitutional change in the form of a possible independent loyalist state and the much more localistic and almost apolitical vigilantism of the emerging Protestant paramilitary groups developed. The politician who temporarily dominated the Protestant reaction was William Craig. He had played a leading role in all the anti-reformist movements that had developed since O'Neill had sacked him from the cabinet. He warned that if the British government abolished Stormont it would be met by massive resistance; a provisional government would be formed and, if necessary, Northern Ireland would go it alone.[58] As the IRA campaign intensified he criticized Faulkner's acquiescence in London's 'interference' in Stormont's security responsibilities and demanded the creation of a 'third force' of loyalists, essentially a return of the B Specials, to deal with the republican threat.[59] In the aftermath of 'Bloody Sunday', with rumours of imminent direct rule abounding, Craig launched Ulster Vanguard on 9 February. Although other leading members of Vanguard, such as the Presbyterian minister and leading Orangeman Martin Smyth, saw the organization as a means of reunifying the Unionist Party around more right-wing poli-cies,[60] Craig's willingness to be associated closely and publicly with loyalist paramilitaries was an embarrassment to the staid and conservative figures who were the backbone of the right within the party. Vanguard's initial role was to scare off any interventionist urges Heath might be planning to indulge by a theatrical politics of threat. Craig was borne in an ancient limousine, complete with motorcycle outriders, to mass rallies stiffened by the presence of paramilitaries in uniform, where he threatened violence: most graphically to a crowd of over 60,000 in Belfast's Ormeau Park on 18 March, where he proclaimed, 'We will do or die. We will not accept direct rule . . . We must build up dossiers on the men and women who are the enemies of Northern Ireland because one day, if the politicians fail, it will be our job to liquidate the enemy.'[61]

When on 24 March Heath announced the suspension of the Stormont parliament after Faulkner and his cabinet refused a demand for the transfer of all security powers to London, Vanguard's response was a two-day general strike. Although it was relatively successful, it did little to obstruct the unfolding of British policy. The introduction of direct rule was hailed by the Provisional IRA as a victory, which they declared 'places us in a somewhat similar position to that prior to the setting up of partition and the two statelets. It puts the "Irish Question" in its true perspective – an alien power seeking to lay claim to a country for which it has no legal right.'[62] But the significance of direct rule was elsewhere: its intro-duction marked the definitive end of the 'Orange state', and it allowed the British government to introduce a strategy of reform from above. Northern Protestants were inevitably divided in their reading of the conflicting interpretations of direct rule put forward within a unionist politics characterized by disarray and confusion.

Craig advocated an independent Ulster as the only defence against the IRA and a Conservative government that a Vanguard pamphlet portrayed as 'tired, even bored with Irish politics from which they wish to extricate themselves'.[63] In a newspaper article he denounced British treachery:

They had experience of Westminster politicians from Gladstone to Wilson. Consistently at every crisis Westminster has produced politicians prepared, for party advantage, to renege on Ulster. If the gentlemen at Westminster are bent on seriously tampering with our constitution, Vanguard will seek a transfer of power from Westminster with the objective of achieving some form of friendly dominion status.[64]

But Vanguard's willingness to contemplate fundamental constitutional change and its association with Protestant paramilitary groups was unappealing to many unionists. Distrust of the British governments was a much more widespread phenomenon amongst unionists than a willingness to contemplate a radical loosening of the constitutional link with the British state.[65] There was also little evidence that the emergence of Protestant paramilitary groups as players in inter-communal conflict had allowed them to develop the sort of political and ideological legitimacy that the Provisional IRA had achieved in the Catholic community.

The Ulster Volunteer Force (UVF) – its name adapted from that of the unionist paramilitary grouping created in 1912 to resist Home Rule – had been formed in 1966 by ex-servicemen who worked in the shipyard and lived in the Shankill district of West Belfast. They had been involved with Ulster Protestant Action, founded in 1959 to ensure that Protestant employers looked after loyalists as redundancies threatened, and were influenced by the anti-ecumenical and anti-republican preaching of Ian Paisley. However, the UVF's murder of two Catholics in 1966 and the arrest of its leader Gusty Spence and two of his associates dealt it a near-fatal blow and left little in the way of enduring organization or support.[66]

It was the communal violence in West and North Belfast in August 1969 and after internment that propelled Protestant paramilitarism from the lumpen fringes of loyalist activity to, at least temporarily, a more central role. Although the UVF would benefit from the violent and febrile conditions post-August 1969, the main organization to emerge was the Ulster Defence Association (UDA). The UDA was established in September 1971 out of the fusion of a number of vigilante groups that had emerged in North and West Belfast. At its peak in 1972 it had a membership of between 40,000 and 50,000 men.[67] The declared motivation of the UDA was the defence of its communities from republican attacks. Most of the membership had full-time employment and so tended to play little part in the day-to-day running of the organization, coming out at night and weekends to man barricades or take part in marches and demonstrations, which were common in the centre of Belfast in 1972. However, a hard core of often unemployed members would work full time for the organization, and, as in the smaller UVF, it was these who were also involved in violent actions under the *nom de guerre* of the Ulster Freedom Fighters (UFF). The object of its attacks was defined as the republican movement, but UFF targets extended well beyond known IRA men to include any Catholic unlucky enough to come into the

path of one of its assassination squads. In the eighteen months after its
first killing of a Catholic vigilante on the Crumlin Road in February
1972 it would kill over 200 people.[68] Although some of the more cerebral of its leaders would rationalize these sectarian killings as an attempt
to dry up the reservoir of popular support and sympathy for the Provos
in the Catholic community, many were ad hoc responses of small groups
of UDA men enraged by an IRA attack and often inflamed by alcohol
and sectarian hatred.

Although the Provisionals had a less nakedly sectarian agenda than
that of the loyalist groups, their campaign was also tainted by sectarianism.[69] Until the onset of the 'Ulsterization' of security policy in the
mid 1970s, the Provisionals had a large and easily identifiable non-
Protestant target in the British Army. Even then their use of car-bombs
in Belfast and other town centres showed a cavalier disregard for the
lives of civilians, the majority of them Protestants. Nor did the IRA hesitate to bomb pubs in Protestant areas: in September 1971 a Provisional
bomb at the Four Step Inn on the Shankill Road killed two people and
injured twenty.[70]

In this situation of political instability and intense violence, Ian Paisley
posed the biggest threat to the position of the Unionist Party. There was
nothing inevitable about this, for down to 1973 it was to William Craig
that most disaffected unionists looked to provide leadership against
Faulkner's 'appeasement' policies. Paisley was by 1971 a member of both
the Stormont and Westminster parliaments, but his coarse and unsophis-
ticated anti-Catholicism made him and his Protestant Unionist Party
appear too extreme for the vast bulk of 'respectable' unionists. His support
was still largely confined to rural Ulster, where he had, in areas such as
north Antrim and north Armagh, a following composed of a mixture of
pietistic Protestants and members of the Orange Order.[71]

However, the hostility he had experienced from other MPs at
Westminster led him to modify the more fanatical features of his public
persona. He was also affected by his friendship with the Ulster Unionist
MP for Shankill, Desmond Boal. Abrasive, intelligent and one of the
North's leading lawyers, Boal emphasized the importance of class issues
if Paisleyism were to become an effective challenge to the Ulster
Unionist Party (UUP). Both he and John McQuade, the ex-docker
and ex-soldier who was MP for Woodvale in North Belfast, personified
the dissident Unionist tradition that had produced previous independent
Unionist MPs such as J. W. Nixon and Tommy Henderson, who
combined ultra-loyalism and strong Orange credentials with a record

of criticism of the Unionist Party on social and economic issues.[72]

Paisley and Boal made a bid to widen their political appeal by the replacement of the Protestant Unionist Party with a new organization, the Democratic Unionist Party (DUP), founded in September 1971. Boal defined it as being 'right wing in the sense of being strong on the constitution, but to the left on social issues'. But although some of its Belfast activists were from the NILP tradition, most of the DUP's belonged to Paisley's Free Presbyterian Church. This provided the party with an infrastructure of dedicated and ultra-loyal activists who in time would emerge as a disciplined and monolithic threat to the defensive and divided Unionist Party. However, for most of the first two years of the DUP's existence the policy stances adopted by Paisley did much to confuse his supporters and limit his appeal. Paisley opposed internment, supported Northern Ireland's full political integration into the UK political system and speculated that changes in the Republic's Constitution might change Protestant attitudes to a united Ireland. These heretical statements created confusion and incredulity amongst his supporters. They also prompted the IRA leadership to praise his 'statesmanship', and evoked a prediction from William Whitelaw, first Secretary of State for Northern Ireland, that he would be 'the future leader of Northern Ireland'.[73]

In the short term his iconoclasm was little short of disastrous for the appeal of the party. When it was revealed that Whitelaw had had leading members of the IRA flown to London for secret talks in July 1972, calls for the full integration into the UK appeared both fatuous and positively dangerous. However, after 'Operation Motorman' had ended the 'no-go' status of the Bogside and the Creggan in July and it became clearer that the objective of British policy was a reformed Northern Ireland and not disengagement, the environment for a DUP take-off became more favourable.

Paisley was assisted by Craig's political ineptitude. In a speech to the right-wing Monday Club in the House of Commons in October 1972, he declared that his supporters were prepared to 'shoot and shoot to kill' and added 'I am prepared to kill and those behind me have my full support.'[74] In February 1973 he told an audience in the Ulster Hall that an 'independent dominion of Ulster' would be economically viable. This vision might have enthused the largely middle-class activists of Vanguard, but it had little appeal to working-class loyalists, who wondered what would happen to the welfare state and many of their jobs in Craig's utopia. In the same month he identified Vanguard with a one-day general strike called by the UDA and the Loyalist Association of Workers (LAW) in protest at the internment of two loyalists, the first Protestants to be interned at a time when there were already hundreds of Catholics 'behind the wire'. LAW was composed of Protestant trade unionists in some of the North's key industries, including the main power stations in Belfast and Larne. The strike, which combined limited industrial muscle with paramilitary intimidation, shut down transport and the electricity supply in Belfast and was accompanied by widespread rioting and destruction of property. Five people died, including a fire-fighter shot by a loyalist sniper. The great majority of unionists were appalled by these events, and in their aftermath LAW fell apart and many on the unionist right turned their backs on Craig.

Paisley exploited this weakening of Craig's position and was able to use the border referendum held in March 1973 to bring the DUP back in from the periphery of loyalist politics.[75] The British government, relying on the poll to reassure unionists that their constitutional position was secure, pressed ahead with plans for a return to devolved government in Northern Ireland. The White Paper *Northern Ireland Constitutional Proposals*, published in March, made it clear that any new administration must be based on some form of executive power-sharing between unionists and nationalists and would also have an 'Irish Dimension': new institutional arrangements for consultation and cooperation between Dublin and Belfast. The new northern arrangements should be 'so far as is possible acceptable to and accepted by the Republic of Ireland'.[76]

At a time when violence, although somewhat lower in intensity than in the previous horrendous year, was claiming around thirty lives a month and with nationalists publicly committed to joint Dublin–London rule over the North as a 'transition' to unity, what is surprising is not the Protestant support for the right but rather the continued existence of a considerable constituency that was prepared to back Faulkner's qualified and ambiguous acceptance of the White Paper. A special meeting of the Ulster Unionist Council rejected an anti-White Paper motion, forcing Craig to lead his followers out of the Unionist Party to form a new organization, the Vanguard Unionist Progressive Party (VUPP).[77] Former allies, including John Taylor, Harry West and Martin Smyth, refused to follow him and resigned from Vanguard. The right was determined not to cede control of the Unionist Party to the Faulknerites and stayed inside to mobilize opinion against 'capitulation' to the British government's 'pro-republican' stratagems. Here they showed more political sense than those liberal Unionists who left the party to join the new non-sectarian Alliance Party. Established in April 1970, Alliance quickly gained support from middle-class unionists in the greater Belfast area who had supported O'Neill. Their defection denuded the ranks of those within the Unionist Party who could most effectively have resisted the onward march of the right and split the pro-power-sharing constituency in the Protestant community as well.[78]

Paisley benefited from the confused and disorganized state of the Ulster Unionist Party. Direct rule had at a stroke removed the UUP's control of governmental and administrative power. No longer was the directing centre of Unionism located in the cabinet, with its access to the substantial resources of the Northern Ireland civil service. Within months of the prorogation, Faulkner's old cabinet had collapsed as an effective political force, and he was faced with an increasingly assertive set of officers from the party's ruling Ulster Unionist Council, within which the older and more traditional elements of the party were strongly ensconced.[79] Senior civil service officials such as Sir Harold Black and Kenneth Bloomfield, who had been at the core of the Stormont system, were now working within the new Northern Ireland Office, created to service William Whitelaw's ministerial team.[80] While Bloomfield was using his sharp political intelligence and considerable drafting skills in the preparation of the British government's constitutional proposals, Faulkner had to rely on the penny-farthing machine that was the Unionist Party's 'research and publicity' department, staffed by a few young graduates almost totally lacking in political experience. Given these exiguous resources, Faulkner's political achievements down to the end of 1973 were considerable.

After winning the support of the Ulster Unionist Council to participate in the constitutional experiment outlined in the White Paper, Faulkner applied all his undoubted resources of energy, courage and verbal dexterity to selling a deal based on power-sharing with the SDLP and what he saw as a 'merely' symbolic concession to nationalist sentiment in agreeing to the setting up of a Council of Ireland. The manifesto on which Faulkner proposed that the party's candidates contest the June 1973 elections for a new Northern Ireland Assembly contained the formula, soaked in ambiguity, 'we are not prepared to participate in government with those whose primary objective is to break the Union with Great Britain.'[81] Preparing to drop his previous opposition to sharing power with constitutional nationalists, he argued that any member of the proposed Executive had to take an oath under the Northern Ireland Constitution Act of 1973 'to uphold the laws of Northern Ireland', which would make them structurally, if not ideologically, Unionist.[82] This was

a relatively subtle distinction for many Ulster Unionists to appreciate at
a time when their predominant emotions were often ones of bewilder-
ment and apprehension at the collapse of the Stormont regime, coupled
with bitter resentment at those they considered responsible, amongst
whom the leaders of the SDLP ranked almost as high as the Army
Council of the Provisional IRA.

Faulkner insisted that all UUP candidates sign a statement committing them to working within the framework of the White Paper. This
statement became known as the 'Pledge', and the thirty-nine Unionist
candidates who signed it became known as 'Pledged Unionists', while
the ten party candidates who refused to sign the pledge were
'Unpledged'.[83] The results of the election on 28 June were, as Faulkner
admitted, 'mixed'. He had topped the poll in South Down, and two of
his main supporters, Roy Bradford and Basil McIvor, had also come first
in East and South Belfast. Craig, by contrast, had come third in North
Antrim, trailing not just Paisley but the 'Pledged' Unionist as well. Overall
the 'Pledged' UUP candidates won 29.3 per cent of the first-preference
vote and twenty-two seats, with the 'Unpledged' Unionists at 8.5 per
cent and ten seats. Despite Craig's prediction of thirty seats, the VUPP
won 10.5 per cent and seven seats, while the DUP took 10.8 per cent
and eight seats.[84] The UUP retained a strong pull on a substantial sector
of the Protestant electorate, and this traditionalist appeal was accentuated by distrust of Paisleyism and Craig's constitutional radicalism.
However, the UUP vote was not necessarily a vote for the White Paper,
and up to three of the 'Pledged' candidates returned had made it clear
that they opposed it. As a result Unionist representation in the Assembly
was fairly evenly divided, and the risks of pressing on with the constitutional proposals were evident. However, together with the SDLP, which
had won 22 per cent of the vote and nineteen seats, and the Alliance's
9 per cent and eight seats, the parties supporting the proposed new
dispensation had a commanding majority in the Assembly. Negotiations
began between delegations of the three parties on the formation of an
Executive. Faulkner, perhaps because of an exaggerated belief in the effect
of the Border poll in generating a sense of constitutional security amongst
unionists, seriously overestimated his ability to sell the prospective deal
to his party. He astounded the supportive but cautious Ken Bloomfield
when, after a visit to his home in October by the Irish Foreign Minister,
Garret FitzGerald, he agreed that the proposed Council of Ireland would
not simply be a consultative body but would have executive powers.[85]
Bloomfield's reaction – that it 'represented the crossing of a significant

Rubicon . . . I wondered if it would not have proved a bridge too far for the unionist community'[86] – accurately predicted the role that an overambitious 'Irish Dimension' would have in destroying reformist unionism's prospects for two decades.

Social Democrats versus Provos: Nationalist Politics 1969–1973

While the dynamic behind the Provisionals was found in the Catholic working class of North and West Belfast and Derry's Creggan and Bogside, the modernized constitutional nationalism of the Social Democratic and Labour Party had its social roots in the post-war educational revolution. Francis Mulhern, who as a teenager from a Catholic working-class background in County Fermanagh took part in the civil rights movement, provides an acute summation of the local effects of the Butler Education Act:

The local leaderships of the civil rights movement were to a striking degree highly educated, with teachers, present, past or future, most prominent in them. These people enjoyed a conventional authority, but unlike an earlier generation of their kind they were not a rarity and unlike the Nationalist notables they now displaced they wore their class differences lightly.[87]

The dominant intellectual influence in the SDLP came from the revisionist nationalist thinking associated first with the National Unity project in the early 1960s and then with the more politicized challenge to the Nationalist Party that emerged with the formation of the National Democratic Party (NDP) in 1965. The NDP's arguments for a participationist strategy that maintained a commitment to unity but only with the consent of a majority in the North, and for a modern democratic party structure, were central to the SDLP at its formation; of the almost 400 people who joined the new party, nearly 80 per cent had been NDP members.[88] The NDP had made little progress because it confined its activities to those areas where the Nationalist Party did not have seats, and it was left to the civil rights movement to create that unprecedented mobilization of northern Catholics that made a frontal challenge to the party possible. In the February 1969 Stormont election the Nationalists lost three of their nine seats to independents, all of whom had played a prominent part in the civil rights movement. Most shattering was the defeat of the Nationalist leader, Eddie McAteer, by John Hume in the

Foyle constituency. Over the next decade Hume would establish himself as the predominant strategic intelligence in non-violent Irish nationalism on the island. This would also be a period in which constitutional nationalism adopted a more implacable position.

In his early thirties when elected to Stormont, Hume had already established a reputation for incisive criticism of the negativity and conservatism of the Nationalist Party combined with a moderate and 'responsible' role in Derry's increasingly disturbed situation after 5 October 1968. From working-class origins, he had been empowered by the Education Act of 1947 to follow the traditional route of many middle-class Derry Catholics through the strict religious and nationalist environment of St Columb's Grammar School to the Catholic seminary at Maynooth. A loss of vocation led him into teaching in his home town and an increasingly prominent role in community politics through his active promotion of 'self-help' schemes such as the Credit Union movement and local housing associations. Hume's politics, while professedly left of centre, had little association with the city's labour tradition, which by the end of the 1960s had become heavily influenced by Eamonn McCann's Trotskyism and leftist republicans. Derry's Catholic middle class of teachers, shopkeepers and publicans looked to Hume and other members of the Citizens' Action Committee to curb the excesses and extremism of the leftists and republicans, who were seen as dangerously influential, particularly on the rioting activities of the young.

During his campaign against McAteer, Hume had committed himself to working for a new political movement based on social democratic principles, which would be 'completely non-sectarian' and animated by the ideal that the future of Northern Ireland should be decided by its people.[89] However, the insurrection in the Bogside in August 1969 and the impetus it gave to the rebirth of physical-force republicanism would put increasing pressure on this project. At Stormont, Hume attempted to unite the divergent elements of anti-unionism into a coherent force. Nationalist Party hostility to this dangerous upstart meant that the focus of his activities was a group of five MPs, comprising former civil rights leaders and two Belfast labourists, Gerry Fitt and Paddy Devlin.

Fitt and Devlin were essential to Hume's project of a serious political challenge to unionism, for without them any new party would continue to replicate the largely rural and border-counties orientation of the Nationalist Party. Without a base in Belfast the party would also be absent from the cockpit of the struggle with resurgent republicanism. But both men, with their powerful personalities and strong labour and socialist sentiments, fitted uneasily into the new formation. Fitt, an ex-merchant seaman who had done convoy duty to the USSR during the war, had built a political base in his native dock ward through a combin-ation of republican socialist rhetoric and clientelism. A councillor from 1958, he had entered Stormont in 1962. But it was his victorious return as Republican Labour MP for West Belfast in the 1966 Westminster general election that allowed him to capture the attention of the British and Irish media as he gave powerful and eloquent expression to the emerging civil rights critique of the Unionist regime. Fitt's seniority, his growing influence in the House of Commons and his friendly relations, not only with members of Wilson's cabinet but also with leading Tories, helped to ensure that this arch-individualist who had little interest in questions of long-term strategy or party management became leader of the new party.[90]

From the start there were tensions. Fitt's predominant orientation towards Westminster-inspired reform of the North was at odds with Hume's increasingly close connections with the southern state. Fitt's almost instinctive class politics led him to be suspicious of Hume's social democratic philosophy and the school teachers and other middle-class Catholics whom he believed dominated the SDLP. This suspicion was shared by Paddy Devlin, a more cerebral socialist but also a fiercely indi-vidualist and prickly individual. A republican internee during the Second World War, Devlin had educated himself out of both nationalism and Catholicism to become a dogged and courageous exponent of socialism and secularism. He had won the Falls constituency for the NILP in the 1969 election. Fitt and Devlin insisted that any new organization should make clear its distance from traditional forms of Catholic nationalism by including in its name an identification with the North's Labour tradition, which both saw as the basis for a cross-sectarian appeal. Hume had to explain to an Irish official that the new formation would include the word 'Labour' in deference to Fitt and Devlin but asked him to assure Jack Lynch that there would be no connection between the new party and the British, Irish or Northern Irish Labour Parties.[91] Fianna Fáil was not to be embarrassed by any outbreak of class politics in the North.

When the SDLP was launched in August 1970, Fitt emphasized its left-of-centre, non-sectarian philosophy. Its nationalism was expressed in a moderate and democratic form: 'To promote co-operation, friendship and understanding between North and South with a view to the even-tual reunification of Ireland through the consent of the majority of the

people in the North and South.'[92] One of the party's first policy-makers
has subsequently outlined the 'dream' of many members in 1970: 'to
participate in a coalition government with the NILP and some liberal
Unionists. Agreement within Northern Ireland might destroy many
Unionists' fears [and] be a preliminary to agreement in Ireland.'[93]

However, just as the violence of August 1969 had pushed Devlin into
rushing to Dublin to call for the defensive arming of northern Catholics,
internment and Bloody Sunday forced a radicalization of the SDLP's
attitudes to the state. In the immediate aftermath of Bloody Sunday,
Hume gave an interview on Irish radio in which he said that, for many
people in the Bogside, 'it's a united Ireland or nothing. Alienation is
pretty total.'[94] In a subsequent interview he claimed that reunification
was 'a lot nearer than many people believed'.[95] Radicalization was obvious
in the party's policy statement, *Towards a New Ireland*, published in
September 1972, which called on Britain to make a formal declaration
of intent in favour of a united Ireland and in the interim proposed that
Northern Ireland be jointly ruled by Dublin and London. The document reflected the fear that the Provisional IRA could challenge the
party for the leadership of the Catholic community.[96]

Although the Provisionals had declared that 1972 would be their 'Year
of Victory',[97] direct rule and the possibility of British-sponsored reforms
created major problems for them. Many Catholics saw direct rule as a
victory and as an antechamber to more radical changes, thus making
further republican violence unjustifiable. Even areas with strong support
for the IRA, such as Andersonstown in West Belfast, developed local
peace groups often linked to the Catholic Church. Such attitudes affected
the IRA, and there were reports that rank-and-file Provos in Belfast and
Derry favoured a truce.[98] Pressure for a Provisional ceasefire was
intensified when the Official IRA announced one in May. The Officials
had been involved in a militarist competition with the Provisionals since
internment. The results had been difficult to reconcile with their pretensions to non-sectarianism and the defence of working-class interests.
The Derry Officials shot dead a prominent Unionist Senator, Jack
Barnhill, in December 1971. Then, in retaliation for Bloody Sunday, the
Officials bombed the officers' mess of the Parachute Regiment in
Aldershot, killing seven people, including five female canteen workers
and a Catholic chaplain. Finally, in April 1972, the Derry Officials
'executed' Ranger William Best, a young Derry Catholic who had joined
the British Army and was home on leave. Convinced that such actions
made political progress in the South impossible and could even allow

the southern state to introduce internment, Goulding and a majority on the Army Council declared a ceasefire in May.[99]

Within the Provisionals there were signs of a North–South divide on a ceasefire. The cutting edge of the armed campaign was being provided by young working-class Catholics in Belfast, whose republicanism was more a product of the conflict with Protestants and the security forces since 1969 than any ideological commitment to a united Ireland or identification with the martyrs of 1916. Here suspicion that a ceasefire would allow the security forces to reassert their control of the IRA's base areas in North and West Belfast was strong and reflected in the scepticism of the IRA's Belfast commander, the former bookmaker Seamus Twomey, and the up-and-coming Provo strategist Gerry Adams. However, for leading members of the largely southern leadership of the Provos, including Dáithí Ó Conaill and Ruairí Ó Brádaigh, the increasingly obvious sectarian effects of the bombing campaign, along with an exaggerated estimation of the British state's willingness to consider radical constitutional change, made a ceasefire attractive, and an indefinite one was declared on 22 June.

The ceasefire was agreed in return for the granting of political status to their prisoners (some of whom were on hunger strike), the temporary release from detention of Gerry Adams and the promise of direct talks at a high level. A six-man delegation led by Seán MacStíofáin was secretly flown to London for talks with Whitelaw and senior officials. Its demands, which included a British declaration of intent to withdraw within three years, offered little to negotiate over. Whitelaw responded to MacStíofáin's shopping list by pointing out that the British government was constrained by the consent provisions of the Ireland Act.[100] Within two weeks the Belfast IRA had brought the ceasefire to an end and launched an intensified campaign, culminating on 21 July in 'Bloody Friday', when it placed twenty-six bombs in Belfast, killing eleven people and injuring 130. Seven people were killed in the city's main bus station, and as the television cameras showed human remains being scooped up into black plastic bags, the Provisionals suffered a major blow to the moral credibility of their campaign. Whitelaw moved quickly to exploit popular revulsion, and the 'no-go' areas in Belfast and Derry were reoccupied with a massive display of military might in Operation Motorman. From this time on the Belfast IRA was subject to attrition, and by the end of 1973 the organization increasingly had to centre its operations in rural areas such as south Armagh and mid Ulster. In the South, Lynch's government closed Sinn Féin's headquarters, and a number of senior republicans were arrested. In November the government dismissed the entire governing body of the Republic's television service after the showing of an interview with MacStiofáin.[101]

The SDLP benefited significantly from the ceasefire and its violent aftermath. Republican willingness to halt their campaign and enter into discussions without an end to internment made it easier for the SDLP to resume negotiations with the British and the Unionists. The utter inflexibility of the republican negotiators when they got their chance to put their demands to Whitelaw allowed them to be politically outflanked by the SDLP. The government's Green Paper, published in October, with its support for power-sharing and an 'Irish Dimension', indicated that, while a united Ireland might not be on the immediate agenda, northern Catholics were being offered the possibility of political gains that would have been inconceivable even two years previously. That these possibilities would not be realized would be in large part a result of the increasingly tough bargaining position that the SDLP adopted and whose main architect was John Hume. Thus on 12 December 1972 Whitelaw met an SDLP delegation led by Fitt and including Hume, Devlin and Austin Currie. The SDLP warned Whitelaw that the government was adopting 'short-term expedients' in treating the province of Northern Ireland as the basis for a settlement: 'A framework of reconciliation should be provided on the basis of absolute equality between the two communities. What was needed was the long-term certainty of political union by 1980 within the context of the European Community.' Whitelaw pointed out that many of the SDLP's proposals would be 'repugnant to the majority in Northern Ireland,' but the SDLP impatiently brushed aside such warnings.[102]

In local government elections in May 1973 the SDLP showed that it had emerged as a political force, with 13 per cent of the vote. For the first time since the death of Joe Devlin in the 1930s, a nationalist party could claim support in both the west and east of Northern Ireland as the influence of Fitt and Devlin ensured the party had a solid base in Belfast. Provisional Sinn Féin had urged a boycott of the elections, and some of its strategists were concerned that the support for both the SDLP and the Republican Clubs, the political wing of the Officials, came from Provo sympathizers who rejected abstentionist tactics. The republican dilemma was even more obvious in the election for a new Northern Ireland Assembly, held in June. In these the SDLP emerged as the second-largest party, with almost 160,000 votes, 22 per cent of the total and nineteen seats.[103] Provisional unease over strategy was manifest in conflicting advice to their supporters, who were urged first to abstain and then to spoil ballot papers. A mere 1.2 per cent of ballots were spoiled, and it was clear that the majority of northern nationalists had put their hopes in radical reform rather than in armed struggle.

Hume, with the support of most of the SDLP Assembly members from constituencies outside Belfast, was convinced that the political fragmentation of unionism and the British desire to build up the SDLP as a bulwark against the Provisionals meant that an 'interim' settlement combining power-sharing with a powerful Council of Ireland should be the only acceptable outcome of any negotiations. When Liam Cosgrave, the Taoiseach in the new Fine Gael–Labour coalition government, told a Conservative meeting in London that any pressure for movement on the partition issue 'would dangerously exacerbate tension and fears',[104] he provoked an angry response from the SDLP. Hume gave a tough speech in which he advised Cosgrave's government not to underestimate its strength or to surrender its position to 'the false liberalism of placating the Unionists'.[105] SDLP delegations arrived in Dublin to emphasize that they saw Cosgrave's position as less robust than Fianna Fáil's[106] and as weakening their negotiating position with the British and the Unionists. Fearful of being portrayed as letting the 'separated brethren' down, the Irish government's official position soon shifted to one of uncritical support for Hume's analysis and prescriptions. By the autumn Garret FitzGerald was pressing the British hard on several fronts. He wanted: agreement on a Council of Ireland before the formation of an Executive in Northern Ireland; the proposed Sunningdale Conference to be co-chaired by an Irish minister or a 'neutral' chairman to be drawn from the European Union; and an all-Ireland police force under the supervision of the Council of Ireland. In the view of the British Ambassador in Dublin, the Irish government, with the exception of Conor Cruise O'Brien and Patrick Cooney, were 'timorous' and 'narrow-minded . . . they cannot lift their eyes above their own domestic politics.'[107]

Sunningdale and the Ulster Workers' Council Strike

As the intense and exhausting process of inter-party talks at Stormont Castle under Whitelaw's chairmanship continued through October and November 1973, the Unionist negotiators were aware that opposition within the Protestant community was growing. On 20 November the Ulster Unionist Council narrowly turned down a proposal to reject power-sharing by 379 votes to 369. Despite the obviously precarious position of Faulkner, Hume, described by one of the most liberal of Faulkner's supporters as 'grim and unbending in negotiations',[108] remained implacable in his commitment to a Council of Ireland with substantial powers. An agreement on the formation of a power-sharing Executive was announced on 22 November. The Executive was to consist of eleven members: six Ulster Unionists, four SDLP and one from the Alliance Party. Brian Faulkner was Chief Executive and Gerry Fitt Deputy Chief Executive. It was the SDLP's insistence that 'nothing is agreed until everything is agreed' that prevented the immediate devolution of power following the successful conclusion of the talks. Instead Faulkner and his Unionist ministers-in-waiting had to participate in a conference with the SDLP, the Alliance Party, and the British and Irish governments to deal with the unresolved issue of the Council of Ireland.

The conference, held at the civil service college at Sunningdale in Berkshire between 6 and 9 December, was an unmitigated disaster for Faulkner's standing in the unionist community. Heath had viewed the deepening of his government's involvement in Northern Ireland affairs after direct rule as a necessary but unfortunate diversion of the time and abilities of some of his most important ministers. With the formation of the Executive his immediate inclination was to reduce the quality of his commitment. This meant the recalling of Whitelaw to Westminster to deal with the pressing problem of industrial militancy, and his replacement by Francis Pym. If Whitelaw had been present at Sunningdale, his almost two years of experience in the North might have allowed him to make Heath more aware of the difficulties of Faulkner's position. As it was, the Unionist negotiators were confronted with an SDLP supported by a heavyweight Irish governmental team led by the Taoiseach; they also found themselves at loggerheads with Heath, who showed little patience with Unionist concerns that they were being asked to sign up to an agreement that would be unsellable at home.

Hume brushed aside the nagging concerns of his party leader: that by pushing the role and powers of the Council of Ireland to the forefront of negotiations, the SDLP would make the position of Faulkner untenable. The only voice that was raised against Hume's agenda was that of Paddy Devlin, who, on seeing the full list of executive functions proposed for the Council of Ireland, exclaimed that it would result in his Unionist colleagues being hanged from the lamp-posts when they got back to Belfast.[109] Heath's overwhelming desire for a deal and his impatience with Unionist concerns, which might have been checked by

Whitelaw's knowledge of Ulster conditions, were unrestrained by Francis Pym. The result was disastrous for the new power-sharing government.

Although the extent of Unionist/SDLP differences on the functions and powers of the Council of Ireland meant that these areas were set aside for further discussion, the final communiqué, by agreeing that the Council would be created, provided Faulkner's enemies with a focus for their attack, while the very lack of a clear definition of powers allowed the most extravagant claims to be made and believed. Faulkner had hoped for compensatory commitments from the Irish government on the removal of Articles 2 and 3 from the Irish Constitution and the extradition of terrorist offenders. He got neither, and even senior members of the Irish delegation feared that nationalism had been too successful at Sunningdale.[110] Whitelaw confided in FitzGerald that in his acceptance of the Council of Ireland Faulkner was 'perhaps further ahead of his party than was quite wise for him'.[111]

On the day that the Sunningdale Conference began, 600 delegates from Unionist Party constituency associations, Vanguard, the DUP and the Orange Order agreed to form the United Ulster Unionist Council (UUUC) to oppose power-sharing and the Council of Ireland, which was described as 'so obvious a preparation for a united Ireland'.[112] The Grand Lodge of the Orange Order had sent an unprecedented letter to all Orange delegates to a special meeting of the UUC on 20 November 1973, urging a vote against power-sharing. Martin Smyth, who was Grand Master of the Order as well as Vice-President of the UUP, along with the new MP for South Antrim, James Molyneaux, also a leading member of the Order, played a central role in the UUUC. Although the UUC meeting rejected the anti-power-sharing motion, it did so by a narrow margin of 379 to 369.[113] The Sunningdale Agreement would ensure that Faulkner lost this remaining narrow margin of support. A special meeting of the UUC on 4 January 1974, just four days after the Executive took office, passed a resolution opposing any Council of Ireland by 427 to 374, and Faulkner resigned as leader of the party. Despite this further blow to the Unionist pillar of the new devolved structures, the SDLP continued to inflame Protestant fears with claims such as that of one Assembly member, Hugh Logue, that the Council of Ireland was 'the vehicle that would trundle Unionists into a united Ireland'. Faulkner's earlier demands for constitutional recognition rebounded when on 16 January the High Court in Dublin ruled that the Irish government's recognition of the North in the agreement was 'no more than a statement of policy' with no constitutional significance.[114]

Faulkner hoped that the effective and mundane working of the new institutions would dissipate the fears of many ordinary Unionists, but Heath's overriding concern with the challenge of industrial militancy in Britain impinged disastrously on Northern Ireland. Ignoring pleas from Faulkner, Gerry Fitt and Pym that an election could be fatal for the Executive, Heath called a general election for 28 February.

The UUUC, mobilizing with the slogan 'Dublin is only a Sunningdale away', won eleven of Northern Ireland's twelve constituencies at Westminster. The power-sharing parties – Faulkner Unionists, the Alliance Party, the NILP and the SDLP – competed against one another. The result was that in South and East Belfast the victorious UUUC candidates got fewer votes than the combination of their power-sharing opponents. There was still a substantial Unionist power-sharing constituency in suburban Belfast and North Down, but it was drowned in the rejectionist tide that flowed through the rest of Northern Ireland.[115] The Executive had lost all legitimacy with the bulk of the Unionist electorate, and this is the key to understanding the British government's reaction to the unprecedented industrial action by the Ulster Workers' Council (UWC), which was the occasion, but not the fundamental cause, of the Executive's collapse.

The UWC had been created in November 1973 by groups of loyalist trade unionists who had been involved in the discredited Loyalist Association of Workers. They were convinced that it would be easier to mobilize support against an unpopular Executive and the spectre of creeping unification associated with the Council of Ireland than it had been to protest about the internment of loyalist paramilitaries. Distrustful of most of the Unionist politicians who were opposed to Faulkner, they were determined to maintain their independence and take action with or without the politicians' blessing. Although the UWC maintained a notional separation from the main paramilitary organizations, its 'co-ordinating committee' (headed by the impressive Derry trade unionist and Vanguard activist Glenn Barr) included UDA and UVF members. Its paramilitary links would be crucial in ensuring the withdrawal of labour in the first days of the strike that began on 15 May 1974. The possible role of intimidation and violence had been one of the factors that had made the main leaders of Unionist opposition to the Executive reluctant to consider industrial action when the UWC issued its first public statement on 23 March. This threatened widespread civil disobedience unless fresh Assembly elections were held. The UUUC's response was to ignore the UWC and to call for a boycott of southern goods by northern consumers instead.[116]

The motley crew of industrial militants and paramilitaries had read the popular mood better than the politicians, although even they did not expect the stunning victory that was to come. The SDLP and some leading Labour and Conservative politicians were to explain the success of the strike in terms of intimidation and the failure of the authorities to act decisively and early to keep roads open and remove the barricades erected by strike supporters. This simply ignored the extent of support for the strike in the unionist community. Most unionists perceived the course of events from 1968 to 1973 as one of continued political retreat, if not defeat. It was unlikely that they would accept in government those whom they considered as instrumental in bringing down the Stormont regime, especially when members of the SDLP still talked as if a united Ireland were an imminent possibility through the Council of Ireland.[117] By the end of the first week of the strike the UWC had shut down the North's main industries and through its control of the Ballylumford Power Station at Larne had a stranglehold on the electricity supply, which put it in a position to bring daily life to a standstill.

The new Labour administration showed no desire to confront the strikers for the sake of a terminally divided Executive; moreover, the army's advice was that it would be disastrous to open up a second front against the Protestant paramilitaries at a time when its resources needed to be fully committed against the Provisionals. Harold Wilson's main contribution to the dénouement of power-sharing was a crassly misjudged national television and radio broadcast in which he denounced the strikers as 'thugs and bullies' and their supporters as those who 'spend their lives sponging on Westminster'. Ken Bloomfield judged the broadcast 'catastrophically unhelpful', and in the days that followed even moderate unionists sported pieces of sponge in their lapels.[118] A plan devised by John Hume, the Minister of Commerce, to use the army to take over a number of petrol stations to break the UWC's control of fuel supplies was leaked in advance by a sympathetic official – an indication of the defection *en masse* of the Protestant middle class – and the UWC announced a total shutdown of services. Faced with the possibility of the closure of hospitals and the probability of raw sewage flooding Belfast streets, the Executive resigned.[119]

Those commentators who saw in the victory of the UWC strike the emergence of a new proletarian leadership for unionism had obviously never read Lenin's *What is to be Done?*, with its powerful dissection of the limits of even the most militant forms of trade union consciousness. After the strike the UWC leadership, faced with decisions about the future, began to fragment. Sarah Nelson has described the various tendencies as follows: 'hardline Loyalists, more conciliatory, socially radical elements and people who had just not thought what constructive alternative they were aiming for'.[120] While Glen Barr, together with some leading members of the UVF, saw the UWC as the possible basis for the development of an independent working-class political grouping, the more influential groups were those dominated by support for Craig and Paisley.

Vanguard and the DUP appeared to be equal contenders in the competition to displace an Ulster Unionist Party that, although it was now firmly under the control of the right, remained enervated and demoralized after almost a decade of internecine conflict. Harry West, the bluff Fermanagh farmer whom O'Neill had sacked and Faulkner reinstated, had been elected leader of the party following Faulkner's resignation. After the Westminster general election of October 1974, when he lost his seat for Fermanagh and South Tyrone, West saw his leadership undermined by the increasingly important integrationist lobby led by the leader of the Ulster Unionists at Westminster, the self-effacing but crafty MP for South Antrim, James Molyneaux, and his intellectual guru, the former Conservative MP for Wolverhampton, Enoch Powell, whose record of support for the unionist cause while a Tory got him the UUUC nomination for South Down in the 1974 general election.

In the wake of the collapse of the power-sharing Executive, the Wilson government arranged elections for a Constitutional Convention to consider what provision for the government of Northern Ireland was likely to command the most widespread support. The results, in May 1975, showed for the first time an Ulster Unionist Party that, though remaining the largest single party, with 26 per cent of the vote and nineteen seats, had less support than the combined strength of Vanguard (13 per cent and fourteen seats) and the DUP (15 per cent and twelve seats).[121] The UUP was weakened by evidence of increasing tensions between those, like West and the Reverend Martin Smyth, who remained convinced devolutionists, as well as by escalating integrationist pressure from Molyneaux and Powell. The divisions showed up when Craig, to the surprise of many observers, launched a proposal for the formation of an 'emergency' coalition government with the SDLP in September 1975. The idea had emerged from discussions between the SDLP and a negotiating team from the UUUC, which had included Craig, William Beattie of the DUP and Austin Ardill of the UUP. It used a section of the proposed UUUC Convention report, which stated that in times of war and similar emergency it was appropriate British practice to form a coalition government. The three had approached the Chairman of the Convention, Sir Robert Lowry, to ask for a report on the idea. Paisley was initially sympathetic,[122] but a hostile response from sections of his party, and possibly the realization that Craig could be isolated, led him to denounce the idea once it became public. Craig was, indeed, isolated, and eventually he was expelled from the UUUC.[123]

During West's leadership of the UUP there were signs that, despite the conflict between its devolutionist and integrationist tendencies, the party had begun to regain some of the self-confidence that had been shattered during the 1968–74 period. In part this reflected the belief that, as the 'middle ground' in Ulster politics, it would benefit from the extremism of its loyalist opponents.[124] When, as Craig had predicted, the UUUC majority report was ignored at Westminster and the Convention shut down in March 1976, the DUP adopted a militant posture. Here it was influenced by the rhetoric of Craig's opponents in Vanguard. A majority within the organization had opposed the emergency coalition proposal and, led by Ernest Baird, had rechristened themselves the United Ulster Unionist Movement. Baird, who owned a chain of chemist shops, was an uncritical Ulster nationalist, and was beginning to talk of militant resistance to direct rule. He was in the forefront of calls for the formation of a loyalist vigilante force to combat terrorism. In March 1976 he and Paisley took the initiative within the UUUC in forming a United Ulster Action Council to oppose direct rule and press the government for tougher security policies. Within a few weeks the UUP withdrew from the Action Council because of the prominent role of Protestant paramilitaries in it. In contrast to the DUP's dalliance with vigilantism, West's party, with the strong support of the leadership of the Orange Order, urged unionists to join the official security forces.

Baird and the DUP gave much credence to the common belief of the period that Britain was disengaging from Northern Ireland, which provoked a clear sympathy for the idea of loyalists going it alone in some sort of independent state. In the interim Baird and Paisley focused on the 'disastrous security policies' being followed by the Northern Ireland Office and in May 1977 attempted a repeat of the UWC strike. The Action Council launched a general strike to force the British government to concede a return to majority rule and tougher security policies. Both the UUP and the Orange Order opposed the strike, as did the crucial group of power workers who had been central to the success of the UWC strike. In September 1976 the ineffectual Merlyn Rees had been replaced as Secretary of State for Northern Ireland by Roy Mason, an altogether blunter and more robust figure. Mason ably exploited the contradiction between the strikers' demand for increased security and their launching of a major disruption of public order. The strike collapsed ignominiously after a few days.[125] In its aftermath the UUUC broke up, and in the local government elections later that year the UUP won 34 per cent of the vote, down on its 1973 share but an improvement on the Convention election. Nevertheless, despite the débâcle of the Action Council strike, the DUP saw a significant increase in support, demonstrating the existence of a growing constituency for its perceived militancy.[126]

The DUP's hard core of Free Presbyterian activists in its rural and small-town base areas was increasingly augmented by a group of youngish Belfast members, some of them graduates, who were extending the party's influence in the Protestant working class through involvement in community politics and local government. Lean and hungry for power, they took as their model Peter Robinson's expanding fiefdom in the Castlereagh area of East Belfast. Robinson, who was twenty-nine when he won his first elected office for the DUP (as a councillor in Castlereagh in 1977), had been a Paisleyite activist since leaving grammar school in 1966, and his intellectual and organizational abilities had led Paisley to make him his secretary at Westminster in 1970. He became the DUP's general secretary in 1975 and played a central role in making it the most coherent and well-organized party in the North.[127] Robinson did not share the scruples of some of the Free Presbyterian members about associating with paramilitaries. While his cultivation of the UDA failed to force a change of British policy in 1977, it contributed significantly to the DUP's winning of its first Belfast constituencies in the Westminster general election of 1979, when Robinson defeated William Craig for East Belfast and his party colleague Johnny McQuade won North Belfast.[128] The tensions between the original hard core of Paisleyism, the conservative fundamentalists of areas such as North Antrim and Robinson's more pragmatic, left-of-centre populism were easily enough contained through a combination of the integrating force of Paisley's personality and the healing balm of electoral success.

The success was certainly spectacular. Between the local government elections of 1973 and 1981 the DUP expanded its number of councillors from twenty-one (4 per cent of the vote) to 142 (26.6 per cent), fractionally ahead of the UUP. From a narrow base, with representation in only seven of the North's twenty-six local authorities, the party was now represented on every council in Northern Ireland. Most spectacular of all was its advance in Belfast: from two seats to fifteen, making it the largest party on the Council.[129] But it was the first direct election to the European Parliament, in 1979, that did most to support Paisley's claim to be the leader of Protestant Ulster. With Northern Ireland treated as one constituency, his own gargantuan appetite for electioneering – he claimed to have covered 122 miles on foot and 4,000 miles by car[130] – and the DUP's polished election machine, he delivered a devastating blow to the UUP, which had put up two candidates, John Taylor and Harry West. Taking 170,688 votes, 29.8 per cent of the total, Paisley topped the poll and claimed that he now spoke for a majority of the Unionist population. Between them the two UUP candidates obtained 125,169 votes, 22 per cent. West's particularly weak performance, which reflected his marked disinclination to pursue an active canvass, led to his resignation as leader of the UUP. His replacement by Molyneaux marked another stage in the increasingly integrationist tone of the party.

Padraig O'Malley, at this time of DUP ascendancy, wrote of Paisley:

he is the personification of the 'fearful Protestant', the embodiment of the Scots-Presbyterian tradition of uncompromising Calvinism that has always been the bedrock of militant Protestant opposition to a united Ireland. It is a tradition shaped by a siege mentality, and the almost obsessive compulsion to confirm the need for unyielding vigilance.[131]

This overplays the religious and irrational component in Paisleyism's success, important though it was, at the expense of those elements of the political conjuncture that were favourable to the DUP. The return of the Tories in 1979 had replaced a period of 'positive direct rule' under the Labour Northern Ireland Secretary Roy Mason with another search for a devolutionary settlement under his successor, Humphrey Atkins. Molyneaux's integrationist agenda – which his friendship with Margaret Thatcher's Northern Ireland spokesman, Airey Neave, had encouraged him to believe would be indulged when the Tories returned to power – had been pointedly ignored. When Atkins's initiative failed, in part because Molyneaux had cold-shouldered it, a resentful Thatcher turned towards an Anglo-Irish framework with a summit in Dublin with Charles Haughey in December 1980, in which she agreed to new institutional structures to reflect the 'unique relationship' between the two islands and to further meetings to give 'special consideration to the totality of relations within these islands'. While Molyneaux continued to reassure his followers that he had the ear of the British Prime Minister, Paisley scented betrayal and launched the 'Carson Trail', a series of paramilitary-style rallies in which he vowed to go to any lengths to resist Thatcherite 'treachery'.

Fighting the Long War: British Policy 1974–1985

Although by the time of direct rule a number of senior Conservative politicians such as Peter Carrington and William Whitelaw had come to agree with Harold Wilson that the only ultimate solution was Irish unity, it was recognized that this would be a long-term process. Power-sharing devolution and an 'Irish Dimension' would, it was hoped, provide interim structures that, while providing stability, could be open to constitutional change. However, when Wilson returned to power in 1974 he asked one of his advisers, Bernard Donoghue, to put forward suggestions for a new initiative. This occurred before the UWC strike and illustrates Wilson's belief that the Sunningdale project was doomed. Donoghue's paper suggested granting Northern Ireland dominion status, with the UK, the US and Ireland acting as guarantors of Catholic rights within the now autonomous Ulster state. By the time of the strike, Wilson had established a small and secret committee in the Cabinet Office to develop new ideas on the North. After the strike, Wilson wrote a memorandum arguing that, as power-sharing was now ruled out, the UK government was in a position of 'responsibility without power' and proposing that his 'Doomsday Scenario' of withdrawal be seriously considered. He proposed dominion status and a tapering off of financial support to the province over five years.[132] Nothing came of these proposals, in part because of the horrified reaction of the SDLP when Wilson put forward the idea of Ulster independence to a delegation in June 1974.[133] The UK Ambassador to the United States also warned that the US 'would most likely follow the lead of the Irish Republic in castigating withdrawal as a loss of will and a betrayal'.[134] Although little hope was vested in the Constitutional Convention and the British government prepared for direct rule for the foreseeable future, Wilson's withdrawal plans had contributed to an air of fevered speculation in the province about the possibility of British disengagement.

Such rumours had their origins also in secret negotiations between British officials and the leadership of the Provisional IRA, which resulted in an IRA ceasefire that lasted for most of 1975. Ruairí Ó Brádaigh and his allies in the leadership of the Provisionals had seen the UWC strike as a watershed that 'threw British policy totally into the melting pot . . . The word coming through was that every solution was up for consideration.'[135] The 'word' was conveyed by various officials from the Foreign Office and the security services, working out of Laneside, a nineteenth-century mansion on the shores of Belfast Lough where the Political Affairs section of the Northern Ireland Office preferred to have its meetings with paramilitaries away from possible media intrusion. The British officials did not discourage the Provisional belief that the Constitutional Convention had been set up in the expectation that it would fail through loyalist intransigence, thus providing the British government with the justification for extrication. There is some evidence that the officials involved may have gone as far as talking about the 'structures of disengagement'.[136]

The British had hoped that a successful political initiative would enable the SDLP to marginalize the republicans politically and make their military defeat easier. Since Operation Motorman the Provisionals' campaign in Belfast and Derry had been curtailed radically, and the political developments of 1973 put the IRA on the defensive. The level of violence had reduced considerably. With 470 deaths and over 10,000 recorded shootings, 1972 was by far the worst year in three decades of the 'Troubles'. By 1974 the number of deaths had fallen to 220 and shootings were down by two thirds. In 1972, 105 British soldiers had been killed, while by 1974 the figure was thirty.[137] However, the IRA compensated for setbacks in its urban strongholds by intensifying its campaign in rural areas such as mid Ulster and south Armagh. It had also initiated a bombing campaign in England in 1973 to compensate for being forced on the defensive in the North and to attempt to galvanize the undoubtedly strong 'troops out' sentiment in British public opinion. The first deaths occurred when a bomb on a coach carrying British soldiers killed twelve people in February 1974. Bombings of pubs that were claimed to be 'military targets' because they were used by soldiers followed, with deaths and dozens of injured at Guildford and Woolwich. The culmination of this first Provisional campaign was the bombing of the Mulberry Bush and the Tavern in the Town pubs in Birmingham on 21 November 1974 in which nineteen people were killed and 182 injured.[138]

Although the republicans were contained militarily, their continued capacity for violence and the resultant communal polarization made the possibility of a ceasefire very attractive for the British. The ceasefire allowed the political embarrassment of internment to be ended. The murder and intimidation of witnesses and jurors had already resulted in the introduction of so-called Diplock courts (named after Lord Diplock who, in 1973, had chaired a commission to investigate alternatives to internment), where persons accused of 'scheduled offences', that is those of a terrorist nature, could be tried in the absence of a jury. The Emergency Provisions Act of 1973, which introduced these courts, also repealed the Special Powers Act while re-enacting many of its provisions. Like the Prevention of Terrorism Act introduced after the Birmingham bombs, which allowed for detention for up to seven days and provided for the exclusion from the rest of the UK of 'undesirables' from the North, it was to apply for one year but was renewable annually. Both pieces of legislation became key components of the state's anti-terrorist strategy. Although they had a real effect in weakening paramilitary structures, they inevitably generated resentment in those Catholic working-class areas where they were often implemented in a heavy-handed and indiscriminate manner.[139]

The ceasefire also allowed the shift to a security strategy of 'Ulsterization' under which the role of the British Army was diminished in favour of the RUC and the Ulster Defence Regiment. While this avoided the possibility of a Vietnam syndrome in British politics, its effect in deepening sectarian divisions in Northern Ireland cannot be over-emphasized. In the early 1970s there were over 23,000 British soldiers in Northern Ireland, compared with 7,000 full-time and part-time police officers and 7,500 in the locally recruited Ulster Defence Regiment. By the end of the 1980s the number of British soldiers had declined to around 10,000, while the RUC had increased to 11,500, with the UDR maintaining its size at 7,500.[140] After 1976, while the IRA was still capable of dealing the British Army occasional major blows – most spectacularly at Narrow Water near Warrenpoint in County Down in 1979, when its bombs killed eighteen soldiers – its most relentless campaign was aimed at local members of the security forces. These were largely Protestant and often, when part-timers, easy targets as they carried out their jobs as bus drivers, milkmen and farm labourers. As the 'anti-imperialist struggle' increasingly killed Protestant members of the Irish working class, its effects on community relations began to concern even some members of the IRA's leadership, who were repulsed by the brutal and casual sectarianism of many of their northern comrades.[141]

Along with Ulsterization went a policy of ending the granting of political status to paramilitary prisoners. Since 1972 political status had allowed prisoners to organize their day-to-day existence in prison, including wearing their own clothes and running education classes instead of performing the prison work required of 'ordinary decent criminals'. During the ceasefire Merlyn Rees announced that political status would be ended for all newly convicted paramilitary prisoners. With the IRA leadership confident that all its prisoners would soon be released as part of the process of British withdrawal, there were only the most formal of protests from republicans.[142]

Rees's successor as Secretary of State, the tough ex-miner Roy Mason, pursued the policies of criminalization and Ulsterization with a crude vigour. At his first press conference in September 1976 he announced that the IRA was 'reeling'.[143] A new Chief Constable, Kenneth Newman, who had come from the Metropolitan Police to implement the policy of police primacy, oversaw a process through which a major expansion of resources was focused on four new regional crime squads targeted at the IRA's most active units. Suspects were held under detention orders for up to seven days at RUC holding centres at Castlereagh in East Belfast and Gough Barracks, Armagh. Making use of Lord Diplock's permissive recommendation that confessions made under interrogation could be accepted unless it was proved that they had been extracted by torture, the RUC was able to deal such serious blows to the IRA that an IRA 'Staff Report' captured by the police in Dublin referred to it as 'contributing to our defeat'.[144] By the end of 1977 Mason was claiming that 'the tide had turned against the terrorists and the message for 1978 is one of real hope'.[145] In fact, 1978 was to see clear signs that the Provisionals had been able to regroup and reorganize.

The prime architect of the strategic redirection of the Provisionals was Gerry Adams. A senior member of the Belfast IRA when he was rearrested in July 1973, Adams spent the next four years in the IRA compounds at the Long Kesh Prison. Here he took an increasingly critical line against the still largely southern leadership of the Provisionals. This in part reflected the hard sectarian edge of northern republicanism that detected in the southerners' *Éire Nua* document a deplorable tendency to accommodate Unionists. There was also a realistic assessment that the British state was not in the process of withdrawing from the North. But the main criticism that Adams and his supporters levelled against the leadership was their support for the ceasefire that had divided and demoralized the IRA. With their main targets temporarily out of reach, sections of the IRA became unofficially involved in violent conflict with the Official IRA, who themselves had recently suffered a split: a more militaristic and ultra-leftist group broke away and founded an Irish Republican Socialist Party with its own military wing, the Irish National

Liberation Army. Even more politically damaging to the Provisionals was their response to the loyalist paramilitaries who had intensified their activities during the ceasefire. Acting under the flag of convenience of 'South Armagh Republican Action Force', Provisionals shot dead six Protestants in Tullyvallen Orange Hall in September 1975 and on 5 January 1976 stopped a minibus carrying workers, separated out the Protestants and machine-gunned them, killing ten. The eruption of support for a grass-roots anti-violence movement, the Peace People – after a car driven by an IRA man attempting to escape from soldiers ploughed into a Catholic mother and her four children in West Belfast, killing three of the children – was also a worrying sign of a potential drying-up of toleration for the 'armed struggle' in Provisional heartlands.

The basis for Adams's rise to a dominant position in the republican movement was his role in ensuring that the IRA recovered from its near defeat in the mid 1970s. He promoted a reorganization of the IRA, replacing its old structure of geographically based brigades, battalions and companies with small Active Service Units, whose members would be drawn from different areas for a specific task such as assassination or robbery. This cellular structure was designed to be less vulnerable to infiltration and disruption by the security forces. A new Northern Command was established, which ensured that Adams and his allies controlled the main area of IRA operations. The northerners made it clear that they did not expect an imminent British withdrawal but were prepared for a 'Long War' that could last for two decades or more. IRA activity would be refined and increasingly take the form of 'armed propaganda' aimed at a process of attrition of the British will to remain in the North.

The 'Long War' would be fought as much politically as militarily, and Adams looked enviously at his rivals in the Officials who were enjoying increasing success as a left-wing political force in the South. He advocated that Sinn Féin become a campaigning political party rather than simply an IRA support organization. Adams and some of his lieutenants, for example Tom Hartley and Danny Morrison, adopted an increasingly left-wing language, which won them allies on the left wing of the British Labour Party. However, their major political breakthrough would come about not because of this rather superficial radicalism but through the unleashing of much more primordial passions in the North.

Mason had tried to buttress his robust security policies with a strong commitment to use the public sector and state investment to undermine the economic and social deprivation that he was convinced exacerbated communal conflict: 'The terrorists needed unhappiness and hopeless-ness.'[146] In the 1960s Northern Ireland had a thriving manufacturing sector, employing over 30 per cent of the workforce and returning the highest rates of productivity growth amongst the UK regions. The engine driving this impressive performance was the large number of multi-nationals that came to the region in this decade and the still-sizeable indigenous industrial base in shipbuilding, aircraft production and textiles. The twin pillars of this success were badly hit by the worldwide economic recession of the 1970s. The multinationals left the region as quickly as they had arrived, employment in manufacturing fell to 18 per cent of the overall workforce, and unemployment rose significantly.[147] In 1976 unemployment in the North, at 10 per cent, was double the UK rate and in some areas in Catholic West Belfast the rate amongst adult males was over 50 per cent.[148]

Mason's response was to try to follow the recommendations of the Quigley Report, produced by four senior civil servants in 1976, which proposed a heavily subsidized economy, with the state playing a much greater role until market conditions improved. Employment in the public sector increased by over 50 per cent during the 1970s, compared to 22 per cent in the UK as a whole, and Mason's period at the Northern Ireland Office accounted for a substantial part of this.[149] So strong was his view of the causes of support for violence that he persuaded the cabinet to support an extremely high-risk venture in which an American entrepreneur proposed to build a futuristic sports car on a green-field site in West Belfast. The project eventually collapsed when Thatcher was in office in part because of a lack of demand for its cars but also because of the embezzling activities of its founder, John DeLorean, who had siphoned off millions of pounds of public money for his private use.[150]

Mason's strong commitment to direct rule as an acceptable interim form of governing Northern Ireland, together with his tough rhetoric on security, endeared him to many unionists but did little to counter an increasingly militant tone in nationalist politics, reflected in John Hume's ascendancy in the SDLP. Hume, who as Minister of Commerce had denounced the UWC strike as a fascist takeover,[151] blamed the Wilson government for political cowardice in not standing firm and in using troops to break it. The SDLP was traumatized by the collapse of the Executive, and in its immediate aftermath Hume told an official from the Department of Foreign Affairs that any hope of Irish unity was gone for ever. The members of the party's Assembly group reported a 'massive swing' of support away from them towards both wings of the IRA, while

Fitt and Paddy Devlin claimed that they no longer had any support in Belfast.[152] The year 1974 now entered the Irish nationalist chronology of shameful British capitulations to loyalist threats, along with 1912 and 1921. Although Fitt and Devlin had been prepared to respond to Craig's proposals during the Convention, Hume was hostile. Even if Craig had been able to win the support of Unionists for voluntary coalition, the SDLP would probably have split over participation in what Hume and many of its members would have seen as a 'partitionist' administration.[153] The defeat of Craig's proposal ensured that the SDLP continued to shift in a more traditionally nationalist direction. At their conference in 1976 a motion calling for a British declaration of intent to withdraw was only narrowly defeated.[154]

Hume, who recognized the dangers for the party of adopting a policy that would make it indistinguishable from the Provisionals, countered with a proposal for a 'third way' between the constitutional status quo and British withdrawal. This 'agreed Ireland' would be the result of a process beginning with a statement from the British government that 'its objective in Ireland was the bringing together of both Irish traditions in reconciliation and agreement'.[155] Subsequent talks amongst the northern parties should be jointly chaired by the British and Irish governments. By this time Hume had begun the process of constructing a coalition of important allies in Europe and the US that he hoped to mobilize to apply sufficient pressure on Britain to bring a shift in policy. All this was too much for Paddy Devlin, who detected behind the language of 'agreement' and 'process' an iron determination to have the British state 'educate' the Protestants as to what their true interests were. For Devlin, the essence of 'Hume-speak' was the desire to impose a settlement over the heads of the unionist population. He resigned from the SDLP in 1977 and was soon followed by Fitt.

The 'greening' of the SDLP in 1978–9 was accelerated by increasing evidence that some RUC officers had brutalized suspects in Castlereagh and the fear that British policy was taking an integrationist direction. The Callaghan government's increasing vulnerability in the House of Commons led to negotiations with James Molyneaux to obtain Unionist votes and produced a commitment to deal with Northern Ireland's under-representation at Westminster. The promise of more seats enraged the SDLP and strengthened Hume's argument that the conflict could be resolved only through a process of internationalization involving the US and the Irish government.

However, even with this alienation of mainstream nationalists, the

Provisionals faced the new Tory government with little evidence that, despite a successful reorganization of their military machine, they had overcome their political weakness. This was in part a reflection of popular revulsion at some of their actions, particularly the fire-bombing of the La Mon House Hotel in County Down on 17 February 1978 when twelve people were incinerated. Gerry Adams recalls being 'depressed' at the carnage and fearing that his two years of work at reviving the Provisionals was in danger of going down the drain.[156] The victory of Hume in the election for the European parliament in June 1979, in which he came second to Paisley, with almost a quarter of the votes cast, seemed to emphasize republicans' political irrelevance. Yet within two years, more by accident than by calculation, Adams would find himself in a position to launch an unprecedented political breakthrough for Sinn Féin.

A hint of what was to come was the 38,000 voters, 6 per cent of the total, in the European poll who had supported the former student revolutionary Bernadette McAliskey, née Devlin. She had stood as an independent supporting the demands of republican prisoners for political status. Since 1976 those convicted of terrorist offences had been placed in new cellular accommodation at what was now called the Maze Prison, although republicans continued to refer to it as Long Kesh. In protest they had first refused to wear prison clothes, covering themselves with blankets, and subsequently radicalized their campaign by smearing the walls of their cells with excrement. By 1978 there were over 300 prisoners involved in the 'dirty protest'. Regardless of the fact that the squalor was self-inflicted and the Provisionals on the outside were carrying on a campaign of assassinating prison officers, in which eighteen were killed between 1976 and 1980,[157] the strongly nationalistic Archbishop of Armagh and Primate of All-Ireland, Dr Tomás Ó Fiaich, denounced the H Blocks at the Maze as 'unfit for animals' and compared them unfavourably with the sewers of Calcutta. Yet, potent though the mixture of religion and nationalism that Ó Fiaich embodied was, it did not acquire an overwhelming power until the IRA prisoners decided, against the advice of their leaders on the outside, to go on hunger strike. The strike, which began in October 1980, was called off after fifty-three days when it seemed that concessions were coming. When they did not materialize, a second, more determined strike led by Bobby Sands, the Provisionals' Commanding Officer in the Maze, began in March 1981.

Marches in support of the prisoners, which prior to the hunger strikes had brought out a few hundred from the republican heartlands, now numbered tens of thousands motivated by what one commentator described as a 'tribal voice of martyrdom deeply embedded in the Gaelic, catholic nationalist tradition'.[158] By dying for their cause in this way, Sands and his comrades succeeded in overlaying the reality of the Provisionals' role as the main agency of violent death in the North with the cloak of victimhood. The death of Frank Maguire, the MP for Fermanagh and South Tyrone who was a republican sympathizer, provided an opportunity for a political breakthrough.

The usually cautious Adams was extremely nervous about putting forward a prisoners' candidate and decided to do so only after Bernadette McAliskey had expressed an interest in running as an independent. Bobby Sands was the choice. In a constituency evenly balanced between nationalists and unionists, a decision by the SDLP to stand would have denied the hunger striker victory. Instead, responding to the emotional upsurge of support for the hunger strikers, the party decided not to enter the contest. With a turnout of 87 per cent, Sands won by 30,492 votes to 29,046 for the Ulster Unionist Harry West.[159] Sands's victory was a propaganda coup of major proportions, and it was soon followed by more gains as first Sands and then nine of his comrades died. By the time the hunger strikes were called off in October 1981, two hunger strikers had been elected to the Dáil and Sands's election agent, Owen Carron, had won the by-election caused by his death. Thatcher had kept an inflexible position throughout, maintaining 'Crime is crime is crime, it's not political.' In doing so, she may have won the battle and lost the war. A more flexible position would have exposed the increasingly rigid position adopted by Gerry Adams and the republican leadership, who sabotaged various attempts by clerics and the Irish government to broker a compromise.[160] Instead the 100,000 who turned out for Sands's funeral on 7 May demonstrated the political harvest that republicans would reap from this series of agonizing and drawn-out suicides. In the election for a new Assembly in Northern Ireland in 1982, Sinn Féin won 10 per cent of the vote to the SDLP's 18 per cent. In a politically even more significant result, they won 13 per cent in the 1983 Westminster election to the SDLP's 17 per cent, and Gerry Adams defeated Gerry Fitt to become MP for West Belfast. The party of constitutional nationalism had paid a heavy price for its loss of nerve in Fermanagh and South Tyrone.

Fears of the imminent demise of constitutional nationalism propelled Thatcher towards the most radical British initiative on Ireland since partition. Ironically, although it was her mishandling of the hunger strikes that had done so much to transform the political fortunes of republic-anism, it would be the unionist community, many of whom had applauded her hard line, who would be the main losers from the political reper-cussions of the ten deaths.

The fact that Thatcher's close friend and former Northern Ireland spokesman Airey Neave had been a staunch ally of the Ulster Unionist Party and a supporter of integration had encouraged James Molyneaux in an uncritical faith in Thatcher's self-proclaimed 'Unionist instincts'.[161] However, there is some evidence that he was aware of the dangers posed to the Unionist position by the return of a Conservative government with a substantial majority. The high point of his time at Westminster had been before he became UUP leader, during the Callaghan admini-stration (1976–9), when the votes of the UUP MPs had been eagerly sought by Labour. This had allowed him to extract a number of conces-sions, most importantly the increase in Northern Ireland seats at Westminster from twelve to seventeen. He explained to those with an anti-Labour bias in his party that it was not necessarily in Unionists' interest that a Tory government be returned: 'The Unionist Party aimed to hold the balance of power. The position could be destroyed by a general election. Do you really believe that we would be listened to by the Conservatives if they had a majority of 200?'[162] Prior to the 1979 election he warned that 'If the Conservatives win we will have to be on our guard and avoid falling into a carefully baited trap. We might be faced with a nicely coated pill in the form of a type of Sunningdale.'[163] Both Molyneaux and Powell were convinced that the Atkins conference was part of a NIO–Foreign Office strategy of extrication from Northern Ireland and that Paisley's participation in the talks would undermine support for the DUP.[164] Molyneaux's self-confidence was maintained despite grass-roots concern that the UUP's focus on Westminster and lack of activism in Northern Ireland was playing into the hands of the DUP. He was encouraged when the Reverend Martin Smyth defeated the DUP's William McCrea in the by-election for South Belfast after the IRA had murdered the sitting MP, the Reverend Robert Bradford, in November 1981. In 1982 the new Secretary of State, James Prior, who had been banished to Belfast because of his leftist brand of Toryism, proposed elections for a new assembly and a scheme of 'rolling devolu-tion'. The SDLP boycotted the assembly because no 'Irish Dimension' was included, and the UUP's attitude was much less enthusiastic than that of the DUP. Ironically for Molyneaux, who persisted in seeing the Prior initiative as part of the extrication process, Thatcher herself had little faith in it and was considering a much more radical approach. But, although she shared Neave's scepticism about a power-sharing deal between parties who had such conflicting national aspirations, she did not believe in the feasibility of any policy initiative that would, like integration, be rejected by the Dublin government. Concerned above all with the fact that Northern Ireland was the only place in the world where British soldiers were losing their lives, she looked to political leaders in the Republic for more cooperation in the intelligence, security and judicial fields. It was this that had motivated her 1980 summit with Haughey and the subsequent agreement with Garret FitzGerald to establish an Anglo-Irish Inter-Governmental Council in November 1981. Although the refusal of Haughey's government to support European Union sanctions against Argentina during the Falklands War in 1982 had temporarily disrupted the emerging Anglo-Irish axis, FitzGerald's return to power, coinciding as it did with the eruption of Sinn Féin into Northern Irish politics, led to a renewed and more intensive engagement.

The negotiations that led to the signing of the Anglo-Irish Agreement by Thatcher and FitzGerald at Hillsborough Castle on 15 November 1985 had taken two years to complete, and, although the leader of the SDLP was kept in close touch with their contents by the Irish government throughout, the leaders of Unionism were excluded from the process. For Thatcher the prize was to be enhanced security cooperation from the Republic and the possibility that the majority of northern nationalists would support or acquiesce in the constitutional framework of the state in which they lived. The price she was willing to pay was a new role for the Republic in the governance of Northern Ireland.

Thatcher was adamant that formal British sovereignty over Northern Ireland was untouchable and ruled out FitzGerald's favoured option of joint authority. However, senior British officials, including the Cabinet Secretary, Sir Robert Armstrong, and the Foreign Secretary, Sir Geoffrey Howe, were in favour of a radical initiative that would undermine the republican challenge even at the cost of unionist outrage. They represented a section of opinion in Whitehall that saw the initiative as a first step in the process of decoupling Northern Ireland from the rest of the UK, precisely because the province was a drain on the political and economic resources of the British state.

At the time of her summit with FitzGerald in November 1984, when she publicly rejected all three constitutional options proposed by the New Ireland Forum, it appeared that Thatcher had turned her back on any notion of a new departure in Northern Ireland policy. It was certainly the case that her increasing conviction that the Republic would not be able to offer constitutional recognition of a new dispensation in Northern Ireland by removing Articles 2 and 3 from its constitution had made her more reluctant to innovate. The IRA's bombing of the Grand Hotel in Brighton during the Tory Party conference in October, which nearly killed her and did kill several leading Conservatives, had the same effect. It was Thatcher's ardent pursuit of the 'special relationship' with Washington that allowed the Anglo-Irish initiative to be resurrected.

Up until the 1960s the 'special relationship' had made US presidents reluctant to voice opinions on Northern Ireland, and the State Department was regarded by Irish diplomats as having a pro-British bias on the issue of partition. However, during the 1970s the Department of Foreign Affairs under FitzGerald had made a concerted effort to increase Irish influence in Washington in order to marginalize support for the IRA and increase the influence of constitutional nationalism. Together with John Hume, FitzGerald and Seán Donlon, the Irish Ambassador, had built up a powerful support base on Capitol Hill centred on four influential Irish-American politicians: Senators Edward Kennedy and Daniel Patrick Moynihan, Governor Hugh Carey of New York and the Speaker of the House of Representatives, 'Tip' O'Neill. The 'Four Horsemen' had issued a joint statement on St Patrick's Day 1978 criticizing the lack of political progress under direct rule and alleging violations of civil rights by the security forces. They had been responsible for President Carter's unprecedented declaration that the US would support a deal in Northern Ireland involving the Irish government. Most worryingly for London, it was their pressure that was behind the decision of the State Department in 1979 to suspend the sale of handguns to the RUC.[165] It was US pressure too that had led Thatcher, very much against her own instincts, to promote all-party devolution talks under her first Secretary of State for Northern Ireland, Humphrey Atkins, and that proved decisive in getting stalled negotiations restarted after Thatcher's post-Forum fulminations. Speaker O'Neill wrote to Reagan shortly before a Thatcher–Reagan summit in December 1984 urging him not to tolerate British retrenchment. O'Neill had unprecedented leverage with Reagan because of his record of opposition to US funding of the 'Contras' – the counter-revolutionaries fighting against the Sandinista government in Nicaragua. The muting of O'Neill's criticism on Nicaragua was the price of the Irish state's most important political advance in relation to Northern Ireland since partition.[166]

At the core of the Agreement was the creation of an Anglo-Irish

Inter-Governmental Council jointly chaired by the Secretary of State for Northern Ireland and the Irish Minister for Foreign Affairs. It was to be serviced by a joint secretariat of Irish and NIO officials based in Belfast. The conference was to deal on a regular basis with political, security and legal matters, including the administration of justice and the promotion of cross-border cooperation. The British government committed itself, in what was an international treaty, to make 'determined efforts' to resolve any differences that arose within the Council. Although all this fell short of joint authority, the British claim that it was simply an 'institutionalization' of normal consultation with Dublin was not taken seriously in the Irish capital, where the Agreement was accurately characterized as giving the southern state 'a foothold in decisions governing Northern Ireland'.[167] Writing in August 1985, John Cole, the BBC's political editor, referred to the 'booby prize' that awaited Anglo-Irish strategy: 'The booby prize is when the Agreement is not good enough to attract the Nationalists and worrying enough to send the Unionists over the top.'[168]

It was soon clear that Thatcher had indeed won the booby prize. The unionist community in Northern Ireland was united in angry rejection of the Agreement, or 'Diktat', as it was almost instantly christened. At the same time, although the expanding Catholic middle class greeted direct rule with a Dublin input as an ideal political framework, the core areas of working-class support for the IRA showed little sign of being impressed with the new dispensation. Although support for Sinn Féin had peaked before the Agreement, there was no indication that it was now threatened by an electoral meltdown, while IRA activity continued unabated and the actual level of violence increased. However, while the Agreement was initially denounced by republicans as part of a British counter-insurgency strategy, it would soon contribute to a major republican rethink of the role of armed struggle.

9. From Crisis to Boom: The Republic 1973–2005

Industrialization by Invitation

In the thirty years after 1970 the economy and society of the Republic underwent a radical transformation that would have, as one of its unintended consequences, the effect of making a historic compromise between the main political traditions on the island a real possibility. The prerequisite for this shift was the Lemass–Whitaker policy watershed in 1958–9 and the subsequent role of the state in the promotion of an export-orientated development strategy and the attraction of foreign direct investment. The structure of employment was transformed. The number at work in agriculture continued its long-term decline and the share of agricultural employment fell from 26 per cent in 1971 to just over 11 per cent in 1995. By 1996 the numbers at work in agriculture had fallen to 136,000, representing a decline of 50 per cent over the twenty-five years since 1971.[1]

The Republic was one of the few EEC countries in which manufacturing employment did not shrink drastically during the 1970s and 1980s. By 1977 the Republic had caught up with the North in terms of manufacturing output per head, and by 1984 it was 60 per cent higher. In the 1980s, while Northern Ireland was labelled a stagnant 'workhouse economy', with growth in manufacturing output averaging 0.1 per cent per annum, the Republic's rate of growth was 6 per cent per annum.[2] This impressive performance, together with a substantial expansion of the public sector, made the two decades after 1960 a period of unprecedented economic expansion and material improvements, particularly in comparison with the bleak and stagnant 1950s. GDP grew at 4 per cent per annum and real personal disposable income more than doubled by 1980.[3]

This improvement in economic performance was largely dependent on the growing number of branch plants of foreign companies attracted to the Republic by an extremely favourable tax regime and relatively low wages. By 1980 foreign-owned firms, predominantly from the USA but with strong representation from other European countries, accounted for one third of employment in the manufacturing sector and 70 per cent of exports of manufactured goods.[4]

The Lynch government's White Paper of January 1972, which presented the case for membership of the EEC, had predicted that any jobs lost in the traditional sectors would be more than compensated for by the additional employment created by foreign investment attracted to Ireland by the prospect of access to the wider EEC market.[5] This proved over-optimistic. By 1980 imports accounted for almost two thirds of the sales of manufactured goods, compared to about a third in 1960. The IDA could point to the development of the foreign-controlled electronics sector, which more than doubled its workforce in the decade after 1973. But in the same period employment in the traditional industries of clothing, textiles and footwear declined by 40 per cent.[6]

Such problems were exacerbated by the more unstable international economic environment in the 1970s and 1980s. The fivefold increase in oil prices after the 1973 Yom Kippur War pushed up inflation and exercised a deflationary effect on demand in oil-importing countries. It had a particularly strong impact on the Republic, which was almost entirely dependent on imported energy sources. A fresh surge in oil prices in 1979 helped to precipitate a major international recession. This reduced the amount of internationally mobile investment at a time when Ireland was experiencing increased competition for foreign capital. The development since the 1960s of a number of low-wage, newly industri-alizing countries as potential sites for investment, combined with rising labour costs, eroded Ireland's attractiveness. Its pull as a low-wage export platform for US firms wanting access to the EEC had been undermined by the accessions of Greece, Portugal and Spain.

This deterioration in the international environment occurred at a time when demographic changes were putting increasing pressure on the economy's job-creating capacity. The census of 1971 registered the first increase in the population for the twenty-six counties since partition, and this trend was maintained through 1981, when the census showed an annual rate of increase of 14.4 per 1,000, compared with 5.5 during the 1960s. The improved economic conditions of the 1960s and early 1970s encouraged more people to remain in the country, and former emigrants and their children also began to return to Ireland, resulting in a net immigration figure of 100,000 for the 1970s. A late Irish baby boom was another by-product of economic optimism that weakened the unique Irish pattern of very late marriage.[7] Ireland's rate of natural increase was six times the EEC average during the 1970s, and by the beginning of the 1980s the Irish birth-rate of 21 per 1,000 was far in excess of the European average of twelve.[8] By the end of the 1970s it was calculated that 20,000 new jobs a year were needed just to deal with new entrants to the labour force. This compared with the annual average of 17,200 new jobs created during the decade.[9]

The National Coalition 1973–1977

The initial response of Fianna Fáil to the signs of deteriorating conditions was to maintain the optimistic assumption of the 1960s that the economic problems would be solved by a new and long-lasting expansion, which it was the responsibility of the state to kick-start. George Colley, who had replaced Haughey as Minister for Finance after the Arms Crisis, ignored the warning of T. K. Whitaker, now Governor of the Central Bank and, despite the existence of rising inflation, made a radical departure from financial orthodoxy in his budget of 1972 by running a deficit on current account. His justifications were that the economy was running well below capacity, that unemployment was high and that 'economic buoyancy' was needed to deal with the demands of adaptation to EEC membership. These arguments were unlikely to be contested by the Labour Party.

More surprising was Fine Gael's enthusiastic endorsement of the new principle.[10] Although the party had been rescued from its dire condition in the 1940s by the experience of coalition government, the radical shift in Fianna Fáil's economic policies had removed one of the party's main areas of policy distinctiveness. Lemass's proclaimed desire for a more positive engagement with the North had a similar effect. The departure from the scene of increasing numbers of politicians from the Civil War generation raised fundamental questions for a party that seemed to have increasingly little left to define it, apart from a widespread perception that it existed to defend the interests of big farmers, merchants and professionals. This unfavourable image was exacerbated by the part-time and often amateurish ethos of many of its TDs.

When de Valera retired, Fine Gael's leadership was still an uneasy duopoly, with Richard Mulcahy as President of the party in the country and John A. Costello as leader in the Dáil when his busy professional life as a barrister permitted. When Mulcahy retired in 1959, a majority of the party in the Dáil rebuffed Costello's plea that he should now combine the two roles while maintaining his legal practice, and James Dillon was elected leader. Dillon had been a critic of the many part-timers in the upper reaches of the parliamentary party and favoured a

modernized and professional party organization. However, his modernizing ideas did not extend much beyond party organization. He favoured
moving Ireland from isolation towards what he referred to as a 'White
Commonwealth Alliance' with Britain, the USA, Canada and the other
dominions. He also favoured membership of the EEC, which, its critics
claimed, would ultimately involve the Republic in some sort of military
alliance. At one with Lemass on the issue of Europe, on issues of economic
and social policy he was, as an American diplomat put it, 'cast in an
Edwardian mould'.[11] He was ideologically and temperamentally out of
tune with the Lemassian themes of industrial development and the need
for planning. His position as Minister for Agriculture in both the inter-
party governments reflected his deep, almost philosophical conviction
that agriculture would always be Ireland's prime source of wealth and
his scepticism about whether a country with few natural resources for
industrial development could entertain the ambitious vistas set out by
Lemass. He was also resolutely pre-Keynesian in his views on the role
of the state in the economy and of anything that smacked of the welfare
state or 'socialism'.

Dillon's leadership was seen as damagingly conservative by an
influential group of younger party members led by Declan Costello. Like
his leading acolyte, Garret FitzGerald, Costello was a son of the party's
aristocracy: his father was a former Taoiseach, while FitzGerald's had been
Minister for External Affairs in the first Cumann na nGaedheal government. Costello was one of that rare breed: an intellectual in Dáil politics.
He had created the Fine Gael Research and Information Centre in 1957,
and through it and the *National Observer*, a newspaper that he had founded,
he promoted the idea that Fine Gael needed a new, left-of-centre
identity.[12] Fine Gael's defeat in two by-elections in 1964 weakened
Dillon's capacity to resist the left, and Costello was able to persuade the
Fine Gael parliamentary party to adopt a resolution supporting a 'more
just social order' and 'a more equitable distribution of the nation's
wealth'.[13] The party accepted Costello's proposals, which he embodied
in what he termed the 'Just Society' programme, as policy during the
1965 general election campaign. It upstaged Fianna Fáil with its proposals
for a new Department of Economic Affairs, an incomes policy, state
control of the credit policies of the commercial banks, and a social
development strategy to complement economic modernization with a
free medical service and higher spending on housing and education.

Although the 'Just Society' caught the popular imagination, especially
among younger voters, there remained a fundamental question mark over

the extent and the depth of the party's commitment to Costello's philosophy. Dillon assured journalists on the day the 'Just Society' document was published that Fine Gael remained 'a party of private enterprise', and many in the party would have agreed with Senator E. A. McGuire, the owner of Brown Thomas, Dublin's major department store, that Costello's proposals were 'pure socialism of the most dictatorial kind'.[14]

If radical policies demanded a radical leader, then Dillon's successor was an undoubted improvement. Liam Cosgrave, son of W. T. Cosgrave, had played an important role in the process by which the party had adopted the 'Just Society' programme. At the same time he was trusted by many of the party traditionalists because of his strongly conservative views on moral issues and his identification with the classically Fine Gael values of law and order and the defence of the institutions of the state against any subversive threats.

Cosgrave's support for Costello's proposals reflected not any left-of-centre disposition but his strong belief that they would provide a more coherent basis for cooperation with the Labour Party in order to displace Fianna Fáil from power. He was prepared to be radical in the pursuit of this goal and had even proposed a merger of the two parties in 1968, which had been rejected by Labour's leader, Brendan Corish, as had Cosgrave's suggestion of a pre-election pact between Fine Gael and Labour in 1969.[15] Labour's failure to make an electoral breakthrough in 1969 put an end to the go-it-alone strategy. Visions of the 1970s as being socialist gave way to a more realistic assessment that, together with the 'social democratic' element of Fine Gael, Labour in coalition could make a real difference to the lives of its working-class supporters.

The 1969 election had produced an important shift in the balance between pro- and anti-coalitionists in the party. Traditionally it had been the rural deputies who were strongly in favour of coalition, while those from urban areas, particularly Dublin, tended towards a rejectionist position based on socialist principles. The 1969 election had brought in a group of new Dublin deputies, including Conor Cruise O'Brien and Justin Keating, who combined an impressive amount of intellectual firepower with the conviction that 'principled socialist opposition' was a recipe for impotence. The Arms Crisis and its revelation of the links between sections of Fianna Fáil and the Provisionals added the argument that the two main opposition parties had a national duty to provide a stable and democratic alternative to Fianna Fáil. A special delegate conference held in Cork in December 1970 allowed the leadership to complete what Conor Cruise O'Brien called 'Operation Houdini' by voting to allow the leader and the members of the Parliamentary Labour Party to make the decision to go into coalition when they were convinced this would allow the implementation of Labour's policies.[16] This was more than enough latitude for a parliamentary party that, with the exception of Noel Browne, was determined to get into government at the earliest opportunity.

When Jack Lynch dissolved the Dáil in February 1973, Labour and Fine Gael hastily concluded a coalition agreement and issued a joint fourteen-point programme that contained few specific promises and that Labour's historian described as 'consisting largely of platitudes'.[17] Due to the success of vote transfers between the two parties, Labour won an extra seat, although it had lost votes compared to 1969, particularly in Dublin, where anti-coalition supporters transferred to Official Sinn Féin, which had fought the election on a fairly left-wing set of policies. But it was Fine Gael who benefited most from the transfer pact, gaining four seats. Thus, despite the fact that Fianna Fáil increased its share of the vote slightly on 1969, it lost the election, and the two opposition parties were able to form a stable coalition government.[18]

To many observers the most remarkable thing about the National Coalition was its unity. It faced economic problems and challenges on the security and Northern Ireland fronts that were far greater than those that the previous inter-party governments had had to endure. Key to this unity was the absence of any major divisions on left–right lines between Labour and Fine Gael members of the government. Much of the credit for this must go to Liam Cosgrave, who from his initial decision to offer Labour five ministries – one more than their electoral performance strictly warranted – had operated as a considerate and fair chairman of government meetings.[19] However, it also reflected the fact that the Labour ministers did little to put a distinctive imprint on the key areas of domestic policy during their time in office.

As Tánaiste and Minister for Health and Social Welfare, Brendan Corish at sixty was running out of steam and lacked the inclination or time to give direction to his colleagues. Three of them were particularly forceful personalities: Justin Keating at Industry and Commerce, Conor Cruise O'Brien at Posts and Telegraphs, and Michael O'Leary at Labour. They had their own departmental agendas and, in the case of Keating and O'Leary, leadership ambitions that took priority over any notion of a common Labour strategy. This would, in any case, not have been easy to develop, given the buffeting that the Irish economy was receiving from the end of 1974. The 1973 manifesto had promised that a 'programme of planned economic development' would be a central feature of the government's policy and that an immediate aim was a stabilization of prices, a halt in redundancies and a reduction of unemployment. The fivefold increase in oil prices removed any possibility of these ambitions being realized. Prices rose by about 90 per cent during the first four years of the coalition's term, an average rate almost twice that experienced during the previous four years of Lynch's government. The combined effect of freer trade and recession caused many firms to cease production or cut their workforces. The number of unemployed rose from 71,435 when the coalition took power in March 1973 to 115,942 four years later, or from 7.9 per cent to 12.5 per cent of the insured labour force.[20]

These dismal figures undermined any possible electoral benefit Labour might have had from the achievements of the coalition in the areas of social expenditure and taxation. Expenditure on social welfare rose from 6.5 per cent of GNP in 1973 to 10.5 per cent four years later and most benefit rates rose by 125 per cent, considerably more than wages and prices. The rate of house building increased by 50 per cent and expenditure on health services increased almost threefold.[21] Taxation was an area in which Fine Gael's left made common cause with Labour. The election manifesto had committed the coalition to a wealth tax, and Garret FitzGerald, who was a member of the cabinet's economic subcommittee, supported his Labour colleagues on the need for taxation of capital gains and wealth.[22] A White Paper published in February 1974 proposed a capital gains tax of 35 per cent and an annual wealth tax on estates of over £40,000. In an attempt to lessen criticism from the large propertied and middle-class element in Fine Gael's traditional support, death duties were to be abolished. The intensity of the reaction to the proposed taxes on capital gains and wealth, led in the Dáil by the only recently rehabilitated Charles Haughey, resulted in the introduction of a higher threshold of £100,000 and a lower rate of 1 per cent. Such redistributive policies alienated the middle class, while their only marginal contribution to the public purse did little to compensate Labour's working-class supporters, many of whom experienced a real drop in their living standards in the last two years of the coalition. Labour's presence in government had made it easier for the leadership of the Irish trade union movement to be persuaded of the need for 'responsible' wage demands. Real pre-tax incomes rose in 1974 and 1975, but then National Wage Agreements were amended to introduce pay curbs, which, together with a heavily regressive tax system, led to a squeeze on working-class living standards.[23]

The apparent lack of division within the coalition on the economy, the issue that would lose them the election in 1977, was in contrast to the open tensions over how best to deal with the reverberations of the northern conflict. Cosgrave, along with Conor Cruise O'Brien, had favoured a low-key approach to Northern Ireland, aimed at a largely internal power-sharing deal between the Ulster Unionists and the SDLP. Garret FitzGerald had been appointed to Foreign Affairs by Cosgrave, who had an uneasy relationship with his voluble and super-confident colleague and had hoped that the many ramifications of EEC member-ship would result in the minister spending a lot of time out of the country. This ignored FitzGerald's formidable energy and his conviction that having a mother from a northern Presbyterian background gave him a particular insight into the mentalities of both communities in the North.

FitzGerald soon assumed a key role in Northern Ireland policy and used it to support the more activist policies favoured by John Hume. O'Brien, who was an increasingly scathing critic of the conventional Irish nationalist analysis of Northern Ireland, was kept on as Labour Party spokesman on Northern Ireland and at Sunningdale tried in vain to argue for a deal more palatable to Faulkner's supporters. After the UWC strike he became the first Irish government minister to state publicly that he was not working actively for Irish unity, as it was not a practi-cable goal. In a document prepared for his party colleagues and leaked to the press, he argued that to prevent a 'doomsday situation' in the North the government in Dublin should adopt a relatively low profile.[24] In fact, the UWC strike's success had forced the Irish government to pay more attention to O'Brien's analysis. Concerned that Harold Wilson might be considering a unilateral British withdrawal, the government established an inter-departmental unit to plan for such a scenario. It warned that British withdrawal would not lead to a united Ireland but to a loyalist-dominated independent state, and that the best that could be hoped for was some form of repartition following inter-communal violence.[25]

O'Brien was criticized at the time and since for an unbalanced approach that demanded from Irish nationalists an intellectual maturity and generosity of spirit that he never demanded from unionists.[26] Yet it was precisely O'Brien's point that much of the rigidity, lack of imagin-ation and simple bigotry associated with the unionist cause was a result of nationalism's refusal to accept that there could be any democratic validity to partition. He was convinced that reform in the North and better North–South relations were a real possibility if the unity issue were put to one side. This inevitably meant that he concentrated his attentions on those best placed to unlock this progressive potential in the North by abandoning positions that, no matter how appealing in Dublin, strengthened the hands of the most reactionary opponents of change in Belfast.

O'Brien's most vociferous critics were within his own party. Justin Keating was in the forefront of those wedded to the republican socialist mantras of James Connolly, demanding British withdrawal at a time when the North was as near to a sectarian civil war as at any time since the 1920–22 period. Anti-partitionists were soon joined in the ranks of critics of 'The Cruiser' by civil liberties groups and a substantial sector of the Dublin print and broadcast media as O'Brien and Cosgrave became identified with a heavy-handed approach to the activities of the IRA in the South.

Cosgrave had outraged his more liberal colleagues and threatened to split the Fine Gael parliamentary party when, in December 1972, he had indicated that he would support Fianna Fáil's amendment to the Offences against the State Act, which allowed the indictment by a senior police officer of those suspected to be terrorists. The explosion of two bombs in the centre of Dublin, killing two people and injuring over a hundred, which was probably the work of loyalist terrorists, led to the withdrawal of Fine Gael's opposition to the amendment and saved Cosgrave's leadership. However, his government was soon faced with intensifying and often sickening reminders that neither republicans nor loyalists would respect the border when the exigencies of the 'war' in Northern Ireland demanded it.

Within a fortnight of the coalition coming into office, the *Claudia*, a fishing boat filled with an IRA arms shipment and with the senior Belfast IRA man Joe Cahill on board, was captured off the Waterford coast as a result of joint British–Irish intelligence work. Over the next two decades the IRA's 'southern command' would use the Republic as the major location for its arms dumps, for the training of its 'volunteers', and as a source of funds through bank robberies, kidnappings and other forms of extortion. In the autumn of 1973 all the members of the government were informed that they and their families were under direct threat of kidnapping by one or other of the republican groups. In 1975 the Dutch businessman Tiede Herrema was taken by the IRA, which demanded the release of its prisoners in Irish jails. The government refused to negotiate. As Conor Cruise O'Brien puts it in his account of the coalition,

'We and Herrema got lucky': police interrogation of a suspected member of the gang revealed where the victim was being held and he was released without physical harm.[27] Others were less fortunate. In March 1974 a Fine Gael Senator, Billy Fox, was visiting his fiancée in the border county of Monaghan when he was shot dead by the Provisionals. Fox, like the family he was visiting, was a Presbyterian, and the motive for the murder was apparently sectarian.[28] Although the IRA had attempted to deny its involvement in Fox's murder, it openly admitted responsibility for the murder of the British Ambassador, Christopher Ewart-Biggs, whose car was blown up by a landmine near his official residence on the outskirts of Dublin on 23 July 1976.

The Dáil was recalled for a special emergency sitting, and Cosgrave proposed a state of national emergency with a substantial increase in the powers of the state in its 'anti-subversive' struggle. A politically embarrassing conflict with the President, Cearbhall Ó Dálaigh, occurred when he referred one of the proposed pieces of legislation to the Supreme Court in September. The Minister for Defence, Paddy Donegan, a strong Cosgrave loyalist, departed from his script in a speech to troops at Mullingar to refer to Ó Dálaigh as a 'thundering disgrace', provoking the President's resignation. It is hard not to agree with the journalist Bruce Arnold in his judgement that Cosgrave overreacted to the murder, in part to wrong-foot Fianna Fáil with the objective of an early election on the law-and-order issue.[29] It is difficult otherwise to explain why similar measures had not been proposed after the appalling atrocity committed by the Ulster Volunteer Force when it exploded car-bombs in the centres of Dublin and Monaghan on 17 May 1974, killing thirty-three people in the worst single loss of life during the 'Troubles'.

If Cosgrave did have an undeclared electoral agenda, the President's resignation frustrated it and intensified the authoritarian and repressive image of the government. Newspaper reports of police brutality in the interrogation of terrorist suspects by what was described as the 'Heavy Gang' were taken so seriously by FitzGerald that he considered pressing for an inquiry and resigning from the government if it were not granted.[30] In 1975 O'Brien amended the Broadcasting Authority Act of 1960 to allow the Minister for Posts and Telegraphs to name certain organizations that would be prevented from making broadcasts and from having their members interviewed. Broadcasting by the IRA and Sinn Féin had been effectively banned from the airways since broadcasting began in the state, although neither organization was referred to in the legislation. Now, for the first time, Sinn Féin was named as a proscribed organization, and the resulting furore only enhanced the government's 'law-and-order' image.

If, as Garret FitzGerald claims, the coalition lost the 1977 election because 'the people were tired of us',[31] then what J. J. Lee calls the 'constipated' image of Cosgrave, as opposed to the amiability of Jack Lynch, may well have played a role.[32] His obvious relish in the fight against subversion, and O'Brien's 'anti-national' views on Northern Ireland, have been seen by some analysts as key elements in the coalition's defeat.[33] The repressive image of the government may have damaged it amongst younger voters. The voting age had been reduced to eighteen for the first time, and a quarter of the electorate was under twenty-six. The coalition's appeal to this group had been hurt by Cosgrave's decision to vote against his own government's legislation on contraception. This had been prompted by a Supreme Court ruling in the McGee case in December 1973, which declared the ban on the importation of contraceptives under the 1935 Act to be unconstitutional. The government's legislation, which aimed to regularize the situation by allowing chemists to sell contraceptives to married couples, was hardly a charter for promiscuity, but worried a number of Fine Gael TDs with rural seats to defend.[34] Cosgrave's vote and a number of other Fine Gael defections killed the bill. Yet, if some younger voters were dismayed by the coalition's failure on contraception, they were hardly likely to turn to Fianna Fáil, which took an unabashedly traditional line on the issue. It is also unlikely that Northern Ireland played much of a role in Cosgrave's defeat. It featured little in the campaign, and if the defeat of Conor Cruise O'Brien was seen by some as a blow struck by the electorate against revisionist views on the North, what then was the significance of Justin Keating's loss of his seat, given his unreconstructed anti-partitionism?

But, while the Irish media's fixation on the repressive and authoritarian features of the coalition and O'Brien's revisionist agenda had little impact on the electorate, it did dent the morale of many of the government's members and contribute to the decision to go to the country in June 1977. This was despite the fact that the government had another six months to run and despite signs that the economy was moving back to rapid growth and inflation was falling.[35] Cosgrave was proud of the coalition's ability to hold together for four and a half years, longer than any government since the Emergency, and hopeful that a radical redrawing of constituency boundaries by the Labour Minister for Local Government, James Tully, would damage Fianna Fáil. While the infamous 'Tullymander' might have been effective against a moderate swing to the

Opposition, what occurred in June 1977 was a massive surge to Lynch's party. For the first time since 1938, Fianna Fáil won over 50 per cent of the vote, and their eighty-four seats represented a gain of fifteen. The combined vote for the coalition parties dropped from 49 per cent to 42 per cent and from seventy-three seats to sixty.[36]

The key to Lynch's success was a sharp turn of working-class voters towards Fianna Fáil. In 1969, 40 per cent of skilled workers voted for Fianna Fáil and 26 per cent for Labour. By 1977 the gap had widened to 54 per cent for Fianna Fáil and 11 per cent for Labour.[37] Disillusion with the coalition on unemployment and falling incomes was decisive, and it was transformed into a surge of support for Lynch through Fianna Fáil's first ever election manifesto, *Action Plan for National Reconstruction*, which was the most extravagant and reckless collection of economic pledges ever made in an Irish election. It promised to create 25,000 jobs a year, when the previous average had been around 4,000 a year. Income tax was to be cut and domestic rates abolished along with road tax. First-time house buyers were to receive a grant of £1,000.

Conor Cruise O'Brien has claimed that this audacious programme 'bore all the hallmarks of C.J. Haughey, now again the rising star of Fianna Fáil'.[38] The manifesto, however, was designed to ensure such a margin of victory that Lynch would once and for all be able to put the 'unconstitutional element' in the party in its place. In this sense Northern Ireland did play a subtle and subterranean role in the election. Haughey had maintained a strong body of support within the party, and after the collapse of the power-sharing executive and the apparently bleak prospects for further political reform in the North there was an upsurge of traditional anti-partitionist sentiment within Fianna Fáil. Michael O'Kennedy, the party's new spokesman on Northern Ireland, was in awe of Haughey and in March 1975 the party published a distinctly hawkish policy document calling for a British commitment to implement an 'ordered withdrawal' from the North.

Haughey's post-1970 public posture of loyalty to the party and his strong performance in the Dáil as a critic of the coalition's wealth tax had led to his return to the opposition front bench in 1975 as spokesman on Health and Social Welfare. He had used his time in the political wilderness to cultivate the party's grass-roots. There was no 'rubber chicken' function in a rural backwater that he was not prepared to grace with his presence. Lynch, aware of Haughey's popularity with the party's foot-soldiers, hoped that a major election victory would allow him to re-establish his authority in the party. It was with this in mind that he had asked Martin O'Donoghue, Professor of Economics at Trinity College, to be a candidate in the election and write the sort of expansionist manifesto that would copper-fasten his leadership.[39] Against his better economic judgement, O'Donoghue delivered the victory. Unfortunately for Lynch, the influx of new TDs included many who would look to Haughey for the strong leadership deemed necessary when O'Donoghue's strategy appeared to threaten the possibility of national bankruptcy.

Charles Haughey and the Fracturing of Fianna Fáil

The strong passions that Haughey aroused in his opponents and allies have tended to result in a version of the political history of the South in the 1980s that pays too much attention to the role of individuals and not enough to the profound economic problems that the Republic faced. If one individual has to be singled out as responsible for the crisis years of the early 1980s, then it would have to be Jack Lynch. One Irish historian's comment that Lynch 'stood for nothing in particular except a kind of affable consensus' has been criticized by J. J. Lee for not recognizing that such a consensus was an achievement if the alternative was the 'breakdown of civilized discourse or government by the elect instead of the elected'.[40] Yet Lynch had displayed severe hesitancy during the Arms Crisis and an unwillingness to confront Haughey and his fellow conspirators until forced to do so by Liam Cosgrave.[41] The consensus he prioritized was that which was within Fianna Fáil, and in 1977 he showed a marked inclination to sustain it with an electoral triumph whatever the ultimate economic cost.

This was apparent to some leading members of the party at the time, with Haughey's ally Brian Lenihan commenting on the manifesto, 'Blessed are the young for they shall inherit the national debt.'[42] Martin O'Donoghue was now in the cabinet heading a new Department of Economic Planning and Development. He set out the government's economic strategy in a White Paper, *National Development 1977–1980*. It was, he admitted, a gamble, relying on a vigorous pump-priming exercise by the state that would create the expansionist environment in which private enterprise would take over, allowing for a reduction in the role of the state and in the level of public expenditure. Two of the basic assumptions underpinning the strategy were dangerously optimistic. One was that the oil price shock of 1973 was a once-and-for-all event and that international economic conditions would continue to recover. The other was that the trade union movement would be prepared to exchange 'responsible' wage demands for job creation.

The second large increase in oil prices at the end of 1978 and the consequent deep international recession dealt a severe blow. Growth of GDP, which had averaged 6 per cent in 1977 and 1978, dropped to 1.5 per cent in 1979 and unemployment and redundancies began to increase sharply. Lynch had said that he would resign if the number of unemployed could not be brought below 100,000 – it was 106,000 when the coalition left office. In the first two years of the new administration over 60,000 new jobs were created and the number of unemployed had fallen to 90,000 by 1979. It then began to rise and reached 100,000 in 1980. By 1983 it would soar to 200,000, or 16 per cent of the workforce, the highest rate in the EEC.[43] The jobs that were created were mostly in a fast-growing public sector and were paid for by a sharp rise in public expenditure financed by government borrowing. By the time Haughey succeeded Lynch as Taoiseach in December 1979, the Exchequer borrowing requirement had doubled and the national debt was more than two thirds higher than when the coalition had left office.[44]

To imported inflation was added the inflationary effect of trade union wage demands. The 1970s had seen a shift towards more centralized collective bargaining between the ICTU and the employers' organizations through a series of national wage agreements. In the second half of the decade the government began to play a formal role in these negotiations. This culminated in the *National Understanding for Economic and Social Development* in 1979, aimed at eliciting union restraint on wages in return for government action on a wide range of issues that included health, education, taxation and employment.[45] However, the fragmentation of the Republic's trade union movement made it difficult for the ICTU leadership to deliver its members' compliance in wage restraint. In 1978 a plea from the Minister for Finance, George Colley, for a national wage settlement of 5 per cent had little effect as average industrial earnings rose by 17 per cent.[46]

Wage discipline was made less likely because of an eruption of urban/rural conflict over taxation. The EEC's Common Agricultural Policy (CAP) had provided Irish farmers with a golden harvest. Guaranteed prices and highly favourable price increases caused by substantial devaluations of sterling had brought Irish farmers unprecedented prosperity. By 1978 real incomes in agriculture had doubled compared with 1970.[47] The fact that farmers were not subject to income tax seemed increasingly intolerable as more and more urban workers were brought into higher tax brackets because of inflation. The exclusion of farmers from the income tax base of the state, together with a very favourable tax regime for companies, meant that during the 1970s there was a considerable increase in the tax burden for those subject to income tax.[48] George Colley had attempted to deal with growing criticism of his government's inaction on farm incomes with a proposal for a 2 per cent levy on farmers' turnover in his 1979 budget. However, by this time the CAP-induced boom had come to an end. Ireland's decision to join the European Monetary System when it was created in 1978 meant the end of favourable currency movements as the link with sterling was broken. EEC concern with over-production under the CAP led to a reduction in the rapid rate of increase in agricultural prices and ushered in a slump in agriculture. A strong reaction from farmers' organizations led to the proposed farm levy being dropped. The result was an explosion of protest from trade unionists, who took to the streets in marches and demonstrations for tax equity, culminating in a one-day national strike on 20 March 1979 with 150,000 protesters in Dublin and another 40,000 in Cork. George Colley, who had criticized the strike as 'unproductive' on the day before it took place, probably sealed his fate in the forthcoming battle for the leadership of the party.

With unemployment and inflation rising, tax protesters on the streets, and a prolonged and bitter strike by postal workers, 1979 was the year in which the direction of economic policy by a small 'inner cabinet' of Lynch's closest supporters sparked off a revolt in the parliamentary party. Some of those involved were new TDs with a background in business and accountancy, including Albert Reynolds and Charlie McCreevy. Others were aghast at the party's poor electoral performance. In the first elections for the European Parliament in June, Fianna Fáil's vote slumped to 34 per cent, and it won only five of the Republic's fifteen seats. Most galling for Lynch was the election of one of his most virulent republican critics, Neil Blaney, as an Independent in the Connacht/Ulster constituency.[49] Then in November the party lost disastrously in two by-elections in Cork, one of them in Lynch's own constituency.

To the economic reverses and electoral rebuffs were added the legacy of the Arms Crisis and Lynch's unpopularity with the unreconstructed republicans in the party. On 27 August 1979 the IRA blew up a yacht belonging to the Queen's cousin, Lord Mountbatten, who was holidaying in County Sligo. Mountbatten and three others of the party were killed. At Narrow Water in County Down on the same day another IRA attack killed eighteen soldiers. Lynch agreed to requests from Thatcher to allow British military aircraft brief incursions into the Republic's airspace in pursuit of terrorists. When news of the 'air corridor' agreement appeared in the press, it produced a paroxysm of traditionalist rage against such 'collaboration' with a Tory government. An attempt to discipline a TD who had claimed that Lynch had lied about the agreement backfired badly, and then Síle de Valera, a granddaughter of de Valera, made an only slightly veiled attack on Lynch's northern policy in an address to a Fianna Fáil commemoration. Lynch, shocked by the extent and bitterness of the backbench revolt, announced that he would resign. It is unlikely that the government's failures on the economy and the election reverses would in themselves have led to Lynch's decision. His administration had another two years to run and previous governments had recovered from similar reversals. It was the extra dimension of bitterness that came from the legacy of the Arms Crisis, the 'sulphurous' atmosphere that a journalist detected in the parliamentary party,[50] that propelled Lynch, a leader who had prided himself in his ability to bring together the different wings of the party, out of politics. In the contest for the leadership that followed, Haughey defeated Colley by forty-four votes to thirty-eight.

Haughey's victory has been depicted by one of his numerous critics as the opening up of 'the most sordid and diseased chapter in Irish political life since the end of the civil war'.[51] One of a number of tribunals of inquiry established at the end of the 1990s to investigate corruption in Irish politics since the 1960s established that Haughey had run up a debt of £1.14 million with the Allied Irish Bank during the 1970s and that he had used his position as Taoiseach to persuade the bank to settle for £750,000.[52] At the time rumours about how he had acquired his fortune in the 1960s abounded, as did those about his current financial problems. It was to these that Garret FitzGerald alluded in his speech on Haughey's nomination as Taoiseach when he referred to a 'flawed pedigree' and a man who, while his abilities were undeniable, should be disqualified from high office as he wanted 'not simply to dominate the state but to own it'.[53]

With a self-image that seemed to blend the Renaissance prince and the Gaelic chieftain, Charles Haughey did not regard himself as bound by the conventional values that applied to ordinary mortals. In the late 1970s bank officials were threatened with his displeasure if they dared to apply the same standards to him as to other debtors. In 1987 Ben Dunne, one of Ireland's leading businessmen and an admirer of the Taoiseach, was approached to bail him out of an even deeper hole of indebtedness and provided him with payments in excess of £1 million over the next few years.[54] The many rumours about how Haughey financed such a lavish lifestyle did not damage his immense popularity with a substantial section of the party and the electorate. Like the 'whiff of cordite' associated with the Arms Trial, such rumours made him seem appealingly dangerous. As the Irish political journalist Stephen Collins has noted, Haughey's popularity revealed the continuing influence of 'deep ambivalence to politics and law, coupled with the atavistic anti-English strain in Irish nationalism' amongst many Irish people.[55]

Haughey had always been dismissive of Lynch's consensual and relaxed leadership style, and his own was characterized by the encouragement of a deferential and at times fearful loyalty amongst his supporters, who called him 'Boss', and the implacable desire to marginalize his opponents. Although some of these, including Colley, who refused to offer Haughey loyalty as leader of the party and demanded a veto on the appointment of the Ministers for Justice and for Defence, were resolute in opposition, others, including Des O'Malley, were open to persuasion.[56] Instead, Haughey looked towards a victory in the next general election as the prerequisite for a final purge of his most irreconcilable critics.

The fixation on obtaining a Fianna Fáil majority was in part responsible for his rapid volte-face on the economy. In his first televised address to the nation on 9 January 1980, he had sounded a stern note: 'as a community we have been living beyond our means . . . we have been living at a rate which is simply not justified by the amount of goods and services we are producing.'[57] Having sacked Martin O'Donoghue and abolished his department, Haughey now proposed cuts in government expenditure and a reduction in borrowing. A large part of the business and financial community, virtually all of the media and most professional economists were enthused at the prospect of a Celtic Thatcherism. It was not to be, at least not yet. A right-wing turn in economic policy made good economic sense but was politically perilous for a party whose recovery from the post-war doldrums had been based on Lemass's mixture of economic expansion and cooperation with the unions. Working-class resentment on the taxation issue had been manifest two weeks after Haughey's television address, in what the BBC referred to as 'the largest peaceful protest in postwar Europe'.[58] An ICTU-organized national strike for tax reform was supported by 700,000 workers, with a mass demonstration of 300,000 in Dublin. For many of those TDs who had supported Haughey, fiscal rectitude seemed a recipe for political suicide.

Haughey's own lavish and debt-financed lifestyle may have made him uncomfortable with demands that the largely working-class electorate of his North Dublin constituency put on hair shirts while his own wardrobe was tailor-made in Paris.[59] His political career and personal fortune had been built in the expansionary 1960s, when the building industry had begun to have an increasingly powerful influence on Fianna Fáil.[60] This was a major sector of the economy that stood to lose badly from neo-liberal policies. Big cuts in public expenditure might be seen as necessary to get the economic fundamentals right by those sections of Irish industry that had successfully made the transition to free trade and selling abroad. However, there remained many Irish manufacturers who were uncompetitive, relied on the domestic market and were directly threatened by the shrinkage in demand that deflationary policies would inevitably produce. Together with the trade union movement, they forced Haughey to backtrack. Within months the government had agreed another National Understanding with the unions, which involved an increase in welfare benefits and job-creation targets along with a promise of more investment in infrastructure and a continuation of high levels of government borrowing. Haughey's former business allies despaired as the budget deficit rose from £522 million in 1979 to £802 million in 1981 and the Exchequer borrowing requirement from 13.8 per cent of GNP to 16.8 per cent,[61] with the Department of Finance forecasting that it would reach 21 per cent by 1982.[62]

With all the main economic indicators deteriorating, Haughey attempted to maintain popular support by a robustly nationalist line on Northern Ireland. Describing it as a 'failed political entity', he announced that he wanted to raise the issue to a 'higher plane' by seeking a solution through direct negotiations with the British government.[63] Despite his public disdain for Thatcher's neo-liberal economic policies, he was obviously attracted by her imperious mode of government and her impatience with the inherited policy of power-sharing devolution. There were hints of a willingness to consider a defence deal with the UK and, more immediately, after his first meeting with Thatcher when he presented her with a silver Georgian teapot, it was announced that there would be a meeting between the Chief Constable of the RUC and the Garda Commissioner.[64] The British hoped that Haughey's solid republican credentials would allow him to act decisively against the IRA. As a result, Haughey did remarkably well in the major Anglo-Irish summit held in

Dublin on 8 December 1980. In their joint communiqué after the talks, Thatcher acknowledged Britain's 'unique relationship' with Ireland and permitted the establishment of joint study groups to find ways of expressing this uniqueness in 'new institutional relations'. The two Prime Ministers agreed to devote their next meeting to considering 'the totality of relations within these islands'. Haughey's subsequent demagogic exploitation of this phrase infuriated Thatcher, and differences over the IRA hunger strikes and the Falklands War further soured relations between the two. However, the logic of Haughey's approach – that the two governments should act over the heads of the northern parties, particularly the Unionists – would come to partial fruition in the Anglo-Irish Agreement.

In the short term the credibility of Haughey's approach to the North was damaged by the hunger strikes and his failure to have an influence on Thatcher's handling of them. Nevertheless, unsure of the electorate's verdict on his economic stewardship, he dissolved the Dáil on 21 May 1981, claiming that he was calling the election 'because of the grave and tragic situation in Northern Ireland'.[65] This was the first time Northern Ireland had been proclaimed the central issue in a southern election. Although Bobby Sands had died on 5 May and other hunger strikers were nearing death, the bulk of the electorate continued to focus doggedly on the domestic issues of taxation, inflation and unemployment. Haughey, who was about equal in popularity with FitzGerald when the election was called, paid a hefty price for such a clumsy diversionary tactic. By giving a high profile to Northern Ireland he provided Sinn Féin with the best opportunity for advance in southern politics since the 1950s. Nine republican prisoners were nominated for the election and the two that were successful took seats that would otherwise have gone to Fianna Fáil.

Any vestigial claim to economic competence or responsibility that his government might have made was undermined by his descent into crude vote-buying in key constituencies, with a commitment to an international airport in a remote part of County Mayo to bring pilgrims to the Marian shrine at Knock and a deal with workers in the Talbot car assembly plant in his constituency that guaranteed them state salaries for life when the plant closed. Both commitments were made without any consultation with his colleagues or the Department of Finance.[66]

The result of the 1981 election was a substantial victory for Fine Gael, whose percentage of the vote increased from 30.5 to 36.5 and seats from forty-three to sixty-five, its best ever result, even considering that the overall number of Dáil seats had increased from 147 to 166. Under Garret FitzGerald's leadership since 1977, Fine Gael had modernized its archaic structure and transformed its culture of genteel amateurism. Youth and women's wings were established, and it was the first of the major parties actively to promote women candidates, becoming home to some of those who had played a prominent role in the development of the Irish women's movement in the early 1970s.[67] The party had waged a professional and aggressive campaign, and its promise of large cuts in income tax had allowed it to make inroads into working-class support for Fianna Fáil. FitzGerald's public persona – that of an amiable and loquacious academic – contrasted sharply with Haughey's tight-lipped and imperious aura.

Fianna Fáil's vote dropped from 50.6 to 45.3 per cent and its seats from eighty-four to seventy-five.[68] The Lynch–Haughey inheritance of debt and inflation led to a sharp decline in middle-class support, while rising unemployment and lack of tax reform produced an only slightly less sharp drop in working-class support.[69] However, its vote in 1977 had been exceptional, and, given the worsening economic situation, its losses were not unexpectedly high. In 1969 Fianna Fáil had won an overall majority of seats with a slightly smaller share of the votes. It was the agreement between Fine Gael and Labour to urge their supporters to give their second preferences to the other party that proved decisive. Without the transfer arrangement Fianna Fáil would have won five extra seats, which, given the absence of the two hunger strike TDs, would have provided it with a clear overall majority.[70] Haughey made use of this to claim that he had not really lost the election: a quirk of the electoral system and the intervention of the hunger strikers had robbed him of victory.[71] That the new government was a minority administration dependent on the votes of three leftist independents encouraged him and his supporters to believe that their loss of office would be brief.

Although still convinced that Fine Gael's only secure future was as a 'social-democratic' party, FitzGerald was soon forced to apply a radical deflationary programme to deal with what his Minister for Finance, the wealthy County Meath farmer John Bruton, termed the threat to national economic independence that was the legacy of the previous government.[72] An emergency budget was introduced in July with increases in indirect taxation and spending cuts aimed at reducing the Exchequer borrowing requirement from 20 to 16 per cent of GNP.[73] The draconian budget created major problems for the junior partner in the coalition: Frank Cluskey, the gruff Dublin trade unionist who had been elected Labour leader in 1977, would probably have led his ministers out of government. However, Labour had lost two seats in the election and one of those was Cluskey's. His successor was the altogether smoother Michael O'Leary, a former student radical who had been a research officer for the ICTU before becoming Minister for Labour in the 1973–7 coalition, where he was seen as the most successful of the Labour ministers.[74]

Labour's performance in the election had been dismal. Given a bad result in 1977 and that it was in opposition at a time of very high unemployment and inflation, it had expected to make gains. But its share of the vote fell to less than 10 per cent for the first time since 1957 and its number of seats to fifteen in a much larger Dáil. Its performance in Dublin was particularly bad, with a reduction of three seats that left it only three, a sad decline on the ten it had won in 1969. The party remained divided over the leadership's support for a coalition strategy. Anti-coalition feeling and a more ideological socialism were strong amongst party members in Dublin, but continued backing for a coalition was guaranteed by the support of rural members. Critics argued that the pursuit of coalition with Fine Gael had blurred Labour's distinctiveness and weakened its independent appeal: 'since a vote for Labour was a vote for a Fine Gael-dominated coalition, then in many ways it may make more sense simply to vote for Fine Gael *per se*.'[75] It now faced a challenge from a number of smaller parties to its left. Noel Browne had changed his party affiliations yet again and was elected as a Socialist Labour Party TD in Dublin; Jim Kemmy, an independent socialist with strongly anti-nationalist views on Northern Ireland, won Limerick East; and Joe Sherlock won East Cork for Sinn Féin–The Workers' Party (SFWP), as the increasingly successful political arm of the Official IRA was now known.

Labour entered the 1981 coalition from a position of weakness. In 1969 it had won half as many votes as Fine Gael; now it had barely a quarter. With four cabinet seats out of fifteen, the Labour ministers could do little to blunt the edges of Bruton's draconian budget except prevent the income tax cuts that would have intensified the regressive effects of the taxation changes. Dissent within the party increased, and in October its ruling Administrative Council declared that the Labour ministers had exceeded their mandate in agreeing to the July budget. However, worse was to come when in January 1982 Bruton proposed an even tougher second budget, with cuts in food subsidies, rises in indirect taxation and new taxes on clothing and footwear. FitzGerald refused to consider an exemption for children's shoes in case it was exploited by women with small feet. This was the last straw for Jim Kemmy, who subordinated his strong dislike of Haughey's position on Northern Ireland to his rejection of such a regressive measure and voted with the Opposition against the budget, thus ensuring the government's defeat by eighty-two votes to eighty-one.

Despite its commitment to austerity, Fine Gael marginally increased its vote in the subsequent inconclusive general election in February 1982, although its number of seats fell by two to sixty-three. Fianna Fáil increased its vote from 45.3 to 47.2 per cent and its seats from seventy-eight to eighty-one. The Labour Party's vote had declined slightly, but it held its fifteen seats, although it now faced a sharp left-wing challenge in the Dáil after the SFWP made a breakthrough to win three seats. The three SFWP TDs and four independents held the balance of power and were assiduously courted by Haughey.[76]

Haughey's failure to win a majority for the second time precipitated a period of intense convulsion in his party. The Opposition front bench was already divided over economic policy when the election was called. In an attempt to mend fences with some of his most prominent critics in the party, Haughey had appointed Martin O'Donoghue as the party spokesman on Finance and had agreed that a more 'responsible' attitude be adopted to the government's proposals for dealing with the dire economic situation. However, as soon as the campaign started he reverted to populist mode and attacked the coalition's 'Thatcherite' approach. FitzGerald, he claimed, was 'hypnotized' by the issue of the national debt, and Fianna Fáil would find 'a more humane way' of running the economy, even if it meant borrowing money. This failed to convince many of his colleagues, and it also had little impact on the electorate. At the beginning of the campaign 51 per cent of those polled preferred FitzGerald as Taoiseach, compared to 31 per cent for Haughey; by the end the respective figures were 56 and 36 per cent.[77]

Even before a new government could be formed, Desmond O'Malley had declared his intention to stand against Haughey for the leadership of the party. O'Malley's distrust of Haughey dated from the Arms Crisis, when he had been a key supporter of Lynch. It was now accentuated by his wholehearted commitment to neo-liberal economics and an identification of Haughey as an irresponsible populist. However, O'Malley's aloof and prickly personality made him an unappetizing alternative to that sizeable section of Fianna Fáil TDs who were wavering in their allegiances, and when Martin O'Donoghue, who had been O'Malley's campaign manager, at the last moment called for unity behind Haughey, O'Malley withdrew his challenge. Haughey then outbid FitzGerald for the support of Tony Gregory, an Independent TD of republican-socialist leanings, who represented an inner-city constituency in Dublin. The 'Gregory deal' involved a government commitment to spend over £80 million in job creation, new housing, environmental works and schooling.[78] The support of the three SFWP TDs for Haughey was a major surprise, given that party's shift to a position on Northern Ireland that accepted the need for unionist consent for constitutional change. The party supported the proposals of James Prior, the Northern Ireland Secretary, for the election of a Northern Ireland Assembly. While Haughey believed the proposals to be unworkable, he agreed to adopt a public position of neutrality. Together with his promise of opposition to the privatization of state-owned companies and his anti-Thatcherite rhetoric, this was sufficient to obtain SFWP support.[79]

The government's short life was dominated by rumours of plots and the unorthodox methods adopted by some of Haughey's supporters to deal with his critics. George Colley was dropped from the cabinet and, with his veto on appointments to the Ministries of Defence and Justice removed, Haughey filled the positions with two of his loyalists, Seán Doherty and Paddy Power. Power was a very traditional republican and when the *Belgrano* was sunk during the Falklands War he embarrassed Haughey by making a speech accusing the British of being the aggressor. However, it was the appointment of Doherty that would have the most devastating long-term effects on Haughey's career. Only thirty-seven when appointed, the County Roscommon TD had been one of Haughey's most strident supporters. An ex-Garda, he showed little inclination to respect the law when it came into conflict with his political or personal priorities. In January 1983 the Garda Commissioner and his deputy were forced to resign when it emerged that they had agreed to Doherty's request for the tapping of the telephones of two journalists. The purpose of the taps was to discover which of Haughey's critics in the party had been talking to the press. Doherty also supplied Ray MacSharry, the Tánaiste and Minister for Finance, with Garda equipment to bug a conversation with Martin O'Donoghue. When in August a suspected murderer was found living in a flat owned by the Attorney-General, who departed on a holiday to New York in spite of the crisis, Haughey described the sequence of events as 'grotesque, unbelievable, bizarre and unprecedented'. Conor Cruise O'Brien turned the description into a telling acronym that became the government's epitaph: GUBU.

The débâcle was to lead to another attempt to oust Haughey in the autumn, which failed, although this time twenty-two TDs openly opposed him. However, the fate of the government had already been decided by yet another turn in economic policy.

Ray MacSharry had initially dismissed the economic policies of the coalition as 'gloom and doom' and promised 'boom and boom'. However, as 1982 progressed, the economic crisis deepened, as more companies collapsed, more redundancies were made, and unemployment rose. At the same time net foreign debt rose from £3.45 billion at the end of 1981 to £5.11 billion a year later.[80] In response MacSharry announced a radical shift in policy in July, with a postponement of an already agreed rise in public sector pay along with a series of spending cuts. The government's apparent conversion to economic realism was complete by October, when it published a major economic policy document, *The Way Forward*, which committed it to phasing out the budget deficit by 1986. The promise of austerity ahead brought an end to SFWP support. The party had already been annoyed by Haughey's denunciation of the Prior proposals for a northern Assembly when they were made public in April. When Garret FitzGerald put down a vote of no confidence in November, the government fell.

The FitzGerald Coalition 1982–1987

The second general election in less than a year saw Fianna Fáil's vote fall from 47.3 per cent to 45.2 per cent, while Fine Gael's rose from 37.3 per cent to 39.2 per cent, and Labour's increased marginally from 9.1 per cent to 9.4 per cent. Fianna Fáil lost six seats, while Fine Gael gained seven and Labour one. Michael O'Leary had resigned as leader of the Labour Party in October after failing to persuade its annual conference to adopt a pre-electoral commitment to coalition. His successor was Dick Spring, a 32-year-old barrister who had been elected to the Dáil for the first time in the 1981 general election. Spring's father, Dan, from whom he inherited his North Kerry constituency, had been typical of the rural TDs who had dominated the party until the 1960s. His son's horizons had been widened through the still-unusual choice of Trinity College Dublin as his university and by two years spent working in the US. The result was that, although Spring maintained his father's distrust of the intellectual left in the party, as personified by the eloquent Galway TD and Chairman of the party, Michael D. Higgins, he was much more sympathetic to those arguing for a liberal agenda on such issues as divorce and contraception than many of his rural-based colleagues.[81]

With Fine Gael's seventy seats and Labour's sixteen, the coalition had a working majority in the 166-seat Dáil. Spring was Tánaiste and Minister for Environment; Frank Cluskey, Minister for Trade, Commerce and Tourism; Liam Kavanagh, Minister for Labour; and Barry Desmond, Minister for Health and Social Welfare. Although Spring developed a good personal relationship with FitzGerald, he came into frequent and sometimes public conflict with Alan Dukes, the Minister for Finance. Like Spring, Dukes had entered the Dáil for the first time in 1981. A former student of FitzGerald, he had been an adviser to the Irish Farmers' Association and was on the right of Fine Gael. Dukes gave strong support to the view of Department of Finance officials that the major task of the government was to cut the budget deficit by the maximum amount possible. Dukes's right-wing radicalism allowed FitzGerald to present himself to Spring and his Labour colleagues as a moderate social democrat trying to contain the Thatcherites in the Fine Gael minister-ial group and parliamentary party. He supported Labour's demand for a residential property tax and for a National Development Corporation to deal with the problem of the growing number of young unemployed.[82]

The unease that this apparent alliance between the Taoiseach and Tánaiste produced within Fine Gael has led some commentators to claim that FitzGerald's government failed to confront the crisis of the public finances.[83] But by taking some account of Labour's concerns in both the 1983 and 1984 budgets, FitzGerald was able to implement what remained quite draconian cuts in public expenditure accompanied by substantial rises in taxation. The coalition thus made an important contribution to the reduction in the Exchequer borrowing requirement from a threat-ened 21.5 per cent of GNP in 1982 to 1.5 per cent in 1989.[84] Inflation was cut from 17 per cent to 4 per cent. The cost was high for many of Labour's traditional supporters. Real personal income after tax fell by 12 per cent between 1980 and 1986, and emigration, after net inflows in the 1970s, averaged 25,000 a year during the 1980s.[85] The Labour Party paid a high electoral price for FitzGerald's economic achievement. It lost its four seats in the European Parliament in the 1984 elections, and in the local government elections of 1985 it did badly nationally and was humili-ated in the capital, where the Workers' Party, as SFWP was now known, won six seats to its two.[86] Spring finally decided to leave the government in January 1987 rather than support cuts in health expenditure.

In the general election that followed, Labour's support dropped to 6.4

per cent – its worst result since 1933 – although it managed to retain twelve seats. Fine Gael dropped from 39.2 per cent to 27.1 per cent and from seventy to fifty-one seats. Despite the unpopularity of the government parties, Fianna Fáil under Haughey failed for the fourth time to win a majority. Its vote fell marginally to 44.1 per cent, although its number of seats increased from seventy-five to eighty-one. The biggest shock of the election was the performance of a new party, the Progressive Democrats, who replaced Labour as the third-largest party, winning 11.8 per cent of the vote and fourteen seats. The party had been formed in early 1986 after a schism from Fianna Fáil led by Des O'Malley. Although its main figures were prominent ex-Fianna Fáilers, including Bobby Molloy and Mary Harney, it was able to attract support from sections of Fine Gael who had disapproved of the 'contamination' of the party's traditional conservative stance by the coalition arrangement with Labour.[87]

Haughey and the Origins of the Boom 1987–1992

The recession had promoted a new left–right polarization in Irish politics, pitting Labour and the Workers' Party against Fine Gael and the Progressive Democrats. Fianna Fáil had fought the election on a centrist platform, renewing its commitment to economic growth, welfarism and social partnership while accepting the need for some degree of fiscal balance. A trade union movement that had felt spurned and neglected by the coalition was happy to have Haughey back in power. In opposition, Haughey had assiduously cultivated trade union leaders. A Fianna Fáil Trade Union Committee was established in 1986 and through it a series of meetings with key union officials laid the basis for the government–union concordat, *The Programme for National Recovery*, concluded in October 1987. As Kieran Allen has pointed out, Haughey was the beneficiary of the decline in trade union strength and militancy that the soaring redundancies, unemployment and rocketing emigration of the early and mid 1980s had produced.[88] Shut out of any role in the framing of public policy on the economy under FitzGerald and Spring, and with the Progressive Democrats keen to import a pure neo-liberal model, it was little wonder that the trade union leadership accepted Haughey's offer to participate in what he skilfully presented as a national stabilization programme based on partnership rather than on a Thatcherite dog-eat-dog philosophy.[89] In return for an agreement for modest wage increases over a three-year period, the unions were tied into cooperation with a government that proceeded to implement a cuts package of £485 million.

The size of the cuts proposed by Ray MacSharry, Haughey's Minister for Finance, so impressed the new leader of Fine Gael, Alan Dukes, that he announced that he would not oppose the government as long as it stuck to its commitment to slash expenditure. Dukes's so-called 'Tallaght Strategy' meant the arrival of a dominant ideological consensus from which only Labour and the Workers' Party were excluded. MacSharry's economic shock therapy, implemented in two budgets, cut public expenditure by £900 million, or 8 per cent, between 1987 and 1989. Within a short period of time the harsh medicine appeared to work. Economists started to talk about 'expansionary fiscal contraction'. The dominant consensus on putting the public finances in order had apparently restored the confidence of investors, and from the second half of the 1980s the Irish economy began to grow at rates that far outpaced the rest of Europe.[90]

Irish GDP rose by 36.6 per cent between 1987 and 1993, compared with an increase of 13.3 per cent in the EU as a whole.[91] Growth accelerated in the period from 1994 to 1999, when GDP rose by 8.8 per cent a year. Ireland had surpassed even the emerging 'Tiger' economies of Asia in terms of growth rates, industrial production and low inflation. Unemployment, which had stood at 17 per cent in the mid 1980s, the second highest in the EU, had fallen to 6 per cent – below the EU average – in 1998 and was reduced further to 4.4 per cent in July 2000.[92] By the end of the decade the Republic's per capita income surpassed Britain's and by 2004 its per capita GDP was the second highest in the EU, behind Luxembourg.[93] The OECD, notoriously a severe judge of national economies, said of the Republic in 1999: 'It is astonishing that a nation could have moved all the way from the back of the pack to a leading position within such a short period, not much more than a decade, in fact.'[94]

The more euphoric accounts of the Republic's 'economic miracle' need to be deflated. Gross National Product, which is the final output attributable to Irish workers, firms and government, has consistently grown less quickly than Gross Domestic Product. This is because an increasing proportion of production within the country accrues to foreigners, mainly in the form of profits going to foreign investors and as interest on the foreign debt. GDP was also overstated because of transfer pricing by multinational corporations who exploited the fact that Ireland was a low-tax jurisdiction for most corporations (10 per cent on the profits of manufacturing firms) by inflating the proportion of their overall profits that they claimed to have been generated in Ireland. Disposable income per head also grew much more slowly, in part because of unfavourable movements in the terms of trade and also because of a fall in the transfer payments from the EU as the Republic's economic success made it less eligible for such assistance.[95]

Ulster Unionist critics made much of the role of these transfers in generating the boom. The EU had created Structural and Cohesion funds to deal with the difficulties that the less developed and poorer members would experience in the process of creating a Single Market that began with the Single European Act in 1987 and was completed with the Maastricht Treaty in 1992. The strong endorsement of both by the Irish electorate reflected government promises of Euro bounty to come. In 1992, promoting a 'yes' vote in the referendum on Maastricht, the Taoiseach, Albert Reynolds, claimed that the Republic would receive £8 billion in the next allocation of Structural and Cohesion funds. Although this claim was inflated and received frostily in Brussels, Ireland did eventually get over £6 billion, and this was reckoned to have raised GNP by between 2 and 3 per cent. Although small in gross terms, the funds did make a very significant contribution to public expenditure in infrastructure projects, which were important in the 1990s take-off.[96]

All serious accounts of the boom agree that it was a product of a number of factors, of which EU funding was a real but in no way decisive one. The Single Market was much more directly important, as it made the Republic an even more attractive location for foreign investors, particularly US ones. The Republic's IDA was already offering high grants, tax breaks, and a young and skilled workforce. It had also proved adept at 'picking winners' – setting out to expand particular industrial sectors, including electronics, pharmaceuticals, chemicals, software and, more recently, financial services and tele-services. By the end of the 1990s leading-edge companies such as Intel, Microsoft, IBM, Dell, Hewlett-Packard and Kodak were all represented in Ireland. The Republic was also benefiting from the substantial increases in investment in education and training dating from the 1960s. As one US commentator noted, 'Ireland's well-educated workforce today offers multinational businesses perhaps Europe's best ratio of skills to wages.'[97]

For all the complexity of the debate on the causes of the unprecedented levels of economic growth, there is little doubt that the reinvigoration of social partnership between unions, employers and the state played a fundamental domestic role.[98] The National Economic and Social Council (NESC), an offspring of Lemass's corporatist initiatives in the 1960s, had in 1986 worked out an agreed strategy to escape from the vicious circle of stagnation, rising taxes and exploding debt. Haughey had used this as the basis for his negotiation of the *Programme for National Recovery* in 1987, which ran to 1990. It was the first of four agreements that brought the Republic through more than a decade of negotiated economic and social governance.[99] The *Programme for National Recovery* was followed by the *Programme for Economic and Social Progress* (1991–3), the *Programme for Competitiveness and Work* (1994–7) and *Partnership 2000* (1997).

In exchange for trade union support for corrective measures in fiscal policy, the government committed itself to maintaining the value of social welfare payments. In return for moderate pay rises, take-home pay was increased through tax reductions. The agreements fixed pay increases and established common ground on a range of issues from tax reform and measures to tackle poverty to exchange-rate policy and measures Ireland was to adopt to prepare for membership of a European Single Currency. Although there was some rank-and-file dissatisfaction with evidence of rocketing corporate profits while wage increases lagged behind, a dramatic drop in the number of strike days from an average of 316,000 a year in the eight years to 1987 to an average of 110,000 a year in the nine years to 1996 was an indication of the success of social partnership.

The evidence that the economic gloom of the coalition years was fast dissipating and the opposition's tacit support for the main lines of his government's economic policy encouraged Haughey to call another general election in June 1989. Although Fianna Fáil's vote dropped only marginally, it lost two seats. More importantly, while its support among middle-class voters increased, there were major losses of working-class support to Labour and the Workers' Party. With fifteen Labour Party TDs and seven from the Workers' Party, together with two left-wing independents, the Irish left had won its highest share of Dáil seats ever. Richard Sinnott noted that 'The story of the election is undoubtedly the polarisation of the voters along class lines.'[100] Fine Gael had improved its position somewhat, with an increase in its vote from 27.1 per cent to 29.3 per cent and in its seats from fifty to fifty-five. More than half of the Progressive Democrats' support was lost to Haughey's new-found economic respectability: the party's vote dropped from 11.8 per cent to 5.5 per cent and its seats from fourteen to six.

Haughey attempted to persuade Fine Gael and the Progressive

Democrats to continue with the 'Tallaght Strategy', but both now demanded a share in government, and he was forced to abandon what had hitherto been proclaimed as a central value of Fianna Fáil: its refusal to consider forming a coalition with another party. By entering into government with the Progressive Democrats in July 1989, Haughey finally ended the pretence that Fianna Fáil was a 'national movement' and not a mere political party. At the time, the deal with their former colleagues that brought Desmond O'Malley and Bobby Molloy into the cabinet represented a deep 'cultural shock' to many in Fianna Fáil.[101] Yet by jettisoning the traditional imperative to form only a single party government, Haughey had placed his party in a better position to maintain a dominant role in what had become a much more fragmented party system. Now it could tack to the right or left, forming alliances with the Progressive Democrats or Labour and the Workers' Party. Ironically, the greatest obstacle to the full development of this new flexibility was Haughey himself. He remained anathema to many on the Irish left. This was not for his economic viewpoint, which, apart from his Thatcherite lapse in 1980, was rhetorically Keynesian, even Peronist. Rather it reflected the fact that the 1980s had witnessed intense debates on moral issues and Northern Ireland during which Haughey had positioned his party on the side of traditional Catholic values and irredentism.

A Church under Pressure

Two decades of rapid economic growth after 1959, urbanization, a new openness to the outside world and sweeping cultural change created the conditions for fierce debates over the Catholic Church's teachings on sexual behaviour and morality. An important factor in promoting change was the increase in the participation of women in the labour force. From partition to the 1960s, the opportunities for female participation in paid employment had been restricted by the South's lack of a significant manufacturing sector, particularly one with industries that tended to employ women.[102] In 1961, 28.5 per cent of women and only 5.2 per cent of married women were economically active in the South, compared with 35.3 per cent and 19.5 per cent in the North. By 1995 the respective figures were 38.5 per cent of women and 36.6 per cent of married women in the South and 62 per cent of women and 64.2 per cent of married women in the North. Thus, even in the 1990s the proportion of women in the labour force in the South was still below the EU average of 45 per cent.[103]

The mass entry of married women into the labour market and the expansion of higher education formed the background in Western developed countries to the impressive expansion of feminist movements from the 1960s on.[104] Ireland's participation in these developments was later and more muted but significant none the less. Together with an urbanized, better educated and younger population in a society less insulated from the materialist values of consumer capitalism, they represented a major challenge to the defenders of traditional Catholic values.

The Irish Catholic Church had shown only very limited signs of responding to the far-reaching alterations in liturgy, theology, Church government and ecumenism promoted by the Second Vatican Council (1962–5). There was a process of liturgical renewal and a limited expansion of a lay role in Church government. Although there was no objection when, in 1972, the government proposed the deletion of Article 44 of the Constitution, which had accorded a 'special position' to the Catholic Church, Ireland experienced no ecumenical revolution, with inter-church activity often restricted to 'rarefied theological discussion'.[105] The Irish Church's conservatism was most obvious in its undeviating support for *Humanae Vitae*, the encyclical of Pope Paul VI, in 1968, which had come out against all artificial means of contraception. The hierarchy was relentless in its opposition to any change in the law on contraceptives despite the Supreme Court decision in the Magee case in 1973 and the fact that opinion polls showed a growing level of public support for legalization.[106]

This stance contributed to the weakening of the Church's moral authority in the 1970s and 1980s. It provided the impetus for the development of the Irish women's movement when, in 1971, feminists took a train from Dublin to Belfast in order to buy contraceptives and import them into the Republic in defiance of the 1935 Criminal Law (Amendment) Act, which proscribed their sale, importation, advertisement and distribution.[107] The failure of the coalition's attempt to reform the law in 1974 led to the formation of a Contraception Action Programme, a pressure group composed of women's groups and Labour Party activists, including Senator Mary Robinson, who forced the coalition's hand by introducing her own, much more liberal bill in the Seanad. It was their activist campaign that began to influence the public mood and made reform an issue in the 1977 election, inducing Fianna Fáil to give a commitment to introduce legislation. The Health (Family Planning) Bill was introduced by Charles Haughey in December 1978 and declared by him to be 'an Irish solution to an Irish problem'. It provided for the availability of contraceptives on prescription where the doctor was satisfied that they were sought '*bona fide* for the purpose of family planning'.[108] It was a minimalist response to a situation where couples were increasingly using birth-control methods without concern for the law.

Despite its limited nature, the legislation contributed to a growing traditionalist backlash. Following the example of 'pro-life' pressure groups in the US and Britain, the initiative came from lay Catholics rather than from the clergy or the hierarchy. The fundamentalists had been given major encouragement by the visit of Pope John Paul II to Ireland in 1979, which the Irish hierarchy had organized with the purpose of stemming what it perceived as the rising tide of materialism and secularism. The Polish pope, smarting after an Italian referendum in favour of divorce and with an ongoing campaign to legalize abortion in Italy (which would be successful in 1981), depicted Ireland as a proud centre of the faith but warned that forces were working to tempt it away from this historic role. In his address at Limerick the Pope called for a continuing Irish witness to 'the dignity and sacredness of all human life, from conception to death'.[109]

Abortion was illegal in Ireland under the 1861 Offences against the Person Act, but was not expressly forbidden in the Constitution. The religious right feared that a successful campaign by feminists and Dublin liberals and leftists might result in its legalization. An Irish branch of the British Society for the Unborn Child was established in the aftermath of the Pope's visit, and in 1981 the Pro-Life Amendment Campaign (PLAC) was founded to push a constitutional amendment to prohibit abortion. Taking advantage of the unprecedented degree of governmental instability in the early 1980s, the PLAC had no problems in getting pledges from both FitzGerald and Haughey that they would support the holding of a referendum on abortion. Before it left office in 1982, the Haughey government introduced its proposed wording for an amendment to the Constitution: 'The State acknowledges the right to life of the unborn and, with due regard to the right to life of the mother, guarantees in its laws to respect, and as far as is practical by its laws to defend and vindicate that right.' Back in government in 1983, FitzGerald rejected the Fianna Fáil wording, but this was eventually endorsed by the Dáil with the support of Fine Gael and Labour Party defectors.

Voting took place on 7 September 1983 following a campaign that reached levels of acrimony 'probably not witnessed in Ireland since the post-Treaty campaigning by rival sides in 1922'.[110] Although the amendment was passed, the referendum was a disappointment for the Church. Of those who voted, 66.5 per cent were in favour of the amendment, but only 54.6 per cent of those eligible had actually voted, reflecting a feeling amongst a sector of the population that the referendum was an unnecessary distraction from more pressing economic and social issues.

At the time some argued that the low turnout and the fact that the amendment was carried with only the slimmest of majorities in Dublin boded ill for the future of traditional Catholic values.[111] It was true that there was continuing evidence of large-scale rejection of the Church's position on contraception, particularly amongst the young and the university-educated urban middle class. It was this that induced the coalition government to introduce new family-planning legislation in 1985. Its most notable provision allowed for the sale of contraceptives to anyone aged over eighteen. It was passed by the Dáil despite the opposition of the Catholic hierarchy, opportunistically tail-ended by Fianna Fáil. Desmond O'Malley refused to vote against the bill, arguing that the Dáil had to prove itself free to legislate on such matters regardless of the teaching of the Catholic Church. For this and his declaration that he would stand by the concept of a secular republic, he was expelled from Fianna Fáil. Within a year he was leading the Progressive Democrats, a party whose main dynamic came from the secularizing impulses of the urban middle class.[112]

That such a secularizing trend was still relatively weak was shown in 1986 when the coalition failed in its attempt to legalize divorce, which was proscribed under Article 41 of the 1937 Constitution. The hierarchy made clear its opposition to the proposed constitutional amendment and the associated divorce legislation in a leaflet delivered to every home in the country. The Archbishop of Dublin, Dr Kevin McNamara, warned that 'divorce would generate a social and moral fallout as lethal as the effects from the recent accident at the Chernobyl nuclear power station.'[113] As in 1983 the traditionalist campaign was spearheaded by a coalition of lay Catholic groups headed by the Family Solidarity organization. It amplified the Church's moral arguments, with an appeal to material insecurities connected with property and inheritance rights and visions of deserted and impoverished mothers with starving children.[114] The result was a second defeat for the liberal agenda. On a turnout of 60.5 per cent, the amendment was rejected by 63.5 per cent to 36.5 per cent. There was little consolation to be drawn from the fact that the amendment was supported by a small majority of Dublin voters. Optimistic liberals argued that the low turnout in both referenda and that concerns about land and property ownership as well as succession rights were important influences in the divorce referendum showed that traditionalism was on the wane. Yet, when a further referendum was held nine years later, the amendment in favour of divorce was carried only by a paper-thin majority.[115]

This was hardly a ringing endorsement of pluralism, particularly given that there had been a number of major blows to the religious right and the moral authority of the Catholic Church in the early 1990s. In 1992 a fourteen-year-old girl who was pregnant as a result of rape was prevented from seeking an abortion in Britain by an injunction obtained by the Irish Attorney-General and a subsequent High Court decision that forbade her to leave the jurisdiction for nine months. An appeal to the Supreme Court produced a ruling that the 1983 amendment did in fact provide for abortion when, as in this case, there was a real threat to the life of the mother through a possible suicide.[116] The 'X' case complicated the 1992 referendum on the Maastricht Treaty, as the government had previously obtained a protocol in the Treaty designed to ensure that future EU law could not override the 1983 amendment. An attempt to regularize the situation with a further and more restrictive amendment failed to satisfy either side of the debate and was rejected.

To the disarray of the religious right was added the discomfiture of the Church as a result of a series of clerical sex scandals that dominated the media and fascinated and repulsed the public. In 1992 the *Irish Times* revealed that the high-profile Bishop of Galway, Eamonn Casey, had fathered a child when he was Bishop of Kerry in the 1970s. He had pressurized the mother to have the child adopted and then used diocesan funds to make payments to ensure the mother's silence.[117] Even more damaging for the Church was a deluge of charges that there had been an institutional cover-up of the sexual and physical abuse of children by priests and members of religious orders. The dam broke in the autumn of 1994 when Father Brendan Smyth was convicted in a Belfast court of sexually abusing children. A subsequent television documentary revealed that he had a record of paedophilia in Ireland, the US and Britain that had been known to his own order and other Church authorities who had shielded him by moving him to another parish whenever complaints arose. Exposures of the physical and sexual abuse of children by members of religious orders, male and female, who had been responsible for running residential institutions quickly followed.

The author of a historical sociology of the Irish Catholic Church described the results of these scandals: 'The media have driven a stake into the heart of the institutional church from which it will recover, but never fully. We will never see the likes of the Catholic Church's moral monopoly again.'[118] Mass attendance rates had remained impressively high throughout the 1970s and 1980s, especially by international standards. As late as 1990, 85 per cent of those surveyed went to mass at least once a week. By 1997 this had dropped to 65 per cent.[119] This was still high by international standards and, as one historian noted, 'it would be wrong to write off the Catholic Church's grip upon the mores and the outlook of its Irish members.'[120]

Yet the Church's capacity to defend its power and influence was even more profoundly sapped by a sharp decline in vocations. Ordinations for the priesthood dropped from 412 in 1965 to forty-four in 1998, while there were even starker declines in the numbers of those entering the religious orders. Between 1967 and 1998 the total number of priests, brothers and nuns in Ireland fell from almost 34,000 to just under 20,000.[121] An ageing, shrinking Church was unable to staff the schools, hospitals and other public services that provided much of the institutional basis of its power. The political significance of this was twofold. First, it removed the 'Catholic card' from electoral politics, to the disadvantage of the party that had been most proficient in using it: Fianna Fáil. Second, it revealed the hollowness of the argument that the main motivation behind Ulster Unionist resistance to Irish unity was a fear of Catholic power, as the weakening of the Church did little to undermine support for partition amongst the northern majority. Despite this, the political leader identified with this analysis, Garret FitzGerald, was responsible for the biggest political advance for Irish nationalism since partition.

The Republic and the Anglo-Irish Agreement

The marginalization of those in the Fianna Fáil leadership identified with a more conciliatory line on Northern Ireland provided Garret FitzGerald with an opportunity to establish Fine Gael as the sensible, moderate alternative on the North and Anglo-Irish relations. At a time of considerable tension over the hunger strikes and the Falklands War, this was an approach that appealed to an electorate that ranked Northern Ireland far down on the list of issues that would influence its vote. It also made FitzGerald seem more the sort of Taoiseach with whom Thatcher might do business.

In September 1981 FitzGerald had announced that he wanted to launch a crusade to create a 'genuine republic' with which northern Protestants would wish to have a relationship. He declared: 'If I were a northern Protestant today, I cannot see how I could be attracted to getting involved with a state that is itself sectarian.'[122] Although FitzGerald's willingness to criticize the Catholic ethos of the Republic and his desire to open up dialogue with unionists, rather than appeal over their heads to London, raised his popularity ratings in Belfast, the honeymoon was short-lived. His 'constitutional crusade' did not survive the pressures of the abortion debate, and the victories of Sinn Féin candidates in the Assembly elections put paid to his earlier objective of seeking a solution to the northern conflict through dialogue with the unionists: 'I had come to the conclusion that I must now give priority to heading off the growth of support for the IRA in Northern Ireland by seeking a new understanding with the British government.'[123]

FitzGerald's decision to establish the New Ireland Forum in 1983 was related to an immediate political crisis: the threat posed by Sinn Féin to the SDLP. It was also prompted by Hume's idea that all the main constitutional nationalist parties on the island needed to produce an agreed statement of the principles believed to be at stake in the Northern Ireland conflict. This statement would then be the basis for an approach to the British government. The Forum comprised representatives of the SDLP, Fianna Fáil, Fine Gael and the Irish Labour Party. Although, contrary to Hume's original idea, it was open to unionist participation, its stated purpose of unifying and revivifying the non-violent nationalist tradition ensured that none of the unionist parties participated, although some unionists gave evidence as individuals.

Professor John Whyte noted that the Forum, with government funding and a full-time staff, was in a position to make a weightier contribution to the discussion on Northern Ireland than any previous body on the nationalist side since the All-Party Anti-Partition Conference in 1949.[124] Given that the latter resulted in little more than a restatement of old nationalist attitudes, this was not a very exacting criterion of success. In fact its final report was an unimpressive document. This in part reflected the need to ensure that Charles Haughey was kept on board. The demands of pan-nationalist unity amongst the constitutional parties ensured that the historical section was untainted by any of the 'revisionist ideas' that had increasingly influenced the professional writing of Irish history. Similarly, it was Haughey's veto power that resulted in all the party leaders agreeing to a unitary thirty-two-county state as the report's preferred constitutional option. It is true that the report referred to two other options – a confederal Ireland and joint authority – and that the latter implied an acceptance that a total British withdrawal might not be necessary for a solution of the Northern Ireland problem. However, as neither constitutional nationalism nor physical-force republicanism was any nearer to achieving British withdrawal in 1984 than they had been in 1949, this might be interpreted as a not very substantial concession.

That was certainly the predictable Ulster Unionist response. However, despite Thatcher's vigorous rejection of all three options at a press conference after her summit meeting with FitzGerald in November 1984, the Anglo-Irish Agreement did for the first time provide the Irish state with considerable leverage on the governance of Northern Ireland. Public opinion in the Republic was supportive of the Agreement and Charles Haughey's denunciation of it as 'copper-fastening partition' was not well received. As leading members of Fianna Fáil announced that the party was proud to be 'the sole party with the nationalist forces', Haughey appeared to take a position on the Agreement that was indistinguishable from that of Gerry Adams. Such extremism was damaging. Support for the Agreement rose from 59 per cent, with 32 per cent supporting Haughey's position in its immediate aftermath, to 69 per cent by February 1986.[125] It was becoming increasingly clear that public opinion in the Republic, while still robustly nationalist, saw the Agreement as achieving a shift in the balance of power in Northern Ireland that favoured the SDLP and Dublin, while still keeping northern passions and violence at arm's length.

The unpopularity of Haughey's negative reaction to the Anglo-Irish Agreement had forced him to backtrack,[126] and by the time of his resignation in 1992 his ambitions for the North did not seem to go beyond joint authority, a position he had execrated when it was supported by FitzGerald in the 1980s. In an analysis of public attitudes in the Republic towards Northern Ireland written two years after the Agreement, Peter Mair demonstrated that, while the aspiration to unity was pervasive, less than a third of the electorate was prepared to pay extra taxes to achieve it. Elections were fought and lost on economic issues. He concluded: 'Irish voters will be primarily concerned about their pocketbooks for the foreseeable future while Northern Ireland will remain a foreign country.'[127] While the Agreement would do much to increase the involvement of the Irish government in the day-to-day governance of the North, it did little to undermine popular aversion to what were seen as its two squabbling and murderous tribes.

The Republic in the 1990s

Although the economic boom that began in the 1990s had its roots in the resurrected social partnership that Haughey's governments had developed from 1987, it did not provide his party with the electoral boost that Lemass's investment in economic programming and corporatism had given Fianna Fáil in the 1960s. Haughey was forced to resign in January 1992 when his former Minister for Justice, Seán Doherty, revealed his complicity in the phone-tapping of two journalists in 1982. However, even before the Doherty revelation, his leadership had been under renewed pressure because of increasing public concern at what became known as the 'Golden Circle': prominent businessmen who had used various sharp practices to make multimillion pound deals and whose accountants and lawyers had created complex structures to conceal their identities and reduce or eliminate their tax liabilities. The 'Golden Circle' had close personal and political connections with leading politicians.[128] At the centre of these concerns was Larry Goodman, the dominant figure in the Republic's meat-processing industry. Goodman was a friend of Haughey and of other leading members of Fianna Fáil, and after Haughey returned to power in 1987 his business had received substantial assistance from the IDA and also from the Ministry of Industry and Commerce for an export credit insurance scheme to cover its beef exports to Iraq.[129] The beef industry had long been the subject of allegations of corruption, and in May 1991 the ITV programme *World in Action* alleged that serious malpractices were commonplace in Goodman's plants. The PD leader in the coalition, Des O'Malley, insisted on a tribunal of inquiry, which revealed that many of the allegations, including millions of pounds of tax evasion, were true.

Haughey's successor, Albert Reynolds, had as Minister for Industry and Commerce restored export credit insurance for the Goodman group's venture into the Iraqi market – insurance that had been withdrawn by the previous Fine Gael minister. A millionaire from Longford who made his money in dancehalls and dog food, there was never any suggestion of personal corruption on Reynolds's part. Nevertheless, the tribunal led to the collapse of the government when Reynolds accused O'Malley of committing perjury in his evidence and the PDs withdrew from the government. The subsequent general election produced a spectacular result for Dick Spring and the Labour Party, whose vote increased by almost 10 percentage points to 19.3 per cent – its highest since 1922 – and whose number of seats increased from fifteen to thirty-three. Fianna Fáil's vote declined to 39 per cent, its worst since 1927, while Fine Gael, which had been shaken by the emergence of the PDs, saw its vote decline by almost 5 percentage points to 24.5 per cent.[130]

Labour's victory had been anticipated in the 1990 presidential elections when, for the first time since the inauguration of the office, Fianna Fáil's candidate had been defeated. Spring had persuaded the constitutional lawyer and champion of divorce and contraception Mary Robinson to stand, even though she had resigned from Labour over the Anglo-Irish Agreement. The first woman candidate for the post, Robinson also gained the support of the Workers' Party, the Greens and many women's groups. Her declarations of support for gay rights and for a radical improvement in the state's family planning services did not endear her to many male voters in rural Ireland, although her sex and some of the crasser attacks on her by male Fianna Fáil politicians may have led their wives and daughters to a different conclusion. There was a strong correlation between support for Robinson and a 'progressive' stance on abortion and divorce, leading one commentator to claim that 'the "new Ireland" had emerged victorious after two referendum defeats.'[131] This exaggerated the implications of Robinson's victory. The only region in which Robinson outpolled the Fianna Fáil candidate, Brian Lenihan, was Dublin city and county, and Lenihan's first-preference vote was 44.1 per cent to Robinson's 38.9 per cent. Robinson's victory came about through the distribution of the second-preference votes of those who supported the Fine Gael candidate, Austin Currie. Moreover, Lenihan was a seriously weakened candidate: during the campaign Haughey was forced to sack him from the cabinet after it emerged that in January 1982, upon the defeat of the coalition government, Lenihan had phoned the President to try to persuade him not to dissolve the Dáil.

Labour's surge in 1992 was in part a product of the 'Robinson effect', but it was also a reflection of widespread public perception of a Fianna Fáil political class embroiled in sleaze. Neither of these factors would continue to favour the party once Spring shocked many of his party supporters by entering into a coalition with Reynolds. After the collapse of the Reynolds government in 1992, Spring had told the Dáil it was impossible to envisage entering into partnership with a party that 'has gone so far down the road of blindness to standards and blindness to the people they are supposed to represent'.[132] However, after the election Spring displayed no real enthusiasm for John Bruton's proposal of a 'rainbow coalition' including Fine Gael, Labour and the Progressive

Democrats. This reflected the deep-rooted hostility of Spring to Bruton, which had its origin in bitter clashes between the two when they were in the 1983–7 coalition. Spring was also concerned that neither Fine Gael nor the Progressive Democrats would countenance the participation of Democratic Left in the coalition. This party had been formed when six of the seven Workers' Party TDs had split from the organization in March 1992 over their disquiet about revelations of the continuing links between leading members of the WP and the Official IRA in Northern Ireland.[133] Labour, watchful of its left flank, went through the motions of negotiating a platform with Democratic Left to construct a centre-left government with Fine Gael, but this became academic when after a series of recounts it was confirmed that the Democatic Left had lost its Dublin South-central seat, robbing the centre-left option of sufficient Dáil support.

Although some of Reynolds's colleagues were hostile to the idea of a coalition with Labour, Brian Lenihan welcomed the possibility of a return to Fianna Fáil's social republican past. Spring had sent Reynolds a paper drawn up by Labour and Democratic Left during their negotiations and Fianna Fáil's response was drafted by the Taoiseach's special adviser, the Oxford-educated historian Dr Martin Mansergh. Although the perceived incongruity between his Protestant, Anglo-Irish background and his strong republican line on Northern Ireland was to make him a figure of fascination for many journalists, another side to Mansergh's intellectual make-up was important in the formation of the coalition. This was his firm conviction that Fianna Fáil's social-republican and corporatist tendencies had been the real source of its hegemony in Irish politics.[134] Such thinking eased Labour's way into government, but the process was also greatly assisted by Reynolds's apparent success at the Edinburgh EU summit, where he claimed to have secured £8 billion for Ireland in structural and cohesion funds up to 1999. This made it easier to implement those elements of Labour's programme that involved a commitment to extra expenditure on health and social welfare, which in turn enabled Reynolds to insist that Labour accept the budgetary constraints imposed by the Maastricht Treaty. All of the Labour demands on the 'liberal agenda' and the issue of sleaze were included in the programme for government, with commitments to an Ethics in Government Bill, Dáil reform, the introduction of divorce, abortion legislation and the decriminalization of homosexuality. Labour's stunning electoral performance was also recognized in an unprecedented profile in government. It had six of the fifteen cabinet posts and a special office of the Tánaiste was created, situated in government buildings, with its own staff and budget, to strengthen Spring's position in the cabinet.

Despite such an apparently auspicious beginning, including a Dáil majority of forty-two, the largest in the history of the state, the coalition was characterized by internal conflict almost from the start. In part this reflected a serious personality clash between Reynolds and Spring: 'The two men were like chalk and cheese and seemed always prepared to think the worst of each other. In contrast to Reynolds's bright and breezy style, Spring was thoughtful and reserved and quick to take offence.'[135] Such tensions were exacerbated by Labour's increasing dissatisfaction with Reynolds's failure to rein in Fianna Fáil's proclivity to favour its business allies and his tendency, when the need arose, to behave as if he were leading a single-party government. Spring, conscious of the shock that his move into government with Fianna Fáil had caused many of those who had voted Labour in 1992, was determined that Labour would play a high-profile and assertive role in government. Labour insisted on a new system of ministerial programme managers whose job it was to ensure that the coalition deal was implemented. The programme managers appointed by the six Labour ministers were all Labour Party activists, and the party shocked some of its supporters in the media by the extent to which political and familial nepotism influenced its appointments from special advisers to secretaries and drivers.[136]

In 1993 Reynolds insisted on a new amnesty for tax evaders, the second in five years, which was opposed by his own Minister for Finance Bertie Ahern and which deeply troubled many Labour supporters already annoyed by the government's first budget in 1993, which had increased taxes on ordinary workers and imposed a 1 per cent income levy.[137] Labour supporters were also uncomfortable with the 1994 Finance Bill, which relaxed the tax regime for wealthy expatriates, and with the so-called 'Masri affair', which also became public in 1994. It was alleged that two members of the Masri family, who had been granted Irish citizenship under a Business Migration Scheme, had invested £1 million in a pet-food company that was owned by the Reynolds family. Reynolds in turn was exasperated with what he regarded as Labour's refusal to face up to hard economic decisions: in his view, the budget was a response to a difficult economic situation, which included a rise in unemployment and a currency crisis that had forced a devaluation of the Irish pound.

He and his colleagues were also deeply resentful about Labour's pose as the moral mudguard of the coalition. This was the context in which Reynolds ignored a cabinet decision that the forthcoming report of the

BeefTribunal would be studied before the government issued its collective response. Instead, fearing that Labour would use the report to undermine him, Reynolds had the report scrutinized by his own advisers and then issued a statement that the report had vindicated his role in the affair. Spring was furious at having been ignored – the Taoiseach refused to accept his phone calls while the report was being studied – and his supporters claim he remained in government only because of the delicate state of the peace process in Northern Ireland.[138]

It was in the area of Northern Ireland policy that the Reynolds–Spring coalition registered its major success. Reynolds had inherited the ongoing contacts that Haughey had initiated with Sinn Féin but was able to develop these within the context of a new engagement with John Major, the British Prime Minister. Taking up John Hume's idea that a joint declaration by London and Dublin on the basic principles of a settlement could create the conditions for an IRA ceasefire, he displayed a ruthless pragmatism and a willingness to accommodate the constitutional concerns of Ulster Unionists. The result was the Downing Street Declaration of December 1993, with its subtle combination of 'green' language and democratic content. Further inducements were proffered to republicans, including an end to their banishment from the airwaves in the Republic and an Irish version of a proposed Anglo-Irish Framework document that provided a 'dynamic' set of North–South institutions that republicans could envisage as 'transitional' to a united Ireland. Reynolds persuaded President Clinton to allow a visa to Gerry Adams for a visit to the US. In return, Reynolds made it clear that the only response he would be satisfied with was a permanent end to violence; the alternative was a deal with Major, the Unionists and the SDLP, which would leave republicans isolated.[139] The IRA's announcement of a 'complete cessation of military operations' on 31 August 1994 was to a large extent Reynolds's achievement: his blunt businessman's approach with its lack of ideological baggage on the North, and above all his willingness to take major risks, had paid off.

This success was double-edged, for it was very much the Taoiseach's, and Spring, despite his role as Foreign Minister and a history of Anglo-Irish involvement going back to 1982, was marginalized. In fact, it is doubtful whether Spring's background and his political base in 'republican' Kerry would have allowed him to deal as robustly with Sinn Féin as Reynolds had done. Meanwhile, radical deterioration in relations between the coalition partners had occurred over Reynolds's treatment of the Beef Tribunal report. A terminal blow was struck in November 1994, when Reynolds insisted on appointing Attorney-General Harry Whelehan as President of the High Court. Spring had opposed Whelehan, who was a conservative with no judicial experience, and when it transpired that the Attorney-General's office had been responsible for a delay in the processing of an extradition warrant for a paedophile priest and that a similar case had occurred in 1993, the Labour ministers resigned from the government and Reynolds stepped down as leader of Fianna Fáil, to be replaced by Bertie Ahern.

Fine Gael, Labour and Democratic Left, whose Dáil strength had increased to six TDs after two by-election victories, were able to form a 'rainbow coalition' in December 1994, with John Bruton as Taoiseach. Labour retained six cabinet seats while the Democratic Left leader, Proinsias de Rossa, became Minister for Social Welfare and three of the party's TDs were appointed Ministers of State. The three parties established a good working relationship, and there was no repeat of the divisions that had been a feature of the previous administration. Tensions did exist between Spring and de Rossa on Northern Ireland because of the latter's hostility to Sinn Féin and his sympathy for mainstream Ulster Unionism. This was particularly so after the coalition's greatest setback: the ending of the IRA ceasefire in February 1996. Republicans blamed Major for allegedly using the question of IRA weapons as an obstacle to 'conflict resolution' and, supported by Albert Reynolds, they criticized Bruton and de Rossa for being accomplices in 'British intransigence'. Spring's most influential adviser, Fergus Finlay, publicly established clear green water between Spring and his government partners by declaring that talks without Sinn Féin were 'not worth a penny candle'.[140]

One of the most notable effects of the peace process after 1992 was the increasing 'Ulsterization' of politics in the Republic, as there was a qualitative increase in the amount of time and energy that the Republic's political class had to invest in the developing political situation in the North. Public opinion in the Republic was also affected as, for the first time since 1969, there appeared to be a real possibility of an end to violence. The effects were complex. On the one hand there was a willingness to jettison more traditional forms of irredentism and, in 1998, support what was essentially a 'two states – one nation' settlement. On the other there was an upsurge in uncritical support for northern nationalism, once it appeared that its violent cutting edge could be discarded. That the IRA went back to war in February 1996 was put down to John Major's indulgence of Ulster Unionist intransigence, an interpretation that was then considered vindicated by the sectarian stand-off over the Portadown Orange Order's desire to march down the mainly nationalist Garvaghy Road. During the 1997 general election campaign Bertie Ahern attacked Bruton's handling of the peace process, asserting that it was the duty of the Taoiseach to act as leader of 'Nationalist Ireland'. Sinn Féin won its first seat since 1957 when its candidate topped the poll in Cavan–Monaghan. Although its overall vote at 2.5 per cent was still small, it had overtaken Democratic Left, and good polls in Kerry and inner-city Dublin showed a substantial potential for growth. This potential was all the greater given the increasingly fragmented nature of party support in the Republic.

Fianna Fáil's performance was not impressive in terms of votes: it was only marginally up on 1992 at 39.3 per cent, although a more effective vote-management strategy brought it an extra nine seats. Fine Gael had been rescued from the doldrums by Bruton's performance in government and its share of the vote increased from 24.5 per cent to almost 30 per cent, gaining it an extra nine seats. Labour paid the price for its embrace of Reynolds, with its vote almost halved to 9 per cent and its number of seats dropping from thirty-three to seventeen. Although the Progressive Democrat vote held up at just under 5 per cent, it lost six of its ten seats. Bertie Ahern was able to construct a minority coalition government with the PDs that was dependent on the support of some of the plethora of independents who had been elected.[141]

Fine Gael had begun to portray itself as the leader of a social democratic alternative to a conservative Fianna Fáil–PD alliance. Bertie Ahern, who had been a trade union activist before entering full-time politics, was unlikely to accept such a right-wing designation for his party, and the strong performance of the economy made it easier to avoid the traditional tough choices between expenditure and tax cuts. His government's position was also strengthened by his role in the Northern peace process and, above all, by the Good Friday Agreement. Fianna Fáil's choice of a northern Catholic, the Queen's University law professor Mary McAleese, as its presidential candidate when Mary Robinson resigned in 1997 was the first indication of how 'Ulsterization' could benefit Fianna Fáil. McAleese was an example of a new breed of younger, upwardly mobile Catholics who had benefited from reformist direct rule. Self-confident in their nationalism, they regarded a non-violent republican movement as a more effective voice than the increasingly tired and middle-aged SDLP.

After the IRA cessation Sinn Féin's leaders had many fewer occasions to appear as apologists for violence and instead projected themselves as calm, reasonable, and earnest men who talked about peace. For younger voters with no direct experience of atrocities like Enniskillen, Teebane Cross or the Shankill Road bombing, Sinn Féin became an increasingly attractive anti-establishment political force. A survey of school students carried out by the National Youth Council of Ireland in 2000 showed that it was the second most popular party after Fianna Fáil and had almost as much support as Fine Gael, Labour and the Greens put together.[142]

Sinn Féin, despite the IRA's bloody history and involvement in criminal activities including armed robberies and smuggling, did not hesitate to denounce the immorality of the Republic's political elite. Certainly the scale of corruption involving senior political figures, most of whom were members of Fianna Fáil, proved substantial, as evidenced by the results of the two tribunals of inquiry set up to investigate first, the finances of Charles Haughey and second, the way the physical planning process had been distorted by developers' payments to Dublin-based TDs and councillors. But its political impact was relatively muted.

Although Fianna Fáil did not win any of the five by-elections held during the new Dáil, it did reasonably well in the local and European elections held in 1999, and there was little evidence of a revival of the main opposition parties. Labour under a new leader, Ruairi Quinn, had merged in 1998 with Democratic Left. The new organization faced a challenge in the most deprived working-class neighbourhoods from Sinn Féin, which imported the potent mixture of populist nationalism and vigilante justice for local drug dealers and petty criminals it had perfected in the North. Fine Gael, which had fought the 1997 election on left-of-centre commitments to a more equitable tax system and the need for radical improvements in public services, did not sustain this dynamic in opposition. As its support in opinion polls slumped,[143] a sizeable section of the party in the Dáil blamed John Bruton's leadership style, stiff and didactic, and his alleged pro-Unionist bias on the North. However, his successor, Michael Noonan, more populist and more nationalist, did not produce any improvement in the party's poll ratings.

Despite his former political association with Haughey and the embarrassment caused by the revelation that his Minister for Foreign Affairs, Ray Burke, had received a £30,000 political donation from a building firm in 1989, Ahern was not damaged by the corruption issue. This must be linked to the astonishing performance of the Republic's economy.

Growth rates at around 10 per cent a year were unprecedented, and unemployment fell from 10 per cent to under 4 per cent for the first time in the history of the state. The result was that, as one financial journalist put it, 'normal rules of budgetary policy did not seem to apply, every budget brought lower taxes, higher spending and the promise of more to come.'[144] The Minister for Finance, Charlie McCreevy, was able over four budgets to make substantial cuts in direct taxation. The main beneficiary was the business community and high earners: corporation tax was cut from 36 per cent to 16 per cent and capital gains tax was halved, while probate tax was abolished. The large surpluses generated by the boom permitted substantial tax benefits to workers as well: there were substantial cuts in the standard and top rates of income tax and a widening of the standard rate band.[145] Increasing private affluence, while it greatly strengthened the goverment's ability to insulate itself from the revelations of sleaze, did not prevent it from being criticized for ignoring the evidence that, while the Republic was now one of the richest countries in the EU, it was also one of the most unequal, with a crumbling infrastructure and seriously underfunded public services. Social spending fell as a share of GDP during the period 1997–2001, and, according to the United Nations Human Development Report, the Republic had the second highest level of poverty in the developed world.[146]

Issues of who benefited from the Celtic Tiger became more pressing when, in 2001, it appeared that the years of spectacular boom might be over. The economic downturn reflected the global slowdown in the information and communications technology sector on which Ireland was particularly dependent. Even before the events of 11 September, the Republic had been hard hit by the recession. As the IDA calculated that 6,500 multinational jobs were lost in 2001 and the economy's rate of growth slumped from 11 per cent in 2000 to 3 per cent,[147] the Governor of the Central Bank declared the era of the Celtic Tiger was indeed over.[148]

The coalition's response was one of ambivalence. Some ministers, including McCreevy and the Tánaiste and PD leader Mary Harney, continued to articulate a strong neo-liberal response, criticizing the EU for its 'outmoded philosophy of high taxation and heavy regulation' and declaring that the Republic was 'spiritually closer to Boston than Berlin'.[149] Others, including the Taoiseach, rediscovered Fianna Fáil's social democratic vocation and Ahern even called himself a socialist.[150] The conflicting messages contributed to the government's major defeat on the Treaty of Nice Referendum in June 2001. The Treaty was designed to make the institutional reforms to EU decision-making structures necessary for enlargement. Supported by all the main parties, the trade unions, employers, farmers' organizations and the Irish Catholic bishops, it was nevertheless rejected by 54 per cent of the third of the electorate who bothered to vote.

The two parties that had been active in the anti-Nice campaign, the Greens and Sinn Féin, put a radical, anti-militarist gloss on the result. However, it appears that the biggest factor leading to a 'no' vote was what one academic labelled a 'growing independence sentiment: the feeling that Ireland should do all that it can to protect its independence from the EU'.[151] With the Republic now too rich to enjoy 'objective one' status and the access to structural funds that it provided and with the prospect of having to compete for EU resources with the prospective new members from the former Soviet bloc, Irish Euro-scepticism reflected insular self-interest more than some radical anti-system agenda. The darker side of Irish Euro-scepticism was also seen in increasing evidence of racism and antagonism to foreign workers and asylum seekers. However, it was also the case that the low turnout had reflected the failure of the political elite to overcome the indifference and lack of interest of a large section of the public in European affairs in general and the Nice Treaty in particular. In a rerun of the referendum in October 2002, the governing parties, and Fianna Fáil in particular, ran a much more intensive and effective campaign. The result was an increase in turnout of 15 per cent and a victory for the 'yes' campaign of 63 per cent to 37 per cent.[152]

Ahern suffered another reversal when the government held a referendum on abortion in March 2002. Hoping to tidy up the situation created by the 'X' case, the government proposed to remove the threat of suicide as a justification for a termination. Ahern had given a pledge to deal with the issue during the 1997 campaign and had made a post-election commitment to hold a referendum to four of the Independent TDs who supported the government. Despite the support of the Catholic Church and the main 'pro-life' groups, the government's amendment was narrowly defeated: 49.58 per cent to 50.42 on a turnout of 42.89 per cent. There was a clear urban–rural divide with Dublin, Cork, Galway and Limerick voting 'no' and the predominantly rural constituencies voting 'yes', and the turnout in urban areas was higher than that in the countryside. As one commentator noted, 'Never before has the electorate refused to yield before the full force of Rome and the Republican Party.'[153]

Despite his setbacks on Nice and abortion, and despite the economic slowdown, Ahern's reputation for competence, even statesmanship, which had been gained through his role in the peace process, remained a major asset to Fianna Fáil. It helped to cement Fianna Fáil's success in the general election in May 2002. Fighting on the slogan 'A Lot Done, More to Do', the party portrayed itself as the only political force large enough and coherent enough to maintain prosperity in a more unstable international environment and at a time of increasing evidence that there had been a serious deterioration in the public finances during 2001.[154]

Fine Gael, which had alienated some of its core support with Noonan's more nationalist stance on the North, further disconcerted them with a manifesto full of spending commitments that allowed Fianna Fáil to attack it for irresponsibility. Fine Gael's incoherence and its low poll ratings led to large-scale defections by its supporters to Labour, Fianna Fáil and the Progressive Democrats, who appealed to the electorate to deny Fianna Fáil an overall majority and ensure that they could continue to act as a governmental restraint on the larger party. Labour refused Noonan's plea for a pre-election pact, but, like Fine Gael, it underestimated the electorate's preference for governmental stability over specific spending commitments. In addition, Labour's implicit commitment to a centrist coalition meant that it failed to benefit from the substantial anti-establishment vote that went to Sinn Féin, the Greens and the Independents.

The result was a triumph for Ahern and a disaster for Noonan. Fianna Fáil's vote rose by over 2 per cent to 41.7 per cent and its number of seats from seventy-seven to eighty-one. Fine Gael's vote fell by 5.5 per cent to 22.5 per cent, while its seats plummeted from fifty-four to thirty-one. In Dublin it was left with only three TDs, putting it in fifth place. Labour's vote fell by 2 per cent to 10.77 per cent, although it returned with the same number of seats: twenty-one. The Progressive Democrats, despite a small decline in their vote (0.72 per cent to 3.96), doubled their number of seats to eight. Sinn Féin's vote increased by 4 per cent to 6.5 per cent and its number of seats from one to five. The Green vote increased by 2 per cent to 3.85 and its seats from two to six. There would be a record number of Independents in the new Dáil: fifteen.[155]

For the first time since 1969 an outgoing government had been re-elected. The election seemed, to some commentators, to portend radical change in the Irish party system. There was much talk of a terminal crisis of Fine Gael.[156] In fact, the key shift in the system had occurred over a decade before, in 1989, when Fianna Fáil had given up its 'principled' opposition to coalition government.[157] Fine Gael's future would depend on the attitude of the Labour Party towards Fianna Fáil, and here the prognosis was not so bleak. Ruairi Quinn, the Labour leader, resigned in August 2002, and his successor, elected by the new system of one-member, one-vote, was Pat Rabbitte, TD for Dublin South-west and a former junior minister in the 1994–7 Rainbow Coalition. Rabbitte had been a leading member of the Workers' Party and its successor, Democratic Left, which merged with Labour in 1999. He brought to the leadership of the party strong intellectual qualities and a reputation as perhaps the Dáil's most effective performer. He was also influenced by the Workers' Party tradition of hostility to traditional Irish nationalism, particularly that associated with Fianna Fáil and Sinn Féin. Here he was in tune with the attitudes of those party members who preferred to seek coalition with Fine Gael and the Green Party, rather than with Ahern's party, and who were hostile to Sinn Féin.[158]

The governing coalition's popularity slumped in the two years after the election. A pre-election spending spree had been followed by a series of cuts in services and the postponement of the implementation of some key election promises in areas like hospital beds and Garda numbers. Fianna Fáil paid a high price for these adjustments in the local and European elections in June 2004. Its share of the vote fell to 32 per cent, its lowest since 1927.[159] While Fine Gael's vote declined slightly, they won a number of extra seats and their new leader, the Mayo TD Enda Kenny, had the added compensation of winning an extra seat in the European elections, where Fine Gael emerged as the largest party, with five of Ireland's thirteen seats:[160] Labour's performance was strong in Dublin, where it emerged as the largest party, and it did well in the east of the country and the larger urban areas. Perhaps most importantly, its vote held up in spite of a surge in support for Sinn Féin. This was the most dramatic feature of the elections, with the party's support more than doubling and the acquisition of a European seat in Dublin.

Sinn Féin's vote was distinctive in geographical and class terms, being particularly concentrated in the working-class districts of major urban centres and in the border constituencies – its largest support was in Monaghan (31 per cent) and Dublin city (18.5 per cent). Its gains were strongly correlated with losses in Fianna Fáil support, suggesting that, although it is often presented as a left-wing alternative in Irish politics, it is more interested in moving into the territory of the mainstream Irish parties. Here it benefited from the media's focus on the central role of its leading members in the northern peace process. Adams ranked as one

of the most popular political figures in the country, getting higher satis-
faction ratings than either the Labour or Fine Gael leaders in an *Irish
Times* poll conducted a month before the Northern Bank robbery in
Belfast that was attributed to the IRA.[161]

After the electoral bruising in June 2004, Bertie Ahern announced
that the government would listen to the voters. One result was his public
declaration that he was a socialist. Another manifestation of Fianna Fáil's
repositioning was a 'think-in' of the parliamentary party, addressed in
September 2004 by Father Seán Healy of the Conference of the Religious
of Ireland, on the subject of 'social inclusion'. Healy's address, which
advocated greater income and wealth redistribution, was followed by the
departure of the Minister for Finance, Charlie McCreevy, for Brussels.
McCreevy was blamed by backbenchers for contributing to the election
losses because of his 'right-wing' tone, and it was hoped that his replacement, Brian Cowen, would re-establish the party's social-democratic
image.[162]

By early 2005 there had been a marked recovery in the popularity of
the government. This reflected an improvement in the economy after
the post-election slippage. But the government still faced high levels of
criticism on a range of issues, from inadequacies in the health service to
ill-treatment of patients in state-funded nursing homes. More important
was the intent on the part of Labour and Fine Gael to work out a pre-
election pact. Ahern's response to the emergence of a more coherent
opposition was to allege that it would be dominated by Labour's 'tax-
and-spend' philosophy and would 'bring us all back to the Third World
in "jig time"'.[163] This pronouncement came during another 'think-in',
which was addressed by the American social theorist Robert Putnam;
his analysis of social capital and the decline and revival of community
in the US was declared by the Taoiseach to be of central relevance to
Ireland. Rabbitte immediately responded to Ahern's attack by making it
plain that a government of which Labour was a part would not increase
income or corporation tax, although it would address the issue of tax
loopholes for the rich and would consider a wealth tax. As one political
scientist noted, there were few significant differences between the policy
positions of Labour, Fianna Fáil and Fine Gael on the economy. But she
also noted, on the basis of a survey of election candidates in 2002, that,
while there was a convergence of economic and social policies, there
remained a long-standing difference in the political identities of Fianna
Fáil and Fine Gael. This difference was a product of the parties' different
positions on the 'national question' and Northern Ireland. Fianna Fáil's

self-image of being more authentically republican than the other main parties was connected with a tendency to appropriate the Northern Ireland issue and suggest that both Fine Gael and Labour were less trustworthy custodians of the national interest.[164] Ahern did not let his eulogy for Putnam divert him from pointing out that Fianna Fáil was "'The Republican Party" devoted to achieving unity by consent . . . because I am an Irish Republican no issue means more than this to me.'[165]

There had been since the 1920s a struggle between Fianna Fáil and Sinn Féin to appropriate the identity of 'true' republicanism. The peace process had given a major boost to Sinn Féin in this competition. Nevertheless, Fianna Fáil could claim to have played a key role in bringing republicans into the process, while the continuing evidence of republican involvement in paramilitary and criminal activity put a limit on Sinn Féin's appeal to the electorate. However, if the IRA statement of July 2005 renouncing armed struggle turned out to be as historic as Ahern claimed, then not only would Sinn Féin be likely to win new Dáil seats at the next general election, but it would also have removed the major objection to its inclusion in government. Already one member of the government, the Minister for Foreign Affairs and TD for Louth, Dermot Ahern, had floated the possibility of Sinn Féin being in government after the next general election. This was a prospect with profound implications for North–South relations and unionist attitudes to the Republic. Although Ahern subsequently proclaimed that Sinn Féin's 'Marxist' economic policies would rule it out as a coalition partner, his decision to revive the official military parade to celebrate the Easter Rising and support for extending speaking rights to Northern Ireland MPs demonstrated the success of Adams's party in 'Ulsterizing' political debate in the Republic. Whether such a tendency would be welcome to an electorate whose patriotism had a traditionally twenty-six-county focus remained to be seen.

10. Between War and Peace: Northern Ireland 1985–2005

Direct Rule with a Green Tinge 1985–1993

Unionism was traumatized by the Anglo-Irish Agreement. Molyneaux had until the last believed that nothing would come from the ongoing Anglo-Irish negotiations.[1] He had been over-impressed by Thatcher's rejection of the three main proposals of the New Ireland Forum and perhaps relied too much on the views of Ian Gow, who had been Thatcher's Parliamentary Private Secretary but was excluded from the small group who negotiated the Agreement. But his miscalculation was buried in a wave of Protestant rage that manifested itself in the massive crowd of over 100,000 that gathered at a protest rally outside Belfast City Hall on 23 November. Tellingly, it was Molyneaux who warned the crowd that the campaign against the Agreement would be a protracted one.[2] The campaign in its various manifestations – from a mass resignation of Unionist MPs to council boycotts and a one-day general strike and 'Day of Action' in March 1986 – had little effect. The institutions of the Agreement had been specifically designed to be impervious to a loyalist reaction à la 1974. The UUP was soon divided over the wisdom of a council boycott, which would in some cases leave its political opponents in control and in others lead to legal action. The Day of Action ended in violence, and in the by-elections caused by the resignations the Unionists lost Newry and Armagh to the SDLP.[3] The Agreement's fundamental unpopularity with Protestants was to remain one of the core facts of Northern Ireland's political life, but this was to co-exist with a growing awareness that the institutions of the Agreement, like the hated Anglo-Irish Secretariat at Maryfield on the outskirts of East Belfast, were becoming more or less permanent features of the governance of the province.

Another notable feature of the post-Agreement landscape was the weakening of the DUP; the party's intransigence could be credibly presented as part of the reason for the imposition of the accord itself. It continued to dabble in the militant fringes of loyalist politics. In 1986, when a group of grass-roots loyalists formed the paramilitary-tinged group Ulster Resistance, Paisley and Peter Robinson were seen parading in the organization's red berets. Robinson got himself arrested in the Republic after leading a farcical loyalist 'invasion' of the County Monaghan village of Clontibret in August 1986.[4] The DUP's practice of resistance to relatively marginal concessions to the Catholic community was in any case rendered futile when such a substantial concession as the Agreement was already in place. The party entered hesitantly into a pact with the UUP from which it emerged in a weakened state, shorn of some of its best-known leaders. In the 1992 general election it achieved a mere 13.7 per cent of the poll, although its decline stabilized somewhat at 17.2 per cent in the May 1993 local government elections.[5] The DUP's difficulties went hand in hand with a steady rise in Protestant paramilitarism: loyalist paramilitaries killed only two people in 1984, but by 1991–2 they were more active agents of death than the IRA.

While the Agreement led to an increase in support for integrationist ideas amongst the Protestant middle class, Molyneaux advocated a strategic minimalism based on twin perceptions of the need to maintain UUP unity and of increasing Conservative disenchantment with the Agreement. While deeply averse to the more traditional NIO objective of power-sharing devolution, Molyneaux was nevertheless determined that mainstream unionism would not be imprisoned within a public posture of inflexibility. If the British government were to raise the possibility of a new and more broadly based agreement, Molyneaux would not adopt a rejectionist stance.[6]

Meanwhile, constitutional nationalism was profoundly divided, and not entirely because the UUP leadership still found it unpalatable to speak of power-sharing devolution. The SDLP had, by 1988, shown signs of moving decisively beyond the demands of Sunningdale. This was, in part, the result of the failure of the Agreement to marginalize Sinn Féin. Although that party's support had peaked before the Agreement, it had consolidated at around 11 per cent of the electorate. While the Agreement had accelerated those tendencies that made direct rule the 'best possible shell' for an expanding Catholic middle class, it had delivered neither the final decisive defeat for unionism nor the concrete economic benefits for the impoverished urban Catholic ghettos that might have reduced republican support in a more substantive way. It was also a reflection of the failure of Hume's own belief during the early phase of the Agreement – from November 1985 to mid 1987 – that since Thatcher had 'lanced the Protestant boil' by imposing the Agreement on the majority community, the unionists would have no alternative but to negotiate with him. He had predicted in an *Observer* interview that this would occur

by the end of 1986.[7] The failure of the prediction and the lack of a Sinn
Féin meltdown impelled Hume towards a political engagement with the
republican movement. The 'pan-nationalist front' was beginning to emerge.

The first sign of this was the seven-month-long dialogue between the
SDLP and Sinn Féin in 1988. This was facilitated by Sinn Féin's desire
to avoid the political isolation and marginalization that were the objective of the Agreement. Gerry Adams recognized that as long as the Sinn
Féin vote was contained at around 30 to 40 per cent of the Catholic
electorate – as seemed likely – the impetus of the 1982 electoral surge
might well dissipate. Adams was also concerned that Sinn Féin's attempt
to build up an electoral base in the Republic had so far proved fruit-
less. The breakthrough of their bitter enemies, the Officials – now known
as Sinn Féin–The Workers' Party – into Dáil politics was noted with
some envy by Adams and his comrades, particularly after the three SFWP
deputies had forced Haughey to cut a deal with them in order to form
a government in 1982.[8] Convinced that the party's maintenance of the
traditional policy of refusing to take their seats in the Dáil was a major
obstacle to political advance in the Republic, Adams and his allies had
waged a campaign against abstentionism, which culminated in the Sinn
Féin Ard-Fheis voting in 1986 to remove the ban on attendance at the
Dáil from the party's constitution.

The removal of the ban had provoked a final break with the traditionalists led by Ruairí Ó Brádaigh and Dáithí Ó Conaill, who resigned
from the party and created Republican Sinn Féin. Adams's critics claimed
that, despite his continued public support for the 'armed struggle', the
logic of increasing political involvement would eventually lead the
Provisionals down the same road as the Officials and Fianna Fáil towards
incorporation in the 'partitionist system'. In 1981, when Adams was
starting the process of building up the political side of the movement,
Danny Morrison had brilliantly anticipated the complaints of the more
militarist elements in a speech to the Sinn Féin Ard-Fheis in which he
asked: 'Who here really believes that we can win the war through the
ballot box? But will anyone here object if, with a ballot paper in one
hand and an Armalite in the other, we take power in Ireland?'[9] Although
tremendously effective as rhetoric, the 'Armalite and ballot box' strategy
put a severe limit on Sinn Féin's capacity to grow electorally in both
states. Adams was soon criticizing IRA 'mistakes' that killed ordinary
people and deterred northern Catholics from voting for his party. In the
first general election in the Republic after the decision to abandon
abstentionism, support for Sinn Féin was a mere 1.9 per cent.[10] The

connection with northern violence was a formidable obstacle to Adams's aim of Sinn Féin acquiring a pivotal role in the Dáil.

It also made impossible the creation of a broad 'anti-imperialist alliance' proposed by Adams and including the SDLP and Fianna Fáil. The aims of such an alliance were to pressurize the British government to declare in favour of a united Ireland and use its influence to move the unionists in that direction. For, although the Anglo-Irish Agreement had been denounced by Sinn Féin as an attempt to build up the SDLP and marginalize republicans, there was a recognition that the British state had made a substantial concession to constitutional nationalism and undermined the unionist position in Northern Ireland.[11] Using his friend Alec Reid, a Redemptorist priest from the Clonard Monastery in West Belfast, as intermediary, Adams informed Haughey that he would support an IRA ceasefire if the Irish government would pursue the issue of Irish unification.[12] During 1988 Adams was involved in secret discussions with Martin Mansergh, Charles Haughey's adviser on Northern Ireland. The price for pan-nationalist negotiations was an IRA ceasefire, and this was, publicly at least, said to be out of the question by Adams, who declared that 'the British will leave only when they are forced to leave.'[13] However, behind this public reiteration of the continued centrality of 'armed struggle' an intense debate on future strategy had opened up amongst the republican leadership.

By the mid 1980s the conflict between the IRA and the British state was stalemated. The reorganized, slimmed-down and militarily proficient terrorist organization – the product of the 'Long War' strategy promoted by Adams and his supporters from 1977 – was far from being defeated by the security forces. Yet its campaign was obviously containable. Its main victims had long ceased to be British troops: as a result of the policy of 'Ulsterization', it was local Protestants in the police and the Ulster Defence Regiment who bore the brunt of Provisional attacks. In the year of the Anglo-Irish Agreement, of the sixty-four deaths from the conflict only two were of British soldiers, whereas twenty-seven were members of either the RUC or the UDR.[14] Adams has subsequently described the situation in which republicans found themselves after the Agreement: 'There was a political and military stalemate. While republicans could prevent a settlement on British government terms, we lacked the political strength to bring the struggle to a decisive conclusion. Military solutions were not an option for either side.'[15] There were, however, still those in the leadership of the IRA who believed that the 'war' could be won.[16] A serious attempt was made to break the stalemate with the help of three shipments of arms and explosives from the Libyan leader Colonel Gaddafi in 1985–6. These included two tons of the powerful plastic-explosive Semtex, surface-to-air missiles, heavy machine-guns, and rocket launchers. The more militaristic of the IRA's leadership, including its Chief of Staff, saw in the Libyan material the possibility of a major shift in the balance of forces that would lead to an end to British rule.[17] In July 1986 the list of IRA 'legitimate targets' was widened to include civil servants, building contractors, caterers and British Telecom employees who did work for the security forces. Republicans had killed forty-two people in 1985, while in 1987 they killed sixty-nine and in 1988, sixty-two.[18] But if the intensification of 'armed struggle' gained it some gruesome head-lines, with the murder of a leading Northern Irish judge and his wife in a car-bomb attack in April 1987 and a landmine at Ballygawley, County Tyrone, in August 1988 that killed eight off-duty soldiers, it also had high military and political costs.

The 'Long War' strategy, by reducing the number of IRA activists, had made it easier for the security forces to concentrate their resources against known activists. The Special Air Services (SAS) was first publicly committed to action in Northern Ireland in 1976 to combat the IRA in south Armagh, an area with a centuries-old tradition of anti-state activities and a republican stronghold that the security forces could only enter in strength and with helicopter backup. Now its activities were expanded to Fermanagh and Tyrone, where the IRA was attempting to create another 'free zone' like south Armagh. In May 1987 it wiped out an eight-man IRA unit that was in the process of attacking the RUC station at Loughgall. This was the IRA's largest loss of 'volunteers' in a single incident since the Civil War and a major blow to its East Tyrone brigade, one of its most effective units. The same brigade was further weakened in August 1988 when the three men responsible for the Ballygawley landmine were killed in an SAS ambush as they attempted to kill a lorry driver who was a part-time member of the UDR. In March 1988 three of the IRA's most experienced operatives had been shot dead in Gibraltar while unarmed. It was alleged that they were preparing a bomb attack on a British Army band.[19]

Controversy over the use of the SAS and their tactics, particularly over whether it was necessary to kill those whom they had ambushed, was inevitable. However, Sinn Féin's ability to exploit it was limited by the IRA's spiralling list of 'mistakes' in which it had to admit that it had killed the wrong people. Most politically damaging was the detonation of a bomb at the Remembrance Day ceremony in Enniskillen on 8 November

1987, which killed eleven people. The IRA admitted that this had dealt a 'body blow' to hopes of a 'broad-based front against imperialism'.[20] The eight-month dialogue with the SDLP in 1988, so important for Adams in his quest for pan-nationalist unity, was called off by John Hume when the IRA accidentally killed two of his constituents.[21] By the end of the decade hopes of military victory had been relinquished, although the republican movement was far from discarding the application of violence or the threat of it as a tool for political bargaining.

The intensification of republican violence after 1986 showed the limitations of the attempt to combine the armed campaign with the search for more electoral support. Sinn Féin lost sixteen seats in the 1989 local government elections and some of its councillors began to point out publicly the irony of its criticisms of direct rule's failure to deal with unemployment levels in West Belfast while the IRA's bombing campaign continued to put people out of work and scare off new investors.[22] The impasse of the 'Armalite and ballot box' strategy and the knowledge of internal republican debate gained by intelligence services led to a two-track approach on the part of the British, by which hints of flexibility in the event of a ceasefire were combined with the threat of inter-party talks aimed at a centrist settlement that would isolate and marginalize republicans.

As early as the end of March 1987, Thatcher felt that the security returns following the Agreement were inadequate: 'I told Tom King [Northern Ireland Secretary] there must be a paper brought forth setting out all the options. I was determined that nothing should be ruled out.'[23] The election of the Haughey government served to cool the atmosphere even further, as did the announcement in January 1988 by the Attorney-General, Sir Patrick Mayhew, that there would be no prosecutions arising out of an inquiry into an alleged 'shoot-to-kill' policy of the RUC that led to the deaths of six unarmed men in County Armagh in 1982. John Stalker, Assistant Chief Constable of Manchester, who had been brought in to conduct the inquiry, complained of resistance and sabotage by some in the RUC and was taken off the inquiry in suspicious circumstances.[24] Although he did find that there was no official policy of 'shoot-to-kill', the controversy surrounding his replacement and the Mayhew decision led to the resurgence of the megaphone diplomacy between London and Dublin that the Agreement was supposed to have consigned to the history books.

Thatcher and Mayhew had little sympathy with an approach to policing that seemed to them to impose standards appropriate to a liberal democracy untroubled with a terrorist campaign on a society in which the IRA's main target was the RUC. Thus in the year that the 'shoot-to-kill' incidents took place, republicans had killed eight members of the RUC and four of the RUC Reserve. In the year that the Anglo-Irish Agreement was signed twenty-three members of the RUC and RUC Reserve had been murdered, nine of them in one IRA mortar attack on the Newry RUC station. In the 1982–5 period republicans were responsible for 70 per cent of the deaths from political violence, while the security forces were responsible for 13 per cent.[25] Even the most right-wing members of Thatcher's cabinet would have accepted that the state should not debase its standards to those of the terrorists, but there was none the less little inclination to see the issues raised by Stalker as more than blemishes on what was fundamentally a disciplined and lawful response to an organization that, as Hume pointed out, had killed twice as many Irish Catholics as the security forces in the first twenty years of the 'Troubles'.[26]

Thatcher's annoyance with Dublin grew as Irish politicians condemned the decision of the Court of Appeal to reject the appeal of the six men convicted of the 1974 Birmingham pub bombings. Convinced that she had signed the Agreement to facilitate more Irish cooperation against the IRA in such key areas as policing and extradition, she now complained that Haughey's government provided less cooperation in the security field than any other European country: 'Our concessions had alienated the Unionists without gaining the level of security cooperation we had a right to expect.'[27] This was the context in which she directed her new Secretary of State for Northern Ireland, Peter Brooke, to begin the search for a new and more broadly based agreement.

As the republican movement both intensified its military campaign and gave public hints of a new-found flexibility over the next five years, British policy assumed an increasingly pro-Union public posture while at the same time giving substantive private signs of an interest in republican revisionism. Peter Brooke launched the search for a new agreement through inter-party talks in January 1990 and managed to achieve some progress by the eve of the 1992 general election. An offer to suspend temporarily the workings of the Anglo-Irish Agreement proved enough to ensure the participation not only of the Ulster Unionists but also of the DUP. After the election the talks continued in a more serious vein with a new Secretary of State, Sir Patrick Mayhew. The UUP approached the talks in a slightly more confident frame of mind: their proposals were certainly considerably more advanced and elaborate. Under John Major, who had succeeded Thatcher in late 1990, the government gave even more explicit signs that it wished to reduce the unionist sense of isolation and anxiety. The Foreign Secretary, Douglas Hurd, told the 1991 Conservative Party Conference that the debate on partition was over. The Anglo-Irish inter-parliamentary tier was presented in early 1992 with a critical British analysis of the working of the Agreement. In the run-up to the election in April 1992, a Tory Prime Minister rediscovered the Union as a political theme. After the election there was the appointment of a team at the NIO that was just about as unionist in political sympathy as the current Conservative Party could produce.

However, the talks process foundered on the rock of the SDLP's refusal to depart from its original policy document, which argued for a form of joint authority with an added European dimension. It was clear during the talks that the NIO was impressed with the flexibility of the Ulster Unionists. Although they had originally insisted on an agreement in 'strand one', which dealt with the internal structures of the North's governance, before the start of 'strand two', dealing with North–South relations, they proved willing to make the crucial transition without agreement having been reached in 'strand one'. The unprecedented willingness of the Ulster Unionists to go to Dublin to discuss North–South relations was made possible by a private letter from Mayhew to Molyneaux indicating the former's lack of enthusiasm for the SDLP document. Nevertheless, Dublin's apparent unpreparedness to respond to the Unionist flexibility, together with Hume's refusal to budge from the original document, led to the collapse of the talks.

Deeply ingrained distrust of unionist motivation and an acute awareness of the potential republican cries of 'sell-out' for anything smacking of an 'internal solution' forced the SDLP away from a historic compromise with unionism. The Anglo-Irish Agreement had created a context in which it became logical, almost compellingly so, for constitutional nationalists to argue for a form of joint authority. British dissatisfaction with the Agreement's domestic failures – nobody questioned its international success in fire-proofing British policy in Northern Ireland – produced the usual frenetic tactical ingenuity, but this simply served to obscure the fundamental shift in terrain that the Agreement had produced. Even if a Sunningdale-type agreement were now possible, it was too 'internalist', too dependent on unionist goodwill, to be attractive from the SDLP's point of view. Both constitutional and revolutionary nationalism were convinced that the Agreement was a clear indication that the tide of history was running their way.

Major's increasingly precarious position in the House of Commons – where he was dependent on the nine UUP votes – brought about an increasingly pro-unionist tone in government statements. Yet the failure of the talks also pushed the government back towards an Anglo-Irish approach and into the intensification of private communications with the republican movement that had been initiated in October 1990.[28] Republican interest had been stimulated by hints of a new flexibility in speeches by Brooke. In an interview to mark his first 100 days as Secretary of State, Brooke had conceded that it was difficult to imagine the military defeat of the IRA. The following year he made a more direct appeal to republican strategists when he declared that the British government had 'no selfish strategic or economic interest in Northern Ireland'.[29] This produced a number of public indications of possible republican flexibility on some of their more fundamentalist postures – particularly that Britain should withdraw in the lifetime of one parliament. A 'scenario for peace' emerged in which an IRA ceasefire might be forthcoming in exchange for a British commitment to withdraw in a 'generation' while, in the interim, structures of joint authority would operate. Ultimately it appears that, despite the intensification of IRA activities in the North and Britain in 1991 and 1992, it was republican rather than unionist flexibility that was found most impressive.

Only the impact of serious intelligence work can explain British willingness to wager on these hints of a new republican flexibility at a time when IRA violence was intensifying. The IRA launched a renewed campaign in England in the early 1990s. At first aimed at 'Establishment' figures and institutions – Ian Gow, MP, a close friend of Thatcher and former adviser on Ireland, was murdered in a car-bomb attack in July 1990, and, in January 1991, 10 Downing Street was mortared while a cabinet meeting was taking place – the campaign developed into devastating bomb attacks on key financial and commercial centres. On 10 April 1992, the day after the British general election, two IRA bombs exploded at the Baltic Exchange in London, killing three people and causing £800 million of damage. More attacks followed over the next year. In March 1993 a bomb in a shopping centre in Warrington killed two young boys, and in April a massive explosion at the NatWest Tower in the City of London killed one person and caused over £1 billion in damage.[30] There was also an upsurge of IRA attacks in Northern Ireland. In 1991 the IRA planted more incendiary devices in commercial premises than it had in the previous nine years, as well as launching some massive car-bomb attacks in Belfast. The year 1992 began with the slaughter of eight Protestant building workers whose van was destroyed by a bomb at Teebane Cross in County Tyrone as they returned from working at an army base. During the year that followed the centres of a number of predominantly Protestant towns were destroyed by IRA car-bombs.

The Provisional campaign was increasingly matched in murderous intensity by the main loyalist paramilitary organizations. The UDA had experienced a palace revolution in the late 1980s as a leadership considered too middle aged and corrupt had been pushed aside by a younger and more single-mindedly ruthless cadre. Working under the *nom de guerre* of the Ulster Freedom Fighters (UFF), it had responded to the Teebane Cross atrocity by an attack on a bookmaker's business on Belfast's Lower Ormeau Road in which five Catholics were murdered. In 1992 and 1993, for the first time since the outbreak of the 'Troubles', loyalists were responsible for more deaths than republicans.[31] The campaigns of the UFF and UVF, although ordinary Catholics were still the main victims, were notable for their successful targeting of Sinn Féin activists as well as, for the first time, IRA members. Claims of security force 'collusion' soon became a major issue. However, the main result of the intensification of loyalist violence was a further weakening of electoral support for Sinn Féin. It lost ground to the SDLP in the 1992 general election, and Adams lost his West Belfast seat to Joe Hendron of the SDLP. Although the immediate cause of his defeat was the decision of a substantial section of the 3,000 unionists in the constituency to vote tactically for Hendron, there could be no disguising the fact that republican complicity in the violent sectarian atmosphere of the early 1990s had cost them votes. However, Adams's disappointment at his loss of West Belfast was mitigated by ongoing negotiations with Hume to construct a pan-nationalist alliance that would apply pressure to the British government for a radical shift in policy on Northern Ireland.

The Origins of the Peace Process

During the 1988 discussions between Sinn Féin and the SDLP the core difference between the parties, apart from the issue of violence, was the SDLP's interpretation of the Anglo-Irish Agreement. In one of their papers for the talks, the SDLP argued that the Agreement showed that Britain was now neutral on the partition issue: 'she has no military or economic interests and if the Irish people reached agreement among

themselves on, for example Irish unity, Britain would facilitate.'[32]
Although even in 1988 the extent of the British financial subvention
made it difficult for republicans to argue that Britain had an economic
interest in maintaining partition, they claimed that a strategic interest
did exist:

Strategic interests are now the most important consideration in Britain's
interference in Ireland. Quite apart from the very real, if somewhat exaggerated fear, among the British establishment that an Ireland freed from
British influence could become a European 'Cuba', even the prospect of a
neutral Ireland is regarded as a threat to British and NATO's strategic interests.[33]

The fall of the Berlin Wall and the collapse of 'actually existing
socialism' in Russia and Eastern Europe instituted a new world order
within which only one hegemonic power, the US, existed. The end of
the Cold War removed any lingering credibility from the notion that
Britain remained in Northern Ireland for strategic reasons. It had a related
effect noted by Michael Cox: 'it was inevitable that as the global tide of
radicalism began to retreat after 1989, this would feed into republican
thinking.'[34] With former 'anti-imperialist' and 'national liberation' forces
in Central America, the Middle East and South Africa opting for negotiations rather than for the continuation of armed struggle, the
international context helped to foster hitherto heretical thoughts amongst
leading republicans. Thus the republican propagandist Danny Morrison
reflected on the fall of the Berlin Wall in a letter from prison:

If there is one thing last year in Eastern Europe should have taught us it
was the bankruptcy of dogmatism . . . The lesson has certainly helped me
rethink my politics and become more pragmatic and realistic in terms of
our own struggle. If we all lower our demands and our expectations a peg
or two we might find more agreement.[35]

But this new realism did not mean that republicans had come anywhere
near accepting that there was a democratic basis for partition, nor even
that they were prepared to countenance Hume's argument that the British
state was neutral on the issue. During their discussions with republicans
in 1993, the British had specifically rejected the republican demand that,
in return for an IRA ceasefire, they should adopt the role of 'persuading'
the North's majority population of the merits of a united Ireland.[36]

However, this notion would be central to what became known as the 'Hume–Adams' negotiations.

Hume had approached Adams in October 1991 with a proposal, the idea for which had come from the same Catholic cleric who had opened up contacts between republicans and Charles Haughey in 1987, for a joint declaration to be made by the British and Irish governments. This would set out the agreed principles that must underlie any final settlement and was aimed to be open enough to republican aspirations to allow for an IRA cessation of its campaign. Republicans were unhappy with Hume's reformulation of the principle of Irish self-determination, which made it dependent upon 'the agreement and consent of the people of Northern Ireland'. This was flawed from a republican point of view, as it gave unionists, who were a majority in Northern Ireland, a 'veto' on the achievement of national unity.[37] But the fact that Hume had obtained the support of Haughey for the draft of the joint declaration encouraged Adams's leadership group to envisage the construction of a pan-nationalist front that might be able to shift the British towards a more proactive position.

A crucial development that affected republican calculations was the election of Bill Clinton as the new President of the USA in 1992. The end of the Cold War had drained the 'special relationship' of much of its significance for Washington and made it easier for Clinton to intervene in what had up until then been regarded as London's business. During the presidential campaign Clinton had supported the granting of a visa to Adams and also the idea of sending an American 'peace envoy' to Northern Ireland. Central to this more interventionist approach was the emergence of a new elite Irish-American lobby that aimed to transcend the existing division between Noraid and other pro-IRA groups and the 'Friends of Ireland' (for instance Senator Edward Kennedy) who were closely allied with Hume.[38] 'Americans for a New Irish Agenda' was a powerful group of well-funded, business-oriented Irish-Americans[39] whose leaders included ex-Congressman Bruce Morrison, Niall O'Dowd, editor of the *Irish Voice*, and two millionaire businessmen, William Flynn and Charles Feeney. A native of Drogheda, O'Dowd believed that Irish-American leverage was weakened by its association with support for IRA violence. A leading member of 'Irish-Americans for Clinton and Gore', he travelled to Belfast early in 1992 to talk to the Sinn Féin leadership about the American scene.[40]

Republican enthusiasm for the injection of an American dimension into the situation was a reflection of the leadership's calculation that

Clinton's support might make it easier to sell a compromise to the more fundamentalist elements of the IRA. The price of the creation of a pan-nationalist front with the blessing of the White House would be a ceasefire, and this was bound to remind the 'republican base' of the last nearly disastrous ceasefire of 1975. In 1986 Martin McGuinness had declared: 'Our position is clear and it will never, never, never change. The war against British rule must continue until freedom is achieved.'[41] Yet by the early 1990s it was clear to Adams and his closest allies that, as Danny Morrison put it in a letter to Adams in 1991, 'I think we can fight on forever and can't be defeated. But, of course that isn't the same as winning or showing something for all the sacrifices.'[42] The purpose of the 'Irish peace process', as Sinn Féin described its deepening involvement with constitutional nationalist parties in both states, was to obtain a settlement amounting to joint sovereignty that could be presented as transitional to the final goal of a thirty-two-county democratic socialist republic. In return the IRA would deliver an open-ended cessation of violence. The devastating bombs in London in 1992 and 1993 were aimed at increasing republican leverage once all-party talks about a settlement got under way.

US involvement was important as a compensatory device that allowed the republican leadership to recover from its profound disappointment with the Downing Street Declaration produced by John Major and Albert Reynolds on 15 December 1993. When Reynolds had dispatched his amended version of the Hume–Adams document to Major in June 1993, it was still heavily republican in content, with references to Britain as a 'persuader' of unionists towards Irish unity and the demand for a specific time-frame within which unity was to be attained.[43] However, this was little more than an opening gambit as Reynolds had accepted that the notion of 'persuasion' was incompatible with the principle of consent. Despite his frustration with Major's much more cautious approach to the possibility of an IRA cessation, Reynolds did not shift on this fundamental point, and he was also concerned, as was Major, that mainstream unionism in the person of figures such as James Molyneaux and the Church of Ireland Primate Robin Eames would not reject any joint declaration.

Republican violence made it all the more necessary for the two Prime Ministers to distance themselves from 'Hume–Adams'. On 23 October an IRA attempt to kill the leadership of the UDA in a bomb attack on the Shankill Road resulted in the death of ten people, nine of them shoppers or passers-by who were killed when the Provisionals' bomb went off prematurely. The day before the carnage Hume had told the House of Commons that his talks with Adams provided 'the most hopeful dialogue and the most hopeful chance of lasting peace that I have seen in twenty years'. He called on the two governments to 'hurry up and deal with it'.[44] Hume now seemed dangerously isolated in his partnership with the republican movement, and Adams further shredded the tattered moral credibility of 'Hume–Adams' by helping to carry the coffin of the IRA bomber killed in the attack. On 30 October the UDA, using its *nom de guerre* of the Ulster Freedom Fighters, wreaked its revenge for the Shankill bombing when two of its men machine-gunned customers in the Rising Sun bar in Greysteel, County Londonderry, killing six Catholics and one Protestant.

On 27 October Dick Spring, as Minister for Foreign Affairs, had announced to the Dáil six democratic principles that should underpin any settlement. These included a rejection of talks with those who used, threatened or supported violence, and no change in the North's constitutional position without the consent of a majority in Northern Ireland.[45] Two days later, after a meeting between Major and Reynolds at an EU summit in Brussels, the Prime Ministers developed the six principles as a seemingly explicit alternative to the Hume–Adams document. As Reynolds privately informed his press secretary, 'Hume–Adams was being declared dead, in order to keep it alive, in the same way as Adams carried the bomber's coffin, because otherwise he couldn't deliver the IRA.'[46] Despite further embarrassment when, in November, news of the 'back-channel' discussions with republicans leaked to the press, Major was still prepared to continue with discussions aimed at producing an IRA ceasefire.[47] At the same time he intensified the process of consultation with Molyneaux and other unionist leaders to attempt to ensure that any joint declaration would at least have the acquiescence of the majority community.

The Joint Declaration was signed at a ceremony at 10 Downing Street on 15 December 1993. It was a relatively brief document of eleven paragraphs, but underneath a certain opaqueness of style there was considerable originality and sophistication. This was particularly so in the complex language of the Declaration's fourth paragraph, in which the British government agreed 'that it is for the people of the island of Ireland alone, between the two parts respectively, to exercise their right of self-determination on the basis of consent, freely given, North and South, to bring about a united Ireland, if that is their wish'.

After the Downing Street Declaration, the 'Hume–Adams' phraseology

continued to dominate the political scene, but its content was dramatically altered. One of the most effective slogans of Irish nationalism had
been given new, decidedly softer conceptual content, and this had been
done by a Fianna Fáil-led government. The self-determination of the
Irish people was conceded by Britain but only on the basis that the Irish
government wished to operate that principle in favour of Irish unity
with the support of a majority in the North. Superficially, the rhetoric
of the 'Hume–Adams' process had been conceded, but the process had
been stripped of its content in a quite dramatic way. The British were
now 'facilitators', not for Irish unity but for an agreed Ireland, and an
agreed Ireland, by definition, could not be a united Ireland until there
was majority consent in the North.

Divisions amongst republicans over how to evaluate the Declaration were
soon apparent. Mitchel McLaughlin, the prominent Sinn Féin leader from
Derry, claimed that the general reaction of republicans was one of disappointment. At a meeting of around 400 republican activists, many
of them ex-prisoners, at Loughmacrory in County Tyrone in December
there was no support for the Declaration.[48] Yet Adams insisted that the
Declaration represented a significant shift by the British, who had for the
first time, if in a heavily qualified manner, recognized the right of the Irish
people as a whole to self-determination. He was even to claim that it
'marked a stage in the slow and painful process of England's disengagement
from her first and last colony'.[49] Tensions within the republican movement
were exacerbated by Major's talk of a 'decontamination period' for Sinn
Féin before they could enter into dialogue with the governments and the
other parties about the way ahead. It was also made clear by the British
government that the IRA would have to decommission its weapons before
Sinn Féin would be admitted to all-party talks.[50] Dick Spring compounded
the republican leadership's problems when he too announced that republican participation in talks would necessitate movement on the arms issue.[51]

Yet, if many rank-and-file republicans saw in the Declaration little
more than the 'Unionist veto' disguised in more 'green' verbiage, Adams
and his supporters in the leadership detected real possibilities of political advance for Sinn Féin, North and South. Reynolds did all he could
to play on Adams's desire for a republican political breakthrough in the
Republic. The ban on Sinn Féin from radio and television in the Republic
was removed in January 1994, and Reynolds announced that a Forum
for Peace and Reconciliation would be set up to allow all the parties in
the Republic to consider ways in which 'agreement and trust' could be
developed between the 'two traditions on the island'. Republicans were

being invited into the mainstream in the Republic; Reynolds also ensured that Adams would be elevated to the status of an international statesman, provided he gave clear evidence that he was committed to 'conflict resolution'. Crucial here was Clinton's decision in January, against the wishes of Major and the US State Department and Department of Justice, to grant a visa to Adams to allow him to attend a high-profile one-day conference on Northern Ireland in New York, organized by leading figures in the corporate wing of Irish-America. Clinton's decidedly 'green' Irish ambassador, Jean Kennedy-Smith, was also important in making Adams and his colleagues understand that with sufficient tactical ingenuity they could look to powerful allies in Washington.

When the leadership of the republican movement prepared IRA volunteers for a ceasefire in the summer of 1994, they emphasized the importance of a powerful pan-nationalist alliance supported by the White House. In a key strategy document entitled 'TUAS' that was circulated at the time, the main factors they identified as favouring an initiative were:

Hume is the only SDLP person on the horizon strong enough to face the challenge.

Dublin's coalition is the strongest government in 25 years or more.

Reynolds has no historical baggage to hinder him and knows how popular such a consensus would be among the grassroots.

There is potentially a very powerful Irish-American lobby not in hock to any particular party in Ireland or Britain.

Clinton is perhaps the first US President in decades to be substantially influenced by such a lobby.

The activists were told that the initials stood for 'tactical use of armed struggle', which implied that, if the ceasefire tactic failed, the armed struggle would resume. The two governments and the Americans were given the more soothing message that TUAS stood for 'totally unarmed strategy'.[52]

The involvement of Reynolds and Clinton was conditional on a radical shift in the IRA's position. Both reacted angrily when, in pursuit of the 'tactical use of armed struggle' in the forlorn hope that the British could still be coerced into acting as 'persuaders' for unity, the IRA mortared Heathrow Airport in March 1994.[53] Back at the time of the spat with Major over Adams's visa, Reynolds had privately declared that 'Sinn Féin will pay a price for going to Capitol Hill. A lot of powerful people went out on a limb for Adams. If he doesn't deliver, they'll have him back in the house with steel shutters [Sinn Féin headquarters on the Falls Road] so fast his feet won't touch the ground.'[54] When the IRA declared a three-day ceasefire in March it was received with cold contempt by Adams's 'allies' in Dublin and Washington; and by the beginning of the August, after some more gruesome loyalist murders of Catholics and with rumours of an imminent IRA cessation that would be time-limited and reserve them the right to defend nationalist communities, Reynolds let Adams know that republicans could be as quickly consigned to the margins as they had been recently brought in from the cold:

I've told them that if they don't do this right, they can shag off . . . Otherwise I'll walk away. I'll go off down that three-strand talks/framework document road with John Major, and they can detour away for another 25 years of killing and being killed – for what?'[55]

The IRA declaration of a 'complete cessation of military operations' on 31 August 1994 was therefore in part the product of a carrot-and-stick strategy on the part of the Irish government aided by the White House. Fear of political isolation if London and Dublin proceeded with the inter-party talks process from which they were excluded was a factor. So was the realistic assessment that 'republicans at this time and on their own do not have the strength to achieve the end goal'.[56] At the core of the leadership's optimism about 'the new stage of struggle' was the information it had obtained from Reynolds about the ongoing discussions with the British on the Framework Document that the two governments were drafting as a basis for a new and decisive round of all-party talks. The document, laden with cross-border institutions, was given an all-Ireland ethos designed to be seductive to republicans. From this perspective a 'transitional' settlement combining strong North–South institutions and a process of radical reform of the northern state would create conditions for unity over a period of fifteen to twenty years. Central to this process was the further fragmentation and weakening of unionism. But could republicans continue to count on unionism remaining inertly divided between Paisleyite rejectionism and Molyneaux's crab-like adjustment to the strategic initiatives of others?

Unionism and the Peace Process

James Molyneaux had tried to counter the lurid doom-mongering of Paisley by stressing his ability to have the unionist position respected at the highest levels in Westminster and Whitehall. His 'friends in high places' approach came near to foundering in 1985, and only the disarray of the DUP in the aftermath of the Agreement saved him. The publication of the Framework Document seemed to many in the UUP to show that their leader had been fooled again because of a naive faith in the goodwill of a British Prime Minister. Molyneaux, who had been denounced by Paisley for going to Dublin during the 1992 talks process, had been confident that the collapse of the talks would consolidate a shift in British government attitudes away from sympathy with nationalism. Given the Major government's precarious position in the House of Commons, he expected that it would give sympathetic attention to unionist concerns, particularly the demand for a Northern Ireland Select Committee to end the situation whereby Northern Ireland legislation was dealt with through Orders in Council. Although he did get satisfaction on this issue, he had seriously underestimated the attractive power of republican revisionism to any British government. When the Framework Document was published, it contained provision for North–South institutions that to many unionists appeared to be alarmingly autonomous and powerful. As Graham Walker notes, 'The Unionist Party now found it difficult retrospectively to justify its acquiescence in the Downing Street Declaration and was roundly condemned by Paisley, who identified this as a key development in encouraging the government to pursue a path inimical to Unionist interests.'[57]

The Framework Document dealt a fatal blow to Molyneaux's leadership. In March 1995 Lee Reynolds, an unknown 21-year-old student, obtained 15 per cent of the votes in an audacious leadership challenge to Molyneaux. In the summer, Molyneaux resigned after his party lost the North Down by-election, a prime UUP seat, to an arch Molyneaux critic, Robert McCartney, QC, leader of the small UK Unionist Party.

North Down was referred to as the North's 'gold coast' because of its high concentration of prosperous Protestants. These were the so-called 'contented classes': those who had in material terms done very well under direct rule. A major factor in the well-being of this group was the growth of the public sector, which had been expanded as a fire damper against political violence. By the 1980s public sector employment accounted for 42 per cent of the total workforce, compared to 27 per cent a decade earlier.[58] Even under Thatcher, government policy in Northern Ireland remained strongly interventionist and quietly Keynesian. The result was a massive expansion in the size of the subvention that was paid by the Treasury to the region and reflected the difference between what was raised locally in taxes and the amount of public expenditure injected into the region. While the subvention was tiny in the early 1970s, by the mid 1990s it had become huge, standing at about £3.7 billion annually.[59]

The economic dependence of the North on the British Exchequer raised a serious practical obstacle to Irish unity and also provided a strong prudential argument against the 'little Ulster' vision of the DUP. The material well-being of the Northern Protestant middle class was another factor that British policy-makers might have hoped would buttress moderate unionism. However, the problem with this economic under-pinning of the Union was that it tended to encourage a largely privatized lifestyle that wanted to insulate itself as much as possible from politics. For many middle-class Protestants the lives of their working-class co-religionists in North and West Belfast were as much an unknown and alien territory as those of the inhabitants of the Falls Road and Ardoyne. The problem facing any attempt to develop a more politically rational and proactive unionism had its social roots here. As the Church of Ireland leader Robin Eames explained to the Opsahl Commission: 'To many the political process in Northern Ireland is already irrelevant. The opting out of the middle class is a definite factor at play. For those whose work, recreation or social life is untouched by the community of fear, there is a reluctance to get involved.'[60]

The 'community of fear' reflected not simply ongoing violence but a broader perception of decline and retreat amongst Protestants. It was the obverse of rising nationalist and republican self-confidence and reflected demographic and electoral trends. The Catholic share of the North's popu-lation increased from a third to at least 40 per cent between 1971 and 1991 and there were unionist fears that the 2001 census might show the Catholic share as 46 per cent.[61] Although demographers disagreed as to the likelihood of a future Catholic majority because of declining Catholic birth-rates since the 1980s, such qualifications did little to calm more atavistic interpretations of imminent victory or defeat in an ethnic breeding contest. A rising nationalist and republican share of the vote – from 31 per cent in the early 1980s to 43 per cent in 2001 – had a similar effect. Even those tendencies that might have been seen as providing sections of the Catholic community with a material stake in partition were read through Orange spectacles. Thus the strengthening of fair employment legislation in 1989, which by the mid 1990s was contributing to an increase in the Catholic share of employment in virtually every occupational grouping,[62] was read as a Dublin government-inspired stratagem for discrimination against Protestants. Such fearful pessimism would remain a major influence in unionist politics throughout the 1990s.

In the leadership contest that followed Molyneaux's resignation, David Trimble was seen as the most articulate and dangerous candidate of the right. This in part reflected his role in the major confrontation between the security forces and the Portadown Orangemen who were blocked from marching from Drumcree Church down the Garvaghy Road in July 1995. The Garvaghy Road was one of a number of areas where Catholic residents claimed that changing demography required that 'offensive' parades be curtailed. Sinn Féin had played an important role in the establishment of such residents' committees, in part as an example of 'unarmed struggle'.[63] The increasing confrontation over marches also reflected unionist fears about the new interventionist role of the Irish state in the North through the institutions and rights agreed at Hillsborough in 1985.[64] As tens of thousands of Orangemen came to give support and others blocked roads and the port of Larne, Trimble, in whose constituency the conflict was taking place, was intensively involved in attempts to resolve the issue. However, the undoubtedly positive role he played in bringing the stand-off to a peaceful conclusion was obliterated by his indulgence in a piece of street theatre with Ian Paisley, when the two clasped hands in what nationalists interpreted as a triumphalist gesture as they greeted the Orangemen after they had been allowed to march down the Garvaghy Road.

His role at Drumcree would certainly have appealed to the many Orangemen who were delegates to the Ulster Unionist Council that met to elect Molyneaux's successor. Yet those in the upper reaches of the NIO who were aghast at Trimble's election misread both the man and the circumstances of his victory. In a party as bereft of intellectual ballast as the Ulster Unionists, it was no great compliment to Trimble to point out that he was by far the most cerebral of the candidates for the leadership. He was the only mainstream unionist figure who had the intellectual and strategic capacity to enter into a serious contest with Hume and Adams.

Trimble had been in William Craig's Vanguard movement and had supported the idea of an emergency coalition with the SDLP in 1976. This willingness to share power with nationalists was one indication of Trimble's basic political realism: his acceptance of the fact that no British government would return devolved institutions to Northern Ireland except on the basis of power-sharing. At the same time he found Molyneaux's trust in Thatcher dangerously naive. A law lecturer at Queen's

University until he won the Upper Bann seat in 1989, Trimble was also an omnivorous reader of books on Irish history and had published two serious works of amateur history.[65] This historical perspective provided him with a useful corrective to the overly pessimistic view of the British state that gripped many in the unionist community in the early 1990s. For if unionists were mistaken to rely on Thatcher's supposed innate sympathy for their cause, it was equally mistaken, if more understandable because of the Anglo-Irish Agreement, to become consumed by fear of British betrayal. Trimble was convinced that only a proactive strategy on the part of unionists would prevent further British concessions to nationalists and republicans.

For Trimble the IRA ceasefire was an admission of the failure of armed struggle:

Even though the cease-fire may be merely a tactic, the fact that they have had to change their tactics is an admission that the previous tactic [armed struggle] has failed. Although there are elements in the republican movement that desire a return to violence, they will be returning to a tactic that was not working . . . So, in that sense the republican movement is being defeated slowly. It is a slow process but that is what is happening. From our point of view, what we have to ensure is that while their campaign is winding up it does not cause any political or constitutional change which is contrary to the interests of the people of Northern Ireland. And we also want to do everything possible to ensure that the Union is strengthened.[66]

This was a sophisticated analysis, too sophisticated for many unionists, who still preferred the Paisley–McCartney vision of a republican movement with almost demonic powers that was moulding Anglo-Irish policies to its will through the continuing threat of force. Such views were strengthened in February 1996 with the exploding of a massive bomb at Canary Wharf in London, marking the end of the IRA ceasefire.

In the autumn of 1995 Major and Bruton had agreed to establish an international body to find a way forward on the arms issue. Chaired by a close Clinton ally, Senator George Mitchell, its report in February 1996 suggested waiving the British government's precondition – the beginning of decommissioning before republicans got into talks – and instead put forward the notion of decommissioning progressing in conjunction with the talks. There had already been signs that the balance of forces within the republican movement had shifted against the ceasefire, as exaggerated hopes for rapid movement towards all-party talks and the creation of 'transitional' structures were disappointed. Despite a demand by President Clinton, on a visit to Belfast in November 1995, for an end to paramilitary 'punishment' beatings and shootings, by the end of the year the IRA, using the *nom de guerre* 'Direct Action against Drugs', had killed six alleged drug dealers. Major's lukewarm acceptance of the Mitchell Report and his emphasis on the way forward being through an election produced a bitter denunciation from Hume in the House of Commons – and, within days, the bomb at Canary Wharf.

Despite Canary Wharf, Trimble maintained that for unionists to retreat into a posture of resistance to dialogue would be disastrous. Neither London nor Dublin had given up on the republican movement and a simple denunciatory response from unionists would guarantee that they became the passive victims of political change. He could also point out that one of the main reasons for the republican relapse was anger at his success in persuading Major of the need for elections as an alternative way into dialogue with republicans.

In the elections for a Northern Ireland Forum held in May 1996, the UUP vote at 24.2 per cent had declined by 5 percentage points, compared to the local government elections of 1993, while support for the DUP at 18.8 per cent had increased by less than 2 points.[67] The limited rise in the DUP vote reflected inroads made into its support base by the two parties linked to Protestant paramilitary organizations: the Progressive Unionist Party (PUP), linked to the UVF, and the Ulster Democratic Party (UDP), linked to the UDA. Both organizations had responded to the IRA's ceasefire with one of their own, declared on 13 October 1994. Then the 'Combined Loyalist Military Command' had declared that assurances had been sought from the British government that no secret deal had been done with the IRA and that 'the Union is safe'. They also offered 'abject and true remorse' to the families of their many innocent victims.[68] Although members of both, particularly the larger and more Balkanized UDA, would soon be involved in sectarian attacks on Catholics and, like the IRA, continue to use violence to defend their many profitable criminal activities from drugs to cross-border fuel smuggling, the ceasefire did enhance the credibility and political acceptability of the PUP and the UDP amongst the Protestant working class.

Concerned that politics could be seen to work for the loyalist paramilitaries, the Northern Ireland Office provided a mixed electoral system for the Forum, which allocated an extra twenty seats to be filled on a regional list system, giving two to each of the ten parties with the highest votes. The PUP with 3.5 per cent, the UDP with 2.2 per cent and the

Northern Ireland Women's Coalition with a mere 1 per cent were all allocated seats. However, the Forum elections also gave a major boost to Sinn Féin, which won its largest-ever share of the vote: 15.5 per cent. The narrowing of the gap with the SDLP and the party's strong performance in the Republic's general election made a second ceasefire very likely. At the same time republicans were waiting for a British general election to deliver a Labour government with a secure majority that would, they hoped, push forward with a settlement that could be portrayed as transitional to Irish unity.

Trimble was untroubled by the prospect of a substantial Labour victory. He had established good relations with elements of 'new Labour'. Shortly before he became Prime Minister in 1997, Tony Blair had sacked Labour's Northern Ireland spokesman, Kevin McNamara, who was seen as being on the 'green' wing of the party, and replaced him with Dr Marjorie ('Mo') Mowlam, who was initially welcomed by unionists. Blair's first trip outside London as Prime Minister was to Northern Ireland, where, on 16 May at Balmoral, he declared that unionists had nothing to fear from his government: 'A political settlement is not a slippery slope to a united Ireland. The government will not be persuaders for unity. The wagons do not need to be drawn up in a circle.' He also declared that he valued the Union and that 'none of you in this hall today, even the youngest, is likely to see Northern Ireland as anything but a part of the United Kingdom.'[69] Such sentiments were profoundly distasteful to republicans, yet they were soon given a very practical compensation when the government declared that a renewed ceasefire would get Sinn Féin into talks within six weeks. The decommissioning precondition had gone.

From the earliest days of Blair's administration the attractive and repulsive aspects of the deal on offer to unionists were relatively clear. Central to any settlement was an acceptance of the consent principle. This was to be copper-fastened by full constitutional recognition of Northern Ireland by the Republic. There would be a return of devolution to the North, now in the context of Labour's commitment to constitutional change in the rest of the UK. This would spell the end of the Irish government's 'interference' in the governance of the North in the form of the Anglo-Irish Agreement. The price to be paid for these political and constitutional gains was an Irish dimension embodied in a North–South Ministerial Council and the insistence of Dublin, London and John Hume that republicans must be integral to any settlement.

The Good Friday Agreement

The IRA did not return to full-scale 'armed struggle' during the sixteen months between Canary Wharf and its declaration of a second ceasefire on 21 July 1997. This was little consolation for the families of Detective Garda Gerry McCabe, shot dead in June 1996 during an IRA robbery of a mail van in County Limerick, or Stephen Restorick, a British soldier shot dead by a sniper in south Armagh in February 1997. Most IRA activity occurred in Britain, with a series of bombs in London and the devastation of the centre of Manchester by a 3,500 pound lorry-bomb in June 1996. As the general election approached, the attacks focused on disrupting road and rail networks as well as the Grand National steeple-chase. Such violence served a number of purposes. It reminded the British government that should a ceasefire be restored, republican demands had to be seriously addressed if the peace process were not to be put in crisis again. Adams's 'peace strategy' continued to have a coercive element. It maintained the unity of the republican movement by showing restive elements in the IRA that involvement in negotiations had not made them redundant. By keeping the level of violence low and mostly outside Northern Ireland, it did not damage the continuing electoral expansion of Sinn Féin. In the 1 May general election Adams won back West Belfast from the SDLP and Martin McGuinness won Mid Ulster from the DUP's William McCrea. Three weeks later in the local government elections Sinn Féin increased its vote to 17 per cent, cutting the margin between it and the SDLP from 75:25 of the nationalist vote in the 1993 local government elections to 55:45 in 1997.[70]

But if republican violence, or the threat of it, continued to perform important functions for Adams's strategy, it was difficult to see it as more than a means of increasing the 'green' façade of what was a partitionist settlement. Adams was now writing about 'renegotiating the Union' rather than ending it.[71] The new Taoiseach, Bertie Ahern, had already declared that 'irredentism is dead' and that it was not 'feasible or desirable to attempt to incorporate Northern Ireland into a united Ireland against the will of a majority there, either by force or coercion'. He also rejected joint authority as a realistic option.[72] It was possible for republican leaders to depict the North–South institutions as mechanisms for creeping in-tegration, but there was no guarantee that their version of North–South links would be the accepted one.

Republican optimism was encouraged by the way the new Labour government downplayed the decommissioning issue. There was also a commitment to 'confidence-building measures' in areas such as the reform of the RUC and the strengthening of fair employment legislation. Although the government had initially proposed to deal with the arms issue along the lines of the Mitchell Report – by decommissioning in conjunction with political negotiations – this was dropped after a flexing of IRA muscle. On 17 June two RUC men were shot dead by the IRA in Lurgan, County Armagh. Within days an Anglo-Irish paper on decommissioning implied that all Sinn Féin would have to do was agree to discuss the issue during the talks.[73] This approach, while it permitted the successful completion of negotiations, could not prevent the issue returning to haunt the early life of the new devolved institutions.

Some on the Tory right had denounced the internationalization of the search for a settlement involved in British acceptance of Senator George Mitchell as chair of the talks process, claiming that American involvement would simply strengthen the nationalist cause.[74] In fact, for Mitchell as well as his sponsor, Clinton, it was accepted that the talks could only be successful if, as well as bringing in republicans from the cold, they did not drive the majority of unionists into the rejectionist camp. At the centre of Adams's pan-nationalist strategy there had been the over-optimistic assumption that Clinton's involvement would follow an Irish-American agenda. While there was no doubting the deeper emotional sympathy of the Democratic administration with nationalist Ireland, Clinton's substantive political interest was the attainment of a deal that could be trumpeted as 'historic', and this necessitated keeping Trimble's party on board.

Paisley and Robert McCartney had led their parties out of the talks when Sinn Féin entered in September 1997, thus making the negotiation of an agreement possible.[75] While the leadership of Sinn Féin claimed a victory over unionist 'intransigence' and British 'prevarication', some members of the IRA, at both leadership and rank-and-file levels, were increasingly apprehensive about the implications of the peace process for traditional republican objectives. To gain entry to the talks process, Sinn Féin had to sign up to the 'Mitchell Principles', which committed them, amongst other things, to 'democratic and exclusively peaceful means of resolving political issues and to the total disarmament of all paramilitary organizations'. They were also committed to urge an end to punishment killings and beatings – the main rest and recreation activity of IRA volunteers on ceasefire – and to take effective steps to prevent them taking place.[76] Decommissioning was to be treated as an issue to be addressed during the talks, and although unionist sceptics predicted that it would be fudged, there were some in the republican movement who feared that the military integrity of the IRA would be sacrificed on the altar of Sinn Féin's electoral and governmental ambitions. To quieten such voices a senior IRA spokesman had told *An Phoblacht* that the IRA 'would have problems with sections of the Mitchell Principles' and that the IRA was not a participant in the talks.[77] This was a fiction, as senior members of the political wing of the republican movement, including Adams and McGuinness, were also members of the Army Council of the IRA, but it did reflect real tensions in the movement created by the political leadership's increasing envelopment by the process of political bargaining.

Already the Continuity IRA, the military wing of Adams's former comrades who had seceded in 1986 to form Republican Sinn Féin, were attempting to attract disgruntled Provisionals by a series of car-bomb attacks on RUC stations. In November an attempt by Adams's supporters in the IRA to centralize control over the ultimate disposition of arms with the IRA Army Council resulted in a split when the IRA's Quartermaster-General and a number of other senior IRA figures in the border area resigned from the movement and went on to form the Real IRA.[78] The dissidents established their own political wing, the 32-County Sovereignty Movement, which, although it initially had the support of only a few disillusioned members of Sinn Féin, made up for this in 'movement' credibility by having the support of a sister of Bobby Sands. Given the epochal resonance of the deaths of Sands and his comrades for the Provisional movement, it was acutely embarrassing for Adams to be condemned by Bernadette Sands-McKevitt for entering a talks process that could only result in a 'modernized version of partition'. As she witheringly put it, her brother did not die for a cross-border tourism authority.[79]

If republicans were going to embrace a settlement that left the North inside the UK for at least the medium term and accept the principle of consent – the 'unionist veto' in the movement's traditional language – then it was important that it should be presented to their supporters as 'transitional'. Acceptance of new devolved structures of government at Stormont needed to be balanced by a set of strong, free-standing North–South institutions along the lines set out in the Framework Document. But in January 1998 even these consolatory structures were put in question by the British and Irish governments' joint document, Heads of Agreement, which, in setting out their understanding of the likely parameters of any final deal, proposed North–South institutions that would be mandated by and accountable to the Northern Ireland Assembly and the Irish parliament. A Belfast-based journalist knowledgeable about republicanism described Heads of Agreement as a triumph for Trimble and a disaster for republicanism.[80] But, as Trimble himself pointed out, the process of bargaining, which led to an agreement and subsequently to the formation of an 'inclusive' government for Northern Ireland, was a 'white-knuckle ride' in which an apparent victory for one side produced such a bitter response from the other that it was soon provided with a compensatory 'victory' of its own.

Republican displeasure was soon evident in another 'tactical use of armed struggle' when first an alleged drug dealer and then a prominent loyalist were shot dead. Although the violence resulted in Sinn Féin being temporarily excluded from the talks, it may have contributed to the determination of Bertie Ahern's government to press the British for a return to the bolder version of cross-borderism of the Framework Document. The result was a final frenetic four days of negotiation, kick-started by George Mitchell's presentation to the parties of a draft of the agreement on 7 April. This included a section on strand two (North–South institutions) that the governments had drafted, which reflected the strong cross-border dimension of the Framework Document. Mitchell himself recognized that this would be unacceptable to Trimble and, with the leader of the Alliance Party, John Alderdice, predicting disaster if the proposals were carried out, Blair and Ahern descended on Stormont for three days and nights of what James Molyneaux disparagingly referred to as 'high-wire act' negotiations.

The final Agreement allowed Trimble to claim that the Union was not only safe but actually stronger because of unionist negotiating successes in strand two and on constitutional recognition. Unionist focus on strand-two issues during the final days of the negotiations had got a result: the North–South ministerial council and its cut-down list of 'implementation bodies' in areas including animal and plant health and teacher qualifications were difficult for either republicans or unionist rejectionists to portray as 'creeping reunification'. For the first time an Irish government had committed itself to the constitutional recognition of Northern Ireland through the amendment of Articles 2 and 3 of its constitution, and all signatories of the Agreement were committed to accepting the principle of consent.

But the strong belief of the two governments and the SDLP that republicans were essential to any final settlement inevitably meant that unionists would have to pay a price for these victories. On devolution itself there was little attempt to defend the original UUP position of administrative devolution, with committee chairs allocated by the d'Hondt rule – a mathematical device usually used for the allocation of seats in legislatures under the additional-member system of proportional representation. The SDLP demand was for a power-sharing cabinet. Republicans still ideologically opposed to devolution had made no contribution to the negotiations in this area while of course demanding 'inclusion' in whatever structures eventuated. The result was described by Robin Wilson: 'Rather like the camel that emerged from a committee designing a horse, a power-sharing executive with positions distributed by d'Hondt was the outcome.'[81]

The lacuna in the Agreement that was to cause Trimble and his party so much subsequent grief was the failure to make Sinn Féin's participation in the Executive dependent on prior action by the IRA in decommissioning its weapons. It was on this issue that Trimble faced a rebellion from members of the UUP's talks team on the final afternoon of the negotiations. Faced by Blair's insistence that the Agreement could not be altered and after a phone-call from Clinton, Trimble extracted a letter of reassurance from Blair. The letter expressed sympathy with the UUP's concerns and promised that if within six months the Agreement proved unsatisfactory in dealing with this issue, the British government would support changes to the Agreement.[82] But, as Frank Millar notes, 'Most people at the time thought, and still think, that the letter was no more than a last-minute attempt to cover Trimble's embarrassment and was otherwise of no value or significance.'[83] It did prove sufficient to win over most of the doubters as the talks neared their conclusion, with the important exception of Jeffrey Donaldson, Molyneaux's successor as MP for Lagan Valley. Ambiguity on the issue of decommissioning was part of the price that unionists had to pay to allow republicanism a soft landing, given that, as one of their leading strategists admitted, the Agreement had legitimized the British state in Ireland.[84] Another last-minute concession to republican unhappiness with the North–South and constitutional dimensions of the deal was the reduction of the period – from three years to two – before which prisoners belonging to para-military groups on ceasefire would be released. This, and what Sinn Féin referred to as the 'Equality Agenda' – involving human rights legislation and safeguards, commissions on policing and criminal justice, and a British commitment to demilitarization – were to act as consolation for what a considerable number of republicans considered an Agreement that enshrined the 'unionist veto'.

These were the issues that dominated the intra-unionist debate on the Agreement in the period leading up to the two referenda on 20 May through which the northern and southern electorates were to express a judgement on what had been agreed on Good Friday. It soon became clear that while nationalists and republicans overwhelmingly supported the deal, unionists were split. At first roughly half were in favour, a quarter against and a quarter undecided. In the weeks leading up to the referendum in Northern Ireland attention focused not on the constitutional aspects of the deal and Trimble's success on domesticating the North–South institutions but on the more emotive issues of early prisoner releases, the presence of 'terrorists' in government, and the supposed threat to the future of the RUC. Unionist rejectionists benefited from the spectacle of the triumphal reception given at a special Sinn Féin Ard-Fheis to recently released IRA men who had been involved in bombings and kidnappings in London in the 1970s. The choreography of this event was staged to give the imprimatur of those who suffered two decades of imprisonment for the 'struggle' to a radically revisionist republican strategy. But it produced a wave of repulsion in the unionist community and threatened major damage to the pro-Agreement cause.

That just over a half of unionists did vote 'yes' in the referendum was in large part the product of frequent trips to the North during the last two weeks of the campaign by Blair, who gave numerous reassurances, particularly on the issue of decommissioning. He was backed up by a cavalcade of British political leaders and international figures, including Nelson Mandela. A strong sense of the 'historic' nature of the choice on offer was also encouraged by the unprecedented attention of the international media and by a heavily funded 'yes' campaign that could rely on the support of Saatchi & Saatchi and even teamed up the staid, besuited and middle-aged figures of Trimble and Hume with the Irish band U2 and the northern group Ash at a rock concert in Belfast in the final days of the campaign.

The result was the mobilization of the Protestant 'comfortable classes' in an unprecedented fashion. Turnout at 81 per cent (in the Republic it was a mere 56 per cent) was the highest ever in Northern Ireland: 160,000 more than had voted in the last Westminster election.[85] This surge was disproportionately drawn from the majority unionist areas east of the Bann, where turnout was traditionally the lowest in the North. Thus, although the 71 per cent 'yes' vote gave the Agreement a strong boost, its basis in the unionist community was shaky. As a leading member of the DUP put it of those who had broken a habit of a lifetime: 'They came out to vote for what they saw as peace and now they will return to political hibernation for another 30 years. But those who voted "No" are not so apathetic.'[86]

The DUP man's prediction appeared vindicated at the election for the new Northern Ireland Assembly on 25 June. Many of those unionists who had voted 'yes' in May now stayed at home, and Trimble's party turned in its worst-ever performance, taking 21.3 per cent of the first-preference vote to the DUP's 18 per cent. Although pro-Agreement parties won 73 per cent of the vote and eighty of the Assembly's 108 seats, there was no disguising the precarious nature of unionist support in the Assembly, where pro-Agreement unionists held thirty seats while the 'antis' had twenty-eight. Nationalist and republican concern with the supposed danger of a unionist majority abusing its position had led to mechanisms for cross-community validation on key decisions that required, at minimum, the support of 40 per cent of each communal bloc. This was now an ever-present threat to pro-Agreement unionism.

Movement on the arms issue by the IRA would have given a substantial boost to Trimble's position in his party and in the wider unionist community. Such movement seemed possible, as Sinn Féin's political successes were seen as giving Adams increased leverage with the IRA. The Assembly elections had been a major victory for Adams's pan-nationalist strategy. The SDLP topped the poll with 22 per cent, and the aggregate vote of the nationalist–republican bloc was at its highest ever, with a Sinn Féin vote of 17.7 per cent. The peace process had put Adams and Martin McGuinness at the centre of national and international attention. Received respectfully in Downing Street, Leinster House and the White House, they were listened to deferentially when they continued to complain of being marginalized. They had before them the heady vision of being the first transnational party in the European Union with seats in the Dáil, Stormont and Westminster and the possibility of being in government in both Belfast and Dublin.

If the massive political benefits of flexibility, compromise and real-politik were obvious, the dire futility of a return to the armed struggle was made abysmally clear on 15 August in Omagh when twenty-eight people were murdered in a Real IRA car-bomb attack. This was the largest loss of life in Northern Ireland during the 'Troubles'. In the words of one former IRA hunger striker, Omagh was 'the end of an era for a certain school of republican thought. What little sympathy was remaining for the physical force element evaporated on that dreadful Saturday afternoon.'[87] The Omagh atrocity offered the leadership of the republican movement the best possible conditions to address the arms issue. However, nothing was done for another year and a half, by which time Trimble's position was substantially weaker within his party and the electorate.

In part this reflected Adams's long-standing caution in edging the movement in a more flexible and political direction while doing his utmost to prevent a split. It was also the case that the substantively partitionist nature of the deal that republicans had accepted made action on arms more difficult: giving ground on political fundamentals made even a gesture on arms more difficult to sell within the IRA. There was also a major obstacle in the strong element of solipsistic self-righteousness so strongly developed in the republican mentality. Republican violence was from this perspective a legitimate response to state and loyalist violence. This was despite the fact that of the 3,633 violent deaths during the 'Troubles', republicans were responsible for 2,139, or 58.8 per cent of the total. In comparison the reviled RUC, the disbandment of which Sinn Féin put near the top of its post-Agreement demands, was responsible for fifty-two deaths.[88] Only a tiny element of the most sophisticated in the leadership would even hint at the possibility that the armed struggle had made an independent and powerful contribution to making Northern Ireland in 1998 more polarized, more segregated and more embittered than it was thirty years before. From this perspective the ceasefire was the fundamental concession made by the IRA, and pressure for it to move on decommissioning was an attempt to 'humiliate' an 'undefeated army'.

Adams had recognized that most unionists 'quite rightly' would not feel any gratitude towards the IRA. He gave his own version of unionist thinking on the issue: 'We are not thanking these people for stopping what they should never have done in the first place.' Yet he did expect an understanding from unionists that any action on weapons would wait until all the aspects of the Agreement had been implemented, particularly the provision for an international commission on policing. Until then the IRA would remain 'on the sidelines'.[89] It did not take a particularly negative cast of mind for many in the unionist community to interpret this as 'the politics of threat'.

From June 1998 to December 1999 Trimble maintained a position of refusing to form an administration that included Sinn Féin until the weapons issue was seriously addressed. A tactically ingenious 'sequencing' proposition was put forward by the two governments at Hillsborough in April 1999, by which a 'shadow executive' would be formed, and within a month, during a 'collective act of reconciliation', some arms would 'be put beyond use on a voluntary basis' and powers devolved to the Executive. Martin McGuinness rejected the proposals as an ultimatum imposed by the British military establishment and Trimble.[90] With republicans talking of the danger of a split, the UUP came under intense pressure to make a 'leap of faith' on the basis of 10 Downing Street's belief that there had been a 'seismic shift' in the republican position. Blair, buoyed up by his central role in the Kosovo conflict and keen to announce an Ulster deal to coincide with the inauguration of the Welsh and Scottish Assemblies, set a deadline of 30 June. If Trimble had felt any inclination to oblige a Prime Minister with whom he had an extremely good personal relationship, this was undermined by another bad election performance. In the European elections in June the Ulster Unionist candidate got 17.6 per cent of the vote, the party's lowest-ever share, and it narrowly avoided an ignominious fourth place behind Sinn Féin.[91]

Trimble's rejection of the two governments' new attempt at sequencing in July led to a reinvolvement of George Mitchell in a review of the Agreement that started in the autumn. Despite a recrudescence of IRA punishment beatings and killings during the summer, Mitchell achieved a breakthrough: an agreement by Trimble to recommend to his party that, in return for a commitment by republicans to address the decommissioning issue by the end of January 2000, an Executive could be formed. However, the souring of the atmosphere as a result of the publication of the Patten Report on policing in September made Trimble's offer conditional. The international commission headed by the ex-Tory politician and former Governor of Hong Kong produced a report that, while it did not recommend the disbanding of the force, as republicans demanded, put forward proposals for radical restructuring that most controversially proposed a change of name and insisted that the force's symbols should not reflect those of the British and Irish states. The report produced fierce denunciations from all shades of unionism.

Believing that he might not win a majority in the Ulster Unionist Council for his proposal to form a government that included Sinn Féin, Trimble promised to recall the Council in February to report on what progress there had been on weapons and deposited a post-dated letter of resignation as leader of the party with its President. Adams now claimed that Trimble had added a new precondition to what had been agreed in the talks chaired by George Mitchell. The result was that, while in January 2000 Northern Ireland had its first government since 1974, it lacked even the rudiments of a common understanding on what was a central issue – after all, under the Agreement the decommissioning of paramilitary weapons was supposed to be completed by May 2000. This experience of devolved government lasted less than two months. While unionists had to get used to republicans running the departments of Health and Education (one of them, Martin McGuinness, popularly believed to have been a member of the IRA's Army Council until very recently), republicans appeared to have calculated that once the institutions of government were functioning, unionists would be reluctant to bring them down.

However, with the support of a more unionist-friendly Secretary of State, Peter Mandelson, who had replaced Mowlam in October 1999, Trimble did not hesitate to use his threat of resignation to force Mandelson to suspend the institutions in February. This hard-nosed approach outraged nationalists, who claimed that Mandelson's assertion of British sovereignty over Northern Ireland violated the spirit of the Agreement. But it steadied nerves in his own party and forced republicans to move on arms. On 6 May an IRA statement committed it to putting its arms 'completely and verifiably beyond use' in a manner that would be acceptable to the International Commission on Decommissioning, headed by the Canadian General John de Chastelain. The return of devolution on 27 May 2000 took place after Trimble had got the support of 53 per cent of the 800 or so delegates to the Ulster Unionist Council, the party's ruling body. His margin of support in the Council had narrowed substantially from the 72 per cent who had voted in favour of the Good Friday Agreement in April 1998. However, neither nationalists nor republicans appeared to have much concern about this attenuation of pro-Agreement unionism. After two IRA arms dumps were independently inspected by a leading member of the ANC and a senior Finnish politician in June, there was little more of substance for General de Chastelain to report. Meanwhile, Sinn Féin and the SDLP criticized the British government for allegedly eviscerating the Patten Report, while Trimble used his powers as First Minister to ban Sinn Féin ministers from attending meetings of the North–South ministerial council and the implementation bodies.

With a senior republican claiming that Trimble's action and the failure of the British government to deliver on Patten and 'demilitarization' (the closing down of British Army installations in strategic border areas such as south Armagh was particularly emphasized) were threatening the peace process,[92] 2001 began gloomily for pro-Agreement Ulster Unionists. The IRA had formally disengaged from contacts with the international decommissioning body, and the UUP's continued involvement in government with Sinn Féin was a source of increasing intra-party conflict, as activists faced a general election with a high probability of losses to the DUP. Reacting to this pressure, Trimble lodged a letter with the Speaker of the Northern Ireland Assembly on 23 May, resigning as First Minister with effect from 1 July 2001 if by then the IRA had not begun to decommission. Despite this action, the UUP lost three seats in the general election while the DUP gained two. Without it, it is possible that the UUP would have lost two more seats: Trimble's own in Upper Bann, where he was hard-pressed by a fairly unknown DUP candidate, and East Antrim. The overall result – UUP, 26.8 per cent and six seats; DUP, 22.5 per cent and five seats; Sinn Féin, 21.7 per cent and four seats; SDLP, 21 per cent and three seats – was interpreted by many commentators as a triumph for the extremes.[93]

This was an oversimplification. Such a judgement was based on a comparison with the 1997 election, thus ignoring the radical effects of the Belfast Agreement on the political environment in Northern Ireland, particularly its destabilizing influence on unionism. A better comparison is with the 1998 Assembly elections, and here the picture for pro-Agreement unionism was not quite so bleak. The UUP vote increased from 21.3 to 26.8 per cent; the DUP's victories were also accompanied by a shift in its discourse towards a more subtle and less hysterical critique of the Agreement. This was most ably accomplished by its victor in North Belfast, Nigel Dodds, who focused not on the influence of Dublin or the Vatican but on the unbalanced nature of the workings of the Agreement, which, he alleged, was hollowing out the 'Britishness' of the North. This took up emotionally powerful issues such as the 'destruction of the RUC' and Sinn Féin ministers' refusal to allow the Union flag to fly over their buildings.

If decommissioning had begun it might have been easier to deal with these criticisms, particularly as the DUP was heavily involved in the institutions of the Agreement: sitting on Assembly committees with republicans and participating in the Executive, although refusing to sit around the cabinet table with 'Sinn Féin–IRA' ministers. The election result, which saw Sinn Féin out-poll the SDLP for the first time, demonstrated the gains from the 'peace strategy'. Yet senior republican figures were still telling the rank and file that there would be no decommissioning.[94] Attempts to justify republicans' refusal to move on arms pointed to an ongoing campaign of pipe-bomb attacks on Catholic homes by elements of the UDA and the challenge of republican dissidents. These justifications were shown to be less than convincing when, in October 2001, the IRA began to decommission, regardless of the continuation of sectarian attacks and the scorn of fundamentalists who claimed the Provos had finally surrendered. That the weapons issue was at last addressed was a product of events in Colombia and New York that put irresistible pressure on the leadership of Sinn Féin.

Despite Irish fears that the new US President, George Bush, would adopt a more distant approach to Northern Ireland, US strategic concerns ensured an engagement that, for the first time since 1994, republicans would find unwelcome. The arrest of three Irish republicans in Bogotá on 6 August 2001 and the claim of the Colombian authorities that they had been training FARC guerrillas was acutely embarrassing for Adams, who was unable to give a satisfactory explanation to either the Bush administration or those wealthy Irish-Americans who had raised millions of dollars for the party in the 1990s. The events of 11 September put irresistible pressure on Adams to demonstrate, beyond contradiction, that republicans were not part of the 'international terrorist network'. Irrespective of the instinctive anti-imperialism of many republicans, Adams moved quickly to accommodate the White House and corporate Irish-America and on 26 October the IRA announced that it had begun the process of decommissioning.[95]

The IRA's action enabled Trimble to contemplate returning to government with Sinn Féin. However, under the terms of the Agreement he needed to be re-elected First Minister with the support of at least 50 per cent of the members of the Assembly who had designated themselves unionist. He failed on the first attempt because of the defection of two UUP Assembly members. Four days later, in a manoeuvre he admitted was 'tacky', he returned to office – courtesy of three members of the Alliance Party and of one from the Women's Coalition who had redesignated themselves as 'unionist' for that purpose.[96] Trimble might assert that 'I'm not a Faulkner, lacking legitimacy',[97] but his loss of a unionist majority in the Assembly was an important symbolic blow, one that was accompanied by increasing evidence of political disaffection in the broader unionist community.

Protestant 'alienation' became a central theme in the speeches of NIO ministers and had a particularly ugly manifestation in the blockade of a Catholic primary school in North Belfast, which began in the autumn of 2001, where declining working-class Protestant communities in areas such as Ardoyne and Tiger Bay felt themselves losing out in a zero-sum territorial conflict with Catholics. A much broader section of the unionist community found it difficult to accept a republican presence in government, even with increasing signs that there was little chance of the Provos going back to war. This did not stem simply, as some commentators claimed, from an unwillingness to accept equality with Catholics. Rather, it rested on a perception that the new dispensation was based on the steady dilution of the North's Britishness as reflected in changes in the name and symbols of the RUC and disputes over the flying of the Union flag on public buildings.

The end of unionist hegemony within the northern state and the associated rise in nationalist and republican self-confidence both contributed to a prevalence of what Steve Bruce has called the 'dismal vision' in the Unionist community:[98] a vision of inexorable decline in terms of demography and economic clout. Yet, looked at from the perspective of the period covered in this book, this seems an overly black picture. The massive economic and social changes that had transformed the Republic since the 1960s have consolidated a twenty-six-county-state patriotism that prioritizes stability over unity. The end of the IRA's armed struggle and the acceptance by Irish nationalists of the 'consent' principle contributed powerfully to the stabilization of the northern state.

However, the Good Friday Agreement was an elite-brokered settlement that balanced precariously on deep reserves of communal distrust and antagonism. This was particularly so in the Protestant community, where Trimble and pro-Agreement unionists found it increasingly difficult to counter a growing mood of sour cynicism about post-Agreement Northern Ireland. Trimble's upbeat portrayal of the constitutional and material gains since 1998 had a solid basis in reality. He had relied on the argument that the Agreement was a partitionist settlement in which the consent principle had been enshrined. Unionists did appear to be more confident about their constitutional future. According to the *Northern Ireland Life and Times Survey*, the percentage of Protestants who believed that there would be a united Ireland in the next twenty years had fallen from 42 per cent in 1998 to 32 per cent in 2003. This may have been influenced by the results of the 2001 Census, which, despite the increasingly triumphalist predictions of Sinn Féin, were distinctly anti-climactic. Although the Protestant share of the population had fallen from 58 per cent in 1991 to 53 per cent, the Catholic share had risen by only 2 per cent to just under 44 per cent. Trimble's main internal critic, Jeffrey Donaldson, commented that 'A united Ireland is not even a remote possibility and it's time for republicans to accept that.'[99] Similarly, DUP propaganda increasingly focused not on creeping reunification but rather on the claim that the Agreement had institutionalized a nationalist agenda and on its supposed marginalization of Protestant and unionist values and culture.

That this message found a ready audience was also clear from the

Northern Ireland Life and Times Survey, which showed a steep decline in
the belief that the Agreement benefited unionists and nationalists equally:
from 41 per cent of Protestants in 1998 to 19 per cent in 2002. At the
same time the view amongst Protestants that nationalists benefited a lot
more than unionists rose from 31 per cent in 1998 to 55 per cent in
2002.[100] This growing alienation was in part a response to specific policies, particularly those to do with the early release of prisoners and
policing. But it also related to the broader conception underlying the
Agreement that institutions and public policies should reflect 'parity of
esteem' for nationalist and unionist identities and allegiances. Decades of
provincial self-government and thirty years of violence had accentuated
a defensive 'little Ulster' mentality that found it extremely difficult to
differentiate between the institutional recognition of Irish national identity and de facto joint authority. The problem was intensified because it
was increasingly Sinn Féin that dominated the tone and idiom of northern
nationalism. Many unionists were only too ready to take republicans at
their word when they depicted their goal of participating in the governance of Northern Ireland as a mere stage in the inevitable transition
to a united Ireland.

Trimble's ability to counteract popular unionist disaffection was weakened by the IRA's reluctance to move beyond its initial acts of
decommissioning and the continuing evidence that, although it was no
longer actively targeting the security forces, it was still a functioning
paramilitary organization involved in punishment attacks, intelligence
gathering and criminality. A raid on the headquarters of Special Branch
in Castlereagh in March 2002 was suspected by the security forces to
be an IRA operation. By June, Blair was privately wondering, 'Are the
Provisionals in transition or are they messing us about?'[101] On 4 October
of that year the Police Service of Northern Ireland carried out a very
public raid on the offices of Sinn Féin at the Parliament Buildings, as
part of an ongoing investigation into an alleged republican spy-ring at
the heart of government. Sinn Féin's chief administrator at Stormont,
Denis Donaldson, was arrested, and John Reid, the Secretary of State
for Northern Ireland, had little choice but to suspend the devolved
institutions.[102]

The depth of the crisis produced a major intervention by Blair in a
speech given at the Harbour Commissioners' Offices in Belfast on 17
October 2002. He praised Gerry Adams and Martin McGuinness: 'I
think they have taken huge risks in order to bury the past.' However,
at the core of his speech was the argument that the republican delay

on complete decommissioning was, by far, the greatest threat to the Agreement:

But the crunch is the crunch. There is no parallel track left. The fork in the road has finally come . . . we cannot carry on with the IRA half in, half out of the process. Not just because it isn't right any more. It won't work any more.

The threat of violence, no matter how damped down, is no longer re-inforcing the political, it is actually destroying it. In fact, the continuing existence of the IRA as an active paramilitary organisation is now the best card those whom republicans call 'rejectionist' unionists have in their hand. It totally justifies their refusal to share power.[103]

The speech demanded the explicit end of all paramilitary activity by the provisionals, a firm commitment and a date for complete decommissioning. But though the next twelve months would show that words and actions could be extracted from republicans, they were, as Paul Bew has said, 'the typical product of the grinding, inch-by-inch approach that had worn away at the legitimacy of the Agreement in the eyes of many and which Mr Blair explicitly disavowed at the Harbour Commissioners'.[104]

For Blair there were limits to the pressures that could be placed on republicans. He did not share the common unionist view that the al-Qaida attacks of 11 September 2001 had transformed the international environment to such an extent that it would be impossible for the IRA to return to armed struggle and that there was therefore no reason to be patient with republicans. The full story of Blair's relationship with the republican movement must await the opening of the official archives, but a preliminary evaluation is possible. One factor in Blair's approach was the importance of the peace process and the Agreement to his own view of the major accomplishments of his premiership. He claimed, with justification, in the Harbour Commissioners' speech that he had spent more time on Northern Ireland than any prime minister since 1922. The end of the IRA and the restoration of an 'inclusive' government at Stormont would rank as substantial achievements. For Blair, Adams and McGuinness had proved themselves essential to accomplishing these goals.

The information that the British security services were able to provide about the balance of forces within the republican movement was a second crucial factor. The role of what republicans dubbed 'securocrats' is inevitably one where speculation, rumour and conspiracy theory are rife. It is clear, however, that state intelligence agencies penetrated the movement at various levels. In 2003 it was revealed that Freddie Scappaticci, a leading figure in the IRA's internal security department, was 'Stakeknife', a British agent since 1978. Even more embarrassing for the republican leadership was the revelation, three years after the PSNI raid on Stormont, that Denis Donaldson, a former comrade of Bobby Sands and a key Sinn Féin apparatchik, had been a British agent for two decades. The outing of Donaldson, whose murder in April 2006 the IRA denied, led republican critics of Adams and McGuinness to allege that the whole peace process had been corrupted by British involvement from the beginning.[105]

The reality is probably more subtle. The security services provided the intelligence that allowed the police and the military to bear down on the IRA's capacity to continue with any sort of effective campaign. In doing so, they reinforced the position of the more strategically minded in the republican leadership, who had themselves become convinced that the military campaign was stalemated and a major obstacle to the political advance of Sinn Féin. The continuing existence of the IRA, albeit in a relatively passive post-ceasefire mode, was useful as a form of leverage on Blair, who feared not a full-scale return to violence but rather some one-off 'spectacular' to register republican displeasure at setbacks in the process of change in Northern Ireland.

Blair was well aware of the difficulties facing Adams and McGuinness in managing the liquidation of the IRA. However, he was also conscious that the resultant protraction of the process was deeply damaging to Trimble's position within the unionist community. It was because of this that he postponed the Assembly elections, due in May 2003, first for a month and then indefinitely. The two governments published a *Joint Declaration* setting out the steps to be taken by them in anticipation of an acceptable IRA statement. Paragraph 13 stated: 'We need to see an immediate, full and permanent cessation of all paramilitary activity, including military attacks, training, intelligence gathering, acquisition of arms, punishment beatings and attacks and involvement in riot.'[106]

While Trimble was prepared to work within the broad framework set out in the *Declaration*, critics like Jeffrey Donaldson and the MP for South Antrim, David Burnside, claimed that it delivered further concessions to republicans. Their opposition led to the twelfth meeting of the Ulster Unionist Council since the Agreement. Donaldson's resolution to reject the *Joint Declaration* was lost by 54 per cent to 46 per cent, and he, Burnside and the Reverend Martin Smyth resigned the UUP whip at Westminster.

Trimble's response to the persistence of deep division in the party was a final major attempt to negotiate a comprehensive deal with the republican leadership in the autumn of 2003. He had been encouraged by successful joint efforts by UUP and Sinn Féin representatives to prevent violent outbreaks during the summer's marching season. So impressed was he by republican efforts that he shook hands with Gerry Adams for the first time. The handshake took place in private in September 2003 at the start of unprecedentedly intense negotiations between Sinn Féin and the UUP,[107] which aimed to reach agreement on a form of sequencing through which IRA actions on weapons and a statement on future intentions would be followed by commitments by the two governments and Trimble. These would involve a decision to hold the postponed Assembly elections, agreement to devolve policing and justice powers within six months, and a unionist commitment to work and maintain the devolved institutions. Although Trimble and his colleagues had made it plain to republicans that there was a need for transparency and visibility in the decommissioning process, the IRA refused to contemplate a 'Spielberg' whereby the acts of decommissioning would be filmed or photographed. Trimble therefore was reduced to relying on a clear declaration from republicans that the IRA was going out of business, plus a detailed statement from General John de Chastelain, the head of the Independent International Decommissioning body.

The two Prime Ministers had planned to come to Hillsborough to announce a deal on 21 October. But Blair rashly anticipated success by announcing that there would be Assembly elections in November, thus depriving himself of his main leverage on Adams. Adams's statement, which the IRA was supposed to endorse subsequently, was an advance on any previous republican formulation, as it implied that the implementation of the Agreement removed any justification for the continuance of the IRA. Blair had demanded that the statement be clear 'in the way any ordinary member of the public can understand', but Adams avoided any reference to the ending of the paramilitary activities of targeting, training and punishment beatings that had been mentioned in the *Joint Declaration*.[108] Trimble's ability to deal with unionist scepticism was now dependent on General de Chastelain revealing that he had witnessed the destruction of a significant amount of IRA weaponry. The IRA, keen to avoid any hint of public humiliation, had insisted that the general's statement contain no inventory of weapons destroyed or any estimate of how much weaponry remained to be dealt with. To the consternation of Trimble, de Chastelain told reporters who asked for a timetable for the decommissioning process that he could not say when the process would finish.[109]

Despite the failure of the negotiations, the UUP performed creditably in the Assembly election held on 26 November. The DUP did emerge as the largest party, with 30 seats and 25.7 per cent of the vote: ten seats up on its performance of 1998. However, most of the DUP gains had been at the expense of the smaller anti-Agreement unionist parties, not the UUP, and Trimble could take some consolation from the fact that the UUP vote was slightly up on its performance in 1998: its vote share was 22.7 and it lost only one seat, coming back with twenty-seven.

Sinn Féin, which had overtaken the SDLP for the first time in the 2001 Westminster election, consolidated their lead, with twenty-four seats and 23.5 per cent of the vote to the SDLP's 17 per cent and eighteen seats.[110] The election was the first that Mark Durkan, the Derry MLA and former assistant to John Hume, had fought as SDLP leader (Hume had retired as leader of the party in September 2001 and announced he would not stand for Westminster again). The party's strategy was incoherent, asking for moderate unionist votes to 'Stop the DUP' while at the same time trying to embellish its nationalist credentials by claiming it would seek a referendum on a United Ireland within the lifetime of the next Assembly. However, its most fundamental problem was the indispensable role that Adams and McGuinness were seen to play in the high politics of the peace process and that no SDLP politician could match.

The election, with its demotion of Trimble and the UUP and the elevation of the DUP, threatened to alter the dynamics of the peace process in unpredictable ways. Within weeks of the election the DUP's position was strengthened by the defection of Jeffrey Donaldson and two other UUP MLAs, which gave Paisley's party thirty-three Assembly seats to the UUP's twenty-three. The implications for the Agreement and the peace process of the DUP's leadership role in unionist politics were viewed with relative equanimity by senior mandarins in Belfast, London and Dublin. Trimble, it was argued, had been too handicapped by a divided party and harassed by the DUP to be able to deliver a sustainable agreement with republicans. When and if Paisley did a deal with Adams, he could not be attacked from the right. The DUP, it was argued, was a more pragmatic party than its more lurid populist Protestant rhetoric might suggest.

Optimistic calculations about the DUP took account of the fact that, while denouncing the Agreement, it had actively participated in all the Northern institutions created by it. Its Assembly members sat on committees with republicans, including committees chaired by members of Sinn Féin. It had taken up the positions in the Executive that it was owed under the d'Hondt rules. Its two ministers did not participate in the meetings of the Executive because of the presence of Sinn Féin ministers but continued to run their respective departments; meanwhile, the party depicted their ministers as 'whistle-blowers – exposing each of Trimble's further concessions to Sinn Féin'.[111] Commentators noted a further public mellowing when they dropped their policy of not sharing a television or radio studio with Sinn Féin members. The problem remained that the DUP had overtaken the UUP precisely by a relentlessly negative campaign, one that depicted the peace process and the Agreement as an exercise in 'appeasement' that was structurally biased against Protestants and the Union. For many DUP activists and supporters, 'Sinn Féin–IRA' was a slouching beast of 'unreconstructed terrorists'. However pragmatic some members of the DUP political class might have become, they would face formidable problems in selling their participation in government with republicans to many of their supporters.

Despite this, Blair was intent on pushing both the DUP and republicans into serious negotiations, and in November the governments gave the parties their proposals for a comprehensive agreement. In the weeks leading up to the arrival of Blair and Ahern in Belfast for what was hoped to be the unveiling of an agreement on 8 December 2004, there were signs that the DUP was prepared to go some distance in accommodating republicans. DUP demands for radical changes in the Agreement were watered down to the provision that all ministers would be voted for as a slate – thereby avoiding the embarrassment for the DUP of its Assembly members having to cast specific votes for republican ministers, as the previous system would have required. For such a fig-leaf the party was prepared to accept the devolution of policing and justice powers within months, with the inevitability of republican control of at least one of these ministries. However, once again, the two Prime Ministers were to be disappointed. The failure of the negotiations was initially blamed by republicans on the DUP demand for photographs of the decommissioning process. Such claims were given some plausibility by a speech of Paisley's to DUP supporters in Ballymena in which he had proclaimed that republicans needed to be publicly humiliated and that the IRA should don 'sackcloth and ashes'. In fact, the photographic documentation of decommissioning was agreed to by both governments with the proviso that the photographs would not be made publicly available until the formation of the Executive in March 2005.

On 20 December, shortly after the breakdown of negotiations, a gang of twenty armed men took over the houses of two officials of the Northern Bank and threatened to kill their families unless they co-operated in removing £26 million from the bank's vaults in the centre of Belfast. On 7 January 2005 the Chief Constable of the PSNI, Hugh Orde, declared that the IRA had been responsible for the biggest bank raid in the history of the UK and Ireland.[112] Sinn Féin was faced with a united front of criticism from London and Dublin as Bertie Ahern contemptuously dismissed Martin McGuinness's attempt to blame the crisis on 'securocrats' in the Northern Ireland Office and Adams's claim that he believed the IRA when it denied involvement in the bank raid.[113] Both Ahern and Michael McDowell, the Republic's Minister for Justice, accused the Sinn Féin leadership of actively misleading them in the December negotiations because of their supposed prior knowledge of the planned robbery. McDowell pointed to the recent hi-jacking of a truck carrying cigarettes worth £1.5 million and the multimillion-pound robbery of a wholesalers in West Belfast – both of which the Garda and the PSNI blamed on the IRA – in his labelling of the IRA as 'a colossal crime machine'.[114]

Republican discomfiture was soon intensified after a dispute in a central Belfast pub on 30 January led to the death of a working-class Catholic from the Short Strand area of East Belfast. Robert McCartney was stabbed to death by a group that included senior members of the IRA in the Markets and Short Strand areas who were returning from the annual Bloody Sunday demonstration in Derry. The murder produced an avalanche of negative media comment on the continuing coercive role of the IRA in working-class Catholic communities. The victim's sisters and partner launched a high-profile campaign to bring his killers to justice in which they were highly critical of Sinn Féin. It was not easy for republicans to label the sisters as working to a 'securocrat' or 'anti-peace process agenda', as they were committed Sinn Féin voters. Internationally the campaign did major damage to the party, ensuring that Adams and McGuinness were excluded from the annual St Patrick's Day jamboree at the White House while the sisters were welcomed by Bush. Domestically, with Westminster and local elections due on 5 May, Adams's ambition to obliterate the SDLP once and for all, something that many commentators had thought likely until the end of 2004, looked increasingly problematic.

As with the first IRA act of decommissioning, which had been brought about by Trimble's success in having Blair agree to the suspension of the institutions, it was a serious threat to Sinn Féin's political ambitions that seemed to be most effective in producing movement from the IRA. On 6 April, as the election campaign opened, Adams made a public appeal to the IRA to abandon violence in favour of politics. In a predictable piece of peace-process theatre, the IRA responded to Adams by promising to give his appeal 'due consideration'.[115] The IRA's 'internal consultation' process would not produce any result before the election, and it was unclear whether it would do much to help Sinn Féin weather the storm created by the Northern Bank and McCartney murder.

Trimble went to the electorate with the less than compelling message that 'Rebuilding a moderate coalition here and refocusing London on what should be done will not be easy.' Paisley, turning his back on the previous December's attempt to do a deal with republicans, provided a traditional Manichaean blast: 'the peace process is in reality a pit of perdition. To enter into government with the terrorists of IRA–Sinn Féin would be treason.'[116] It was only too easy for the DUP to use the bank robbery and the McCartney murder to depict Trimble as the unwitting stooge of an unreconstructed republican movement. Trimble knew better: that they reflected the disreputable side of a movement in transition. He had little doubt that, like many other national liberation movements with which republicans liked to compare themselves, Sinn Féin would end up comfortably ensconced in power, albeit within a partitionist context. But it was the UUP who would pay the price for the protracted nature of the republican movement's move away from militarism. The UUP's vote slumped by 9 per cent to 17.7 per cent, and it lost all but one of its seats. At 33.7 per cent, the DUP's vote was almost double that of the UUP.

The SDLP's performance was the surprise of the election. Widely expected to be reduced to one seat, Eddie McGrady's in South Down, it won three. Although it lost Newry and South Armagh to Sinn Féin, Durkan easily retained Hume's seat in Foyle, while the party also won South Belfast because of a split in the unionist vote. The party had fought a tough campaign that focused on the recent graphic examples of republicans' continued linkages with criminality and violence. It was doubtful, however, that the 'McCartney' effect would sustain the party in the longer term. Sinn Féin's support – 24.3 per cent of the vote and five seats – had continued to grow. Nevertheless the result was a major disappointment for republicans who had confidently expected to win Foyle and reduce the SDLP to a sole MP at Westminster. This would have allowed them to claim with some foundation to be the party that represented the nationalist community in Northern Ireland.

The reverberations of the bank robbery and the McCartney murder were decisive in bringing some sort of closure to the long-drawn-out process of haggling over IRA arms. On 28 July the IRA issued a statement that its Army Council had 'ordered an end to the armed campaign'. All IRA units had been commanded to dump arms and Volunteers instructed to 'assist the development of purely political and democratic programmes through exclusively peaceful means'. The governments' concern about republicans' previous reluctance to fully embrace democracy was reflected in the instruction that 'Volunteers must not engage in any other activities whatsoever.' There was also a commitment to put its arms 'beyond use as quickly as possible'. Unionist sceptics would still be refused any photographic verification and would have to be satisfied with two clerical witnesses, one of them a Protestant.[117] The process culminated in late September, when General de Chastelain and his staff, together with the two clergymen, witnessed the disposal of what the General referred to as 'the totality of the arsenal of the IRA'.[118]

Despite its historic significance the announcement of the decommissioning of IRA weapons received a muted response. In part this reflected unionist suspicion of anything the IRA said or did. The DUP questioned the credentials of the witnesses: one was Father Alec Reid, a long-time confidant of Gerry Adams, and the other a liberal Methodist. Others, while accepting that the IRA had rid itself of much of its arsenal, argued that it was far from going out of business. Sceptics could point to the reports of the body set up by the two governments in 2004 to monitor the paramilitary ceasefires. The *Fifth Report of the International Monitoring Commission* in May 2005 claimed that the IRA was still recruiting and training new members. It was heavily engaged in organized crime, including the smuggling of fuel and tobacco and sophisticated money laundering. It concluded 'the Provisional IRA remains a highly active organisation.'[119] However, by the end of 2005, there were indications that the organization had become dormant. This reflected the governments' insistence that, despite decommissioning being what Blair had described as a 'step of unparalleled magnitude',[120] unionist confidence in republican intentions would need to be consolidated by further reports from the IMC.

Had the IRA, two years earlier, said and done what it did in July and September 2005, Northern Ireland may well have had a functioning and inclusive government by the end of 2003. In the intervening period Trimble's brand of unionism, which had demonstrated an ability to deal directly and flexibly with republicans, had been displaced by the DUP's more absolutist and populist variety. But it remained possible that, having displaced the moderates, the DUP would end up on very similar political territory to that formerly occupied by Trimble. For the party had moved far from a root-and-branch denunciation of the Agreement. Its demand now was not that it be scrapped but that it be operated in a more balanced manner. The party had been in negotiations with Sinn Féin, although indirectly. Even after the McCartney–Northern Bank storm, it was careful not to rule out entering government with republicans if Sinn Féin could demonstrate a complete break with paramilitarism. This was the pragmatic face that it put forward in negotiations with other parties and governments. The message to its supporters and the broader unionist community was more unreconstructed. It was that a vote for the DUP was a vote to end concessions, for an alternative to the 'push-over unionism of David Trimble'. The DUP had depicted every significant development since 1998 as part of the piecemeal dismantling of the Union. The problem for the party was that, having blamed Trimble's leadership for acquiescing in this process and boasting, as Peter Robinson, deputy leader of the DUP, did, that 'unionism is now under new management', there was little evidence that DUP dominance would produce any major rethink in British policy.

After the IRA's statement the British government announced a dramatic programme of 'demilitarization' that would see the number of British troops reduced to a maximum of 5,000 within two years, together with rapid movement on the closure of security installations along the border. The four 'home' battalions of the Royal Irish Regiment were also to be disbanded. The successor to the UDR, the RIR battalions were 4,000 strong, and the announcement produced a wave of street protests and Protestant paramilitary violence.[121] In early September the rerouting of an Orange march on the Springfield Road led to the most intense period of loyalist violence for well over a decade. Fusillades of shots were fired at the police, roads throughout loyalist areas in Belfast were blocked with burning vehicles, and there was widespread anti-police rioting.

The violence led the new Secretary of State, Peter Hain, to declare that he took unionist concerns seriously.[122] But there was no indication that the main lines of government policy would be more than tweaked at the edges. There was more unionist angst over proposed legislation to provide an amnesty for 'on the runs': IRA members who were outside the UK evading arrest. The government was also considering further police reform plus the official legitimation of restorative justice schemes that republicans had promoted as an alternative to the presence of the police in Catholic working-class areas. While the idea behind such initiatives was to make it possible for Sinn Féin to support the new policing structures, their short-term effect would be to make it unlikely that the DUP would risk going into government with republicans in 2006. Some elements of the DUP and many of those who voted for them preferred the continuation of direct rule to the return of devolution with Martin McGuinness in government. But such a disposition came up against the aversion of the British political class to the prospect of decades more of direct involvement in the running of the province. It also clashed with the strong 'little Ulster' mentality of many unionists, who resented local decisions being made by outsiders. Most fundamentally it ignored the fact that, although the Agreement helped to accommodate the republican movement to partition, it was also associated with the consolidation of a more confident and assertive northern nationalism. In the absence of devolution this would push direct rule towards shared decision-making between London and Dublin, further limiting unionists' involvement in the governance of Northern Ireland.

There are therefore strong negative incentives for the DUP's political class to deal with republicans, apart from the attractions of salaries, status and patronage that the return of devolved government would bring. The amount of agreement reached in December 2004 demonstrated a capacity for pragmatism at the top of the party. However, the powerful components of anti-Catholicism and demonization of republicans in the party's ideology will make the selling of such a deal to grass-roots members and supporters difficult. If it succeeds, the result will not be the 'new Northern Ireland' that Trimble looked forward to in the optimism of 1998.[123] In many ways it will, as some progressive critics of the Agreement claim, institutionalize sectarianism. But underpinning it will be an implicit recognition by the two most obdurate forms of unionism and nationalism that the future of Northern Ireland cannot be settled on their own terms. In that at least the drafters of the Agreement might be able to claim a victory.

Notes

Introduction

1. Eric Hobsbawm, *Age of Extremes: The Short Twentieth Century 1914–1991* (London, 1994), ix.
2. John Peck, *Dublin from Downing Street* (Dublin, 1978), 18.
3. Martin Mansergh, 'Taoiseach Serious in Ruling Out SF Support', *Irish Times*, 26 November 2005.
4. Jonathan Haughton, 'The Dynamics of Economic Change', in William Crotty and David E. Schmidt (eds.), *Ireland and the Politics of Change* (London and New York, 1998), 27.
5. Quoted in Paul Bew, Henry Patterson and Paul Teague, *Between War and Peace: The Political Future of Northern Ireland* (London, 1997), 228.
6. Bernadette Hayes and Ian McAllister, 'Public Support for Political Violence and Paramilitarism in Northern Ireland and the Republic of Ireland', *Terrorism and Political Violence*, 17, 2005.
7. Bew, Patterson and Teague, 90.
8. *Irish Echo Online*, 16–22 November 2005.

1 The Legacy of Partition

1. David Officer, 'In Search of Order, Permanence and Stability: Building Stormont 1921–1932', in Richard English and Graham Walker (eds.), *Unionism in Modern Ireland* (Dublin, 1996), 142.
2. Paul Bew, Peter Gibbon and Henry Patterson, *Northern Ireland 1921–1996: Political Forces and Social Classes* (London, 1996), 28.
3. Paul Bew, *Ideology and the Irish Question: Ulster Unionism and Irish Nationalism 1912–1916* (Oxford, 1994).
4. Enda Staunton, *The Nationalists of Northern Ireland 1918–1973* (Dublin, 2001), 7.
5. Austen Morgan, *Labour and Partition: The Belfast Working Class 1905–1923* (London, 1991), 269.
6. Michael Farrell, *Arming the Protestants* (London, 1983), 168.
7. Graham Ellison and Jim Smyth, *The Crowned Harp: Policing Northern Ireland* (London, 2000), 23.
8. ibid., 23.
9. Memorandum by S. G. Tallents, Colonial Office Papers, PRO, CO 906/24.
10. Paul Bew, 'The Political History of Partition: The Prospects for North–South Cooperation', in A. F. Heath, R. Breen and C. T. Whelan (eds.), *Ireland North and South: Perspectives from Social Science* (Oxford, 1999), 408–9.
11. Bew, Gibbon and Patterson, 241–2.

12. J. J. Lee, *Ireland 1912–1985: Politics and Society* (Cambridge, 1989), 238.

13. Tallents's memorandum, CO 906/30.

14. Michael Farrell, *Northern Ireland: The Orange State* (London, 1976), 84.

15. Letter from Adrian Robinson to F. M. Adams, Press and Publicity Officer, Stormont Castle, 21 November 1944, PRONI, HA/32/1/649.

16. Dominions Office comment on Home Office views, 18 November 1938, PRO, DO 35/893/XII/251.

17. Bew, Gibbon and Patterson, 49.

18. ibid., 57.

19. Quoted in Patrick Buckland, 'The Unity of Ulster Unionism', *History*, 60 (1975).

20. W. A. Maguire, *Belfast* (Keele, 1993), 136.

21. Henry Patterson, *Class Conflict and Sectarianism: The Protestant Working Class and the Belfast Labour Movement 1868–1920* (Belfast, 1980), 20–23.

22. D. S. Johnson, 'The Northern Ireland Economy 1914–1939', in Liam Kennedy and Philip Ollerenshaw (eds.), *An Economic and Social History of Ulster 1820–1939* (Manchester, 1985), 192.

23. ibid., 199.

24. David Fitzpatrick, *The Two Irelands 1912–1939* (Oxford, 1998), 208, and Johnson, 190–91.

25. Fitzpatrick, 178.

26. Bew, Gibbon and Patterson, 69.

27. Christopher Norton, 'Creating Jobs, Manufacturing Unity: Ulster Unionism and Mass Unemployment 1922–1934', *Contemporary British History*, 15, Summer 2001, 9–10.

28. Graham Walker, 'Protestantism before Party: The Ulster Protestant League in the 1930s', *Historical Journal*, 28, 1985, 961.

29. Brian Barton, *Brookeborough: The Making of a Prime Minister* (Belfast, 1988), 84.

30. ibid., 85–7.

31. Thomas Hennessey, *A History of Northern Ireland 1920–1996* (Dublin, 1997), 63.

32. Bew, Gibbon and Patterson, 58.

33. Dennis Kennedy, *The Widening Gulf: Northern Attitudes to the Independent Irish State 1919–1949* (Belfast, 1988), 143.

34. Oliver P. Rafferty, *Catholicism in Ulster 1603–1983* (Dublin, 1994), 230.

35. Sean T. O'Kelly, Vice-President of the government, declared in March 1932: 'We will make every effort to establish a republic of 32 counties. This is our aim and if the gun is necessary, the people have the government to direct the army and they have the volunteer force behind them.' Kennedy, 199.

36. Bew, Gibbon and Patterson, 70.

37. 'The Impact of Ethnic Violence: The Belfast Riots of 1935', in A. C. Hepburn, *A Past Apart: Studies in the History of Catholic Belfast 1850–1950* (Belfast, 1996), 183.

38. John M. Regan, *The Irish Counter-Revolution 1921–1936* (Dublin, 1999), 378.

39. ibid., 377.

40. ibid., 374.

41. Paul Bew, Ellen Hazelkorn and Henry Patterson, *The Dynamics of Irish Politics* (London, 1989), 26.

42. Dermot Keogh, 'The Role of the Catholic Church in the Republic of Ireland', in *Building Trust in Ireland: Studies Commissioned by the Forum for Peace and Reconciliation* (Belfast, 1996), 103.
43. Peter Hart, *The IRA and Its Enemies* (Oxford, 1998), 286.
44. Regan, 254.
45. ibid., 137.
46. Nicholas Mansergh, *The Unresolved Question: The Anglo-Irish Settlement and Its Undoing 1912–1972* (New Haven and London, 1991), 136.
47. ibid., 237.
48. Peter Mair, *The Changing Irish Party System* (London, 1987), 20.
49. Richard Dunphy, *The Making of Fianna Fáil Power in Ireland 1923–1948* (Oxford, 1995), 83.
50. Bew, Hazelkorn and Patterson, 33.
51. Mair, 17.
52. Dunphy, 82.
53. ibid., 79.
54. K. A. Kennedy, T. Giblin and D. McHugh, *The Economic Development of Ireland in the Twentieth Century* (London, 1988), 45.
55. Enda Delaney, 'State, Politics and Demography: The Case of Irish Emigration 1921–1971', *Irish Political Studies*, 13, 1998, 30.
56. Bew, Hazelkorn and Patterson, 75.
57. Dunphy, 178–9, and Lee, 193. James Craig was created Viscount Craigavon of Stormont in 1927.
58. Lee, 193.
59. Between 1933 and 1939 the number of Irish industrial concerns quoted on the Dublin stock exchange trebled and their aggregate capital doubled: Cormac Ó Gráda, *A Rocky Road: The Irish Economy since the 1920s* (Manchester, 1997), 109.
60. Emmet O'Connor, *A Labour History of Ireland* (Dublin, 1992), 130.
61. ibid., 130.
62. Delaney, 30.
63. In 1935–7, some 75,150 emigrated to the UK: Dunphy, 163.
64. James Meenan, *The Irish Economy since 1922* (Liverpool, 1970), 41.
65. Arthur Mitchell, *Labour in Irish Politics 1890–1930* (Dublin, 1974), 246.
66. ibid., 258.
67. Mair, 20.
68. Enda McKay, 'Changing the Tide: The Irish Labour Party 1927–1933', *Saothar Journal of the Irish Labour History Society*, 11, 1986.
69. Mansergh, 304, and Paul Canning, *British Policy towards Ireland 1921–1941* (Oxford, 1985).
70. Canning, 201–2.
71. ibid., 233–5.
72. Dermot Keogh, *Twentieth-century Ireland: Nation and State* (Dublin, 1994), 104.
73. Lee, 215–16.
74. Paul Bew, Peter Gibbon and Henry Patterson, *Northern Ireland 1921–2001: Political Forces and Social Classes* (London, 2002), 66.

2 War and the Welfare State

1. Brendan Lynn, *Holding the Ground: The Nationalist Party in Northern Ireland 1945–72* (Aldershot, 1997), 4.

2. Oliver P. Rafferty, *Catholicism in Ulster 1603–1983: An Interpretative History* (Dublin, 1994), 223.

3. Michael Farrell, *Northern Ireland: The Orange State* (London, 1976), 143.

4. The Prime Minister departed for a family holiday in Scotland in the month of the riots and did not return until September: A. C. Hepburn, *A Past Apart: Studies in the History of Catholic Belfast 1850–1950* (Belfast, 1996), 196.

5. Letter from Cahir Healy to the Secretary of the County Cavan Executive of Fianna Fáil, 28 October 1938, 'An Taoiseach wants the pressure to be from within the Six Counties rather than from without at the moment', PRONI, Cahir Healy Papers, D2991/B/98/1–2.

6. Brian Barton, *Northern Ireland in the Second World War* (Belfast, 1995), 123.

7. *Round Table*, 32, 125, December 1951.

8. Chris Norton, 'The Politics of Exclusion: Nationalism in Northern Ireland' (unpublished paper).

9. Hepburn, 193.

10. *An Phoblacht*, 20 August 1932, and Ronaldo Munck and Bill Rolston, *Belfast in the Thirties: An Oral History* (Belfast, 1987), 184.

11. Neil Jarman and Dominic Bryan, *From Riots to Rights* (Coleraine, 1998), 28.

12. Laura K. Donohue, 'Regulating Northern Ireland: The Special Powers Acts 1922–1972', *Historical Journal*, 41, 4, 1998, 1,094.

13. Jarman and Bryan, 46.

14. Sir Charles Wickham to the Secretary, Ministry of Home Affairs, 3 December 1938, PRONI, Ministry of Home Affairs, HA/32/1/1649.

15. Brian Barton, *Brookeborough: The Making of a Prime Minister* (Belfast, 1988), 129.

16. Barton, *Northern Ireland in the Second World War*, 124.

17. *Irish News*, 5 September 1939.

18. *Irish News*, 17 September 1940.

19. J. J. Lee, *Ireland 1912–1985: Politics and Society* (Cambridge, 1989), 267.

20. *Irish News*, 24 June 1940.

21. Barton, *Northern Ireland in the Second World War*, 120.

22. Rafferty, 242.

23. *Belfast Newsletter*, 20 June 1940.

24. One journalist claimed that in parts of Northern Ireland 'Catholics have joined the army at the rate of anything from eight to fourteen Catholics to one Protestant'; see Gertrude Gaffney's comments in *Orange Terror* by 'Ultach', a reprint from the *Capuchin Annual*, 1943 (Dublin, 1998), 39.

25. *Irish News*, 21 September 1940.

26. J. Bowyer Bell, *The Secret Army: A History of the IRA 1916–1970* (London, 1972), 239.

27. Denis Sampson, *Brian Moore: The Chameleon Novelist* (Dublin, 1998), 47.

28. T. D. Williams, 'A Study in Neutrality' (V), *Leader*, 28 March 1953.

29. Barton, *Northern Ireland in the Second World War*, 200.
30. Graham Walker, *The Politics of Frustration: Harry Midgley and the Failure of Labour in Northern Ireland* (Manchester, 1985), 132.
31. Brian Lacy, *Siege City: The Story of Derry and Londonderry* (Belfast, 1990), 238–43.
32. Barton, *Northern Ireland in the Second World War*, 123.
33. Lacy, 243.
34. Enda Staunton, *The Nationalists of Northern Ireland 1918–1972* (Dublin, 2001), 54.
35. MacEntee's criticisms were in a speech on 15 April 1944 that provoked protests from leading northern nationalists: see correspondence in PRONI, Cahir Healy Papers, D2991/B/23/46.
36. Spender was to end his days as an integrationist: a supporter of Northern Ireland's total political and administrative assimilation into the rest of the UK; see Paul Bew, Kenneth Darwin and Gordon Gillespie, *Passion and Prejudice: Nationalist–Unionist Conflict in Ulster in the 1930s and the Founding of the Irish Association* (Belfast, 1993), x.
37. Bew, Darwin and Gillespie, 50.
38. Farrell, 147.
39. Barton, *Brookeborough*, 269.
40. Barton, *Northern Ireland in the Second World War*, 17.
41. ibid., 18–19.
42. Barton, *Brookeborough*, 159.
43. *Belfast Newsletter*, 19 June 1940.
44. Quoted in Barton, *Northern Ireland in the Second World War*, 116.
45. *Belfast Newsletter*, 29 May 1940.
46. See letter from Dr James Little, MP, *Belfast Newsletter*, 23 June 1940.
47. Barton, *Brookeborough*, 159–62.
48. Thus in his resignation speech Warnock denounced the government as 'pathetic, with the exception of the Minister of Agriculture they had done nothing', *Belfast Newsletter*, 19 June 1940.
49. Bew, Darwin and Gillespie, 40.
50. Barton, *Northern Ireland in the Second World War*, 44.
51. Robert Fisk, *In Time of War: Ireland, Ulster and the Price of Neutrality* (London, 1983), 51.
52. Ian Budge and Cornelius O'Leary, *Belfast: Approach to Crisis* (London, 1973), 194.
53. W. A. Maguire, *Belfast* (Keele, 1993), 147.
54. Walker, 127, and Paul Addison, *The Road to 1945* (London, 1975).
55. Letter from Maynard Sinclair, Brian Maginess and Wilson Hungerford, quoted in John Ditch, *Social Policy in Northern Ireland 1939–1950* (Aldershot, 1988), 68.
56. 'Northern Ireland's Manpower Resources', a report by Harold Wilson, 17 December 1940, PRONI, Ministry of Commerce, COM 61/440.
57. ibid.
58. D. S. Johnson, 'The Northern Ireland Economy 1914–1939', in Liam Kennedy and Philip Ollerenshaw (eds.), *An Economic and Social History of Ulster 1820–1939* (Manchester, 1985), 194.

59. 'The Manpower Position in Northern Ireland', 24 March 1941, PRONI, Ministry of Commerce, COM 61/440.
60. M. Moss and J. R. Hume, *Shipbuilders to the World: 125 Years of Harland and Wolff, Belfast, 1861–1986* (Belfast, 1986), 347.
61. Johnson, 201, and Barton, *Northern Ireland in the Second World War*, 81.
62. Barton, *Northern Ireland in the Second World War*, 189.
63. 'When Peace Breaks Out in Ulster', *Bell*, 5, February 1943.
64. For intellectual life in the North in the period, see Robert Greacen, *The Sash My Father Wore: An Autobiography* (Edinburgh, 1997); John Boyd, *The Middle of My Journey* (Belfast, 1990); and 'Regionalism: The Last Chance', in Tom Clyde (ed.), *Ancestral Voices: The Selected Prose of John Hewitt* (Belfast, 1987).
65. Johnson, 208.
66. Paul Bew, Peter Gibbon and Henry Patterson, *Northern Ireland 1921–1996: Political Forces and Social Classes* (London, 1996), 82.
67. Ditch, 80.
68. Barton, *Brookeborough*, 213.
69. R. R. Bowman to Cabinet Secretary, 6 April 1945, PRONI, Cabinet Secretariat, Cab 9C/22/2.
70. See Malachy Gray, 'A Shop Steward Remembers', *Saothar Journal of the Irish Labour History Society*, 11, 1986.
71. Barton, *Brookeborough*, 186–7.
72. E. H. Cooper, Ministry of Commerce, to H. R. Chapman, Ministry of Aircraft Production, 14 October 1942, in file on 'Labour Disputes', PRONI, Ministry of Commerce, COM 61/655.
73. Mike Milotte, *Communism in Modern Ireland* (Dublin, 1984), 201.
74. *Belfast Newsletter*, 15 October 1942.
75. During a dispute at Short and Harland, Tommie Watters, a Communist Party militant, deplored the strike 'during this critical period for freedom loving people of the world', *Belfast Newsletter*, 19 October 1942.
76. Minutes of Cabinet Committee on Manpower, 6 August 1942, PRONI, Ministry of Commerce, COM 61/266.
77. Minister of Labour to Prime Minister, 5 November 1942, 'Arbitration in Strikes and Industrial Disputes', PRONI, Cabinet Secretariat, Cab 9C/22/1.
78. Emmet O'Connor, *A Labour History of Ireland 1824–1960* (Dublin, 1992), 187.
79. Andrews and the Minister of Labour supported the reduction of fines on strikers at Short and Harland and Harland and Wolff against the advice of Brooke and the Inspector-General of the RUC. See letter from Gransden, Cabinet Secretary, to Montgomery of Home Affairs, 3 April 1942, PRONI, Cabinet Secretariat, Cab 9C/22/1.
80. See file on Labour Disputes in PRONI, Ministry of Commerce, COM 61/655.
81. Barton, *Brookeborough*, 203.
82. Letter from Hugh Douglas to Prime Minister, 27 March 1943: 'the current of abuse against the government from the business and middle class people of the Province'. 'Arbitration in Strikes and Industrial Disputes', PRONI, Cabinet Secretariat, Cab 9C/22/2.

83. W. D. Scott, Regional Controller of Ministry of Supply, Belfast, to E. M. Bowen, Ministry of Supply, London, 31 March 1944, 'Labour Disputes', PRONI, Ministry of Commerce, COM 61/655, and *Belfast Newsletter*, 4 April 1944.

84. Telegram from Brooke to Churchill, 9 March 1944, and Churchill's response, 15 March, on this 'most serious and lamentable strike'. 'Arbitration in Strikes and Industrial Disputes', PRONI, Cabinet Secretariat, Cab 9C/22/2.

85. *Northern Whig*, 7 April 1944.

86. See Lowry's report of a meeting with a deputation from Belfast Trades Council on 24 May 1944, 'Arbitration in Strikes and Industrial Disputes', PRONI, Cabinet Secretariat, Cab 9C/22/2.

87. Letter from J. F. Gordon, Minister of Labour, to Andrews, 15 January 1942, 'Infiltration of Workers from Eire', PRONI, Ministry of Finance, FIN 18/22/37.

88. Conclusions of Cabinet Subcommittee on Infiltration, 5 February 1942. PRONI, Ministry of Finance, FIN 18/22/37.

89. Letter from Dawson Bates to Herbert Morrison, 26 March 1942, PRONI, Ministry of Finance, FIN 18/22/37.

90. 'Infiltration of Eire Workers', PRONI, Cabinet Secretariat, Cab 9C/47/2.

91. Memorandum from Minister of Labour on labour for stone quarries, 18 April 1942, PRONI, Ministry of Finance, FIN 18/22/37.

92. Letter from F. A. Clarke, Ballinamallard, to Sir Basil Brooke, 11 March 1944, and Cabinet Conclusions, 6 April 1944, 'Infiltration of Eire Workers', PRONI, Cabinet Secretariat, Cab 9C/47/2 (3).

93. Figures from memorandum on the Residence in Northern Ireland (Restriction) Order, October 1946, PRONI, Cabinet Secretariat, Cab 9C/47/3.

94. Terry Cradden, *Trade Unionism, Socialism and Partition* (Belfast, 1993), 46. In the 52-seat parliament, the Unionist Party had thirty-three seats and the Nationalists had ten. Sydney Elliott, *Northern Ireland Parliamentary Election Results 1921–1972* (Chichester, 1973), 92.

3 'Minding Our Own Business': Éire during the Emergency

1. Speech to the Dáil, 18 June 1936, 'Notes on the Work of the Irish Section of the Security Services 1939–1945', PRO, KV 4/9 59761.

2. Cornelius O'Leary, *Irish Elections 1918–1977* (Dublin, 1979), 102.

3. T. Ryle Dwyer, *De Valera: The Man and the Myths* (Dublin, 1992), 219.

4. T.D. Williams, 'A Study in Neutrality', *Leader*, 31 January 1953.

5. Speaking on supplementary army estimate in the Dáil, *Irish Times*, 17 February 1939.

6. G. R. Sloan, *The Geopolitics of Anglo-Irish Relations in the Twentieth Century* (Leicester, 1998), 184.

7. Eunan O'Halpin, 'The Army in Independent Ireland', in Tom Bartlett and Keith Jeffery (eds.), *A Military History of Ireland* (Cambridge, 1996), 419.

8. Tony Gray, *The Lost Years: The Emergency in Ireland 1939–1945* (London, 1998), 49.

9. Dermot Keogh, *Twentieth-century Ireland: Nation and State* (Dublin, 1994), 109.

10. Maurice Moynihan (ed.), *Speeches and Statements by Eamon de Valera* (Dublin and New York, 1980), 418, and Gray, 2.

11. O'Halpin, 'The Army in Independent Ireland', 418.

12. Garret FitzGerald, 'Myth of Irish Neutrality Not Borne out by Historical Fact', *Irish Times*, 24 April 1999.

13. O'Halpin, 'The Army in Independent Ireland', 420.

14. 'Notes on the Work of the Irish Section of the Security Services 1939–1945'.

15. J. J. Lee, *Ireland 1912–1985: Politics and Society* (Cambridge, 1989), 234.

16. Sloan, 201.

17. David O'Donoghue, *Hitler's Irish Voices: The Story of German Radio's Wartime Irish Service* (Belfast, 1998), 19.

18. C. S. Andrews, *Man of No Property* (Dublin, 1982), 162.

19. O'Donoghue, 19.

20. Lee, 247.

21. Brendan Barrington (ed.), *The Wartime Broadcasts of Francis Stuart 1942–1944* (Dublin, 2000), 32.

22. Eunan O'Halpin, *Defending Ireland: The Irish State and Its Enemies since 1922* (Oxford, 1999), 239–45.

23. Conor Foley, *Legion of the Rearguard: The IRA and the Modern Irish State* (London, 1992), 191.

24. Lee, 223.

25. ibid.

26. *Round Table*, 119, June 1940.

27. Account of Plant's trial by Military Court, NAD, Department of the Taoiseach, S12682.

28. John Horgan, *Seán Lemass: The Enigmatic Patriot* (Dublin, 1997), 108.

29. 'Notes on the Work of the Irish Section of the Security Services 1939–1945'.

30. *Round Table*, 119, June 1940.

31. Letter from Maurice Moynihan to Patrick Kennedy in the Department of the Taoiseach with enclosures detailing the extent of wartime cooperation with the British government, included as an Appendix in Tim Pat Coogan, *De Valera: Long Fellow, Long Shadow* (London, 1995), 748–9.

32. Coogan, 549.

33. 'Notes on the Work of the Irish Section of the Security Services 1939–1945'.

34. ibid.

35. Sloan, 210.

36. ibid., 227.

37. Geoffrey Roberts, 'Three Narratives of Neutrality: Historians and Ireland's War', in Brian Girvin and Geoffrey Roberts (eds.), *Ireland and the Second World War: Politics, Society and Remembrance* (Dublin, 2000), 167.

38. Coogan, 568.

39. ibid., 173.

40. See for example O'Halpin, *Defending Ireland*, 151.

41. The Irish Association, established in 1938 largely on the initiative of some liberal unionists, published a pamphlet on neutrality, *Ireland and the War*, in 1940, which took up this theme. It is included in Bew, Darwin and Gillespie, *Passion and Prejudice: Nationalist–Unionist Conflict in Ulster in the 1930s and the Founding of the Irish Association* (Belfast, 1993), 84–104.

42. The Earl of Longford and Thomas P. O'Neill, *Eamon de Valera* (Dublin, 1970), 354.

43. Brian Girvin, 'Politics in Wartime: Governing, Neutrality and Elections', in Girvin and Roberts, 27.

44. *Round Table*, 121, December 1940.

45. Maurice Manning, *James Dillon: A Biography* (Dublin, 1999), 172.

46. Robert Fisk, *In Time of War: Ireland, Ulster and the Price of Neutrality* (London, 1983), 160.

47. ibid.

48. ibid., 165.

49. Memorandum signed by James Dillon and T. G. O'Higgins, 14 June 1940, 'Fine Gael and Neutrality', NAD, Department of Justice, S14213.

50. John Bowman, *De Valera and the Ulster Question* (Oxford, 1985), 229.

51. Lee, 248. MacDonald reported that de Valera wanted to know: 'What guarantee . . . did the British have that the Northern Ireland Government would agree, even if they had accepted the plan in principle, to join a United Ireland in practice?' Coogan, 552.

52. Fisk, 186.

53. 'Notes on the Work of the Irish Section of the Security Services 1939–1945'.

54. Longford and O'Neill, 349.

55. Manning, 163.

56. Notes on a conference held in the Taoiseach's room, 16 July 1940, NAD, 'Fine Gael and Neutrality', Department of Justice, S14213.

57. Moynihan, 373.

58. Report of contents of German Foreign Office documents in *Irish Independent*, 3 August 1957.

59. Lee, 247.

60. T. D. Williams, 'A Study in Neutrality', *Leader*, 28 March 1953.

61. *Round Table*, 126, March 1942.

62. Hempel reported to Berlin that de Valera's 'democratic principles' were sympathetic to Britain: German Foreign Office documents reported in the *Irish Times*, 18 October 1958.

63. *Round Table*, 120, September 1940.

64. Arland Ussher, *The Face and Mind of Ireland* (London, 1949), 68.

65. Manning, 160.

66. *Irish Times*, 14 November 1941.

67. Donal Ó Drisceoil, *Censorship in Ireland 1939–1945* (Cork, 1996), 121–5.

68. *Round Table*, 125, December 1941.

69. *Irish Times*, 14 November 1941.

70. Roberts, 176–7.

71. F. S. L. Lyons, *Ireland since the Famine* (London, 1973), 557–8.

72. Brian Fallon, *An Age of Innocence: Irish Culture 1930–1960* (Dublin, 1998), 214.

73. 'One World', *Bell*, 7, 4, January 1944.
74. *Parliamentary Debates: Dáil Éireann* (PDDE), vol. LXXXII, col. 1,118, 2 April 1941.
75. *Bell*, 2, 4, July 1941.
76. ibid.
77. 'Notes on the Work of the Irish Section of the Security Services 1939–1945'.
78. Lee, 224.
79. Richard Dunphy, *The Making of Fianna Fáil Power in Ireland 1923–1948* (Oxford, 1995), 220.
80. Enda Delaney, 'State, Politics and Demography: The Case of Irish Emigration 1921–1971', *Irish Political Studies*, 13, 1998, 33.
81. Ó Drisceoil, 257.
82. Special Branch report of unemployed workers' meeting, 'Unemployed Workers' Organizations', 4 April 1941, NAD, Department of Justice, JUS 8/46.
83. Dunphy, 223.
84. Fallon, 8, and Ó Drisceoil, 100.
85. One example from Garda reports was a Belfast militant who told a meeting of the Dublin unemployed that anti-partitionism would have to engage with economic realities: 'since the unemployed in Northern Ireland were better treated than those in Eire, it made their lot of convincing them to unite with Eire more difficult': Part 1, 21 January 1940, NAD, Department of Justice, S42/39.
86. Dunphy, 180–81.
87. Lee, 216, and Kieran Allen, *Fianna Fáil and Irish Labour: 1926 to the Present* (London, 1997), 77.
88. Allen, 77.
89. Cormac Ó Gráda, *A Rocky Road: The Irish Economy since the 1920s* (Manchester, 1997), 17, and Emmet O'Connor, *A Labour History of Ireland 1824–1960* (Dublin, 1992), 136.
90. Ó Gráda, 16.
91. Lee, 233.
92. Ó Gráda, 6, and Gray, 143.
93. Special Branch report of public meeting held by Dublin Central Branch of the Irish Labour Party, 17 September 1942, where the government was attacked for allowing fuel merchants to charge high prices for turf, NAD, Department of Justice, JUS 8/884.
94. Greta Jones, *'Captain of all these men of death': The History of Tuberculosis in Nineteenth and Twentieth Century Ireland* (Amsterdam and New York, 2001), 188.
95. O'Connor, 140; police report of a meeting of 200 labourers at Foynes, Newcastlewest, 6 March 1941, NAD, Department of Justice, JUS 8/746.
96. Horgan, 121.
97. O'Connor, 133.
98. ibid., 134.
99. Special Branch report of meeting at College Green, 22 June 1941, NAD, Department of Justice, JUS 8/884.

100. Allen, 77.
101. Peter Mair, *The Changing Irish Party System* (London, 1987), 20.
102. O'Leary, 35.
103. Terry Cradden, *Trade Unionism, Socialism and Partition* (Belfast, 1993), 65.
104. John P. Swift, 'The Last Years', in Daniel Nevin (ed.), *James Larkin: Lion of the Fold* (Dublin, 1996), 86.
105. O'Leary, 35.
106. Dunphy, 288.
107. Dunphy, 285, and John de Courcy Ireland, 'As I Remember Big Jim', in Nevin, 454.
108. Horgan, 124.
109. Brian Girvin, 'Politics in Wartime: Governing, Neutrality and Elections', in Girvin and Roberts, 39–41.
110. *Irish Press*, 20 January 1944, in Special Branch report, NAD, Department of Justice, JUS 8/917.
111. Mike Milotte, *Communism in Modern Ireland* (Dublin, 1984), 199.
112. Report on Communists in the Labour Party, 20 April 1944, in papers deposited by John Horgan with the Irish Labour History Museum, Dublin. My thanks to Paddy Gillan for bringing this report to my attention.
113. Allen, 80.
114. Mair, 20.
115. The most reliable estimate is of 72,000 members for the ITUC and 53,000 for the CIU: Cradden, 112.
116. Debate on the Beveridge Plan, 13 December 1942, NAD, Department of the Taoiseach, S13053a.
117. Andrews, 171.
118. Flinn was in charge of the Emergency turf campaign for the Turf Development Board. He was a detested figure amongst those of the unemployed who had been forced to experience the low wages, military discipline and poor food in the labour camps set up on Clonsast and other boglands in County Kildare. Andrews refers to the 'atmosphere of labour unrest in the camps', 174–8, and Peadar Cowan, later a leader of Clann na Poblachta, who was a Labour Party organizer at the time, claimed to have set up more than sixty labour branches in turf-producing counties: see his speech denouncing Flinn at a meeting of the Central Branch of the Labour Party, 3 July 1940, NAD, Department of Justice, JUS 8/884.
119. Brian Girvin, *Between Two Worlds: Politics and Economy in Independent Ireland* (Dublin, 1989), 150.
120. Memorandum on Full Employment Policy, 17 January 1945, NAD, Department of the Taoiseach, S13101a.
121. Dunphy, 231.
122. *Round Table*, 121, December 1940.
123. Charles Townshend, *Ireland: The Twentieth Century* (London, 1999), 155.
124. See, for example, Lee, 334. An editorial in the *Bell* in April 1941 provided an early critique: 'We tried to establish a network of decentralised factories . . . we had an idealised vision of little industries in the small towns and villages . . . The census returns replied in the name of realism with the flow

from the fields to the cities, the decay of small villages and our smaller towns.'

125. Mair, 25.

126. See his suggestion for the 'displacement' of the worst farmers in 'Memorandum on Full Employment Policy', 17 January 1945, NAD, Department of the Taoiseach, S13101a.

127. Sheila May, 'Two Dublin Slums', *Bell*, 7, 4, 1944.

128. Deirdre McMahon, 'John Charles McQuaid of Dublin, the Politician: A Reassessment', *Studies*, 87, 348, Winter 1998, and J. H. Whyte, *Church and State in Modern Ireland 1923–1979* (Dublin, 1984), 76–9.

129. Whyte, 78.

130. Paul Bew and Henry Patterson, *Seán Lemass and the Making of Modern Ireland* (Dublin, 1982), 30.

131. Whyte, 102.

132. Lee, 234.

4 Stagnation: Ireland 1945–1959

1. Enda Delaney, 'State, Politics and Demography: The Case of Irish Emigration 1921–1971', *Irish Political Studies*, 13, 1998, 36.

2. *Mayo News*, 10 January 1931.

3. 'Post-War Policy and the Programme for the Land Commission', 21 August 1942, NAD, Department of the Taoiseach, S13301a.

4. Paul Bew and Henry Patterson, *Seán Lemass and the Making of Modern Ireland* (Dublin, 1982), 5.

5. See his dialogue with Lemass in Cabinet Committee on Economic Planning, NAD, Department of the Taoiseach, S13026b.

6. 'Memorandum on Full Employment Policy', 17 January 1945, NAD, Department of the Taoiseach, S13101a.

7. 'Position of the Minority in the 26 Counties', NAD, Department of Foreign Affairs, 305/14/351A.

8. Cormac Ó Gráda. *A Rocky Road: The Irish Economy since the 1920s* (Manchester, 1997), 22.

9. Ó Gráda, 22.

10. *Economic Development* (Dublin, 1958), PR 4803, 153.

11. Terence Brown, *Ireland: A Social and Cultural History* (London, 1981), 184.

12. K. H. Connell, 'Catholicism and Marriage in the Century after the Famine', in K. H. Connell, *Irish Peasant Society* (Oxford, 1968).

13. James Meenan, *The Irish Economy since 1922* (Liverpool, 1970), 112.

14. Richard Dunphy, *The Making of Fianna Fáil Power in Ireland 1923–1948* (Oxford, 1995), 211–12.

15. 'Discussions with Eire Ministers on UK–Eire Economic Relation', note by Commonwealth Relations Office, 17 September 1947, PRO, Prem 8/824.

16. Bew and Patterson, 40.

17. 'Eire and Western Europe', June 1948, PRO, Prem 8/824.

18. 'Working Party on the Irish Republic', 1957, PRO, MAF 40/471.

19. 'Memorandum on Full Employment Policy'.

20. Liam Skinner, *Politicians by Accident* (Dublin, 1946), 63.
21. *Irish Times*, 12 February 1947.
22. Alvin Jackson, *Ireland 1798–1998: Politics and War* (Oxford, 1999), 308.
23. Ironically, McCaughey blamed MacBride for his capture for he was arrested soon after he had reluctantly agreed to meet MacBride at his office in Dublin to show him extracts from the confession he had recently helped to beat out of the alleged informer Stephen Hayes: see Raymond J. Quinn, *A Rebel Voice: A History of Belfast Republicanism* (Belfast, 1999), 71.
24. Kevin Rafter, *The Clann: The Story of Clann na Poblachta* (Dublin, 1996), 25.
25. Eithne MacDermott, *Clann na Poblachta* (Cork, 1998), 61, and David McCullagh, *A Makeshift Majority: The First Inter-party Government* (Dublin, 1998), 10.
26. M. J. Kennedy to Frank Gallagher, 18 December 1946, National Library of Ireland, MS 18336.
27. Rafter, 39.
28. MacDermott, 19.
29. Dunphy, 39.
30. Rafter, 35–6.
31. MacDermott, 35.
32. McCullagh, 26–9.
33. Peter Mair, *The Changing Irish Party System* (London, 1987), 54.
34. McCullagh, 30.
35. *Irish Times*, 18 May 1944.
36. *Round Table*, 136, September 1944.
37. MacDermott, 33.
38. McCullagh, 182.
39. See Ronan Fanning, *The Irish Department of Finance* (Dublin, 1978), 456–60, and Patrick Lynch, 'More Pages from an Irish Memoir', in Richard English and J. M. Skelly (eds.), *Ideas Matter* (Dublin, 1998), 133.
40. Brian Girvin, *Between Two Worlds: Politics and Economy in Independent Ireland* (Dublin, 1989), 170.
41. Lynch, 133.
42. McCullagh, 145.
43. F. S. L. Lyons, *Ireland since the Famine* (London, 1971), 571.
44. McCullagh, 158–9.
45. Greta Jones, *'Captain of all these men of death': The History of Tuberculosis in Nineteenth and Twentieth Century Ireland* (Amsterdam and New York, 2001), 230.
46. Noel Browne, *Against the Tide* (Dublin, 1986), 35.
47. Browne, 124.
48. McCullagh, 205–6.
49. Ruth Barrington, *Health, Medicine and Politics in Ireland 1900–1970* (Dublin, 1970), 182–8.
50. J. H. Whyte, *Church and State in Modern Ireland 1923–1979* (Dublin, 1980), 305.
51. The letter of 10 October 1952 is reprinted in Paul Blanshard, *The Irish and Catholic Power* (London, 1954), 76–7.
52. McCullagh, 217.

53. Blanshard, 74.
54. McCullagh, 223.
55. J. J. Lee, *Ireland 1912–1985: Politics and Society* (Cambridge, 1989), 318.
56. McCullagh, 198.
57. Whyte, 238.
58. McCullagh, 199.
59. Ronan Fanning, 'McQuaid's Country on Bended Knee', *Independent on Sunday*, 12 April 1998.
60. ibid.
61. Whyte, 43.
62. ibid., 158.
63. Delaney, 39.
64. Emmet O'Connor, *A Labour History of Ireland 1824–1960* (Dublin, 1992), 136.
65. Whyte, 166.
66. ibid., 173.
67. ibid., 268.
68. McCullagh, 157.
69. 'The Year in Retrospect', *Irish Times*, 1 January 1954.
70. McCullagh, 230.
71. Quoted in Blanshard, 15.
72. Rafter, 77.
73. *Round Table*, 136, September 1944.
74. Commonwealth Relations Office to Attlee, 23 October 1947, PRO, Prem 8/824/4487.
75. Report by Lord Rugby, 28 October 1947, PRO, Prem 8/824/4487.
76. Troy D. Davis, *Dublin's American Policy: Irish American Diplomatic Relations 1945–1952* (Washington, DC, 1998), 151.
77. Lynch, 127.
78. They regularly breakfasted together in MacBride's office in Iveagh House: Rafter, 108.
79. Davis, 96.
80. ibid., 127.
81. *Belfast Newsletter*, 8 March 1951.
82. McCullagh, 114.
83. Dermot Keogh, *Twentieth-century Ireland: Nation and State* (Dublin, 1994), 186.
84. Conor Cruise O'Brien, *Memoir: My Life and Themes* (Dublin, 1998), 146.
85. 'Mr Blythe's Suggestions for a Revised Policy on Partition', Memorandum by Conor Cruise O'Brien to the Secretary, Department of External Affairs, 12 August 1949, NAD, Department of Foreign Affairs, 305/14/62.
86. Speech by Colonel Topping, Unionist Chief Whip, on 18 September 1950, reported in 'Position of the Minority in the 26 Counties', NAD, Department of Foreign Affairs, 305/14/351A.
87. Letter from R. C. Geary, Central Statistical Office, to the Secretary, Department of External Affairs, 23 October 1951, in 'Position of the Minority in the 26 Counties', NAD, Department of Foreign Affairs, 305/14/351A.

88. Whyte, 169.
89. Dennis Kennedy, *The Widening Gulf: Northern Attitudes to the Independent Irish State* (Belfast, 1988), 182–4.
90. 'Protestants Denied Positions in Eire', *Belfast Newsletter*, 17 January 1951.
91. Annual Report of the Ulster Unionist Council, 1951, PRONI, Ulster Unionist Council Papers, D1377/20/2/34.
92. Report on a meeting at the London Embassy, 8 August 1952, NAD, Department of Foreign Affairs, 313/3.
93. Boland to the Secretary, Department of External Affairs, 23 October 1953, NAD, Department of Foreign Affairs, 313/3.
94. Lord Brookeborough, 'Diaries', 4 April 1956, PRONI, Ulster Unionist Council Papers, D3004/E/21.
95. Ó Gráda, 25.
96. Meenan, 112.
97. Barry Brunt, *The Republic of Ireland* (London, 1988), 13.
98. Ó Gráda, 27.
99. 'Economic Relations with the Irish Republic', note by the Chancellor of the Exchequer, 5 February 1960, PRO, Cab 129/100.
100. Liam Kennedy, *The Modern Industrialization of Ireland* (Dublin, 1989), 9.
101. Girvin, 197.
102. Tom Garvin, *Preventing the Future: Why was Ireland So Poor for So Long?* (Dublin, 2004), 11.
103. Meenan, 112.
104. Bew and Patterson, 56–8.
105. Seamus Cody, John O'Dowd and Peter Rigney, *The Parliament of Labour: One Hundred Years of the Dublin Council of Trade Unions* (Dublin, 1986), 200.
106. Bew and Patterson, 61.
107. Cody, O'Dowd and Rigney, 201.
108. Girvin, 184.
109. *Round Table*, 44, October 1953.
110. Bew and Patterson, 69.
111. Garret FitzGerald, 'Turning Point', *Irish Times*, 1 January 1957.
112. Bew and Patterson, 87.
113. *Irish Times*, 23 February 1957.
114. Mair, 32.
115. Horgan, *Seán Lemass: Enigmatic Patriot* (Dublin, 1997), 175.
116. *The Times*, 17 September 1957.
117. T. K. Whitaker, 'Capital Formation, Saving and Economic Progress', *Journal of the Social and Statistical Inquiry Society of Ireland*, 19, 1955–6, 196–9.
118. Horgan, 165.
119. *Irish Press*, 12 October 1955.
120. Lee, 343.
121. Girvin, 192.
122. Lee, 344, and Bew and Patterson, 115.
123. Girvin, 192–3.
124. Lee, 354.
125. Garvin, 53.

5 Modernization and Resistance: Northern Ireland 1945–1963

1. A. J. Kelly (Home Office) to A. Gransden (Cabinet Office, Stormont), 2 April 1946, PRONI, Cabinet Secretariat, Cab 9J/53/1.
2. Peter Rose, *How the Troubles Came to Northern Ireland* (Basingstoke and New York, 2000), 2.
3. Note of a meeting with Rt Hon. Herbert Morrison, MP, 15 September 1946, PRONI, Cabinet Secretariat, Cab 9J/53/2.
4. G. C. Duggan, 'Northern Ireland: Success or Failure?', *Irish Times*, 19 April 1950. Duggan was Comptroller and Auditor General at Stormont.
5. Memorandum on 'The Constitutional Position' by R. Nugent, 6 January 1946, PRONI, Cabinet Secretariat, Cab 9J/53/1.
6. Memorandum by Minister of Health and Local Government, 9 July 1946, PRONI, Cabinet Secretariat, Cab 9J/53/2.
7. John Ditch, *Social Policy in Northern Ireland 1939–1950* (Aldershot, 1988), 105.
8. Letter from Lieutenant Colonel J. M. Blakiston-Houston, Beltrim Castle, Gortin, to Basil Brooke, 9 April 1948, PRONI, Cabinet Secretariat, Cab 9J/53/1.
9. *Belfast Newsletter*, 27 November 1947.
10. Note on Dominion Status from Robert Gransden, Cabinet Secretary, to the Prime Minister, 31 October 1947, PRONI, Cabinet Secretariat, Cab 9J/53/2.
11. Sir Alexander Maxwell to the Home Secretary, 25 October 1945, included in the file 'Infiltration of Éire Workers into Northern Ireland', PRONI, Cabinet Secretariat Cab 9C/47/3.
12. Paul Bew, Peter Gibbon and Henry Patterson, *Northern Ireland 1921–1996: Political Forces and Social Classes* (London, 1996), 107.
13. Letter from Henry McCay, Secretary of the City of Londonderry and Foyle Unionist Association, to McCoy, 29 March 1951, PRONI, McCoy Papers, D333/A/1.
14. Madge MacDonald to McCoy, 24 February 1948, PRONI, McCoy Papers, D333/A/1.
15. May Knox-Browne, Aglinton Castle, Fivemiletown, to McCoy, 9 September 1952, PRONI, McCoy Papers, D333/A/1.
16. *Belfast Newsletter*, 22 December 1945.
17. Bew, Gibbon and Patterson, 103.
18. Sabine Wichert, *Northern Ireland since 1945* (London, 1991), 72.
19. F. H. Boland, Irish Ambassador, London, to Seán Nunan, Secretary, Department of External Affairs, 6 January 1954, NAD, Department of Foreign Affairs, 305/14/249. Brooke was created Viscount Brookeborough in 1952.
20. Sir Basil Brooke, 'Diaries', 18 February 1951, account of Ulster Unionist Council Meeting, PRONI, Brookeborough Papers, D 3004/D/44.
21. Letter from Maginess to Brooke, 21 August 1951, PRONI, Cabinet Secretariat, Cab 9J/53/2.
22. 'Roman Catholic Electors Seeing the Light', *Northern Whig*, 20 October 1951.

23. *Belfast Newsletter*, 13 July 1946.
24. Statement showing scope and amount of social services in Northern Ireland and Éire, October 1946, PRONI, Cabinet Secretariat, Cab 9C/47/3.
25. F. S. L. Lyons, *Ireland since the Famine* (London, 1971), 742.
26. *The Ulster Year Book 1947* (Belfast, 1948), 76, and *The Ulster Year Book 1963–1964* (Belfast, 1965), 213.
27. From 2,026 in 1945–6 to 4,708 in 1963–4, *The Ulster Year Book 1963–1964*, 234.
28. John Ditch, *Social Policy in Northern Ireland 1939–1950* (Aldershot, 1988), 107.
29. *The Ulster Year Book 1960–1962* (Belfast, 1963), 229.
30. J. H. Whyte, 'How Much Discrimination was There under the Unionist Regime 1921–1968?', in I. T. Gallagher and James O'Connell (eds.), *Contemporary Irish Studies* (Manchester, 1983), 20.
31. Graham Gudgin, 'Discrimination in Housing and Employment under the Stormont Regime', in P. Boche and B. Barton (eds.), *The Northern Ireland Question: Nationalism, Unionism and Partition* (Hampshire, 1999), 103.
32. Memorandum by the Minister of Home Affairs on the Civil Authorities (Special Powers) Act, 22 February 1950, PRONI, Cabinet Secretariat, Cab 4/846/10.
33. See Henry Patterson, 'Party versus Order: Ulster Unionism and the Flags and Emblems Act', *Contemporary British History*, 13, 4, Winter 1999, 104–29.
34. *Belfast Newsletter*, 13 July 1946.
35. Report of the Proceedings of the Half-yearly General Meeting of the Grand Lodge of Ireland, Sandy Row Orange Hall, 14 December 1949, in the Library of the Orange Order, Belfast.
36. Michael McGrath, 'The Narrow Road: Harry Midgley and Catholic Schools in Northern Ireland', *Irish Historical Studies*, 30, 119, May 1997, 439.
37. ibid., 440.
38. Oliver P. Rafferty, *Catholicism in Ulster 1603–1983: An Interpretative History* (Dublin, 1994), 247.
39. Belfast LOL 958 resolution, which protested against grants to sixteen Catholic schools under the 1947 Act: Meeting of the Grand Lodge of Ireland, 8 June 1949, the Library of the Orange Order, Belfast.
40. *Ulster Protestant*, October 1957.
41. 'Position of the Minority in the 26 Counties', 24 October 1950, NAD, Department of Foreign Affairs, 305/14/351A.
42. *Ulster Protestant*, August 1951.
43. Memorandum from the Inspector-General of the RUC, 30 December 1953, PRONI, Ministry of Home Affairs, HA/32/1/956.
44. Patterson, 120.
45. ibid., 108.
46. Lord Brookeborough, 'Diaries', 6 June 1956, PRONI, Brookeborough Papers, D3004/D/45. In 1956 the Prime Minister met a delegation of leading unionists from Derry who, wrongly believing that Catholics were 40 per cent of the population – the 1951 census figure was 35 per cent – predicted a 'disloyal majority by 2000'. Minute prepared for meeting with the Prime Minister, 13 September 1956, PRONI, PM 5/95/10.

47. ibid., 13 September: 'Deputation headed by Teddy Jones [MP for Londonderry city] on industries. They are anxious that we should not get an invasion from the other side.'

48. This was after a letter from Teddy Jones that warned that if the position 'falls into the wrong hands, the situation in Londonderry City will go from bad to worse and ultimately destroy us'. Letter from Jones to A. J. Kelly, PRONI, Cabinet Secretariat, Cab 9C/5/4.

49. Harry Diamond, a Republican Labour MP, quoted in *Irish News*, 15 October 1953.

50. Whyte, 10.

51. Lord Brookborough, 'Diaries', 24 February 1956, PRONI, Brookeborough Papers, D3004/D/45.

52. ibid., 5 September 1956.

53. Paul Teague, 'Discrimination and Segmentation Theory: A Survey', in Terry Cradden and Paul Teague (eds.), *Labour Market Discrimination and Fair Employment in Northern Ireland: International Journal of Manpower*, 13, 65/7, 1992.

54. The seminal article on the topic is E. A. Aunger, 'Religion and Occupational Class in Northern Ireland', *Economic and Social Review*, 7, 1, 1975.

55. Whyte, 21–3.

56. Letter from Brian Maginess to R. A. Butler, 15 December 1954, PRONI, Cabinet Secretariat, Cab 4A/38/21.

57. Memorandum of the Minister of Commerce on Advanced Factories, 28 March 1956, PRONI, Cabinet Secretariat, Cab 4A/38/25.

58. Letter from Brian Maginess to R. A. Butler, 15 December 1954, PRONI, Cabinet Secretariat, Cab 4A/38/21.

59. This depressing story is, not surprisingly, easier to follow in the Prime Minister's diaries than in the cabinet papers. 30 April 1957: 'Cabinet subcommittee on Derry employment problem in new industries. There are two lines we can help – getting good labour relations people into the factories . . . Housing is important and getting Derry men from other parts of the Province and from England to return to the city.' 17 May 1957: 'Met Executive of the party at Glengall Street and told them we had made arrangements for Derry about new industries.' 26 June 1957: 'Teddy Jones saw Labour and Commerce about employment in Derry. He says there is a row with the Apprentice Boys that no Protestants are being employed in the building operations [for Dupont plant].' Extracts from 'Diaries', PRONI, Brookeborough Papers, D3004/D/45.

60. Campaign for Social Justice in Northern Ireland, *The Plain Truth* (Dungannon, 2nd ed., 1969).

61. Niall Ó Dochartaigh, *From Civil Rights to Armalites: Derry and the Birth of the Irish Troubles* (Cork, 1997), xvi–xvii.

62. Lord Brookeborough, 'Diaries', 23 September 1958, PRONI, Brookeborough Papers, D3004/D/45.

63. Copy of telephone message from Brookeborough to the Home Secretary, 7 February 1958: 'The unemployment rate in Londonderry is 17% and the closing of the station will completely cancel the volume of additional work

being provided by new industry in the area.' PRONI, Cabinet Secretariat, Cab 4A/38/29.

64. Brendan Lynn, *Holding the Ground: The Nationalist Party in Northern Ireland 1945–1972* (Aldershot, 1997), 4.

65. 1951 election address of Gerald Annesley, APL candidate in South Down, NAD, Department of Foreign Affairs, 305/14/109/4/1.

66. In a memorandum on the state of northern nationalism, 1 May 1958, NAD, Department of Foreign Affairs, 305/14/2/4.

67. Lynn, 37.

68. ibid., 55.

69. Visit by Conor Cruise O'Brien to anti-partitionist centres in Northern Ireland, 23–5 March 1953, NAD, Department of Foreign Affairs, 305/14/2/3.

70. ibid.

71. J. Bowyer Bell, *The Secret Army: A History of the IRA 1916–1970* (London, 1972), 296.

72. Report by F. H. Boland to Seán Nunan, Department of External Affairs, 26 November 1953, NAD, Department of Foreign Affairs, 305/14/249.

73. Conor Cruise O'Brien report on a visit to Ulster, 21–2 June, NAD, Department of Foreign Affairs, 305/17/2/3.

74. *Round Table*, 177, December 1954.

75. Report on a visit to Ulster, 21–2 June, NAD, Department of Foreign Affairs, 305/17/2/3.

76. Bowyer Bell, 313–15.

77. Thus Seán Rafferty to a Sinn Féin meeting in Belfast: 'They had a far greater weapon in the ballot box than in bullets, bayonets and bombs.' *Irish News*, 16 May 1955.

78. An intercepted communication from Eamon Timoney, an IRA officer in Derry, to his commanding officer was revealing: 'Our boys are anxious to let the "B" patrols have it, but I have objected . . . If you say the word "let them have it" we will not say "no".' Quoted at his trial, *Belfast Newsletter*, 20 June 1957.

79. Examples were the killing of Sergeant Ovens by a booby-trap in August 1957 and the shooting of an off-duty RUC constable by an IRA team in Fermanagh in January 1961. Bowyer Bell, 367, 391.

80. Seán Cronin, *Irish Nationalism* (Dublin, 1980), 171.

81. Target list included in documents found on IRA man tried in Belfast, *Belfast Newsletter*, 16 March 1957.

82. 'Belfast Man Jailed for Possessing IRA Documents', *Belfast Newsletter*, 11 December 1956.

83. Inspector-General's office, Crime Branch Special, 'Subversive Activities: Reports and Correspondence', PRONI, Ministry of Home Affairs, HA/32/1/1349.

84. Department of External Affairs memorandum on meeting with Michael O'Neill, 19 May 1955, NAD, Department of Foreign Affairs, 305/14/2.

85. Conor Cruise O'Brien, report on visit to Ulster, 21–2 July 1954, NAD, Department of Foreign Affairs, 305/17/2/3.

86. J. G. Nelson, RUC headquarters, to R. F. R. Dunbar, 26 September 1958, PRONI, Ministry of Home Affairs, HA/32/1/1349.

87. Henry Patterson, *The Politics of Illusion: A Political History of the IRA* (London, 1997), 92.
88. 'Subversive Incidents in Northern Ireland since 12 December 1958', PRONI, Ministry of Home Affairs, HA/32/1/1349.
89. 'Proposed Winding Up of the APL in the Six Counties', NAD, Department of External Affairs, 305/14/2/4.
90. Memorandum on Publicity by Eric Montgomery, Director of Publicity, 7 April 1957, PRONI, Cabinet Publicity Committee, Cab 4A/26/75.
91. Government of Northern Ireland, *Report of the Joint Working Party on the Economy of Northern Ireland*, Cmnd. 446 (Belfast, 1962) (hereafter referred to as the *Hall Report*, after Sir Robert Hall, who chaired it), para. 23.
92. G. P. Steed, 'Internal Organization, Firm Integration and Locational Change: The Northern Ireland Linen Complex 1954–1964', *Economic Geography*, 47, 1971.
93. Report by officials on employment policy, December 1960, PRONI, Cabinet Employment Subcommittee, Cab 4A/38/43.
94. *Hall Report*, para. 21.
95. ibid., para. 26.
96. ibid., para. 44.
97. Bew, Gibbon and Patterson, 119.
98. *Hall Report*, para. 25.
99. Bew, Gibbon and Patterson, 118.
100. *Hall Report*, para. 26.
101. Minute from the Prime Minister to the Home Secretary, 29 December 1949, in 'Industrial Development and Employment in Northern Ireland, Measures by British Government', PRONI, Cabinet Secretariat, Cab 9F/188/1.
102. Note by Sir Frank Newsam of the Home Office of a meeting to discuss unemployment in Northern Ireland, PRONI, Cabinet Secretariat, Cab 9F/188/3.
103. PRONI, Cab 4/970/830 April 1955.
104. 'Employment Policy: Report by Officials', December 1960, PRONI, Cabinet Secretariat, Cab 4A/38/43.
105. ibid.
106. 'Industrial Development and Employment in Northern Ireland, Measures by British Government', PRONI, Cabinet Secretariat, Cab 9F/188/72.
107. Terry Cradden, *Trade Unionism, Socialism and Partition* (Belfast, 1993), 179.
108. 'The Economic Survey of Northern Ireland', memorandum by the Minister of Commerce, 16 October 1957, PRONI, Cabinet Secretariat, Cab 4/1049.
109. Bew, Gibbon and Patterson, 126.
110. See O'Neill's comments at meeting of Cabinet Employment Committee, 3 April 1958, PRONI, Cabinet Secretariat, Cab 4A/38/21.
111. 'Observations on the 1953 Election', PRONI, Ulster Unionist Council Papers, D1327/16/3/51.
112. Cabinet Employment Committee, 19 November 1958, PRONI, Cabinet Secretariat, Cab 4A/38/34.
113. Personal note from Minister of Finance to Cabinet Employment Committee, 12 February 1958, PRONI, Cabinet Secretariat, Cab 4A/38/29.

114. Bew, Gibbon and Patterson, 128.
115. Sydney Elliott, *Northern Ireland Parliamentary Election Results 1921–1971* (Chichester, 1973), 43.
116. *Belfast Newsletter*, 2 June 1962.
117. This was the opinion of Jack Sayers, the liberal editor of the *Belfast Telegraph*, who in his column in the *Round Table* noted, 'It begins to appear that Northern Ireland's failure to recruit to the political field men and women of greater stature, capacity and breadth of vision is at last coming home to roost.' *Round Table*, 185, December 1956.
118. 'Future of Messrs. Short Brothers and Harland', memorandum by Minister of Defence and Minister of Aviation, 2 October 1962, PRO, Cab 127/110. Wilson's remark is from a meeting with Terence O'Neill and other members of the Stormont cabinet, 4 November 1968, PRONI, Cabinet Secretariat, Cab 4/1413/10.

6 Expansion: Ireland 1959–1973

1. 'Economic Relations with the Irish Republic', 5 February 1960, PRO, Cab 129/100.
2. Symposium on *Economic Development, Journal of the Social and Statistical Inquiry of Ireland*, 19, Part 2, 1958/59.
3. Paul Bew and Henry Patterson, *Seán Lemass and the Making of Modern Ireland* (Dublin, 1982), 114.
4. 'Economic Relations with the Irish Republic', 5 February 1960, PRO, Cab 129/100.
5. John Horgan, *Seán Lemass: The Enigmatic Patriot* (Dublin, 1997), 216.
6. Garret FitzGerald, *All in a Life: An Autobiography* (Dublin, 1991), 58.
7. Bew and Patterson, 136.
8. ibid., 184.
9. 'The Political Implication of an Anglo-Irish Free Trade Area', 1 January 1965, NAD, Department of the Taoiseach, S16674 Q/95.
10. Peter Mair, *The Changing Irish Party System* (London, 1987), 182.
11. Susan Baker, 'Nationalist Ideology and the Industrial Policy of Fianna Fáil', *Irish Political Studies*, 1, 1986, 61.
12. ibid., 64.
13. Lemass in a speech to the Dublin South-central branch of Fianna Fáil, *Irish Times*, 13 May 1961.
14. Report of a meeting between the Minister for Industry and Commerce and the Linen, Cotton and Rayon Manufacturers' Association, 13 July 1961, NAD, Department of the Taoiseach, S6272 C/61.
15. Cormac Ó Gráda, *A Rocky Road: The Irish Economy since the 1920s* (Manchester, 1997), 29.
16. All the figures in this paragraph are from Liam Kennedy, *The Modern Industrialization of Ireland 1940–1988* (Dublin, 1989), 14–16.
17. Liam Kennedy, 15.
18. Kieran Allen, *Fianna Fáil and Irish Labour: 1926 to the Present* (London, 1997), 108.

19. Allen, 109.
20. Niamh Hardiman, *Pay, Politics and Economic Performance in Ireland 1970–1987* (Oxford, 1988), 48.
21. Horgan, 230.
22. Bew and Patterson, 173.
23. Horgan, 229.
24. Finola Kennedy, *Public Social Expenditure in Ireland*, Economic and Social Research Institute, Broadsheet No. 11, February 1975.
25. Mair, 30.
26. F. S. L. Lyons, *Ireland since the Famine* (London, 1971), 623–4.
27. J. J. Lee, *Ireland 1912–1985* (Cambridge, 1994), 367.
28. Jonathan Bardon, *A History of Ulster* (Belfast, 1992), 629.
29. *New York Times*, 29 April 1957.
30. Martin Mansergh, 'The Political Legacy of Seán Lemass', *Études Irlandaises*, No. 25–1, Printemps 2000, 160.
31. Lemass in his Presidential Address to Ard-Fheis, 20 November 1962, in 'Partition: Government Policy', NAD, Department of the Taoiseach, S9361 K/63.
32. In 1956–7, when ill with phlebitis, he sent a note to T. K. Whitaker: 'Dev wants me to brush up my Irish – please send me some books on economics and finance', in Horgan, 302. The same book records his view on the after-life: 'This is all nonsense. When it's over, it's over' (325).
33. *Round Table*, 196, September 1959.
34. Henry Patterson, 'Seán Lemass and the Ulster Question 1959–1965', *Journal of Contemporary History*, 34, 1, 1999, 151–2.
35. After a meeting with northern Nationalist MPs and Senators on 19 July 1962, Lemass asked the Minister for Transport and Power, Erskine Childers, to raise these issues with the two state companies: 'Government Policy on Partition', NAD, Department of the Taoiseach, S9361 K/62.
36. Presidential Address to Ard-Fheis, 20 November 1962.
37. *Irish Times*, 16 October 1959.
38. At his first meeting in November 1963 with Sir Alec Douglas-Home, the British premier suggested a meeting with Lemass: Andrew Gailey, *Crying in the Wilderness. Jack Sayers: A Liberal Editor in Ulster 1939–1969* (Belfast, 1995), 81–2.
39. Gransden, who was Cabinet Secretary from 1939 to 1957 and Northern Ireland Agent in London from 1957 to 1962, had become friendly with Hugh McCann, then Irish Ambassador in London and subsequently Secretary of the Department of External Affairs. His views were expressed during a holiday in Ireland in June 1963 and recorded in a note by McCann on 15 July 1963, 'Partition: Government Policy', NAD, Department of Foreign Affairs, DFA 313/31K.
40. *Irish Times*, 30 July 1963.
41. Robert Savage, *Seán Lemass* (Dublin, 1990), 40.
42. *Irish Press*, 12 September 1963.
43. Letter from Seán Lemass to all cabinet ministers, 10 September 1963, NAD, Department of the Taoiseach, S1627 E/63.

44. 'Suggested Civil Service Level Discussions with Six-County Representatives', 28 September 1963, NAD, Department of the Taoiseach, S1627 E/63.
45. *Irish Times*, 17 October 1963.
46. *Irish Press*, 18 October 1963.
47. See his 1962 speech to Ard-Fheis: 'I am convinced that British action in expanding freedom throughout Africa and Asia will eventually have its effect in bringing partition to an end.' 'Government Policy on Partition', NAD, Department of the Taoiseach, S9361 K/62.
48. Patterson, 150
49. 'Suggested Civil Service Level Discussions with Six-County Representatives', 28 September 1963, NAD, Department of the Taoiseach, S1627 E/63.
50. *Irish Times*, 2 November 1967.
51. Horgan, 267.
52. 5 July 1967, NAD, Department of External Affairs, 305/14/360.
53. Horgan, 267.
54. ibid., 197.
55. Erskine Childers to Seán Lemass, 1 March 1961, NAD, Department of External Affairs, 305/14/360.
56. Comments by B. Gallagher on proposed discrimination pamphlet, 12 August 1964, NAD, Department of External Affairs, 305/14/303.
57. Memorandum by B. Gallagher, 6 July 1967, NAD, Department of External Affairs, 305/14/360.
58. Horgan, 298.
59. Allen, 123.
60. Aidan Kelly and Teresa Brannick, 'The Changing Contours of Irish Strike Patterns 1960–1984', *Irish Business and Administrative Research*, 8, 1, 1986, 84.
61. Allen, 127–33.
62. Kieran Allen's analysis is a good example of this approach: see p. 123 of *Fianna Fáil and Irish Labour*.
63. Michael Gallagher, *The Irish Labour Party in Transition: 1957–1982* (Dublin, 1982), 4.
64. Emmet O'Connor, *A Labour History of Ireland: 1824–1960* (Dublin, 1992), 172.
65. Gallagher, *The Irish Labour Party in Transition*, Appendices 1 and 2.
66. ibid., 42.
67. Conor Cruise O'Brien, *Memoir: My Life and Themes* (Dublin, 1998), 317.
68. Figures from Mair, 117, 120, Appendix 3.
69. Gallagher, 87.
70. ibid., 89.
71. ibid., 95.
72. Conor Cruise O'Brien, 321.
73. James Wickham, 'The Politics of Dependent Capitalism: International Capital and the Nation State', in Austen Morgan and Bob Purdie (eds.), *Ireland: Divided Nation Divided Class* (London, 1982), 62.
74. J. H. Whyte, *Church and State in Modern Ireland 1923–1979* (Dublin, 1984), 195.

75. Tom Garvin, 'Patriots and Republicans: An Irish Evolution', in William Crotty and David E. Schmitt (eds.), *Ireland and the Politics of Change* (London, 1998), 150.
76. Christopher Whelan, 'Class and Social Mobility', in Kieran Kennedy (ed.), *Ireland in Transition* (Dublin, 1986), 85.
77. Garvin, 152.
78. John Cooney, *John Charles McQuaid: Ruler of Catholic Ireland* (Dublin, 1999), 338–9, 358.
79. John Sheehan, 'Education and Society in Ireland 1945–1970', in J. J. Lee (ed.), *Ireland 1945–1970* (Dublin, 1979), 62.
80. The figures for the North are from *The Ulster Year Book 1947* (Belfast, 1947), 76, and *The Ulster Year Book 1963–1964* (Belfast, 1964), 213, and Sheehan, 65.
81. Whyte, 343–6.
82. Robert J. Savage, *Irish Television: The Political and Social Origins* (Cork, 1996), 46.
83. J. J. Lee, 'Continuity and Change in Ireland 1945–1970', in J. J. Lee (ed.), *Ireland 1945–1970* (Dublin, 1979), 172.
84. Bew and Patterson, 168.
85. Maurice Manning, *James Dillon: A Biography* (Dublin, 1999), 380.
86. James Downey, *Lenihan: His Life and Loyalties* (Dublin, 1998), 55.
87. T. Ryle Dwyer, *Charlie* (Dublin, 1987), 8–9.
88. 'The Berry Papers: The Secret Memoirs of the Man Who was the Country's Most Important Civil Servant', *Magill*, June 1980, 48.
89. Feargal Tobin, *The Best of Decades: Ireland in the 1960s* (Dublin, 1996), 159–60.
90. Horgan, 333–6.
91. *Irish Times*, 4 November 1966.
92. 'GAA Salutes Lynch's Unique Sporting Record', *Irish Times*, 21 October 1999.
93. Horgan, 330.
94. Ryle Dwyer, 67.
95. *Irish Times*, 3 October 1968.
96. *Irish Times*, 6 December 1968.
97. Cornelius O'Leary, *Irish Elections 1918–1977* (Dublin, 1979), 68.
98. Máire Geoghegan-Quinn, 'Lynch: Gentle Leader with a Core of Tempered Steel', *Irish Times*, 23 October 1999.
99. 'Government Information Bureau – Future Activities in Relation to the 6 Counties', 25 January 1969, NAD, Department of the Taoiseach, 2000/6/497.
100. John Bowman, *De Valera and the Ulster Question* (Oxford, 1982), 324.
101. Ronan Fanning, 'Playing It Cool: The Response of the British and Irish Governments to the Crisis in Northern Ireland 1968–1969', *Irish Studies in International Affairs*, 12, 2001, 68.
102. Horgan, 342.
103. Ronan Fanning, 'Living in Those Troubled Times', *Sunday Independent*, 2 January 2000.
104. Ronan Fanning, 'Bank Chief was Architect of Government's NI Policy', *Sunday Independent*, 16 January 2000.
105. The address is printed in full in the inquiry of Lord Scarman, 'Violence

and Civil Disturbances in Northern Ireland in 1969', Report of a Tribunal of Inquiry, HMSO Belfast, Cmnd. 556, 1972, Vol. 2, 43–4.

106. Recommendation of the Planning Board, SITREPS-OPSFILE 4, 13 October 1969, SCS 29, Irish Military Archives, Cathal Brugha Barracks, Dublin.

107. ibid.

108. 'The Berry Papers: The Secret Memoirs of the Man Who was the Country's Most Important Civil Servant', *Magill*, June 1980, 48.

109. See his speech to the London Irish Club banquet: 'the prosperity of these islands as a region is indivisible', *Irish Times*, 18 March 1965.

110. Rachel Donnelly, 'Haughey Seen as "Shrewd and Ruthless"', *Irish Times*, 1, 3 January 2000.

111. Ryle Dwyer, 3.

112. The comment was made in an interview for RTÉ's epic history of the Irish state, *Seven Ages, Sunday Tribune*, 26 March 2000.

113. Horgan, 335.

114. Denis Coghlan, 'Lack of Political Direction on North Ended in Arms Trial', *Irish Times*, 10 January 2000.

115. Details of the men and of the expanded activity of the Irish state in Northern Ireland can be found in 'Government Information Bureau – Special Section Arising out of Distress in 6 Counties', NAD, Department of the Taoiseach, 2000/6/497.

116. Michael Kennedy, *Division and Consensus: The Politics of Cross-border Relations in Ireland 1925–1969* (Dublin, 2000), 346.

117. James Kelly, *The Thimble Riggers: The Dublin Arms Trial of 1970* (Dublin, 1999), 12.

118. The report is quoted in Justin O'Brien, *The Arms Trial* (Dublin, 2000), 58.

119. Kelly, 95.

120. 'Situation in Northern Ireland', in 'Summary of Events 13 August 1969–1 May 1970', SCS 18/1, Irish Military Archives, Cathal Brugha Barracks, Dublin.

121. O'Brien, 69.

122. 'Efforts Made by Colonel Delaney to Have Captain J. J. Kelly Transferred from the Intelligence Service', SITREPS-OPSFILE 4, Military Intelligence File 50.

123. Quoted in O'Brien, *The Arms Trial*, 222.

124. Bruce Arnold, *What Kind of Country? Modern Irish Politics 1968–1983* (London, 1984), 78.

125. Ryle Dwyer, 88.

126. Ronan Fanning, 'Bank Chief was Architect of Government's NI Policy', *Sunday Independent*, 16 January 2000.

127. Arnold, 46–7.

128. Memorandum 'Policy in Relation to Northern Ireland', 28 November 1969, NAD, Department of the Taoiseach, 2000/6/658.

129. Report of a discussion on the Northern Ireland situation between the Minister for External Affairs and the Chancellor of the Duchy of Lancaster, George Thompson, at the Foreign and Commonwealth Office, 20 February 1970, NAD, Department of Foreign Affairs, 2000/14/185.

130. Report on the Six Counties by Eamonn Gallagher, 7 April 1970, NAD, Department of the Taoiseach, 2000/14/185.
131. Arnold, 89–90.
132. Address to Ard-Fheis, 17 January 1970, in 'Partition: Government Policy', 29/12/69–23/4/70, NAD, Department of the Taoiseach, 2000/6/151.
133. Paddy Doherty, *Paddy Bogside* (Cork, 2001), 224.

7 Terence O'Neill and the Crisis of the Unionist State

1. *Irish Times*, 12 October 1959.
2. 'Changes in Unionist Thinking', *Irish Times*, 3 November 1959.
3. 'Will Nationalists Ever Join Unionists?', *Northern Whig*, 2 November 1959.
4. Lord Brookeborough, 'Diaries' 4 November 1959, PRONI, Brookeborough Papers, D3004/D/45.
5. *Belfast Telegraph*, 10 November 1959.
6. Lord Brookeborough, 4 November 1959, PRONI, Brookeborough Papers, D3004/D/45.
7. Ed Moloney and Andy Pollak, *Paisley* (Dublin, 1986), 82.
8. Denis P. Barritt and Charles F. Carter, *The Northern Ireland Problem: A Study in Group Relations* (Oxford, 1962), 93.
9. Although the RUC Special Branch kept National Unity under close observation, it had to report that it had no subversive intent: 'Report on National Unity Organization' by D. I. Fanin for Inspector-General of the RUC, 21 January 1960, PRONI, Ministry of Home Affairs, HA/32/1/1361.
10. Barritt and Carter, 76. Gerry Adams, who would have been twelve in 1960, records that people from Catholic West Belfast shopped on the Protestant heartland of the Shankill Road for bargains and that his new racing bike was bought there. He also relates that the early sexual experiences of himself and his friends from the Catholic Ballymurphy estate were with Protestant girls from neighbouring estates. Gerry Adams, *Before the Dawn: An Autobiography* (London, 1996), 47, 49.
11. 'Belfast Letter', *Irish Times*, 16 January 1960.
12. See the discussion of the 1962 Stormont election in PRONI, Ulster Unionist Council Papers, D1327/16/13/61.
13. W. A. Maguire, *Belfast* (Keele, 1993), 169. As early as the 1953 election an analysis of loss of support in Belfast by Glengall Street refers to this factor. See 'Observations on the 1953 election', in PRONI, Ulster Unionist Council Papers, D1327/16/3/51.
14. See Robert J. Savage, *Irish Television: The Political and Social Origins* (Cork, 1996), 434–45, and Rex Cathcart, *The Most Contrary Region: The BBC in Northern Ireland 1924–1984* (Belfast, 1984).
15. Cathcart, 146.
16. John Boyd, *The Middle of My Journey* (Belfast, 1990), 163–7.
17. He persuaded his colleagues in the cabinet's publicity committee to have an analysis made of the content of questions asked on *Your Questions* and of the political complexion of the panel: Minutes of Cabinet Publicity Committee, 8 March 1961, in PRONI, Cabinet Secretariat, Cab 4A/26/103.

18. Cathcart, 190–3.
19. Barritt and Carter, 61.
20. *Belfast Newsletter*, 2 June 1962.
21. David Bleakley, *Faulkner: Conflict and Consent in Irish Politics* (London, 1974), 26.
22. Michael Farrell, *Northern Ireland: The Orange State* (London, 1976), 208.
23. This was how Sayers saw him: Andrew Gailey, *Crying in the Wilderness. Jack Sayers: A Liberal Editor in Ulster 1939–1969* (Belfast, 1995), 51.
24. Farrell, 222.
25. *Irish Times*, 7 November 1959.
26. At a cabinet meeting on 2 November 1960 a request by the President of the Association, the prominent Ulster linen industrialist Sir Graham Larmour, that its annual meeting pay its respects to the Governor, the monarch's representative in Northern Ireland, was considered and rejected after Faulkner claimed that both Larmour and the Association favoured a united Ireland. PRONI, Cabinet Secretariat, Cab 4/1143.
27. Letter from Connolly Gage to Jack Sayers, 16 September 1963. Gailey, 90.
28. Marc Mulholland, *Northern Ireland at the Crossroads: Ulster Unionism in the O'Neill Years* (London, 2000), 25.
29. Thus at the height of the Dominion Status controversy he wrote to the Prime Minister criticizing the way some ministers were dealing with grass-roots concerns. Letter from O'Neill to Sir Basil Brooke, 23 November 1947, and Brooke's positive response, 26 November 1947: 'Relations with Labour Government (Dominion Status)', PRONI, Cabinet Secretariat, Cab 9J/53/2.
30. Ken Bloomfield, *Stormont in Crisis: A Memoir* (Belfast, 1994), 27.
31. ibid., 26–89.
32. Gavan McCrone, *Regional Policy in Britain* (London, 1969), 120.
33. Government of Northern Ireland, *Belfast Regional Plan*, Cmnd. 451 (Belfast, 1963).
34. *Belfast Newsletter*, 6 April 1963.
35. ibid.
36. Interview with Mervyn Pauley, *Belfast Newsletter*, 12 January 1965.
37. *Economic Development in Northern Ireland*, Cmnd. 479 (Belfast, 1964).
38. ibid., para. 14.
39. The key role of Derry Unionists in sabotaging the city's bid for the university was first publicly stated by the maverick Unionist MP for North Down, Robert Nixon, and set out fully in an article by Ralph Bossence in the *Belfast Newsletter*, 19 February 1965.
40. Gerard O'Brien, '"Our Magee Problem": Stormont and the Second University', in G. O'Brien and W. Nolan (eds.), *Derry and Londonderry: History and Society* (Dublin, 1999), 681–2.
41. *Belfast Newsletter*, 14 August 1964.
42. ibid., 23, 24 July 1964.
43. *The Autobiography of Terence O'Neill* (London, 1972), 61.
44. *Belfast Newsletter*, 5 March 1965.
45. ibid., 21 January 1965.

46. A point made by the right-wing Unionist MP for Shankill, Desmond Boal, in the Stormont debate on the summit, *Belfast Newsletter*, 4 February 1965.

47. *Belfast Newsletter*, 15 January 1965.

48. Within a few weeks of the meeting Lemass made a speech offering unionists a 'realistic' recognition of the continued existence of a Northern government and parliament in a united Ireland and praised Labour's Foreign Secretary for declaring that the British government had no longer any desire to intervene in Ireland. *Belfast Newsletter*, 27 January 1965.

49. His chief critic was the iconoclastic former minister Edmond Warnock, who issued a statement criticizing O'Neill 'for doing within a couple of months what all our enemies failed to achieve in 40 years. He has thrown the whole Ulster question back into the political arena.' *Belfast Newsletter*, 6 April 1965.

50. *The Autobiography of Terence O'Neill*, 47.

51. J. A. V. Graham, 'The Consensus Forming Strategy of the NILP', M.Sc. thesis, Queen's University (Belfast, 1972), 183.

52. *Round Table*, 216, March 1964.

53. *Belfast Telegraph*, 3 April 1964.

54. Mulholland, 63–4.

55. The quotation is from a *Guardian* article by Charles Brett that is included in a British Labour Party Research Department document prepared for discussions between the Wilson government and an NILP delegation: PRONI, HO 5/186.

56. Barritt and Carter, 57.

57. The claim that was made by Brett in his *Guardian* piece: 'Today there are very many respectable Catholics including professions men, members of the business community and trade union officials who are both qualified and willing to serve . . . lists of suitable names have been submitted to the authorities and even to the Cabinet Secretariat, without result.'

58. *Belfast Newsletter*, 15 March 1965.

59. ibid.

60. Bob Purdie, *Politics in the Streets: The Origins of the Civil Rights Movement in Northern Ireland* (Belfast, 1990), 82–102.

61. John Whyte, 'How Much Discrimination Was There under the Unionist Regime 1921–1968?', in Tom Gallagher and James O'Connell (eds.), *Contemporary Irish Studies* (Manchester, 1983), 30–31.

62. Purdie, 83.

63. Graham Gudgin, 'Discrimination in Housing and Employment under the Stormont Administration', in P. Roche and B. Barton (eds.) *The Northern Ireland Question: Nationalism, Unionism and Partition* (Hampshire, 1999), 103.

64. The system was described in the Campaign for Social Justice's pamphlet, *Northern Ireland: The Plain Truth*, second edition, 1969. The town was divided into three wards, each of which returned seven councillors. East Ward: 1,729 electors, comprising 543 Catholics and 1,186 Protestants; seven Unionist councillors. West Ward: 1,031 electors, comprising 844 Catholics and 187 Protestants; seven Nationalist councillors. Central Ward: 659 electors, comprising 143 Catholics and 516 Protestants; seven Unionist councillors.

65. *Northern Ireland: The Plain Truth*, 27.
66. Brendan Lynn, *Holding the Ground: The Nationalist Party in Northern Ireland 1945–1972* (Aldershot, 1997), 165.
67. Conn McCluskey quoted in *Holding the Ground*, 171.
68. Purdie, 104.
69. ibid., 105.
70. 'Allegations of Religious Discrimination in Northern Ireland. The Position of the United Kingdom Government in Respect of Matters Transferred to the Government of Northern Ireland', memorandum by A. J. Langdon of the Home Office, 5 November 1964, in 'Northern Ireland: Religious Intolerance', PRONI, HO 5/186.
71. Peter Rose, *How the Troubles Came to Northern Ireland* (Basingstoke and New York, 2000), 26.
72. A copy of the report, 'An Assessment of Irish Republican Army Activities from 10 December to Date', was sent by the Home Office to Cecil Bateman, Secretary to the Northern Ireland Cabinet. It was sent by Bateman to the Ministry of Home Affairs on 24 November 1964, 'Subversive Activities – Reports and Miscellaneous Correspondence', PRONI, HA/32/1/1349.
73. Rose, 17–18.
74. Thus he was the first British Prime Minister since partition to address the Irish Club's St Patrick's Day banquet in London, infuriating O'Neill by his support for a tripartite meeting between himself, Lemass and the Northern PM in London. *Irish Times*, 18 March 1965.
75. See Purdie, 107–20.
76. Rose, 44.
77. 'Discussions at Downing Street on 5th August', PRONI, Cabinet Secretariat, Cab 4/1338.
78. 'Irish Concerns Raised in Lynch–Wilson meeting', *Irish Times*, 1, 2 January 1997.
79. All the quotes are from Eamon Phoenix, 'Growing Hostility of Labour MPs Put Stormont Under Pressure', *Irish Times*, 1, 2 January 1998.
80. Purdie, 118.
81. Henry Patterson, *The Politics of Illusion: A Political History of the IRA* (London, 1997), 108.
82. Government of Northern Ireland, *Disturbances in Northern Ireland*, Cmnd. 532 (Belfast 1969), 15.
83. Lynn, 129.
84. ibid., 177.
85. Purdie, 133.
86. Lynn, 201.
87. The woman was engaged to be married, but her husband-to-be was a resident of Monaghan and hence ineligible for the council waiting list. She did live in overcrowded conditions with the rest of her family and the case was not such a glaring injustice as Currie alleged, but, given that she was the secretary of a solicitor who was a Unionist parliamentary candidate, the council's decision was even more blinkered than usual. See Purdie, 135, and Graham Gudgin.

88. Purdie, 136.

89. Devlin quoted in Paul Kingsley, *Londonderry Revisited* (Belfast, 1989), 133.

90. Eamonn McCann, *War and an Irish Town* (London, 1980), 41.

91. The *Sunday Times* Insight Team, *Ulster* (London, 1972), 52.

92. Michael Farrell, 'The Long March to Freedom', in M. Farrell (ed.), *Twenty Years On* (Dingle, 1988), 56.

93. See his contribution to the *New Left Review*'s special issue on Ulster, where he refers to 'Catholic-based power of a socialist form', *New Left Review*, 55, May/June 1969.

94. PRONI, Cabinet Secretariat, Cab 4/1406, 14 October 1968.

95. In a cabinet discussion on 23 October, Craig claimed that a change in the local government franchise 'could have disastrous political repercussions', while Faulkner claimed that he 'did not share the reservations which some members of the Party felt'. PRONI, Cabinet Secretariat, Cab 4/1409.

96. PRONI, Cabinet Secretariat, Cab 4/14013/10, 4 November 1968.

97. PRONI, Cabinet Secretariat, Cab 4/14013, 7 November 1968.

98. PRONI, Cabinet Secretariat, Cab 4/1418, 20 November 1968.

99. ibid.

100. PRONI, Secretary's Correspondence, Ulster Unionist Council Papers, May 1968, D1327/18/496.

101. Report on discussion forum at Unionist headquarters with rank-and-file members, September 1968, PRONI, Secretary's Correspondence, Ulster Unionist Council Papers, D1327/18/500.

102. The speech was given to a packed Ulster Hall, *Belfast Telegraph*, 29 November 1968.

103. The text of the broadcast can be found in *The Autobiography of Terence O'Neill*, 145–9.

104. See letter from Miss Noreen Cooper, a leading Unionist in Enniskillen, to J. O. Bailey, Secretary to the Ulster Unionist Council, January 1969: 'It is very easy to be snug in and around Belfast by virtue of superiority in numbers but the lean counties have no such security and they already feel abandoned. It was made quite clear to me at the last standing committee that the feeling was that our three western counties were lost anyway and therefore the concentration from Belfast would be on winning over the moderate Nationalists.' PRONI, Secretary's Correspondence, Ulster Unionist Council Papers, D1327/18/504.

105. Paul Arthur, *The People's Democracy 1968–1973* (Belfast, 1974), 40.

106. The author was present at a meeting of PD leftists in Farrell's house in the Stranmillis area of Belfast in December 1968 when the prediction was made.

107. *The Autobiography of Terence O'Neill*, 112–13.

108. Arthur, 41.

109. Jonathan Bardon, 'O'Neill Warning Went Unheeded', *Irish Times*, 1, 2 January 2000.

110. The interchange of letters can be found in *The Autobiography of Terence O'Neill*, 150–54.

111. Paul Bew, Peter Gibbon and Henry Patterson, *Northern Ireland 1921–1996: Political Forces and Social Classes* (London, 1996), 179.

112. Bloomfield, 106.

113. Niall Ó Dochartaigh, *From Civil Rights to Armalites: Derry and the Birth of the Irish Troubles* (Cork, 1997), 40–47.

114. ibid., 51.

8 Northern Ireland from Insurrection to the Anglo-Irish Agreement

1. Henry Patterson, *The Politics of Illusion: A Political History of the IRA* (London, 1997), 123.

2. The Sunday Times Insight Team, *Ulster: A Penguin Special* (London, 1972), 116.

3. Eamonn McCann, *War and an Irish Town* (London, 1974), 57–8.

4. *Ulster: A Penguin Special*, 119.

5. Ken Bloomfield, *Stormont in Crisis: A Memoir* (Belfast, 1994), 112.

6. Niall Ó Dochartaigh, *From Civil Rights to Armalites: Derry and the Birth of the Irish Troubles* (Cork, 1997), 122.

7. Bloomfield, 114.

8. See Gerry Adams, *Before the Dawn: An Autobiography* (London, 1996), 109–10.

9. Rachel Donnelly, 'Wilson Weighed up Direct Rule in North', *Irish Times*, 1, 2 January 2000.

10. Ronan Fanning, 'Living in Those Troubled Times', *Sunday Independent*, 2 January 2000, and his 'Playing It Cool: The Response of the British and Irish Governments to the Crisis in Northern Ireland 1968–1969', *Irish Studies in International Affairs*, 12, 2001, 62.

11. Paul Bew and Gordon Gillespie, *Northern Ireland: A Chronology of the Troubles 1968–1999* (Dublin, 1999), 21.

12. Kenneth O. Morgan, *Callaghan: A Life* (Oxford, 1997), 352.

13. Ronan Fanning, 'New Dispatches from the 1969 Frontline', *Sunday Independent*, 27 February 2000.

14. Brian Faulkner, *Memoirs of a Statesman* (London, 1978), 66.

15. Fanning, 'New Dispatches from the 1969 Frontline'.

16. ibid.

17. Letter from Oliver Wright to J.H. Waddell, Home Office, 16 September 1969, 'Reports and Correspondence', PRO, CJ 3/18.

18. *Irish Times*, 27 March 1970.

19. Report of a discussion of the Northern Ireland situation between the Minister of External Affairs and the Chancellor of the Duchy of Lancaster, 20 February 1970, NAD, Department of Foreign Affairs, 2000/14/185.

20. Anthony McIntyre, 'A Structural Analysis of Modern Irish Republicanism 1969–1973', D. Phil., Queen's University (Belfast, 1999), 96. Dr McIntyre provided me with access to a copy of his thesis.

21. R. H. S. Crossman, *The Diaries of a Cabinet Minister. Volume III: 1968–1970* (London, 1977), 636.

22. Ciaran De Baroid, *Ballymurphy and the Irish War* (London, revised edition, 2000), 37.

23. Desmond Hamill, *Pig in the Middle: The Army in Northern Ireland 1969–1985* (London, 1985), 28.

24. De Baroid, 5. At the height of the riots 1,000 soldiers saturated an area of one square mile.
25. Peter Taylor, *Provos: The IRA and Sinn Féin* (London, 1997), 77–83.
26. Morgan, 353.
27. Hamill, 35.
28. ibid., 36.
29. De Baroid, 47.
30. 'Consequently, the potential for IRA recruitment amongst the nationalist young could only be enormous.' McIntyre, 151.
31. The words are those of the prominent Fermanagh Unionist Noreen Cooper at a special meeting of the Standing Committee of the UUC, 16 January 1970, Archives of the UUC, D1327/7/79.
32. ibid.
33. Clive Scoular, *James Chichester-Clark: Prime Minister of Northern Ireland* (Belfast, 2000), 101.
34. Faulkner, 78–80.
35. Meeting between Northern Ireland Cabinet and GOC, 6 July 1971, G2.20–G2.623, material released by Ministry of Defence for Saville Inquiry into Bloody Sunday.
36. Ó Dochartaigh, 234.
37. Faulkner, 110.
38. ibid., 119.
39. Meeting at Downing Street on 5 August 1971, G5.50–G5.55, material released by Ministry of Defence for Saville Inquiry into Bloody Sunday.
40. Hamill, 60–61.
41. John McGuffin, *Internment* (Tralee, 1973), 119–20.
42. Bew and Gillespie, 37.
43. 'Meeting to Consider Briefing for Mr Faulkner's Visit', 6 October 1971, G15.87–G15.91, material released by Ministry of Defence for Saville Inquiry into Bloody Sunday.
44. 'Future Military Policy for Londonderry. An Appreciation of the Situation by the Commander of the Land Forces', 14 December 1971, G41.263, material released by Ministry of Defence for Saville Inquiry into Bloody Sunday.
45. Ford's analysis of the situation in Derry on 7 January 1972 is quoted in Professor Paul Bew's 'Report to the Saville Inquiry' as one of its two historical advisers.
46. Quoted in Professor Bew's 'Report to the Saville Inquiry'.
47. Visit of Chief of the Defence Staff, 24 January 1972, G70.433, material released by Ministry of Defence for Saville Inquiry into Bloody Sunday.
48. Eamonn McCann, 'Post-Bloody Sunday, It was All to Play For', *Sunday Tribune*, 26 September 1999.
49. Bloomfield, 161.
50. Notes of a cabinet discussion, 21 March 1972, PRONI, Cabinet Secretariat, Cab 4/1646/16.
51. 'Points Made by Mr Heath at the Downing Street Meeting on 22 March 1972 about the Situation in Northern Ireland', PRONI, Cabinet Secretariat, Cab 4/1646/17.

52. 'Later Statement by Mr Heath in which He Defined the United Kingdom's Government's Ideas', PRONI, Cabinet Secretariat, Cab 4/1646/18.
53. Faulkner, 153–4.
54. Sydney Elliott and W. D. Flackes, *Northern Ireland: A Political Directory 1968–1999* (Belfast, 1999), 681–5.
55. Seán MacStiofáin, *Revolutionary in Ireland* (Farnborough, Hants, 1974), 243.
56. *Belfast Newsletter*, 21 March 1972.
57. *Ulster a Nation* (Belfast, 1972). This was a pamphlet produced by Craig's Vanguard movement.
58. Bloomfield, 137.
59. Paul Bew and Henry Patterson, *The British State and the Ulster Crisis: From Wilson to Thatcher* (London, 1985), 62.
60. See interview with Smyth in David Hume, 'The Ulster Unionist Party in an Era of Conflict and Change', D.Phil., University of Ulster (Jordanstown, 1994), Vol. II, 325.
61. *Belfast Newsletter*, 20 March 1972.
62. Bew and Patterson, 49.
63. Ulster Vanguard, *Ulster a Nation* (Belfast, 1972).
64. *Belfast Newsletter*, 20 March 1972.
65. Sarah Nelson, *Ulster's Uncertain Defenders: Loyalists and the Northern Ireland Conflict* (Belfast, 1984), 94–8.
66. Steve Bruce, *The Red Hand: Protestant Paramilitaries in Northern Ireland* (Oxford, 1992), 14–22.
67. Bew and Gillespie, 39.
68. Bruce, 55.
69. See Alvin Jackson, *Ireland 1798–1998* (Oxford, 1999), 402.
70. Bruce, 42.
71. Clifford Smyth, 'The Ulster Democratic Unionist Party: A Case Study in Political and Religious Convergence', Ph.D. thesis, Queen's University (Belfast, 1983), 36.
72. Smyth, 31.
73. Paul Bew, Peter Gibbon and Henry Patterson, *Northern Ireland 1921–1996: Political Forces and Social Classes* (London, 1996), 170.
74. *Fortnight*, October 1972.
75. The poll, intended to be taken every ten years, was held on 8 March 1973. The SDLP and republicans urged a boycott, and the bulk of nationalists did not vote. The result was that out of an electorate of 1,030,084, some 591,820 voted in favour of the Union and 6,463 in favour of a United Ireland. Thus 57.5 of the total electorate link – probably an under-recording of the pro-Union vote as pro-Union Catholics in largely nationalist areas might have felt reluctant to be seen entering a polling station. Elliott and Flackes, 186.
76. Bew and Gillespie, 61.
77. For a 'class analysis' of Vanguard, see Belinda Probert, *Beyond Orange and Green: The Northern Ireland Crisis in a New Perspective* (London, 1978), 117–28.
78. For the account of a liberal Unionist who rejected the Alliance option, see Basil McIvor, *Hope Deferred: Experiences of an Irish Unionist* (Belfast, 1998), 58.

79. Faulkner, 174.

80. Bloomfield, 168–9.

81. Faulkner, 194.

82. This was certainly the objective of Ken Bloomfield, who drafted the oath. *Stormont in Crisis*, 180–81.

83. Faulkner, 195.

84. Elliott and Flackes, 533.

85. Garret FitzGerald, *All in a Life* (Dublin, 1991), 200.

86. Bloomfield, 152.

87. Francis Mulhern, *The Present Lasts a Long Time: Essays in Cultural Politics* (Cork, 1998), 13.

88. Gerard Murray, *John Hume and the SDLP* (Dublin, 1998), 4.

89. Paul Routledge, *John Hume* (London, 1997), 78.

90. Paddy Devlin, *Straight Left: An Autobiography* (Belfast, 1993), 140.

91. Eamonn Gallagher, 'Report on Conversation with John Hume', 16 February 1970, NAD, Department of Foreign Affairs, 2000/14/185.

92. Routledge, 98.

93. Murray, 6–7.

94. Routledge, 112.

95. Barry White, *John Hume: Statesman of the Troubles* (Belfast, 1984), 127.

96. Murray, 18.

97. *Republican News*, 2 January 1972.

98. *The Times*, 23 June 1972.

99. Patterson, 153–5.

100. Taylor, 142.

101. Bew and Patterson, 54.

102. Eamon Phoenix, 'Whitelaw in Clash of Views with SDLP', *Irish Times*, 2 January 2004.

103. Election results from Elliott and Flackes, 533.

104. *Irish News*, 3 July 1973.

105. White, 142.

106. Bew and Patterson, 72.

107. Richard Bourke, 'Heath was Told Irish Ministers were "Timorous"', *Irish Times*, 2 January 2004.

108. Basil McIvor, *Hope Deferred: Experiences of an Irish Unionist* (Belfast, 1998), 93.

109. FitzGerald, 215.

110. McIvor recalls a conversation with the Taoiseach and his ministerial colleague, Conor Cruise O'Brien, towards the end of the conference: 'Both of them sadly agreed that . . . we Unionists were not going to sell Sunningdale to our people at home.' *Hope Deferred*, 91.

111. Eamon Phoenix, 'Painful Progress to Power-sharing', *Irish Times*, 2 January 2004.

112. Report of the Grand Orange Lodge of Ireland, December 1973, Archives of the Orange Order, Schomberg House, Belfast.

113. Bew and Gillespie, 69.

114. Bew and Gillespie, 77.

115. Elliott and Flackes, 537.

116. Faulkner, 251.
117. Gordon Gillespie, 'The Sunningdale Agreement: Lost Opportunity or an Agreement Too Far?', *Irish Political Studies*, 13, 1998.
118. Nelson, 157.
119. Bloomfield, 219.
120. Faulkner, 276.
121. Nelson, 157–8.
122. David Hume, *The Ulster Unionist Party 1972–1992: A Political Movement in an Era of Conflict and Change* (Belfast, 1996), 56.
123. ibid., 57.
124. Graham Walker, *A History of the Ulster Unionist Party* (Manchester, 2004), 227.
125. Hume, 63.
126. Walker, 226.
127. Ed Moloney and Andy Pollak, *Paisley* (Dublin, 1986), 288–9.
128. Smyth, 112.
129. Elliott and Flackes, 532–3, 550–51.
130. Smyth, 143.
131. Padraig O'Malley, *The Uncivil Wars: Ireland Today* (Belfast, 1983), 170–71.
132. Bernard Donoghue, *The Heat of the Kitchen* (London, 2003), 136–7.
133. 'Impotent PM Considered Doomsday Scenario', *Guardian*, 3 January 2005.
134. Richard Bourke, 'Wilson Clearly Wanted to Disengage from the North', *Irish Times*, 1, 3 January 2005.
135. Quoted in Taylor, 171.
136. Taylor, 191.
137. Elliott and Flackes, 681–5.
138. Taylor, 175.
139. Brice Dickson, 'Criminal Justice and Emergency Laws', in Seamus Dunn (ed.), *Facets of the Conflict in Northern Ireland* (London, 1995), 64–71.
140. Kevin Boyle and Tom Hadden, *Northern Ireland: The Choice* (London, 1994), 85.
141. See Sean O'Callaghan, *The Informer* (London, 1998), 118.
142. Bew and Patterson, 85.
143. *The Times*, 28 September 1976.
144. Taylor, 211.
145. *Irish Times*, 30 December 1977.
146. Roy Mason, *Paying the Price* (London, 1999), 218.
147. Paul Bew, Henry Patterson and Paul Teague, *Between War and Peace: The Political Future of Northern Ireland* (London, 1997), 88.
148. Bob Rowthorn and Naomi Wayne, *Northern Ireland: The Political Economy of Conflict* (Oxford, 1988), 117.
149. Bew and Patterson, 90.
150. Mason, 219.
151. Hume in a *Radio Éireann* interview on 25 May, reported in *The Ulster General Strike: Strike Bulletins of the Workers Association* (Belfast, 1974).
152. 'Scenario of Civil War and Re-partition Dominated Thinking of Demoralized SDLP', *Irish Times*, 1, 3 January 2005.

153. Murray, 37.
154. ibid., 48.
155. *Irish Times*, 16 February 1978.
156. Adams, 266.
157. David Sharrock and Mark Devenport, *Man of War, Man of Peace: The Unauthorized Biography of Gerry Adams* (London, 1997), 168.
158. Patterson, 193–4.
159. Bew and Gillespie, 146.
160. Sharrock and Devenport, 182–92.
161. Margaret Thatcher, *The Downing Street Years* (London, 1993), 385.
162. Leader's report from Westminster to meeting of Executive Committee of UUP, 5 November 1976, PRONI, Ulster Unionist Council Papers, D1327/6/174.
163. Meeting of Executive Committee of UUP, 26 September 1980, PRONI, Ulster Unionist Council Papers, D1327/6/186.
164. 'We would not accept a system of devolved government that would lead to a united Ireland. The government's intention was not to improve the government of Northern Ireland but rather to get the majority to shift their stance and move out of the UK. The DUP had swallowed this hook, line and sinker'. Molyneaux to meeting of UUP Executive, 26 September 1980, PRONI, Ulster Unionist Council Papers, D1327/6/186.
165. Seán Donlon, 'Bringing Irish Diplomatic and Political Influence to Bear on Washington', *Irish Times*, 25 January 1993, and see also Andrew J. Wilson, *Irish America and the Ulster Conflict* (Belfast, 1995).
166. 'US Speaker O'Neill's Role on Ulster is Highlighted', *Belfast Telegraph*, 1 July 2000.
167. *Irish Times*, 16 November 1985.
168. Quoted in Paul Bew, 'Agreement or a Booby Prize?', *Irish Times*, 22 April 1995.

9 From Crisis to Boom: The Republic 1973–2005

1. Philip J. O'Connell, 'Sick Man or Tigress? The Labour Market in the Republic of Ireland', in A. F. Heath, R. Breen and C. T. Whelan (eds.), *Ireland North and South: Perspectives from Social Science* (Oxford, 1999), 219.
2. Liam Kennedy, *The Modern Industrialization of Ireland 1940–1988* (Dublin, 1989), 48–9.
3. Peter Mair, *The Changing Irish Party System* (London, 1987), 211.
4. Paul Bew, Ellen Hazelkorn and Henry Patterson, *The Dynamics of Irish Politics* (London, 1989), 103.
5. J. J. Lee, *Ireland 1912–1985: Politics and Society* (Cambridge, 1989), 462.
6. Bew, Hazelkorn and Patterson, 104.
7. D. A. Coleman, 'Demography and Migration in Ireland, North and South', in Heath, Breen and Whelan, 83–4.
8. D. A. Gillmor, *Economic Activities in the Republic of Ireland: A Geographical Perspective* (Dublin, 1985), 27.

9. OECD, *Economic Surveys: Ireland*, May 1978, 30.

10. Lee, 465.

11. Maurice Manning, *James Dillon: A Biography* (Dublin, 1999), 329.

12. Garret FitzGerald, *All in a Life: An Autobiography* (Dublin, 1991), 68.

13. Mair, 186.

14. Manning, 362.

15. Bruce Arnold, *What Kind of Country? Modern Irish Politics 1968–1983* (London, 1984), 85.

16. Michael Gallagher, *The Irish Labour Party in Transition 1957–1982* (Dublin, 1982), 186.

17. ibid., 118.

18. Michael Gallagher, *Political Parties in the Republic of Ireland* (Dublin, 1985), 156–8.

19. Conor Cruise O'Brien, *Memoir: My Life and Themes* (Dublin, 1998), 342.

20. Gallagher, *The Irish Labour Party in Transition*, 198.

21. ibid., 200.

22. FitzGerald, 298.

23. Niamh Hardiman, *Pay, Politics and Economic Performance in Ireland 1970–1987* (Oxford, 1988), 99.

24. Gallagher, *The Irish Labour Party in Transition*, 210.

25. Stephen Collins, 'Doomsday Plan Gave Parts of the North to the Republic', *Sunday Tribune*, 2 January 2005.

26. Lee, 477–8.

27. O'Brien, 355.

28. FitzGerald, 311: the raiders threw family bibles into the fire.

29. Arnold, 122.

30. 'I allowed myself to be persuaded to leave this sensitive issue over for several months.' FitzGerald, 313.

31. FitzGerald, 320.

32. Lee, 483.

33. Kieran Allen, *Fianna Fáil and Irish Labour: 1926 to the Present* (London, 1997), 149–50.

34. O'Brien, 345–6.

35. FitzGerald, 320.

36. Mair, 30, 33.

37. Allen, 150.

38. O'Brien, 357.

39. The anti-Haughey agenda behind the 1977 manifesto was first pointed out by the political journalist Olivia O'Leary: 'How Haughey Swung the Forum', *Magill*, August 1984.

40. Lee, 498.

41. Vincent Browne, 'Lynch Partly Responsible for the 1970 Arms Crisis', *Irish Times*, 27 October 1999.

42. James Downey, *Lenihan: His Life and Times* (Dublin, 1998), 105.

43. Bew, Hazelkorn and Patterson, 121.

44. FitzGerald, 353.

45. Bill Roche, 'Social Partnership and Political Controls: State Strategy and

Industrial Relations in Ireland', in M. Kelly, L. O'Dowd and J. Wickham (eds.), *Power, Conflict and Inequality* (Dublin, 1982), 63.

46. *Irish Banking Review*, December 1978.
47. Lee, 474.
48. Bew, Hazelkorn and Patterson, 115.
49. Arnold, 136.
50. Dick Walsh, *The Party inside Fianna Fáil* (Dublin, 1986), 142.
51. Kevin Myers in an obituary of Jack Lynch, *Irish Times*, 27 September 1999.
52. Stephen Collins, *The Power Game: Fianna Fáil since Lemass* (Dublin, 2000), 123.
53. FitzGerald, 340.
54. Report of the Tribunal of Inquiry (Dunnes Payments), 25 August 1997.
55. Collins, 127.
56. Walsh, 146.
57. Allen, 158.
58. ibid., 159.
59. The Moriarty Tribunal heard evidence in 1999 of how he spent over £16,000 a year on shirts from the exclusive Charvet shop in Paris: Collins, 125.
60. Dick Walsh, 'Next Election Most Significant since 1930s', *Irish Times*, 12 August 2000.
61. Lee, 502–3.
62. Garret FitzGerald, 'Some Perspectives on the Economic Records of Governments in the 1980s', *Irish Times*, 26 June 1999.
63. Downey, 110.
64. Eunan O'Halpin, *Defending Ireland: The Irish State and Its Enemies since 1922* (Oxford, 1999), 332.
65. Arnold, 158.
66. Joe Joyce and Peter Murtagh, *The Boss: Charles J. Haughey in Government* (Dublin, 1983), 33.
67. Stephen O'Byrnes, *Hiding Behind a Face: Fine Gael under Garret FitzGerald* (Dublin, 1986), 73.
68. Mair, 303.
69. ibid., 41.
70. Gallagher, *The Irish Labour Party in Transition*, 240.
71. Joyce and Murtagh, 14.
72. Arnold, 166.
73. FitzGerald 367.
74. Bew, Hazelkorn and Patterson, 156.
75. Mair, 56–7.
76. Joyce and Murtagh, 31.
77. ibid., 22.
78. FitzGerald, 404.
79. Joyce and Murtagh, 53–4.
80. Lee, 508.
81. Stephen Collins, *Spring and the Labour Story* (Dublin, 1993), 97.
82. FitzGerald, 435–6.
83. This is Stephen Collins's opinion: see *Spring and the Labour Story*, 107.

84. Garret FitzGerald, 'Some Perspectives on the Economic Records of Governments in the 1980s', *Irish Times*, 26 June 1999.

85. John Kurt Jacobsen, *Chasing Progress in the Irish Republic* (Cambridge, 1994), 161.

86. Collins, *Spring and the Labour Story*, 130.

87. Brendan O'Leary, 'Towards Europeanization and Realignment? The Irish General Election, February 1987', *Western European Politics*, 10, 3, July 1987.

88. Allen, 171.

89. See Paul Teague and John McCartney, 'Industrial Relations in the Two Irish Economies', in Heath, Breen and Whelan, 349.

90. Cormac Ó Gráda, *A Rocky Road: The Irish Economy since the 1920s* (Manchester, 1997), 32–3.

91. ibid., 33.

92. *The Irish Times*, 5 August 2000.

93. Robert Kuttner, 'Ireland's Miracle: The Market Didn't Do It Alone', *Business Week*, 7 July 2000.

94. Paul Sweeney, *The Celtic Tiger: Ireland's Continuing Economic Miracle* (Dublin, 1999), 8.

95. Jonathan Haughton, 'The Dynamics of Economic Change', in W. Crotty and D. E. Schmitt, *Ireland and the Politics of Change* (London, 1998), 29–30.

96. Sweeney, 87.

97. Kuttner, 'Ireland's Miracle'.

98. Denis O'Hearn, *Inside the Celtic Tiger* (London, 1998) is an example.

99. Rory O'Donnell, 'The New Ireland in the New Europe', in Rory O'Donnell (ed.), *Europe: The Irish Experience* (Dublin, 2000), 177.

100. *Irish Times*, 19 June 1989.

101. The term was used by one of the party's negotiators. *Irish Times*, 14 July 1999.

102. Yvonne Galligan, *Women and Politics in Contemporary Ireland: From the Margins to the Mainstream* (London, 1998), 31.

103. Pat O'Connor and Sally Shortall, 'Variations in Women's Paid Employment, North and South', in Heath, Breen and Whelan, 288–9.

104. Eric Hobsbawm, *Age of Extremes: The Short Twentieth Century 1914–1991* (London, 1994), 311.

105. James S. Donnelly, Jr, 'A Church in Crisis: The Irish Catholic Church Today', *History Ireland*, 8, 3, Autumn 2000, 13.

106. Basil Chubb, *The Government and Politics of Ireland* (London, 1982), 29.

107. Galligan, 53.

108. ibid., 149–50.

109. M. A. Busteed, *Voting Behaviour in the Republic of Ireland: A Geographical Perspective* (Oxford, 1990), 182.

110. Dermot Keogh, 'The Role of the Catholic Church in the Republic of Ireland 1992–1995', *Building Trust in Ireland: Studies Commissioned by the Forum for Peace and Reconciliation* (Belfast, 1996), 177.

111. Lee, 654.

112. Galligan, 152–3.

113. Cited in Busteed, 201–2.

114. Emily O'Reilly, 'The Legion of the Rearguard', *Magill*, September 1986.

115. Brian Girvin, 'The Irish Divorce Referendum, November 1995', *Irish Political Studies*, 11, 1996.

116. Gene Kerrigan and Pat Brennan, *This Great Little Nation: The A–Z of Irish Scandals and Controversies* (Dublin, 1999), 310.

117. ibid., 53.

118. Tom Inglis, *Moral Monopoly: The Rise and the Fall of the Catholic Church in Modern Ireland* (Dublin, 1998), 257.

119. Niamh Hardiman and Christopher Whelan, 'Changing Values', in William Crotty and David E. Schmitt (eds.), *Ireland and the Politics of Change* (London, 1998), 79.

120. K. Theodore Hoppen, *Ireland since 1800: Conflict and Conformity* (London, 1999), 283.

121. James S. Donnelly, Jr, 'A Church in Crisis: The Irish Catholic Church Today', *History Ireland*, 8, 3, Autumn 2000.

122. FitzGerald, 378.

123. ibid., 462.

124. John Whyte, *Interpreting Northern Ireland* (Oxford, 1991), 138.

125. Brian Girvin, 'Nationalism and the Continuation of Political Conflict in Ireland', in Heath, Breen and Whelan, 381.

126. ibid.

127. Peter Mair, 'The Irish Republic and the Anglo-Irish Agreement', in Paul Teague (ed.), *Beyond the Rhetoric: Politics, the Economy and Social Policy in Northern Ireland* (London, 1987), 109.

128. Kerrigan and Brennan, 134.

129. Collins, *The Power Game*, 182.

130. Paul Mitchell, 'The 1992 Election in the Republic of Ireland', *Irish Political Studies*, 8, 1993, 116.

131. Eoin O'Sullivan, 'The 1990 Presidential Election in the Republic of Ireland', *Irish Political Studies*, 6, 1991, 96.

132. Collins, *The Power Game*, 242.

133. Henry Patterson, *The Politics of Illusion: A Political History of the IRA* (London, 1997), 258.

134. He once explained to me that this was the reason why the best books on Fianna Fáil had been written by Marxists.

135. Collins, *The Power Game*, 257.

136. Sean Duignan, *One Spin on the Merry-Go-Round* (Dublin, 1996), 88.

137. Fergus Finlay, *Snakes and Ladders* (Dublin, 1998), 170–71.

138. ibid., 235.

139. Duignan, 147.

140. Paul Bew and Gordon Gillespie, *Northern Ireland: A Chronology of the Troubles 1968–1999* (Dublin, 1999), 328.

141. Gary Murphy, 'The 1997 General Election in the Republic of Ireland', *Irish Political Studies*, 13, 1998, 131.

142. Fintan O'Toole, 'How the Celtic Tiger's Cubs Find Sinn Féin Reassuring', *Irish Times*, 14 January 2001.

143. Garret FitzGerald, 'A Duty to Show Upheaval was Worthwhile', *Irish Times*, 3 February 2001.

144. Cliff Taylor, 'Value for Money in Public Finances Key in Mind of Voters', *Irish Times*, 15 April 2002.

145. Denis Coghlan, 'Low-tax Low-spend Policy Leaves Social Service in Its Wake', *Irish Times*, 16 April 2002.

146. Kieran Allen, 'Hypocrisy of Social Partnership', *Irish Times*, 14 February 2001.

147. John Murray Brown, 'Celtic Tiger Aged as US Technology Sector Falters', *Financial Times*, 19 December 2001.

148. *Irish Times*, 8 November 2001.

149. Dick Walsh, 'Crucial Debate on How We Run Our Country', *Irish Times*, 23 September 2000.

150. Mike Allen, 'Attempt to Steal Labour's Clothes Will Not Work', *Irish Times*, 10 January 2001.

151. Jane O'Mahony, '"Not So Nice": The Treaty of Nice – The 2001 Referendum Experience', *Irish Political Studies*, 16, 2001, 208.

152. Katy Hayward, '"If at first you don't succeed": The Second Referendum on the Treaty of Nice 2002', *Irish Political Studies*, 18, 1, Summer 2003.

153. Fintan O'Toole, 'No Longer Yielding to Party or Pulpit', *Irish Times*, 8 March 2002.

154. Garret FitzGerald, 'We Need a Tough Minister for Finance to Sort Out the Financial Mess', *Irish Times*, 11 May 2002.

155. 'Election 2002', *Irish Times*, 20 May 2002.

156. Michael Marsh, 'The End of Politics as We've Known It', *Irish Independent*, 20 May 2002.

157. Eoin O'Malley and Matthew Kerby, 'Chronicle of a Death Foretold? Understanding the Decline of Fine Gael', *Irish Political Studies*, 19, 1, Summer 2004.

158. E. Kennedy et al., 'The Members of Labour: Backgrounds, Political Views and Attitudes Towards Coalition Government', *Irish Political Studies*, 20, 2, June 2005, 182–3.

159. Adrian Kavanagh, 'The 2004 Local Elections in the Republic of Ireland', *Irish Political Studies*, 19, 2, Winter 2004.

160. Aodh Quinlivan et al., 'The 2004 European Elections in the Republic of Ireland', *Irish Political Studies*, 19, 2, Winter 2004.

161. 'The *Irish Times* TNSmrbi Poll', *Irish Times*, 8 October 2004.

162. Mark Brennock, 'Silver Lining', *Irish Times*, 29 December 2004.

163. Mark Brennock, 'Short-term Approach Dominates Edgy FF Think-in', *Irish Times*, 7 September 2005.

164. Karin Gilland Lutz, 'Irish Party Competition in New Millennium', *Irish Political Studies*, 18, 2, Winter 2003.

165. 'Taoiseach Promises Not Only Prosperity But Vision', *Irish Times*, 6 September 2005.

10 Between War and Peace: Northern Ireland 1985–2005

1. Dean Godson, *Himself Alone: David Trimble and the Ordeal of Ulster Unionism* (London, 2004), 85.

2. Graham Walker, *A History of the Ulster Unionist Party* (Manchester, 2004), 235.

3. David Hume, *The Ulster Unionist Party 1972–1992: A Political Movement in an Era of Conflict and Change* (Belfast, 1996), 111.

4. Hume, 133.

5. Sydney Elliott and W. D. Flackes, *Northern Ireland: A Political Directory 1968–1999* (Belfast, 1999), 572, 575.

6. Ann Purdy, *Molyneaux: The Long View* (Antrim, 1989), 147.

7. The interview is quoted in Paul Bew and Henry Patterson, 'The New Stalemate: Unionism and the Anglo–Irish Agreement', in Paul Teague (ed.), *Beyond the Rhetoric: Politics, the Economy and Social Policy in Northern Ireland* (London, 1987), 46.

8. Ed Moloney, 'Adams Played a Pivotal Role for Peace', *Sunday Tribune*, 28 May 2000, where he recalls a conversation in 1983 with a key Adams aide to this effect.

9. Paul Bew and Gordon Gillespie, *Northern Ireland: A Chronology of the Troubles 1968–1993* (Belfast, 1993), 157.

10. Henry Patterson, *The Politics of Illusion: A Political History of the IRA* (London, 1997), 206.

11. ibid. 200.

12. Gerard Murray, *John Hume and the SDLP* (Dublin, 1998), 171.

13. *Irish Times*, 24 February 1989.

14. Elliott and Flackes, 681.

15. Gerry Adams, *Free Ireland: Towards a Lasting Peace* (Dingle, 1995), 194–5.

16. Murray, 176.

17. Sean O'Callaghan, *The Informer* (London, 1999), 281.

18. Elliott and Flackes, 683.

19. Patterson, 211.

20. *An Phoblacht*, 26 January 1989.

21. Paul Bew, Peter Gibbon and Henry Patterson, *Northern Ireland 1921–1996: Political Forces and Social Classes* (London, 1996), 220.

22. Patterson, 215–16.

23. Margaret Thatcher, *The Downing Street Years* (London, 1993), 402–15.

24. Graham Ellison and Jim Smyth, *The Crowned Harp: Policing Northern Ireland* (London, 2000), 132.

25. Kevin Boyle and Tom Hadden, *Northern Ireland: The Choice* (London, 1994), 71.

26. Hume's attack on the IRA was made at the SDLP's annual conference in 1988, *Irish Times*, 28 November 1988.

27. Thatcher, 415.

28. The republican version of this exchange is in *Setting the Record Straight: A Record of Communications between Sinn Féin and the British Government October 1990–November 1993* (Belfast, 1993).

29. Patterson, 226.

30. Bew and Gillespie, 298.

31. Elliott and Flackes, 683.

32. *Irish Times*, 19 September 1988.

33. From Sinn Féin document 'A Strategy for Peace', *Irish Times*, 7 September 1988.

34. Michael Cox, 'Cinderella at the Ball: Explaining the End of the War in Northern Ireland', *Millennium: Journal of International Studies*, 27, 2, 1998, 325–42.
35. Danny Morrison, *Then the Walls Come Down: A Prison Journal* (Cork, 1999), 91.
36. Patterson, 244.
37. Eamonn Mallie and David McKittrick, *The Fight for Peace: The Secret Story behind the Irish Peace Process* (London, 1996), 120.
38. Conor O'Clery, *The Greening of the White House* (Dublin, 1996), 61.
39. John Dumbrell, '"Hope and History": The US and Peace in Northern Ireland', in Michael Cox, Adrian Guelke and Fiona Stephen (eds.), *A Farewell to Arms? From 'Long War' to Long Peace in Northern Ireland* (Manchester, 2000), 216.
40. Mallie and McKittrick, 280.
41. Bew and Gillespie, 294.
42. Morrison, 241.
43. Peter Taylor, *Provos: The IRA and Sinn Féin* (London, 1997), 335–6.
44. Bew and Gillespie, 277.
45. Mallie and McKittrick, 207.
46. Sean Duignan, *One Spin on the Merry-Go-Round* (Dublin, 1996), 106.
47. Anthony Seldon, *Major: A Political Life* (London, 1997), 422–3.
48. Bew and Gillespie, 286.
49. Patterson, 250–53.
50. In an interview in the *Irish News* on 8 January 1994, Adams criticized Sir Patrick Mayhew's post-Declaration statement that talks between the government and Sinn Féin would be concerned with decommissioning.
51. Duignan, 136.
52. Ed Moloney, *A Secret History of the IRA* (London and New York, 2002), 413. The TUAS document is printed as an appendix in Mallie and McKittrick, 381–4.
53. Duignan, 137, 140.
54. ibid., 139–140.
55. ibid., 147.
56. Quote is from the TUAS document.
57. Walker, 248.
58. Paul Bew, Henry Patterson and Paul Teague, *Between War and Peace: The Political Future of Northern Ireland* (London, 1997), 91–2.
59. ibid., 90.
60. Andy Pollak, *A Citizens' Inquiry: The Opsahl Report on Northern Ireland* (Dublin, 1993), 7.
61. Kevin Boyle and Tom Hadden, *Northern Ireland: The Choice* (London, 1994), 30–32, and Graham Gudgin, 'A Catholic Majority is Far from Certain', *Belfast Telegraph*, 15 February 2002.
62. Bew, Patterson and Teague, 144–5.
63. Ruth Dudley Edwards, *The Faithful Tribe: An Intimate Portrait of the Loyal Institutions* (London, 1999), 283.
64. Eamon Delaney, *An Accidental Diplomat: My Years in the Irish Foreign Service 1987–1995* (Dublin, 2001), 289.
65. Henry McDonald, *Trimble* (London, 2000), 87–90.

66. Rogelio Alonso, *Irlanda del Norte: Una historia de guerra y la búsqueda de la paz* (Madrid, 2001), 390–1 (translation by Henry Patterson).
67. Elliott and Flackes, 580.
68. Bew and Gillespie, 298.
69. The text of the Balmoral speech can be found in Bew, Patterson and Teague, 217–24.
70. Elliott and Flackes, 594.
71. Patterson, 289.
72. Speech to the Irish Association, 2 February 1995, reprinted in Bew, Patterson and Teague, 225–31.
73. Paul Bew, 'Decommissioning', in Robin Wilson (ed.), *Agreeing to Disagree? A Guide to the Northern Ireland Assembly* (Norwich, 2001), 139–42.
74. 'But is There an Agreement on Northern Ireland?', *Daily Telegraph*, 17 April 1998.
75. 'Reaching an agreement without their presence was extremely difficult, it would have been impossible with them in the room.' George Mitchell, *Making Peace* (London, 1999), 110.
76. Bew and Gillespie, 318.
77. ibid., 348.
78. Deaglan de Breadun, *The Far Side of Revenge: Making Peace in Northern Ireland* (Cork, 2001), 74.
79. ibid. 84–5.
80. Ed Moloney, 'Triumph and Disaster', *Sunday Tribune*, 18 January 1998.
81. Robin Wilson, 'The Executive Committee', in Wilson (ed.), *Agreeing to Disagree*, 76.
82. Thomas Hennessey, *The Northern Ireland Peace Process* (Dublin, 2000), 169–70.
83. Frank Millar, *David Trimble: The Price of Peace* (Dublin, 2004), 70.
84. Mitchell McLaughlin in an interview in *Parliamentary Brief*, May/June 1998, quoted in Hennessey, 171.
85. Richard Sinnott, 'Historic Day Blemished by Low Poll', *Irish Times*, 25 May 1998.
86. Suzanne Breen, 'United No Parties Set their Sights on Assembly', *Irish Times*, 25 May 1998.
87. Tommy McKearney, 'There is No Support for IRA Physical Force Any More', *Sunday Tribune*, 15 August 1999.
88. Paul Bew, 'Reckoning the Dead', *The Times Literary Supplement*, 28 January 2000.
89. 'Keep IRA on Sidelines, Says Adams', interview of Adams by Geraldine Kennedy, *Irish Times*, 20 May 1998.
90. *Irish Times*, 8 April 1999.
91. Frank Millar, 'No Way to Soften the Impact of Paisley's Defiant Triumph', *Irish Times*, 15 June 1999.
92. Anne Cadwallader, 'Peace Deal on Its Last Legs, Says IRA', *Ireland on Sunday*, 24 December 2000.
93. For a good critique, see Jyrki Ruohomaki's analysis of the election results in a Democratic Dialogue discussion paper: http://www.democratic dialogue.org/working/Elect.htm

94. Jim Cusack, 'Decommissioning Pace Forced by IRA's Colombian Links', *Irish Times*, 27 October 2001.

95. ibid.

96. Millar, *David Trimble: The Price of Peace*, 183.

97. Godson, 698.

98. Steve Bruce, *The Edge of the Union: The Ulster Loyalist Political Vision* (Oxford, 1994), 37–71.

99. 'A United Ireland Doesn't Figure', *News Letter*, 20 December 2002.

100. Roger MacGinty, 'Unionist Political Attitudes after the Belfast Agreement', *Irish Political Studies*, 19, 1, Summer 2004, 88.

101. Godson, 713.

102. Godson, 732.

103. The full text of the speech is available on *Guardian* Unlimited/Special Reports: http://www.politics.guardian.co.uk/northernirelandassembly.

104. Paul Bew, 'Why Agree to Meet When You Know They Won't Show', *Sunday Times*, 26 October 2003.

105. Anthony McIntyre, 'More Spies May Be Lurking in Sinn Féin's Cupboard', *Irish Times*, 20 December 2005.

106. Godson, 755.

107. Millar, *David Trimble: The Price of Peace*, 142.

108. Godson, 788.

109. Godson, 790.

110. Christopher Farrington, 'The Northern Ireland Assembly Election 2003', *Irish Political Studies*, 19, 1, Summer 2004, 85.

111. DUP document of 2000 quoted in Conor McGrath, 'The Northern Ireland Ministerial Code', *Irish Political Studies*, 20, 2, June 2005, 115.

112. *Irish Times*, 8 January 2005.

113. 'Robbery is being Used to Kill Peace Process': Gerry Moriarty interview with Gerry Adams, *Irish Times*, 14 January 2005.

114. Mark Brennock, 'Is the Party Over?' *Irish Times*, 19 February 2005.

115. 'A Farewell to Arms', *Sunday Times*, 31 July 2005.

116. Both quotes are from the leaders' final election platforms, *News Letter*, 4 May 2005.

117. 'IRA Statement', *Irish Times*, 29 July 2005.

118. Tom Clonan, 'General Spoke Volumes about Arms Destruction', *Irish Times*, 27 September 2005.

119. *Fifth Report of the International Monitoring Commission*, 24 May 2005, 13.

120. 'Questions That Give Rise to Scepticism', *Irish Times*, 29 July 2005.

121. 'Demilitarization', *Irish Times*, 2 August 2005.

122. 'Hain to Address Unionist Concerns', *Irish Times*, 19 September 2005.

123. David Trimble, *To Raise Up a New Northern Ireland* (Belfast, 2001).

Index